Interpersonal Growth Through Communication

Interpersonal Growth Through Communication

Second Edition

Gerald L. Wilson
University of South Alabama

Alan M. Hantz
University of North Carolina
at Asheville

Michael S. Hanna
University of South Alabama

Wm. C. Brown Publishers
Dubuque, Iowa

Cover design by Dale Rosenbach

The credits section for this book begins on page 437, and is
considered an extension of the copyright page.

Library of Congress Catalog Card Number: 88–71393

ISBN 0–697–01470–3

Printed in the United States of America by Wm. C. Brown Publishers
2460 Kerper Boulevard, Dubuque, IA 52001

10 9 8 7 6 5 4 3 2 1

To Lin, Mimi, and Nancy

Contents

UNIT 20
Defensiveness in Relationships 272

UNIT 21
Supportiveness in Relationships 283

UNIT 22
Managing Power in Relationships 296

UNIT 23
Managing Intrapersonal Conflict 307

Preface

The second edition of *Interpersonal Growth Through Communication* has been thoroughly revised in response to feedback from individuals who used the first edition and from our reviewers. These readers asked us to bring the underlying theme of relationship management more clearly to the surface and to integrate it as thoroughly—and as obviously—as possible. We believe we have accomplished this goal. The book is written for students in an introductory course in interpersonal communication. In this edition, we have tried to present both theory and practice, carefully grounded in research and carefully focused on the variables that influence interpersonal relationships, in a more exciting format.

New Format

Our colleagues asked us to organize the book into units to help them adapt more easily to the shifting needs of their students, for students are better prepared for class when instructors assign smaller units. At the same time, this approach does not change the breadth of coverage of the work.

No two communication events are alike, and no two classes have the same needs and interests. The students in one class, for example, might be very concerned about nonverbal messages. A second class might be more interested in conflict management. This second edition reflects the need for brief units and well-focused narratives designed to teach basic concepts. Throughout, we specify the communication behaviors that are implied by and based on the supporting research presented in the unit.

Specific Features

Our coverage and our sequencing of the material are designed for use in introductory interpersonal communication courses as they are generally taught. Our understanding of these courses is based on much feedback from our colleagues across the country, some of whom used the first edition and some of whom did not. In addition, Wm. C. Brown Publishers has conducted both quantitative and qualitative market research in this area. Thus we are confident that our general organization and the particular sequence of the units will be compatible with most introductory courses. However, because professors often like to teach materials in varying sequences, our units are self-contained and cross-referenced to permit alternative presentations.

Content Features

We believe that learning to manage interpersonal relationships is as important to a person's health as diet. But *the skills involved in managing relationships are not always consistent with the "common wisdom" of our society*. For example, our society teaches competition and a "win-lose"orientation as the underlying assumption of play. However, such an approach is entirely inappropriate in managing a relationship. In this text, we have directly addressed this and similar problems.

Part I focuses on the basic issues and concerns in interpersonal communication. It recognizes that messages serve two functions, communicating meaning and defining relationships. Units 1, 2, and 3 unite the ideas of interpersonal communication and relationship management and present the foundation for our suggestions in the remainder of the text for managing various parts of relational communication. Units 4 through 9 treat particular aspects of an individual's communication behavior—the "intrapersonal" communication system—including how interpersonal needs develop, how perception occurs, how to avoid perceptual error, how to listen and to provide feedback, how self-concepts emerged and can be changed, and how to disclose oneself with greater confidence and success in relationships with others.

Part II focuses on language and its use in relationships. Units 10 and 11 explore the nature of language; Units 12 and 13 address talking about feelings, needs, and expectations; and Unit 14 speaks to several questions: What are the pitfalls of language? What can be done about them? How does language influence relationship style? How can problems of language usage in relationships be overcome?

The enormous complexity of the nonverbal message system has caused most of the problems in relationship management. Part III tries to simplify that complexity for the student. Unit 15 focuses on general and particular body cues and tells the student what to do and what to avoid. Our advice, of course, is carefully based in research. Unit 16 deals with touching, space, and features of the environment. Unit 17 concentrates on silence, time, and so-called vocalic cues, such as tone of voice, rate, and pitch.

Part IV discusses effective relationship management. Units 18 and 19 emphasize the knowledge and skills involved in initiating and developing a relationship. Units 20 and 21 explain why defensiveness occurs and what to do about it. Unit 22 explores power use and abuse in relationships and the management of power games. Units 23 and 24 discuss *intra*personal and *inter*personal conflict, respectively: what conflict is, how we tend to respond to it, and how to intervene in conflicts more intelligently than the common social wisdom teaches. The entire book is about relationship management, but Units 25 and 26 integrate the remainder of the text. Unit 25 explains why relationships deteriorate, how to identify the stages of relationships, and how to manage the loss of a relationship. Unit 26 teaches the skills directly involved in promoting relational growth. Here the student will learn appropriate self-disclosure, how to give support, how to achieve role agreement, and how to demonstrate affection. Most importantly, this unit shows how to guard against stagnation.

Learning Aids

Experiences

At the back of the book is a set of experiences, arranged according to unit sequence, that offer the teacher a broad range of interesting, directly applicable, and easily used in-class activities. We have more than doubled the number of these pedagogical devices, directing them toward the units they support and showing how each relates to some aspect of relationship management and growth. In this, as in other changes in the second edition, we are responding to the requests of our colleagues. Additional experiences are collected in the Instructor's Manual that accompanies the text.

Unit Opening Pedagogy

Each unit in our text opens with a Preview, a brief list of Key Terms, and a statement of Objectives. These are designed to give the student the clearest possible insight into the nature and content of the unit.

End of Unit Pedagogy

At the end of each unit is a Summary of the most important ideas in the unit. The Discussion Questions may be used by the student privately to study the unit or by the teacher to lead the class in practicing the analytical and performance skills described. The Endnotes following each unit include carefully selected references to the literature. We have tried to present a manageable number of both classic and current works.

Self-Help Guide

The Self-Help Guide is presented as a kind of index that organizes the text materials around the questions students most frequently ask about managing their relationships, *expressed in terms the students use*. We believe this guide can lead to wider access to the materials.

Glossary

In the Glossary the important terms used in interpersonal communication courses, and in this book, are compiled. Today's students have come to expect and depend upon a glossary and are willing to express their gratitude when one is presented.

Acknowledgments

We wish to thank the following people who reviewed the first edition of *Interpersonal Growth Through Communication:*

Lois Almen
College of San Mateo

John C. Countryman
University of Richmond

James Crocker-Lakness
University of Cincinnati

Robert C. Dick
Indiana University, Indianapolis

William Douglas
University of Houston

Jackson Huntley
University of Minnesota, Duluth

Bernadette M. MacPherson
Emerson College, Boston

Judy C. Pearson
Ohio University, Athens

Sharon A. Ratliffe
Golden West College, Huntington Beach, CA

We are especially grateful to those colleagues who provided insightful comments and suggestions that improved the second edition:

Allan Broadhurst
Cape Cod Community College, West Barnstable, MA

James Crocker-Lakness
University of Cincinnati

Reese Elliott
Austin Peay State University, Clarksville, TN

Jack Frisch
University of Wisconsin, Green Bay

William Griese
De Anza College, Cupertino, CA

Randall Koper
University of the Pacific, Stockton, CA

Clarice Lowe
Texas Southern University, Houston

Bonnie Miley
Iowa Western Community College, Council Bluffs

Jo Young Switzer
Indiana—Purdue University at Fort Wayne

Gerald L. Wilson
Alan M. Hantz
Michael S. Hanna

Interpersonal Growth Through Communication

Interpersonal
Communication: The Basics

≫|≪
UNIT 1

Interpersonal Effectiveness in Relationships

Preview

We believe that you would not choose to study interpersonal communication if you did not want to increase your relational effectiveness. You are right to believe that your best means to increase such effectiveness is to increase your communication competence. This is the central theme of *Interpersonal Growth Through Communication*. The goal of this unit is to provide a foundation for the remainder of the text. In this unit you will learn a useful definition of *interpersonal communication*. Each main idea in that definition is also defined and explained.

Key Terms

communication
communication competence
communication effectiveness
information
interpersonal
messages
persuasive
process
relationship
self-expressive
sign
symbol
transactional

Objectives

1. Explain why variability is a characteristic of relational life, using examples from a particular relationship.
2. Define and explain *interpersonal communication*.
3. Define and explain each main idea in the definition of interpersonal communication, including:
   information
   messages
   process
   relationship
   transactional
4. Contrast nonpersuasive intentional, self-expressive, and persuasive messages.
5. Contrast the terms *communication competence* and *relational effectiveness* and then explain their relationship.

You may limit your interactions with your boss to formal, task-related talk.

Think about some of the many different relationships that you experience. You have a relationship with each of your parents, if they are living, and with each of your friends. You may even differentiate among your friends on the basis of the degree of intensity or quality of these relationships. If you have brothers and sisters, your relationships with them will undoubtedly differ from your relationships with your friends. If you have a job, your relationships there will include elements of subordination and power that distinguish them from your relationships with your friends.

You will certainly agree that your relationships are characterized by *variability*. For example, you may limit your interactions with your boss to formal, task-related talk, preferring to keep her at a distance because of the power component in your relationship. At the same time, you may engage in a broad range of interactions with your best friend: At one moment you may take out your frustrations on your friend, at another you may turn to your friend for support and comfort or extend support and comfort, and at still another moment you may seek information from your friend to reduce your uncertainty[1] or strengthen your concept of yourself. This enormous variability in interpersonal communication has led scholars to try to define and illustrate the term precisely.

What Is Interpersonal Communication?

Interpersonal communication is the transactional process of exchanging messages and negotiating meaning to convey information and to establish and maintain relationships. This definition makes clear that our focus is not only on the exchange of messages but also on their joint interpretation and negotiation. The definition includes some key ideas that bear further explanation.

Interpersonal

The term *interpersonal* means between people. Interpersonal communication usually, but not always, occurs face to face.

Communication

There are generally two basic understandings of the term *communication*. Perhaps the most common is that it is a process of transferring messages. With this definition in mind, scholars have developed important models of message transmission, which have been very helpful as modern man has evolved highly technical communications systems such as radio, television, and computer-assisted, voice-activated interactive teaching machines.

A second common yet more complex (and more interesting) understanding is that communication involves the meaning of messages—their interpretation as well as transmission. Meaning is thus a function of the interaction of the communicators. It is this second focus that is more interesting to us as we study interpersonal communication.

Transactional

The term *transactional* defines instantaneous, mutual negotiation. We include it to emphasize that each interpersonal communication is a mutual event whose meaning is negotiated by the participants. In fluent conversation, we use signs and symbols as we talk with each other. A *sign* is something that stands for something else, when there is a natural relationship, as in dark clouds to rain. A *symbol* is something that stands for something when there is no natural relationship, as in the word *chair* to the actual object. Our use of signs and symbols depends on our unique, individual understanding of them. The concept of transaction makes clear that the individuals must arrive at some mutual agreement about the meanings for communication to be effective.

When you talk with someone, the act of talking changes both you and the other person.

Process

The word *process* is used to suggest that interpersonal communication is a continuing and continually changing phenomenon. When you talk with someone, the act of talking changes both you and the other person. As you grow, as you learn, as your self-concept evolves, and as your image of the relationship develops, you change your basic assumptions, as does the other person.

One teacher, trying to explain the notion of process, asked a student to try to tell another how she felt and then to report on how she attempted to communicate her feelings. The result was that student's report was obsolete by the time it was finished because the act of telling how she felt changed the way she felt.

Messages

A *message,* another key idea in our definition, is any symbol or combination of signs or symbols that functions as a stimulus for a receiver. These messages may be auditory, such as language and vocal cues, or visual, such as body, face, and eye movements. They may also be tactile if we communicate by touch. We may generate messages by using the environment (for example, how we place objects or arrange furnishings) or the clothing we wear. When we arrive for an appointment or date at a particular time, we express our view of the situation.

Messages are intentional means of achieving **a goal.** Sometimes we are not as aware of our purposes as we might be, as in when we say or do something and later regret it. But, even when this happens, others assume that we are acting with intention. We expect people to mean what they say and do and say and do what they mean. The more intentional we can be in our communication, the more likely we will be able to select messages appropriate to our purposes. Competence in interpersonal communication implies just that. It implies that we are aware of our goals and how to communicate so that we are most likely to achieve them.

Certain verbal and nonverbal messages, known as *self-expressive* messages, point to the sender's emotional state. If you walk near a playground you will be able to see and hear many examples of such messages. The child who jumps up and down just because he is excited is sending a powerful nonverbal message about his excitement. The child who shouts for joy is using his voice for the same purpose.

Similar observations can be made when you watch your friends on the dance floor. Some will be sending messages for a persuasive reason, but many

The Joy of Self-Expression

more will be moving their bodies and occasionally vocalizing just for the joy of self-expression.

Some people use language merely to express their emotional states, not pausing to think about the denotative implications of their word choice. These people frequently choose strong language without intending anyone to take them literally. For example, a teen-age girl was recently overheard saying to her best friend, "I'm going to kill you if you do that again." The statement was made in the kitchen, while the two girls were doing the dishes. The friend had just used the rubber spray hose at the sink to soak the first girl in a surprise attack. Such excessive use of language is probably common in your experience, too.

Sometimes extravagant uses of language can create grave problems in a relationship. How you talk with someone says a lot not only about yourself but also about your concept of the other person. Excessive language may well be giving messages that create relationship problems. For example, you may have known an unhappy person who habitually uses strong, negative language to describe his experience of the world and appears to believe that you see the world in the same way. "It's awful at this school," he says. "The teacher is a jerk. The quarter system is dumb. The student newspaper is stupid. The dormitory is a pigsty. The campus is a dump." Clearly, this language says that the speaker does not like the school. If you were to ask him about the literal meaning of each of his strong words, he might be surprised, for he is thinking metaphorically. Even so, you would undoubtedly grow weary of such a person.

A second category of messages is *persuasive* messages. If you set out to change the thoughts, feelings, or behavior of someone, you have sent persuasive messages. Change is thus an important component of persuasive communication. As you will see, learning to set appropriate, well-defined, positive goals is a valuable persuasive skill.

Not all persuasive messages are consciously structured for the particular communication event. For instance, we believe that individuals carefully nurture the images and impressions they project, although they may not deliberately select the message at the moment they send it. For example, a woman may carefully choose the clothing she buys to conform to certain standards she holds. The clothes thus become part of the image she projects. On some occasions her selection of items from her closet may be very deliberate; at other times—as when she is late for class—her choice may be relatively unconscious. Even at such moments, however, the woman's impression management is intentional.

Persuasive messages operate in at least two ways. When you manage your relationships, that management can take a positive, nurturing, and maintaining direction or it can move in the direction of conflict. In either case, effective goal setting seems a critical interpersonal communication skill.

Information

The term *information* has spurred much interest in communication studies. Some scholars believe information deals with the amount of uncertainty and unpredictability that exists in a situation.[2] When a situation is completely predictable, no new information is present. This view of information is often a little confusing, however, for it has nothing to do with message, facts, or meaning. It suggests instead the number of messages required to eliminate all uncertainty in a situation. Others have argued that information must be more human. They focus on the notion that anything conveyed in a communication that reduces uncertainty and increases predictability is information.[3]

This second understanding of information is closer to our definition of the term as anything in a communication event that helps or causes us to attach meaning. Thus talk and the nonverbal messages that surround it and allow you to know how to interpret the talk are information.

Relationship

We will let *relationship* mean any connection, involvement, or association between two people, regardless of its source. Relationships can be permanent, such as by blood, or transitory. Most of your relationships are transitory and therefore also tentative. Whether by blood or by any other connection, the quality of your relationships is a matter of choice, for to sustain them in a mutually satisfying way, you have to nurture and reinforce them.

Competence and Effectiveness

There are important differences between the terms *competence* and *effectiveness*. Throughout this book we argue that interpersonal effectiveness flows from communication competence. It seems a good idea, therefore, to explain our concept of their differences.

Communication competence has been defined by a number of scholars. The definition we like best is the one by Carl Larson and his colleagues, who define it as "the ability of an individual to demonstrate knowledge of the appropriate communicative behavior in a given situation."[4]

Throughout this book we use the term *communication effectiveness* to mean communication that gets you to your goals. *Communication* is *effective* when you create in the mind of someone else the idea you wanted to create. Communication is *not* effective when the receiver gets a meaning different from the one you intended.

Notice that a person who has not communicated effectively has, nevertheless, communicated. Notice, too, that the person may be a highly competent communicator. It is possible to be a competent communicator and still not get the effect you want.

We entitled this unit "Interpersonal Effectiveness in Relationships" to convey our interest in communication behavior that helps you get the desired results in your relationships. The best way to achieve such interpersonal effectiveness is to develop communication competence.

> **The best way to achieve interpersonal effectiveness is to develop communication competence.**

For the rest of your life, you will want to polish your analytical and performance communication skills. You will continually ask such seemingly simple but crucial questions as: How can I start a conversation with this person? How can I get other people to open up? How can I let another person know who I truly am? How can I issue an invitation that is likely to be accepted? Is there something I can do to handle criticism more constructively? How can I reduce my anxiety in social situations? Is there a way to know where I stand with someone? Can I change a relationship for the better? Can I change a relationship without damaging it? These questions and countless others about relational effectiveness will be the focus of your study in interpersonal communication.

Summary

Your relationships are enormously varied but all rest upon interpersonal communication—the transactional process of exchanging verbal and nonverbal messages to convey information and to establish and maintain relationships. Each term in this definition has been defined and explained. We want you to understand that the study of interpersonal communication is complex but well worthwhile. Your goal is to manage your relationships with increasing effectiveness. The best way to do this is to increase your communication competence.

Congratulations! Your choice to study interpersonal communication is an important step in that lifelong journey.

Discussion Questions

1. Working with a small group of your classmates, try to construct a *taxonomy*, or classification system, of as many different kinds of relationships as possible (for example, a father-daughter relationship). Base the taxonomy on one of these criteria: degree of intimacy, amount of time spent, degree of importance, or activities engaged in. List your group's taxonomy on the chalkboard and compare it to the lists

generated by other groups in your class. What similarities and differences do you find in the *approach* and the *results* of the various group efforts? Can you draw out of this exercise a lesson about relationship effectiveness?

2. Apply each term in our definition of interpersonal communication to an important relationship in your life.

3. With one or two classmates, act out what you think might happen in the first few minutes of a blind date. Afterward, try to identify examples of auditory, visual, tactile, and environmental messages. Then classify them as nonpersuasive intentional, self-expressive, and persuasive messages.

Endnotes

1. For a thoughtful and thorough development of this idea of uncertainty reduction, see C. R. Berger and J. J. Bradac, *Language and Social Knowledge: Uncertainty in Interpersonal Relations* (London: Edward Arnold Publishers, 1982).

2. This difficult concept has been very influential. For further discussion, see three classic works: N. Wiener, *Cybernetics, or Control and Communication in the Animal and Machine* (Cambridge: MIT Press, 1948); W. Weaver, "The Mathematics of Communication," *Scientific American* 181 (1949): 11–15; and C. Shannon and W. Weaver, *The Mathematical Theory of Communication* (Urbana: University of Illinois Press, 1949).

3. Y. Bar-Hillel and R. Carnap, "Semantic Information," *British Journal of the Philosophy of Science* 4 (1953): 147–57.

4. C. E. Larson, P. M. Backlund, M. K. Redmond, and A. Barbour, *Assessing Communication Competence* (Falls Church, VA: Speech Communication Association, 1978), 16.

>>|<<
UNIT 2
Understanding the Interpersonal Communication Process

Preview

In this unit you will study four models of the communication process to discover how the various components of the process work and how they interact with each other. This information will help you communicate effectively because you will be much more sensitive to the enormous complexity of the process and more aware of where communication difficulties usually occur.

Key Terms
channels
context
decoder
encoder
feedback
frame of reference
inter-
intra-
messages
noise
perceptual sensitivity
receiver
risk
self-disclosure
source
trust

Objectives
1. First, draw from memory and label the components of a process model of interpersonal communication. Then define and explain the components.
2. Define and give an example of each of the following parts in the interpersonal communication process:

channels	perceptual
context	sensitivity
decoder	receiver
encoder	risk
feedback	self-disclosure
messages	source
noise	trust

3. Explain each step in the interpersonal exchange model of the communication process.

We have defined interpersonal communication as the transactional process of exchanging messages to convey information and to establish and maintain relationships. This definition is the result of a good deal of thinking about communication by scholars from many different backgrounds and ages. Occasionally someone develops a model of the communication process that is very influential. One of the first models, proposed by C. E. Shannon and W. Weaver in 1949, has sometimes been referred to as the "telephone" model.

The Shannon and Weaver Model

Shannon and Weaver were engineers interested in how messages were transmitted from place to place electrically, and their model reflects that interest. But the model is also valuable in the study of interpersonal communication (see figure 2.1),[1] for it describes communication as a process in which an information source "inputs" a message into a transmitter. The transmitter sends a signal through a channel, where it is received and converted back into a message at its destination. A very important component of the model is noise, which is any disturbance in the channel that interferes with the fidelity of the transmission.

What a simple—and helpful—conceptualization of communication! But, for our purposes, the model has some limitations. Notice that the model flows in one direction, from source to destination, and depicts only one channel. Finally, notice that the model assumes noise to reside in the channel—a physical

Figure 2.1 The Shannon and Weaver Model of Communication

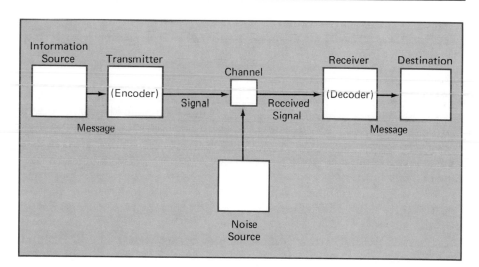

Figure 2.2 A Process Model of Communication

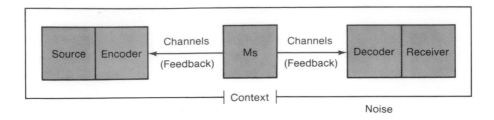

phenomenon. These limitations make it hard to apply the model to the inter-personal communication process. We have said the communication process is transactional, which means that each party is at once sending and receiving messages.

A Process Model of Communication

The limitations of the Shannon and Weaver model gave rise to a number of other models,[2] which, like all models, are useful and also limiting. They are useful because they focus attention on some feature or some set of relation-ships in the process. They are limiting because, in focusing attention, they dis-tract attention away from other features.

Figure 2.2 is a process model that may be more useful in your study of interpersonal communication. Although it resembles the Shannon and Weaver model, it avoids the limitations of its earlier counterpart in showing two-directional flow, multiple channels, and more than one message.

The Process Model of Communication

The model is labeled to indicate that two individuals are working together in one setting. The *source* is the location of an idea. Obviously, in interpersonal contexts, the source of the idea is an individual. The next term, *encoder,* is used in the same box to show that individuals must translate ideas into codes. The most common, but by no means the only, code is language. You can also encode into many different nonverbal message systems. For example, you can communicate with muscle changes, with peculiar use of space, with the clothes you wear, or with your gestures and tone of voice.

Notice that, at the other side of the model, another individual must *decode* the messages sent. Since these messages do *not* have meaning in and of themselves (meaning is in the minds of those who use the codes), messages must be decoded to be meaningful. Skill in decoding is just as important as skill in encoding.

The source/encoder transmits messages—plural. Since more than one code is used every time you communicate, you must be sending more than one message. The *M*s in the middle of the box suggest these multiple messages.

These messages have to be transmitted through *channels*. A person talking with you is using vibrations in the molecular structure of the air as a channel. If this person is visible as well as audible, you will pick up many nonverbal messages, too. In that case, light waves are being used as channels. If a phone is used, electrical impulses over a wire are being used to send messages. Even in a phone call more than one message is sent. Words, phrases, tone, stress, and emphasis are all communicated.

Notice the arrowheads at either end of the middle line labeled *channels*. These arrowheads suggest that messages travel in both directions at the same time. This special feature of the model is *feedback*. A decoder feeds back what is heard so that the encoder can control and correct the message if it is wrong. Feedback also suggests that messages flow in both directions at the same time. This two-way flow allows the encoder to know what is being received. This in turn allows for modification in action during communication.

Reexamine figure 2.2. Notice that all components of the model are enclosed in the context of the communication event. Everything available to the communicators in that event—including all that the participants brought with them—affects the message exchange. Health, attitudes and opinions, emotional condition, and inhibitions all come into play at the moment.

An important feature of both the Shannon and Weaver model and this is *noise*. But we do not want to limit your understanding of this term to physical, channel noise, for it refers to any sensory or perceptual interference that disrupts or distorts communication. Noise can be both physical (disturbances in the channels) and emotional. Sometimes called *semantic,* emotional noise is anything going on inside the participants that upsets the accuracy of message reception or transmission.

A potential for noise is in the source/encoder. If the encoder has a biased perception or uses strong language, for example, noise is introduced. Or there can be noise in the channels. Hear that air conditioner or furnace working? Is anything happening in the next room? If so, you are aware of it because of the noise. If not, you have checked that out, too, by examining the noise in the environment.

Noise is any sensory or perceptual interference that disrupts or distorts communication.

There is also the potential for noise in messages, especially when people of different cultures try to talk with each other. Offensive language is also sometimes used by people speaking the same tongue. Noisy nonverbal signs and signals are likewise transmitted. These problems are compounded when the

Figure 2.3 The Communication Process with Noise Added

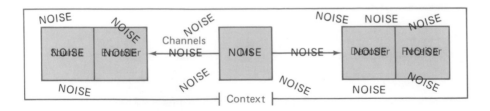

expectations of other cultures are introduced. Often very noisy results are produced.

To illustrate, Tim was working as a busboy in a restaurant that also employed an Iranian student on the same shift. One day Tim gestured a friendly O.K. sign to mean "Everything is good. You did well." The Iranian was working a double shift and had been up most of the night before writing a paper. Thus, he was experiencing a good deal of noise. In his exhausted state, he mistook the sign for an obscene message and knocked Tim down. Noise played an important part in distorting this message from what had been intended.

Let us add noise to the model, then, in all the places where it can occur, namely in the source, the encoder, the channels, the messages, the decoder, the receiver, and the context (see figure 2.3). In sum, the communication process can be a very noisy business.

Notice that in the model the arrow points at either end of the channels to show that feedback is an important and inherent part of the process. Feedback, which is a receiver's response to a message, can take a verbal or nonverbal form or both at the same time. It can also occur instantaneously or some time after the message has been received. Feedback most commonly comes in the form of an instantaneous combination of vocal and nonverbal cues. For example, a smile, a vocalized hum, or a nod may signal agreement, understanding, and the like. Clearly, feedback is central to interpersonal communication. It allows for correction and control of error.

The critical components of interpersonal communication, then, are *source, encoder, messages, channels, decoder, receiver, feedback, context,* and *noise.*

Filtering Screen Model

Meaning is not contained in words but rather is generated by those who use words. Examine figure 2.4, a model that focuses on the filtering process that occurs during communication.

All *S*s to the left of the figure stand for stimuli. This term is used because

Figure 2.4 Filtering Screen Model

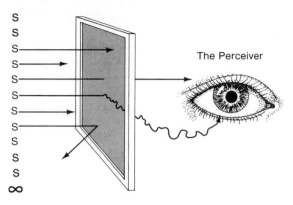

Frame of Reference—A Filter for One's Experience

once a message—such as a word—is sent, it becomes a part of the environmental stimuli. Until it is received, it is only one of an infinite number of such stimuli, which become significant only if they are permitted through the filter. To illustrate this point, think about your left ear. Until your attention was called to it, you may not have been aware of it although it was always there. How does the ear feel? Can you test its temperature with your attention only? Can you check to see if it itches or if there's a hint of an earache? Can you become aware of the sense of hearing in that ear? You can probably do all of these things because of the *filtering system* that allows you to attend to certain stimuli and to ignore others. If your ear began to hurt, you would no longer ignore it; that data would become significant.

For another example, look more closely at the actual ink on the page you are now reading. Center on the formation of the letters. You have been reading along without really paying attention to either the ink or the letters. Look at the enlarged letter in figure 2.5. Why didn't you pay attention to the height of the *t* relative to other letters? The information was always there, but you didn't pay attention to it because, until now, it wasn't important. The features on the letter

Figure 2.5

"t" go unnoticed until something calls attention to them. Besides, you are processing the symbols on this page in ways that prohibit an examination of individual letters. You are looking for groupings and for patterns, not for letters.

Y O U C O U L D R E A D T H I S L I N E O F T Y P E only if you studied
the individual letters and then imposed a grouping and pattern on them. This
is necessary since the line of type violates your perceptual expectations. But
this   line is   somewhat   different   and, no doubt,
is easier for you to read. Although this pattern of ink on paper is also a violation of what you would expect, the groupings make sense.

Thisl   ine,ont   heoth   erhand,i   safarmo   redifficult
line to examine because the groupings and patterns are a complete violation
of perceptual expectations. The stimuli are essentially changed, but not because of the ink on the paper. The change is in the pattern of ink on paper.
You probably weren't aware of the pattern or the shape of the various letters
within it. You were, however, aware of your understanding of the pattern. You
filtered the data, paying attention only to those that seemed important to you.

To provide you with still another example, did you notice those two dots
in the upper margin of this page?

Return to the model in figure 2.4. The eye to the right of the screen symbolizes all of the ways you can take in data: through your eyes, ears, nose,
mouth (both by taste and touch), and skin. The perceptual process is a system,
and you will almost always involve more than one way of receiving data in any
perceptual moment. You are looking at this sheet of paper, but you are probably also touching the book. Perhaps you are sitting in a chair under a lighted
lamp. You may be playing music. Your brain is always monitoring ways of sensing. But at the unconscious level, you are filtering what gets through to your
awareness. It is in that context that you are processing our messages. They
become merely additional data for you to perceive. You have the responsibility
to select those you will attend to and those you will ignore.

The communication models introduced here are useful. The process model
shows that the components of the communication process always exist in a
context. There is always a process of encoding and decoding when people are
communicating. Feedback is important to the model. And noise is a continuing
problem. In fact, the control of noise—either physical or psychological—dif-
ferentiates effective and ineffective communication.

The filtering screen model helps you understand the essence of meaning
inside your head. Outside of you is a stimulus field into which all sent messages
must fall. What gets through your own filtering devices is up to you. The meanings you generate from what you allow through your filters are your realities.
They are your understanding. They are what is real—and all that is real—for
you. Thus, your meanings are in you and not in the messages sent to you.
There are no meanings in words, there are only meanings in the people who
use words.

An Interpersonal Exchange Model

The models you have studied so far have shown the components of every communication event and something of what goes on inside an individual communicator, which scholars describe as *intrapersonal*. The prefix *intra-* means within, as in intramural; intrapersonal thus means "within the individual." Communication includes both *intrapersonal* and *interpersonal* processes. Remember, *inter-* means between. Interpersonal communication can occur between two people and in contexts, such as small groups, that include more than two people. In addition, there are a number of one-to-many settings in which this communication plays an important part. A public speech is such a context.

Figure 2.6 First Part of a Model of Interpersonal Exchange

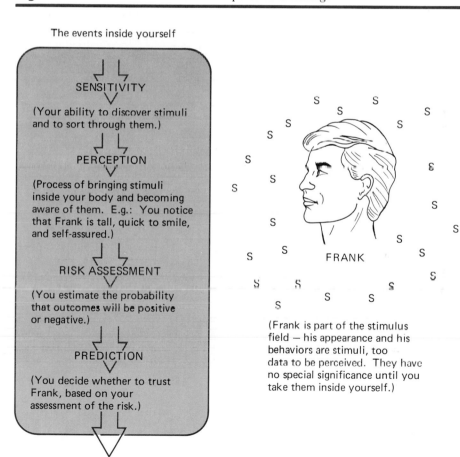

The events inside yourself

SENSITIVITY

(Your ability to discover stimuli and to sort through them.)

PERCEPTION

(Process of bringing stimuli inside your body and becoming aware of them. E.g.: You notice that Frank is tall, quick to smile, and self-assured.)

RISK ASSESSMENT

(You estimate the probability that outcomes will be positive or negative.)

PREDICTION

(You decide whether to trust Frank, based on your assessment of the risk.)

FRANK

(Frank is part of the stimulus field — his appearance and his behaviors are stimuli, too data to be perceived. They have no special significance until you take them inside yourself.)

Now we want to examine a slightly more complicated model of communication, which we have called the *interpersonal exchange model*. It is presented in complete form in figure 2.8, but because it is fairly complex, we first want to break it into parts.

Recall that, through the perception process, you must bring information inside yourself to make it meaningful and that there is no inherent meaning in the stimuli until you do that. Thus, for you Frank is merely part of the stimulus field. His appearance and behaviors have no intrinsic meaning. The meaning is inside Frank, perhaps, and inside yourself. Figure 2.6 shows part of what occurs within you during an interpersonal encounter.

You first recognize Frank as part of your stimulus field and then decide the level of risk in the moment. Having made that risk assessment, you decide

Figure 2.7 Second Part of a Model of Interpersonal Exchange

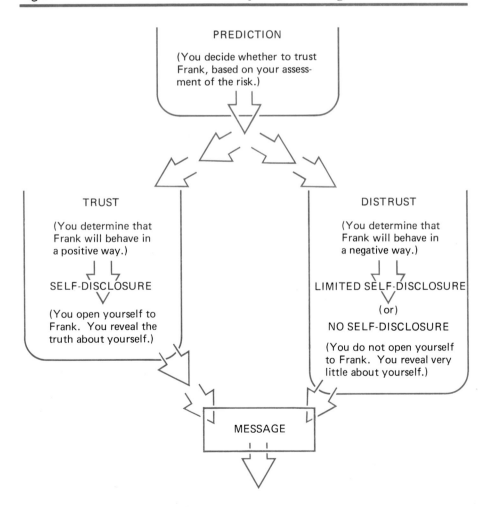

whether or not to trust Frank. At this point, at least in terms of any potential relationship you may have with Frank, you have an important choice to make to trust or to distrust. If you decide to trust, you will disclose yourself. If you decide to distrust, you will limit your self-disclosure, perhaps to the point of no self-disclosure (see figure 2.7).

In either case you will send some combination of verbal and nonverbal messages. At that point, you and your messages are merely part of the stimulus field for Frank. It is now his turn to take up the processing. He will go through the same sequence you have just finished.

Figure 2.8 displays the complete model of interpersonal exchange.

Figure 2.8 Complete Model of Interpersonal Exchange

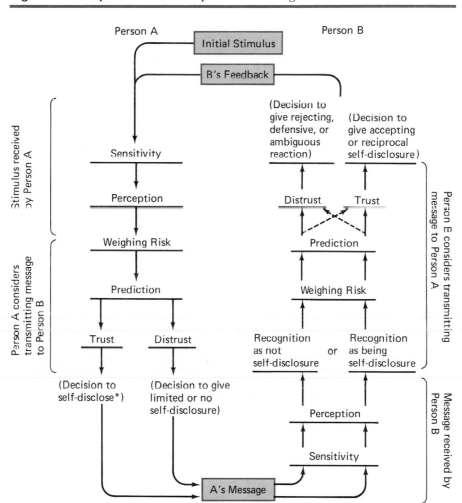

*Intimacy related to appropriate stage in the relationship.

Let yourself be Person A and let Frank be Person B. Frank has provided the initial stimulus that brought you to a decision about the kind of message you would send. Now it is up to Frank, Person B, to go through essentially the same sequence you did. But notice that there is a subtle difference. Frank must decide whether or not you disclosed yourself to him. If he recognizes self-disclosure on your part, he will probably behave in an accepting and self-disclosing way. If Frank understands your self-disclosure as an invitation to greater intimacy, he will almost certainly provide you with feedback. It is your turn again. If that happens, your relationship has a good chance of growing. But if he understands that your message does not disclose yourself and so behaves in a rejecting way, or if he understands your self-disclosure but rejects you anyway, the relationship probably will not grow. You will probably disengage.

We have already identified the critical components of interpersonal communication to be *source, encoder, messages, channels, decoder, receiver, feedback, context,* and *noise.* The exchange model identifies additional terms—*sensitivity, self-disclosure, trust,* and *risk*—that are central to the process of developing relationships.

Sensitivity

Sensitivity is an individual's skill and ability to perceive and to interpret what is perceived with empathy. That is, you are sensitive to the extent that you skillfully observe and make guesses that consider another person and reflect your ability to empathize. No two people can experience an event identically, but you can experience the moment in essentially similar ways. The key to sensitivity is the awareness that you are guessing and that the guess needs to be checked. Sensitive people empathize because they are willing and able to take others into account frequently. Sensitivity thus deals with the perceptual mechanisms and the interpretations that are made of those perceptions.

Self-Disclosure

Self-disclosure is the process of revealing the truth about oneself, including desires, needs, and goals. You self-disclose when you report your honest attitudes about another or another's ideas or about yourself and your ideas. You self-disclose when you respond candidly, daring to display your images.

Trust

Trust is a reliance on another person's behavior. But what is the behavior we rely on in interpersonal communication? We trust that the other person will receive the information we give in a relatively accepting, confirming, and positive way. In our interpersonal relationships, our concern is often with how our self-disclosure will be received. Here too we are relying on the other person to be accepting, confirming, and positive as we share a part of who we are. Because we rely on the other person not to use the information to be hurtful, trust is the foundation of self-disclosure. You trust that your self-disclosure will be received and accepted. Indeed, the bases of trust include another's character, competence, and judgment as you perceive them.

To trust is to rely on another person's behavior.

If a person is open, honest, and discrete and behaves consistently, and if you perceive the person's motives and intentions to be confirming, you trust the other's character. If this person has a record of successes, you trust her competence. And if you think this individual makes the right decisions, you trust the person's judgment. If all of these are combined in your image of this person, you trust and will be able to risk disclosing yourself.

Risk

Risk is the process of deciding to accept adverse outcomes that may result from trusting another. The greater the risk, the more you must trust. "Taking the risk" usually expresses a decision to gamble that you will receive positive, not negative, consequences from your actions. In its simplest form, to risk is to weigh payoffs and costs and to determine that the payoff for certain behavior is likely to be greater than its cost. When the decision is about self-disclosure, you risk being damaged by trusting another enough to disclose yourself.

Summary

Models help scholars study the components of the communication process and the relationships among them. We described four such models. One of the earliest was developed by Shannon and Weaver to examine how messages are electronically transmitted. Although their model was highly linear and one-way, and although it always placed noise in the channels of communication, it nevertheless was very important, for it identified several parts of the process that have since been taken up by other scholars.

A process model of communication, based on the Shannon and Weaver prototype, emphasizes the two-way flow of messages. It also incorporates such central concepts as context and feedback, making it clear that people always send more than one message and that noise can be both physical and semantic. One important implication of such a model is that communication occurs both inside and between individuals.

We also described a filtering screen model of communication to illustrate how a person *selectively* filters the data in the world outside. But the filtering

screen model is not transactional, nor does it allow study of message exchange. We therefore developed an exchange model of the interpersonal communication process, which establishes that what goes on within an individual
is profoundly important not only to communication in the content dimension
but also, more importantly, to communication about our relationships.

Discussion Questions

1. Working with a small group of classmates, develop an original model of
    the interpersonal communication process, labeling each part. Try to
    present as complete a picture of the variables that influence
    communication as you can. Does your model focus attention on certain
    aspects of communication while minimizing others? Present your
    finished product to the class for consideration and comments.
2. Using your group's model or the process model presented in this unit,
    decide whether the model is complete. If not, what changes or
    additions are needed?
3. Together with one or two classmates, discuss whether you believe the
    interpersonal exchange model is accurate. If not, what changes would
    you make? Why?

Endnotes

1. From C. E. Shannon and W. Weaver, *The Mathematical Theory of
    Communication* (Urbana: University of Illinois Press, 1949), 98.
2. For very well written summaries of the better known models, see D. C.
    Barnlund, *Interpersonal Communication: Survey and Studies* (Boston:
    Houghton Mifflin Company, 1968); and S. W. Littlejohn, *Theories of
    Human Communication,* 2d ed. (Belmont, CA: Wadsworth Publishing
    Company, 1983).

›)|‹‹
UNIT 3
An Agenda for Talking About Relationships

Preview

Although it is impossible to know for certain, it seems reasonable to suppose that most of the trouble people get into when they talk with each other has little to do with objects and events in the world. People are fairly skillful at talking about topics and objects. The difficulty is far more likely to occur in the relationship itself. In this unit you will learn how to differentiate between messages about content and messages about relationships. You will also learn how to identify what is going on in a relationship.

The key ideas in the unit are: (1) A communication event has two dimensions—a content dimension and a relationship dimension. (2) The most important part of relationship management is learning to talk about the relationship dimension. (3) A relationship is always a present-tense phenomenon. (4) A relationship exists only inside people, not in the physical space between them. That is, it exists as a concept in the world of words. (5) We live in a society that does not teach us how to talk about relationships very well. (6) It is useful to identify the components that can occur in a relationship because such a list can function as an agenda when we want or need to talk about the relationship.

Key Terms
absolute present
agenda for talking about relationships
check-out
content dimension
expectations
feelings
images
inferences
intentions
observations
openness
personalizing
relationship dimension
wants

Objectives

1. Repeat from memory, in the sequence given in this unit, the agenda for talking about relationships:

Content Dimension	Relationship Dimension
Objects	Observations
Phenomena	Inferences
Events	Feelings
Topics	Wants and expectations
	Intentions
	Openness
	Images
	Check-out

2. Explain the principle of the absolute present and describe its importance to relationship management.
3. Explain the concept of personalizing talk about relationships and then give examples of both personalized and nonpersonalized talk.

27

In a profoundly influential book published in 1967, Paul Watzlawick, Janet Beavin, and Don Jackson argued persuasively that every communication event has two dimensions, a *content dimension* and a *relationship dimension*.[1] In the content dimension are all the objects, phenomena, and events in the world but outside ourselves as well as some objects, phenomena, and events inside ourselves. For example, discussions with a friend about the weather, last night's ballgame, or the movie you saw together are in the content dimension.

Each time we talk with someone, we also send and receive messages about how to interpret what is said or how to perceive the other person. These messages may be carried in gestures, facial expression, tone of voice, or variations in the rate or force of speech. Rarely do we talk directly about the relationship, although we are always aware of it during our conversation because we continually monitor, either consciously or sometimes relatively unconsciously, the range of messages in the exchange. Most of the time this system works well, and we make our way in the world without too much difficulty.

Sometimes, however, we need or want to talk directly about the relationship. Of course, you would not want to talk about your relationship with everyone or even all the time with the most important people in your life. But it may seem necessary, if, for example, we wish to pay a compliment, to assert one of our rights, or to express our anger or resentment. When such a need occurs, most of us are at a loss. We know the relationship issue is there, but we don't quite know how to identify it and bring it out. We don't want to offend, we certainly don't want to do further damage to a shaken relationship, and we don't want to cause people to become defensive. We also feel awkward because talking about relationships is not done much in our society.

This unit focuses on a system and several communication skills that make thinking and talking about relationships easier. The system and skills rest on certain fundamental assumptions, the first of which concerns the *absolute present*.

Absolute Present

One way to improve the accuracy of talk about relationships is to accept the fact that you live in the present. This idea is absolute. You cannot live at any other time, either future or past. But you can remember the past because you have language.

A college student who talks and acts as if his high school experiences are the present is trying to live in the past. The person who lives for and as if she is the physician she is studying to be is trying to live in the future. Both situations cause problems in relationships and communication because most people experience others in the present.

This idea of the absolute present can be greatly liberating. Since you can only live in the present and since you cannot take back the past, all that has come before is history. You can choose—in the present—how you will respond emotionally to past events. This choice can allow you to influence how others view your past. It can also allow you to guide their perceptions of you while you are in contact. You can choose from among many possibilities, not just one!

What you want and what you can expect involve the future. You can learn to deal with others in relationship to what you want—mostly free of your ties to the past—if only you choose to do so.

Personalizing

To *personalize* your verbal communication is to make clear by your choice of language that you are taking responsibility for your own statements and judgments.

This is a fairly complicated notion. For example, suppose your instructor walks up to a person in your class who has just presented an outstanding analysis of a case study. He says, "You are wonderful." Clearly, he is making a judgment about the woman. He is responsible for the decision to judge those stimuli coming into him as "wonderful." Put another way, the idea "wonderful" is a function of his own value system.

But look at his statement again: "You are wonderful." The form of the sentence appears to say that the woman is intrinsically wonderful. Anyone hearing her analysis would judge her to be wonderful if that were true, regardless of their preferences for subject matter or style or their listening ability and expertise in the area addressed by the case study. The "wonderfulness" would be something born into her. The instructor, listening to her, would have nothing whatever to do with her wonderfulness. The form of this sentence makes it incorrect. It denies the truth—that the instructor, and not the woman, is responsible for his judgment about her analysis.

So long as there is no socially sensitive component in the sentence, "You are wonderful," it is a compliment. So is, "You are beautiful." Another student in the class might walk up to the woman and say, "You are beautiful." Although the speaker might be considered forward, you do not notice that the form of the sentence is wrong.

The focus is not on the fact that the judgment actually belongs to the speaker if the judgment does not call attention to itself. But suppose the speaker said instead to that young woman, "You are, without a doubt, the ugliest and most repulsive-looking beast I have ever seen." Ah! That's another story, isn't it?

The woman would not ignore that sentence. She would undoubtedly be offended by it. She would instantly say the sentence is offensive, perhaps wrong, clearly inappropriate. But she might have some difficulty identifying *why* she felt that way. The fact is, the form of this sentence shifts the responsibility for the other student's judgment onto her. ''Ugly'' is not his responsibility, but hers! Ugliness is a function of some intrinsic quality in her if the form of the other student's sentence is correct.

For some personal experience with this idea, study the following two paintings. To determine which is more beautiful, you must call upon an internal set of criteria. That is, you must *judge* which of the two is more beautiful. This judgment is a function of your own nervous system. But if you *say* that one of the pictures *is* more beautiful, you have used language that places the beauty in the picture rather than in yourself.[2]

Likewise, to personalize your talk is to state clearly that your judgments are your responsibility. Personalizing talk is also acknowledging your responsibility. Sentences such as, ''You make me mad,'' ''You're crazy,'' ''It's important that we follow this procedure,'' and ''Don't you think that . . .'' are problematic because none is personalized. Each places responsibility for your nervous system on someone or something outside of you. But they can be improved—and made much more accurate and meaningful—by personalizing them.

On the next page are sample statements. Those on the left are not personalized. That is, the speaker shifts the responsibility for the idea expressed to someone else. The sentences on the right are correctly personalized. You

Which painting is more beautiful? Your answer is a function of your nervous system.

Pablo Picasso, *Seated Woman,* 1926–27, oil on canvas, 51½'' × 38½'', Ontario Art Museum.

Leonardo da Vinci, *Mona Lisa,* Three Lions, New York.

can see at a glance that the speakers are assuming responsibility for their own judgments and opinions.

Not Personalized	**Personalized**
You're beautiful.	You seem beautiful to me.
You're ugly.	I don't like the way you look.
You make me angry.	When I see that behavior I respond with anger.
You're crazy.	That behavior seems crazy to me.
It's important that we. . . .	I think it is important that we. . . .
Don't you think that. . . .	I think that . . . and I would like you to think so, too.

If you can learn to stay in the present when it is helpful to do so—and that is almost all the time when you are working on your relationships—and if you can learn to personalize your talk when necessary, you will already be a more efficient and more effective communicator than most of the people you will ever meet. These are relatively simple skills to learn, but it takes some practice to integrate them into your behavior patterns.

Agenda for Talking About Relationships

Table 3.1, which presents the components of the relationship dimensions, provides a convenient agenda for talking about relationships. The components can be summarized into eight categories: observations, inferences, feelings, wants and expectations, intentions, openness, images, and check-out. Note that five of these eight components are in boldface type, which indicates that they are the primary components of the agenda.

Table 3.1 The Components of the Relationship Dimension of Talk Provide an Agenda for Talking About Relationships

Content Dimension	Relationship Dimension
Objects	Observations
Phenomena	Inferences
Events	**Feelings**
	Wants and expectations
Topics	**Intentions**
	Openness
	Images
	Check-Out

Observations

Observations are any information from outside that you take inside and process as you are communicating with another person. This includes how a person stands, how she looks, how she sounds, or how she feels. You can observe nothing that is inside the other person; your ability to observe stops with the data available at the level of the other person's skin.

You thus cannot "read" someone's mind; you can only make observations and draw inferences from them.

Inferences

Inferences are your guesses about the meaning of your observations. Unfortunately, people often make an observation, guess what another person is thinking, and then act on the guess as though it were correct beyond question. This has been called *fact-inference confusion,* and it can be a very critical communication problem. Perhaps you have had an experience similar to this one:

Said	**Thought**
He: Hello. How are you?	Hmmmm. Not bad looking. Nice eyes.
She: Hi. (Smiles) I'm just fine, although I think I am a little lost.	Thank goodness. Someone to help. Hmmmm. Nice build. Must be an athlete.
He: Can I help you? I. . . .	Nice smile. I'll help her. . . .
She: I'm trying to find the Drum Room. I've been up and down the street and. . . .	I'm late. Hope he knows how to get there. His voice has command. I like that.
He: My name is David. I'm going there myself. Are you in the AMA?	I can help. Maybe she'll walk along with me. That smile lights up her face. The AMA is having a meeting. She must be a doctor!
She: Yes. I'm Jennifer. Are you in the AMA too?	Maybe he'll ask me to walk along with him. That'd be pleasant. His suit must have been expensive.
David: Would you like to walk with me? It isn't far.	Me, a doctor? I haven't even graduated from college yet. But there's no sense spoiling this opportunity. I'll see if I can find something else to talk about with her.
Jennifer: I sure would. . . .	
David: Are you making some kind of presentation?	Dumb question. Why did I say that? For that matter, why didn't I just tell her I'm not a member?

Jennifer: I'm reading a paper at the 3:00 session. And I think I'm late as well as lost.

David: You're not late. You're quite a bit early. It's just a quarter until two. . . .

Could I buy you a drink?

Jennifer: I'd like that very much. Shall we go to the coffee shop here?

David: Sure. Where are you from?

Jennifer: I teach at the University of Iowa. Do you know where Iowa City is?

David: Yes. Where did you go to medical school?

Jennifer: Medical school! I'm a teaching assistant in the Marketing Department working on my Masters.

He's not a member, but he's very good-looking. Wonder what he's going to do at the convention.

Well, I'm not the only one who makes mistakes. Wonder where she's from to be an hour off the time. Hmmm. White Shoulders—or is it Charlie?

I wonder if she's attached?

No ring. I wonder if he's attached? I don't want to get mixed up with. . . . He's surely not single. But then, maybe he is. . . . It won't hurt to have a cup of tea. I'm tired from the trip. Shouldn't have treated myself to that can of beer on the plane.

Dumb question again. Why couldn't I have said something like. . . .

So what if I am a teaching assistant in my first term. He's probably a wealthy attorney or something.

I'll make small talk. She's out of my league. . . .

Where'd he get this idea?

From this short dialogue you can see that what people *say* is only a small part of what they experience at the moment. A good deal of what is experienced is guesswork—and often, wrong. For example, David felt he couldn't trust Jennifer. He didn't respond to her questions. He may have thought that the AMA (we can suppose he saw a sign so he knew there was a meeting) was the American Medical Association. This guess would justify his next guess that Jennifer is a doctor. We can't know what was going on beyond what is provided, but notice that when Jennifer asked him if he was in the AMA, too, he responded with a question. Was he embarrassed by his own lack of education? He talks about not graduating from college—to himself. Does he equate his lack of formal education—his lack of a degree—with being not adequate? He doesn't want to spoil an opportunity with Jennifer so he evades the issue by looking for another topic. Moreover, he chastises himself for asking Jennifer if she is making a presentation. Was he comparing himself to his image of Jennifer and coming out badly in the comparison?

And what about Jennifer's reaction to David? It would seem she is attracted to him. But how do you account for her devaluation of her own position as a teaching assistant in her first term? How do you account for her guess that David is a well-to-do professional? How do you account for her surprise that David asked the name of her medical school? The answer is obvious by now. They were operating on their own guesses as though the guesses were the truth. David and Jennifer were suffering from fact-inference confusion.

Relationships consist of observations and inferences, always in the present tense. You observe the other person, then infer what the observations mean. Sometimes you check them out, and sometimes you don't. Not checking them out can obviously create problems in a relationship.

If you only know four or five words to describe a particular feeling state, you will be able to experience only four or five emotions when that state is present.

Feelings

Feelings deal with the physical condition of individuals. Feelings are always physical, unlike *emotions,* which exist in the words we use to describe feelings. You cannot feel words, but you can feel your body. Then you attach words to those feelings. As you will see, this difference between feelings and emotions is important in learning to improve your communication skills. For now it is enough to say that because we do not have much language to talk about our feelings, we tend to have a limited emotional range and we use our language habits to understand our feeling states in a very limited and limiting way. For example, if you only know four or five words to describe a particular feeling, you will be able to experience only four or five emotions when that state is present.

Feelings are extremely important because contextually we assign language to them that has significance in a relationship. For instance, the physical feeling you get when experiencing anger may include an increased pulse and respiratory rate, elevated temperature, and increased endocrinal juices in the bloodstream. The resulting physiological evidence may include higher energy levels, ''butterflies'' in the stomach, or similar sensations. That physical feeling is sometimes called anger. But isn't this also the physical feeling you call sexual excitement in other contexts? Isn't it essentially the same thing you know as fear at still other times?

In interpersonal contexts, what you call your physical experience is critical to the relationship. If you experience these sensations and you term them fear, what does that say about the nature of your fear? If you're calling them anger, can you see that another's wrong guess has damage potential? Thus one factor in a relationship is a guess about feelings.

Wants and Expectations

Wants and expectations are also part of a relationship. *Wants* are our wishes, needs, and desires for relationships. *Expectations* are anticipations of some occurrence. An expectation is a prediction—an assumption that an event is likely to occur. In our relationships we anticipate how others are likely to respond partly because of the roles we assign to them and partly because of the images we hold of them. In the relationship dimension, there is never a time when you do not want or expect something from the other person. An instructor speaks with you, for example, requesting the loan of a textbook. In the content dimension, she would like you to lend your text to her. But there is a want in the relationship dimension, too. She wants you to confirm your relationship, or at least her image of the relationship. This instructor wants you to show that you trust her. The intent of the request is not only to borrow the text but also to confirm the relationship.

Now consider what the instructor *does not want*. Remember, the task is to borrow the book. This is in the relationship dimension. She does not want you to answer, "Well . . . uh . . . I guess it'll be all right. Uh, look, last time I lent you a book it came back all messed up. You can borrow the book, but don't use a highlighter, and make sure you don't pour coffee all over it." This statement would disconfirm her image of your relationship. Although she would have been able to borrow your book, she would not have received what she wanted in the relationship dimension.

We always expect something from a partner in a relationship. Typically, the expectation is behavior, but sometimes it is *lack* of behavior. If you think about it, when you feel betrayed, the chances are that you thought you had a contract with the one you feel betrayed you. You did not get what you expected. To illustrate, put yourself back to the age of about sixteen. Suppose your father lets you take his car, after asking what time you will return it. You say, "I'll be back by 7:00." He accepts that at face value and makes plans accordingly. "Honey," he says to your mother, "how'd you like to see that movie? We could go tonight and be there in time for the 8:00 show." She answers, "Great." They make a date, and both get set for an evening out together. They have done so because your father believed—expected—that you would return the car by 7:00.

At 7:15, you're still not home. Nor are you home by 7:45. All the while the tension is rising. You made a commitment and your father is feeling betrayed. But your parents can still make the 8:00 show if you return the car. You return at 8:20 to a disappointed mom and a fuming dad. He is feeling betrayed because he expected something from you that he did not get. Obviously, then, wants and expectations are important in any relationship.

From your point of view, however, you probably had a good reason for not getting home earlier. *The other person in a conflict always has a good reason from her own point of view.* You might, for instance, have been caught in a traffic jam. You might have had to change a flat tire, with no phone nearby so you could call for help or tell your father you were delayed. Or the car may have run out of gas, and you had to walk to the nearest intersection to buy some.

The other person in a conflict always has a good reason for her view.

Your father's sense of betrayal is utterly inside himself. It is involved with his perceptions of the situation and his wants and expectations as the events of the evening played out. If he guesses that you were being irresponsible and becomes angry with you on the basis of that guess, your relationship is at risk. If he acts on his wrong guess, that you deliberately betrayed him, you two are liable to become involved in one of the classic conflicts of our time—the parent-child generation gap argument.

Intentions

If there are always wants and expectations in a relationship, there are always intentions too. An *intention* is the will or determination to act or to achieve some end. You can intend to pass a course with the grade of *A*, you can intend to graduate from college *cum laude,* or you can have much less lofty intentions. A professor lecturing to a class wants the students to learn the material. In the relationship dimension, the professor wants to be thought of by the students

The intention to be liked by students will influence the professor's behavior in the classroom.

as a skillful and personable lecturer, competent, knowledgeable, and able to make the subject matter lively so that the learning experience is pleasant. The instructor wants to be regarded as a someone to be trusted, to be respected as a person, and to be identified with positively as a role model. The professor is willing to do certain things in order to get what he wants. He *intends* to prepare in order to be knowledgeable about the subject matter. His intent is to polish an act so that the lectures flow smoothly. A student-centered approach to teaching is intended—one that takes the learner into account. Interactions with students, both in the classroom and outside of it, are intended to be warm—to the extent that this warmth is sustainable. And, really, the professor *intends* to pay attention to his personal habits of dress and grooming so that he manages his image consistently. There is not a lot that can be done beyond this set of intentions except to follow through with appropriate behavior as consistently as possible. *Thus intentions, too, are part of an existing relationship.*

Openness

In a relationship, you guess about the other's openness to your ideas and to yourself. *Openness,* sometimes called "latitude of acceptance," is the willingness of individuals to receive and consider ideas from another. Everyone has a degree of openness toward the other or the other's ideas and attitudes. The latitude continually changes in response to conditions in the environment and in yourself, as you perceive them. If you are open, if you have a broad latitude of acceptance, you are likely to be open to proposals from another. You will probably enjoy interacting with that other person. If you are closed, if you have a narrow latitude of acceptance, you probably will not want to interact with that person. You may even avoid contact altogether. Or, if contact is unavoidable, you may shut out this person, not hearing any proposal.

In a relationship, you usually, consciously or not, estimate the other's latitude of acceptance by observation and guess. You accommodate that estimate by choosing communication strategies that will be most effective under the circumstances you believe exist.

Images

An *image* is a mental representation, idea, or form. In a relationship images are always operating, as they are developed and sustained about all sorts of factors at the same time. Images of self are developed in certain contexts, as are images of others. It is possible to place those images into the same contexts into which you place yourself. When you are interacting with another, you are most likely interacting with your image of that person at that moment.

Friends never directly talk with each other!

Kenneth Boulding developed a notion of image that applies directly.[3] He believed that the total effect of experience was a person's image, *subjective knowledge*. Thus, according to him, what is true is what is believed to be true.

Image is not static but constantly changing. It interacts with what is perceived. A message may leave the image unaffected, add to an image, change an image, either slightly or quite dramatically, or clarify or confuse an image.

Perhaps the most interesting thing about image for the study of interpersonal communication is that people never truly interact in a direct way. That is, we never directly talk with each other! We talk with our images of each other! We get an image of what the other person is like, and we adapt to that image. To illustrate, assume that you wanted to borrow money, say, $20.00. How would you approach your parent? your brother or sister? your professor? your uncle? your boss? your best friend? Would your various approaches differ? Why? You can see that your adaptations to these different people result from your image of them and their likely response to your request.

Check-Out

The last element of the agenda for talking about relationships is called the *check-out* to help you remember to check out your inferences. Check-out is a colloquial term for feedback—messages we send back to a source so that errors in our understanding, can be corrected or controlled. Feed back to the other individual what you have observed and what your inferences are. This feedback provides the other person the opportunity to verify the impression you have formed or to correct it if it is wrong.

We have said that to know what is going on inside another person, you must get that person to tell you. Accept that you cannot read the other's mind. Check out your inferences. (We will address this issue of feedback further in Unit 6.)

To know what is going on inside another person, you must get that person to tell you.

Using the Agenda for Talking About Relationships

Most of the time you will not want to talk about your relationships as they are occurring. For example, when things are going very well between you and another person, you probably will not want to talk about the relationship. More likely, you will want to live it and to enjoy the reality of it. Also, in casual acquaintances you probably will not want to talk about your relationships. We have always had a system for not being clear about your feelings, wants, and images. What we need, however, is a system for talking about relationships when they are at risk.

Consider, for example, the following exchange. At the left is the actual talk, at the right are our comments. Notice that the components of a relationship are always present; what causes us to focus on and talk about them varies with the situation. At any given moment one of the items in the agenda may seem more important than the others. (Review table 3.1 to help you follow the dialogue.) We have chosen a conversation that has the potential for conflict because that most easily illustrates using the agenda. Here Bill assumes responsibility to manage the relationship. He has just arrived late to pick up his friend Jack.

Jack: You're late again.	This statement is in the present tense, but it includes a "hook"—the word "again."
Bill: Sorry. Are you upset?	This statement calls for a *check-out.* Bill does not assume that Jack is upset. He checks out his observation of the word "again" and perhaps how it was delivered.
Jack: Well, yes. You do this to me a lot. Last week you were late three times. You know how I hate it when you do that.	There is a lot of information here, but Jack has not asked for any response. Bill will confirm Jack without engaging in argument. Thus he is *personalizing* by understanding that Jack is talking about himself.
Bill: Um humm. . . .	
Jack: Well? What do you have to say for yourself this time?	Bill has the ball. He can either take a defensive position or build the relationship. Using the agenda, he decides to talk about his own *feelings, wants,* and *intentions.*
Bill: I'm sorry, Jack. I don't want to be the cause of trouble. And I didn't mean to be late this time.	Bill stays in the present tense, and he talks about himself, not Jack. This illustrates both the principle of the *absolute present* and *personalizing.* Jack has no need to be defensive because Bill has not defended himself with an attack.
Jack: So, where were you? You promised to pick me up twenty minutes ago.	Jack has asked for information and has tacked on a reminder of Bill's shortcoming. Bill cannot erase the past, so he won't try (the principle of the *absolute present*). He will stay with the request and let the reminder pass. He shifts to the *content dimension.*

Bill: The left front tire went flat. I changed it, and thought I had enough time to get the tire fixed. Anyway, I got stuck in traffic, and. . . .

Now Jack has some important information he did not have before. If he believes Bill, he can no longer attribute some evil motive to him. Still, he has been inconvenienced.

Jack: Well, I wish you would have called me to tell me you were running late.

He asks for something—a *want*—from Bill. Notice that he has not yet acknowledged the flat tire nor Bill's repair work. Bill can choose to let that pass, and he does. Bill can choose to give Jack what he wants. If he does this, he will make a contract for the future, since he cannot go back to the past and make the phone call. He chooses to talk about Jack's *wants.*

Bill: Yes, I can see that would have been a good idea. I promise to be more careful next time.

Bill confirms Jack again and gives him what he wants—a contract to behave differently in the future. This promise also makes clear that Bill assumes there will be a future relationship. It is upbeat and positive.

Jack: Okay. How bad was the flat?

Jack can now talk about the tire. He shifts to the *content dimension* because, for him, the relationship issue has been managed.

Notice that Bill never assumes or attributes any motive to Jack. He stays in the present tense. He talks about himself. He presents any guesses about Jack tentatively and checks them out. He stays with the relationship issues until Jack asks for information in the content dimension. Even then, Bill gives the information and returns to the relationship as soon as Jack states a want.

Being clear about relationship issues may not always get you what you want, but that is not our point. Rather, we argue that following this agenda for talking about your relationships will help you clarify the issues involved. Moreover, if you stay in the present tense and personalize your talk, you help the other person see things more clearly and you do not create defensiveness.

Summary

Relationship issues are the most common bases for conflict. Thus a taxonomy of the components of a relationship provides an agenda for talking about a relationship when that seems like a good idea. The system rests on two fundamental notions—that relationships are always in the present tense and that they are always inside people, existing as concepts rather than as physical entities.

Since you cannot read another person's mind, talking about a relationship implies recognizing your observations and inferences and then verifying their accuracy. The inferences, or guesses, will be about feelings, wants and expectations, intentions, openness, and images. Learning to stay in the present tense and to personalize talk about relationships constitute two important skills in talking about relationships.

Discussion Questions

1. Can you think of an example of a relationship that does not exist exclusively in the present tense? How are the past and the future tied to the present?

2. We have said that relationships exist inside people, as concepts that are couched in language. Working with three or four classmates, focus your attention on one of these people: the president of the United States, the governor of your state, the mayor or manager of your city, the president of your university, or the professor of your interpersonal communication class. Do you have any present-tense *feelings* toward this person? Do you have any present-tense *wants* or *expectations* of this person? What *images* do you have of this person?

3. Working with one or two classmates, role play each of the following situations, trying to stay in the present tense and personalize your talk. Talk about yourself—your observations and your inferences. Give and ask for feedback often to check out your guesses.

   Situation 1: You are very tidy. Your roommate is, in your opinion, careless about keeping the place neat. You decide to confront the roommate.

   Situation 2: You came to work late this morning. You had taken work home last night, stayed up too late, and overslept. The boss gives you a hard time about being late when you walk into the office.

   Situation 3: You have pooled your resources with your friend on a canoe and camping vacation. You believe that your friend is selfishly taking more than a fair share of the resources when you stop for lunch and other breaks. You are unhappy with this for two reasons: It does not seem fair, and you are afraid you may run out of money before the end of the trip. You determine to say something about it.

Endnotes

1. P. Watzlawick, J. H. Beavin, and D. D. Jackson, *Pragmatics of Human Communication: A Study of Interactional Patterns, Pathologies, and Paradoxes* (New York: W. W. Norton & Company, 1967), 51. Watzlawick

and his associates were among the first to divide communication into these two dimensions. Our treatment of the relationship dimension does not follow theirs.

2. We are aware that we have loaded this exercise somewhat by appealing to the cultural assumptions with which everyone must live. We have skewed your perceptions with an awareness of the assumptive reality you learned while growing up with American cultural traditions.

3. K. E. Boulding, *The Image* (Ann Arbor: University of Michigan Press, 1956).

>>|<<
UNIT 4
Interpersonal Needs

Preview

What motivates communication in our relationships? One reason we communicate is to express and fulfill our needs. For example, we may need to hear someone tell us that we belong, that we are part of a group, that someone likes us, or that we are in charge of something, perhaps the relationship itself.

We also communicate for more unconscious reasons. Sometimes we speak out or avoid communicating to protect the self-concept, or we may avoid changing because it may mean an adjustment in a relationship. This unit explores our interpersonal needs, which will help explain why we communicate as we do in our relationships and how we might adjust to promote relational growth.

Key Terms

abdicrat
adaptable-social
autocrat
democrat
going unconsciousness
interpersonal needs
need for affection
need for control
need for inclusion
openness to change
overpersonal
oversocial
personal
survival orientation
underpersonal
undersocial

Objectives

1. Explain how interpersonal needs affect our communication.
2. Identify and give an example of each component of Maslow's hierarchy of needs.
3. Discuss how each of Maslow's needs might be met through an interpersonal relationship.
4. Define the need for inclusion, and give an example of how it motivated your communication.
5. Define the need for control, and cite an example of how it motivated you to communicate.
6. Define the need for affection, and give an example of how it motivated your communication.
7. Cite an instance in which the need to survive prompted your communication in a relationship.
8. Explain and practice the kind of language that represents the appropriate expression of interpersonal needs.

Most significant interpersonal communication deals with an issue at hand as well as a deeper interpersonal need.

Interpersonal Needs and the Self-Concept

The complex system of beliefs, attitudes, and values that defines our self-concept determines the starting point for our interactions with others. It is also the control system for our interactions. For every interaction there is something that we and the other person wants. Each want is an expression of who we believe we are and how we wish to be seen.

We are more likely to know how to express ourselves in ways that the other person will understand when communicating in an ongoing relationship. We present ourselves to the other person in a style that has developed from past interactions with that person. The greater our experience with the other person, the more accurate our predictions are likely to be. We will also have

The greater our experience with the other person, the more accurate and confident our predictions are likely to be.

more confidence that the other person will behave in ways we can anticipate as we develop more history with a relational partner. An examination of what motivates our communication can help us understand why we behave as we do in our relationships and how to respond to the messages of others.

Usually, our communication is about some issue of concern to us, perhaps the relationship itself or other feelings. Most significant communications within a relationship deal with issues at hand as well as a deeper reason, which quite often is an *interpersonal need*. An interpersonal need is an urgent want that another person can provide.

We will focus on two useful classifications of needs, first, the hierarchy Abraham H. Maslow[1] has suggested and, second, the three areas of need identified by William C. Schutz.[2] Interpersonal needs relate to the development and projection of both self-concept and self-disclosure. We see ourselves in terms of our needs. For example, if we describe ourselves as well organized, we might be saying that our need to control is important to us. We thus communicate to satisfy our interpersonal needs. It must follow that our self-disclosures are selected by what we feel we need. Suppose we are with a group of friends, and one of them spills a drink in another's lap. We might tell a story about a time when we were embarrassed to satisfy our need to communicate that this behavior is acceptable for a member of this group.

Our interpersonal needs are tied directly to the images we hold of who we are. In addition, they act to preserve and protect the self-concept through communication that expresses these needs.

Maslow's Hierarchy of Needs

Maslow's work has had a significant impact on our understanding of needs. The hierarchy of individual needs he suggested is displayed in figure 4.1. He argues that we all have the potential to experience five kinds of needs: We have a need to have our physiological necessities met. We need to feel secure and safe. In our relationships, we need to feel that we belong and are held in esteem. Finally, we need to feel self-actualized. Maslow contends that these needs generally follow a hierarchical order—that lower level needs must be met for higher level needs to become important. For example, if you are starving, it would be somewhat difficult for you to be very concerned about esteem. You might even risk your safety to obtain food.

Physiological needs are our most basic, for they deal with survival. We need food, water, sleep, and shelter to survive. The biological origin of these needs, in that they are important to the life of any organism, gives them their strength. Sometimes we form relationships to help us meet these needs.

Figure 4.1 Maslow's Hierarchy of Needs

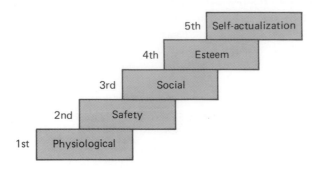

Safety needs are the next level of needs in this hierarchy. We need to feel secure and free from fear. We need structure and order to feel that there is some predictability in our lives. Basically, these needs are related to self-preservation—both present and future protection from bodily harm. These needs, too, can be provided by certain relationships, either through financial contributions or physical strength.

Social needs, Maslow's third category, are represented by two distinct sets of needs. The first are those related to the need to accept, associate with, and be accepted by others, the second are those relating to belonging to a group. The first is a more intense socialization need. At this level, you want to exchange signs of love, affection, or friendship in appropriate interpersonal relationships. The quest for this kind of relationship finds its outlet in informal groups as well as in marriage and other committed relationships.

The second of these needs, association with and acceptance by others, is primarily an affiliation need. Members of groups want to say and believe that they are a part of the group. They do not want to feel alone and set apart.

The fourth level of needs, *esteem need,* is the need to be recognized and rewarded. This need is fulfilled by the respect and recognition of our associates. We may satisfy this need by being a part of a relationship in which our partner gives us status, respect, recognition, and appreciation. We authors believe that self-esteem may be the most important of all the human needs.

The top of Maslow's hierarchy, *self-actualization,* is a need for self-fulfillment, for achieving our potential, for self-development, and for creativity. Maslow suggests that this is a "desire to become more and more what one is, to become everything one is capable of becoming."[3] It is difficult for most people to satisfy this need. We may achieve fulfillment in a relationship with those who give us the freedom to be what we are capable of becoming. We might also receive encouragement to reach our potential by our circle of friends and acquaintances.

Schutz's Interpersonal Needs

Maslow's hierarchy of human needs is supplemented by Schutz's analysis of needs, which places the understanding of needs for inclusion, control, and affection in a framework of interpersonal relationships.

Need for Inclusion

The *need for inclusion* includes our desire to be accepted, to feel wanted, and to be a part of groups, both at work and in our personal lives. It also includes our need to accept others. Yet, clearly, all of us do not experience all these needs in the same way. Some of us demand a great amount of inclusion, while others avoid closeness and interpersonal contact almost entirely. Schutz recognizes these varying degree of need and labels them accordingly.

Undersocial people have little need for inclusion, isolating themselves from group involvement. *Oversocial* people behave in the other extreme, continually seeking to join and feel a part of many groups. The *adaptable-social* person, on the other hand, balances needs for inclusion and privacy, realizing at times each is desirable.

Consider co-workers Greg, Tom, and Julie. Each day Greg comes in and gets right to work. He speaks only when spoken to, takes his breaks and his lunch alone in his office, and never volunteers for any assignment that involves working with other people. Tom, on the other hand, socializes a great deal in the office. He seeks out group assignments, always goes to lunch in the company cafeteria, and frequently initiates conversations with co-workers. During breaks he goes out of his way to find company. Julie seems to have a different need for inclusion. She socializes with others and works well with them, but when she is given an assignment to do on her own, she closes her office door and starts to work. She finds working with Greg difficult, because it is hard for her to communicate with him. Julie believes that she has to carry too much of the burden of the conversation with Greg. Working with Tom can be rewarding but also frustrating. At times, he wants to talk about everything but the task at hand, which makes work take much longer than it should. Sometimes Julie finds it difficult to get her point of view across, as Tom tends to monopolize the conversation.

Undersocial individuals like Greg and oversocial people like Tom often experience difficulties in their work. The undersocial person may be seen as aloof, arrogant, or indifferent. The oversocial person may be seen as superficial, dominating, or demanding of time and attention.

Understanding inclusion as one part of everyone's need structure offers insight into their motivation. Greg, for example, does not respond to messages of inclusion because he does not need to feel accepted as part of the team. Tom may need considerable reassurance in this area and Julie only a moderate amount. In communicating with the undersocial person, it is important to keep the possibility of inclusion open. We must make it clear that if the person wants to develop the relationship, we are willing to do so. We might say to Greg, ''I am glad we are working on this project together. We will do a good job if we both contribute to it. So I want to know what you think about it as we go along. O.K.?''

As we communicate with the oversocial person, we must be clear that the other is included in the relationship. More importantly, we must create language that will communicate our intentions and expectations about the relationship and the task, and the other person must acknowledge that he understands what we want from the relationship. Julie might have to set some ground rules in working with Tom by saying something like, ''Tom, I'm glad we're working on this together because I have some ideas about the way this project ought to go and I know you do too. I want to be sure that at each stage we both have our say about it. Can we do that?''

The need for inclusion is critical because we may seek new relationships, sometimes abandoning current ones, if it is not satisfied. Communicating clearly about how much contact or inclusion we expect in a relationship can help us fulfill this need and allow the relationship to grow.

Need for Control

The *need for control* is our desire both to exercise power and authority and to be controlled. The need to control is based on two strict principles: We have the need to control our environment and the destiny of our relationships, and our partners in relationships have this same need.

There are differing degrees of this need for control. Schutz describes an *abdicrat* as someone with little need to control. This person abdicates all power and responsibilities to his partner in a relationship. This person's opposite, the *autocrat,* dominates others and feels the need to rise to the top of a power hierarchy in relationships. A person who takes the middle ground is called the *democrat.* This person can either take charge or allow others to be in control as appropriate.

The need to overcontrol can cause serious problems in relationships, as autocrats may try to control everything. Abdicrats, on the other hand, can also create problems. For example, the professional who cannot or will not assume control when needed leaves more work for co-workers. This lack of leadership can often mean failure to a business in which efficiency is critical.

The need *for* control can affect relationships as well. Jim and Sally have been married for several years and have had frequent problems in their relationship. Jim would be characterized as an abdicrat, while Sally might be considered an autocrat. She takes charge of most issues in the relationship and often makes decisions without consulting Jim. One year, she made all the arrangements for them to vacation in the Caribbean. By the time they arrived, she was frantic. By taking on too much, she had ruined the trip for herself. Jim did not understand her problem. He thought she should be enjoying herself. After all, she got exactly what she wanted. The next year Sally asked Jim to plan their vacation. He missed the dates for booking an economy flight and waited too long to get reservations at a good hotel. As a result, they did not take a vacation that year.

Jim and Sally might work toward a more democratic control of their relationship. Having one person take all responsibility and the other person none is not working for either partner. Understanding this problem may help them avoid it.

Our awareness of this dimension in others will help us focus still closer on how they function in our relationships. In dealing with the autocrat, we must be clear about what aspects of the relationship we want to control and what aspects we would prefer to share in controlling. Again, expressing what we want from the relationship is the key. We might say to an autocrat, "I know that you want to take care of all this, but I'd like to do some of it too—not so much for you as to satisfy my own needs. Can we work out some way to share the responsibilities for this?" Communicating with an abdicrat can be more difficult. We may try to motivate, while remaining clear about how much we are willing to do. For example, "This event can affect both of us, and we can both benefit from it. I am willing to do X, Y, and Z, and I would like you to agree to do A, B, and C. But I don't want you to say you'll do them if you won't. If that is the case, I will take charge of them and have the event alone."

The need to control is powerful in both its presence and its absence. It is important to know when to take on responsibility and when to give it up. We can only learn this through the experiences we have as a relationship develops. We need to watch for it to address this need in ourselves and our partner appropriately.

Need for Affection

The *need for affection* is the desire to like and be liked by others. It is reflected in the development of loving relationships. We often find ourselves identifying more with the person whom we like when we fulfill this need, for the result of liking is personal closeness and positive feelings. When a person has little need for affection, neutrality is displayed in relationships, and all others are viewed in the same way. Some of us may even respond with hostility to avoid closeness. Schutz refers to people who have a low need for affection as *underpersonal*. Unlike the undersocial person, who avoids contact with others, the underpersonal individual will avoid not contact but self-disclosure. On the other hand, a person with a high need for affection is considered *overpersonal,* and will take special pains to avoid being disliked by anyone. An overpersonal individual may become too concerned with the social dimension and thus often spend far too much time talking about his own feelings or inquiring about the feelings of others. A *personal* individual holds the middle ground. She can bal-

When a person has little need for affection, neutrality is displayed in relationships.

ance situations in order to be liked when affection is desirable but can also maintain distance when affection is not needed. This balance allows people to manage their relationships more productively.

An understanding of others' need for affection will help us determine how to talk with and listen to the partners in our relationships more effectively. We can vary our approach depending on whether the other person is underpersonal, overpersonal, or personal.

Interpersonal Needs and Communication in Relationships

A better understanding of how interpersonal needs differ from relationship to relationship can be quite useful. We may know ourselves better if we analyze each of our need areas: Does our basic needs structure correspond to roles we have chosen? Can we conduct our relationships and have our needs fulfilled? We should not necessarily play amateur psychologist or select roles based solely on our needs, but this information might assist us in making choices about relationships.

We are communicating effectively when we understand how all parties

operate to satisfy their needs in our relationships. When we do this we learn
how to motivate and reward others, which is critical to the effective development of our relationships.

    We all possess these needs to some degree, and that may vary from one
relationship to another. So far, we have examined how each need alone influences communication. But sometimes more than one need is at work, as figure
4.2 depicts.

    Figure 4.2 is a cube, with one of the three interpersonal needs making
up each plane. Every cell in the cube represents a different combination of
interpersonal needs. For each cell, try to imagine how such a person might

Figure 4.2 Interpersonal Needs Matrix

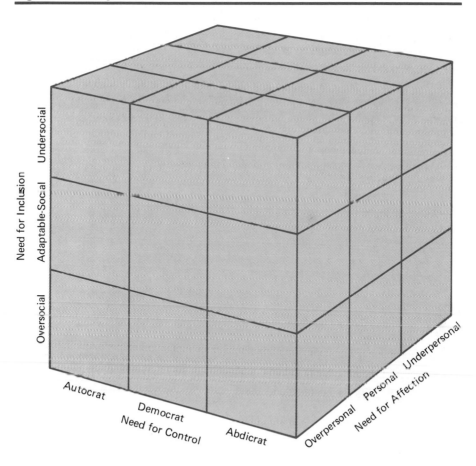

behave in a relationship. For example, what would it be like talking with an undersocial, underpersonal abdicrat? Can you imagine two such people having a growing and healthy relationship? Do you know anyone who seems personal, adaptable-social, and democratic? What is it like to talk with this person? In which cell do you seem to find yourself most often? Do any cells apply to you in only one particular relationship?

Self-Concept Maintenance

We are often reminded that the characteristic that most distinguishes humans from other creatures is our ability to communicate. Indeed, this enabled us to survive in the most hostile of environments. At first, people developed their communication skills to withstand the threats of other creatures. In the modern world, we depend on others and our communication with them more than ever. Improving communication in our relationships is thus essential for further development.

Although our survival instinct remains, it serves a somewhat different function than it did in the past. Now the instinct helps us protect our self-concepts as well as our bodies. At times, the mind works to protect itself from change. This can be beneficial, but also can inhibit the growth of an individual. We find ourselves behaving without awareness and in a way quite inconsistent with our goals when this instinct takes over. When we act to defend ourselves without much thought, this behavior is called *going unconscious*. When our self-concept feels threatened, we will defend it. This affects both our expression and our perception. We are moved to do or say whatever is necessary to emerge from a situation with our self-concepts intact.

The self-concept is a relatively stable structure on a day-to-day basis yet is changeable over time. Have you ever had a professor who encouraged students to ask questions but then ridiculed the questions they offered? This same professor may later complain that students never ask questions. We might interpret this criticism as his way of emerging from the situation with his self-concept intact. After all, he could still (unrealistically) view himself as open and competent if he believed that the students would not participate because they had a problem. Because his self-concept is geared to survival, it moves him to resist changing his behavior, even when change might be desirable.

The survival orientation usually involves self-concept structures that are centrally and intensely held. The most serious problem that may arise from protecting the self-concept is that defensiveness may become a habit that we are not even aware of.

There is an alternative orientation that is active, conscious, and supportive, which we call *being conscious*. With this orientation, our communica-

The most serious problem that may arise from protecting our self-concept is that defensiveness can become a habit.

tion asserts our self-concepts and stimulates the growth of our relationships, thereby helping the self-concept to change in a way that facilitates the realization of our goals. The key to being conscious is *openness to change.* We must be willing to listen to and learn from others. The greater the trust in a relationship, the easier it is for us to maintain this attitude.

We must also be honest with ourselves about who we are, who we can be, and who we want to be to present an image that will work in our relationships and will help us to satisfy our interpersonal needs.

Summary

Understanding why we express ourselves the way we do can help us more carefully choose the language we use to communicate in our relationships. Our relationships are formed to fulfill needs. Maslow suggests that we have physiological, safety, social, esteem, and self-actualization needs. Schutz focuses on three interpersonal needs: the need for inclusion, the need for control, and the need for affection. We experience these needs in different degrees, and our communication frequently relates to one or more of them. We must be sensitive to the needs that motivate the communication of others, using language that addresses these needs while allowing us to express what we need to about ourselves.

The need to survive is internal. We protect our self-concept by using the frame of reference to screen threatening information. This survival need makes changing either the self-concept or our communication style difficult, although we can make adjustments that will allow us to communicate effectively in our relationships through an attitude of openness.

Discussion Questions

1. When and how has the survival need helped you in a relationship?
2. Imagine yourself in each of these roles: a religious person, a political person, a student, a partner in a special relationship, a member of a family, and a volunteer in public service. How might your role and your relationships be affected by their contribution to your self-image?
3. Which of the interpersonal needs discussed in this chapter are most likely to be expressed in the behavior associated with each role mentioned above?

Endnotes

1. A. H. Maslow, *Motivation and Personality* (New York: Harper & Row, 1954).
2. W. C. Schutz, *The Interpersonal Underworld* (Reading, MA: Addison-Wesley Publishing Company, 1969).
3. Maslow, *Motivation,* 82.

>>I<< UNIT 5
The Perception Process

Preview

The world that exists outside us is not the same as the world within us. Our communication and relationships do not depend on the outside world as much as on our perceptions of that world. This unit explores the ways we select, organize, and interpret the information that we use as a basis for action and communication in our relationships. First, we explore the frame of reference, the filter through which we view and understand the world. Next, we examine the perception process. We also look at how our perceptions are organized and how this organization affects our views of relationships. Through perception, we adjust information to fit our frames of reference, and this unit explains how that works as well. Finally, we suggest ways to improve the accuracy of your perception through heightened awareness and concentration.

Objectives

1. Define "frame of reference" and give an example of how different frames of reference affected your communication in a relationship.
2. Explain how perceptions affect the frame of reference.
3. Cite examples of the active, inductive, and unconscious characteristics of perception.
4. Provide examples of the way selective exposure and selective attention work in the process of perception.
5. Define "closure" and explain its importance to organizing perception.
6. Describe an experience that shows the impact of assimilation and accommodation on your frame of reference.
7. Define "leveling," "sharpening," and "perceptual distortion."
8. Discuss the improvement of perceptual ability through concentration and attention.

Key Terms

accommodation
assimilation
closure
frame of reference
leveling
perception
perceptual distortion
perceptual interpretation
perceptual organization
selective attention
selective exposure
selectivity
sharpening

The Nature of Perception

Perception is a fundamental aspect of interpersonal communication. Perception gives meaning and stability to the communication in our relationships because it is a process through which we select and organize information to explain what has happened around us. Understanding perception can help us comprehend our responses to others and the formation of our views of relationships. Perception is not only a process but also a skill. After working with this unit you will be able to improve your ability to perceive.

Perception is not only a process but also a skill.

The basic tools of perception are our senses. The information we take in through our senses is the raw data from which experiences are constructed. Remember that we receive information through all five senses simultaneously. Our other senses are not shut down while we may be looking at something and thinking about what we are seeing. This means that, as we communicate, we are tasting, smelling, seeing, hearing, and feeling the touch of our relationships as well.

We perceive through a *frame of reference*—a set of interlocking facts, ideas, beliefs, values, and attitudes.[1] This frame of reference is the basis for our understanding of people, events, and experiences. It has a structure in that we order our experiences to fit together in a way that is sensible to us. As we take in new information, we use our frame of reference to process it in one of three ways: We may reject it because it doesn't fit with our frame of reference; we may use it to support the frame of reference; or we may use it to expand that structure. Figure 5.1 illustrates the way the frame of reference screens and organizes information to provide meaning.

Frame of reference also provides stability for our perception. Rather than seeing our experiences as constantly shifting in response to various senses, perception within our frame of reference gives them a flowing quality. For instance, try this experiment. Hold your hand at arm's length and examine it for a moment. Now move it quickly toward you and then back out. Although the movement of your hand created sensory differences in size and color, you probably experienced it as the same size and color when you were moving it as when you were not. Your frame of reference contains an understanding of the size of your hand, and it will not let your senses fool you about that.

This same principle of stability applies to our perceptions of people in our relationships. Perhaps you have had the experience of encountering a friend who has changed his appearance somewhat, maybe by getting a haircut or shaving off a mustache. If you did not notice this change at first it is because your perception was acting to maintain your frame of reference for this person.

Figure 5.1 Frame of Reference: Screening and Organizing Information

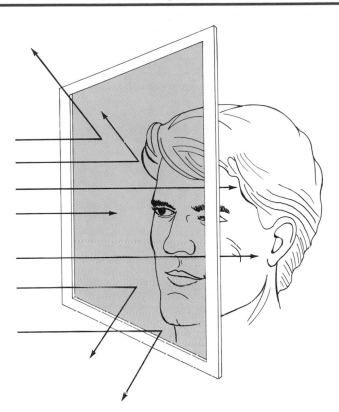

Once the change is called to your attention, your frame of reference adjusts to accept a new vision.

The events that occur around us may be but are not necessarily connected. However, for us to understand groups of sensory events as whole experiences, they must be interrelated and placed within our frame of reference. Perception allows us to connect separate experiences.

Imagine, for example, your standard morning routine. You awaken to a voice talking to you from your clock-radio, telling you the news of the day. You roll over and feel the warmth of your blanket, thinking about having to wake up. You become more alert as the voice describes what the weather will be like, and then you rise quietly. You move to the bathroom, turn on the light, use and flush the toilet, measure the temperature of the shower with your left hand while you adjust it with your right. You step under the shower head, where the needle-like jets of water massage your body and increase your circulation. You turn off the water, draw back the shower curtain, find your towel (noticing that it is your favorite yellow one), and rub your skin vigorously, enjoying the clean, fresh, stimulating feeling that results. All of these perceptions—separate sensory events—are connected in your head. Together they comprise the single reality of a morning routine.

This same idea applies to your relationships. Think about what it feels like to hold someone you love. You feel the smooth touch of his skin, smell the fragrance of his clean hair, hear his breathing and heartbeat, and see his calm, relaxed expression as you draw him close. All of your senses operate and combine to produce sensations that you summarize as the feeling called love.

Characteristics of the Perceptual Process

Although research on perception continues, scientists have clearly identified several aspects of the process.[2] These shed light on the way we perceive ourselves and others. First, perception is active. Because we cannot take in and accept all of the stimuli available to us, we must sort, screen, and sometimes reach out for information. We must perceive selectively to maintain our sense of structure and stability as we use the perceptual process to fit it together.

Perception is active.

Second, the perception process works inductively. Through perception, we generate whole images of things and people built from the observation of their parts. Our perception process takes in clues about the way things are and then puts the clues together to form a conclusion representing the whole thing.

Perception works inductively.

Third, perception generally occurs relatively unconsciously. We usually think no more about perception while we are engaging in the process than we think about our heartbeats or breathing patterns. Unlike the latter, however, we cannot even focus on the act of perceiving because attention is one of our tools of perception. We can, however, focus on *what* we are perceiving, and this focus is very important to accurate perception.

Perception generally occurs unconsciously.

Perception Involves Selection

Selectivity is choosing information. Even with all five senses operating at optimum efficiency, there is just too much going on around us for our senses to absorb and interpret everything. We must, therefore, select from available stimuli. We select what we will expose ourselves to and we select what we will pay attention to.

Remember the first day of class? Certain people captured your attention more than others. You were exposed to the messages of those people and paid attention to some of those messages more than the messages of other people in the class. After several classes, you began to notice more people as well as more *about* them. This is because repeated exposures tend to increase our knowledge of the people around us. There are some things about people in the class—habits, manners of speaking, physical attributes—that you may not have noticed until several weeks had gone by. Although the information was there at every meeting, your perception process ignored it if it was not needed to accomplish your goals in the class.

Selective exposure and selective attention are two types of selectivity that are important to our interpersonal communication. These processes occur in order, with exposure first, followed by attention.

Selective Exposure

When we turn on the radio and tune in a frequency, we are engaging in *selective exposure* as we expose ourselves to some information and exclude other. When we participate in any conversation, we make a similar choice, becoming open to some stimuli while disregarding others. Sometimes selective exposure can help us both avoid unwanted communication and receive needed communication. For example, you may find yourself in a meeting with a group of people that includes someone with whom you frequently argue. When he speaks, you may look away or read something to avoid exposure to him and his communication. On the other hand, you may be at a crowded gathering looking for a particular person you expect to see there. Amid the noise and confusion, you see her across the room, and she sees you. As you concentrate your senses on her and struggle to communicate clearly, you try to shut out much that is happening around you. If you are successful, you may not even notice who was standing by you or what they said. By limiting your exposure to the verbal and nonverbal messages your friend sent across the room, you shut out everything else.

There are more subtle bases for selective exposure to people and things; many are personal preferences. For example, we may choose to expose ourselves to information coming from someone who uses our name. (Direct mail advertisers assume we make this choice when they have their computers insert our names in the appropriate spaces on their form letters.) In the example above, your exposure to your friend across the room might have been interrupted if the person next to you spoke your name. We may not be aware that the news we read tends to report on the issues that we think are important, but research finds that we do choose it for that reason. We thus expose ourselves to ideas and people selectively, although such exposure does not necessarily result in communication. It does, however, provide the opportunity for perceiving. To perceive, we must not only be exposed, we must also attend.

Selective Attention

Selective attention occurs when we choose to attend to one or more of the stimuli to which we are exposed. Even though our senses operate simultaneously, we focus best when we focus on one at a time. At this moment, for example, you may see the page in front of you. You may also taste and smell a cup of freshly brewed coffee, hear the faint hum of the air conditioner, and feel both the hardness of your chair and tightness of your shoes. But you must select one of these sensations for attention at a time. If you decide to see the printed page, for example, and the smell of the coffee is overpowering, you will have difficulty reading. Your concentration will flash rapidly back and forth between the sensations, and you will find it hard to concentrate on either.

Suppose again that you are in the meeting with the person with whom you often argue. When that person is speaking, you may choose to expose yourself to his communication but selectively attend to only some of the points he makes or to the way he says it, listening for a point to break in without seeming rude.

In the case of finding your friend in a crowded room, you may have engaged in two levels of selectivity. While you looked around for her you may have been exposing yourself to communication in your immediate surroundings, picking up on some of what was being said. But when you spotted your friend, you very finely narrowed the focus of both exposure and attention.

Exposure and attention are related in important ways. Through exposure we select information to which we will attend either now or later. Exposure occurs in the present—we are exposed to current people, events, and relationships. We attend to some of these now and store the rest for possible attention later. For example, consider meeting your friend at the crowded gathering. After you are united, she may ask, "Who was that person you were talking with when I found you?" Although at the time you did not pay attention to that person because you were focusing on your search, you will probably recall some details of the conversation to which you were exposed but not attending.

Take some time now to explore your own selective exposure and attention processes in terms of people and relationships. Are there people in your interpersonal communication class with whom you talk often? Are there any who you seem to find yourself avoiding?

Perception Involves Organization and Interpretation

Different people may view the same event in different ways. One reason for this is that people may attend to different parts of the event. Even if they attend to similar facets of the experience, they may *understand* it differently. Since what we do depends on what we perceive, our perception is actually more important to our communication than what the other person intended or what really happened. For example, we may believe that we see two friends arguing. Another observer may view them as joking. We cannot know which perception is true without investigating. The action we take with regard to our friends will differ according to our perception, and can significantly affect our relationship with them. Our willingness to act without investigation may be greater if we do not understand perception.

Our responses to our relationships are based on our perceptions. Sometimes we communicate a distorted view of events because of the way we have organized and interpreted them. We turn to these topics now—organization and interpretation—to show how they contribute to the perceptual process.

The stimuli we receive through the perception process are limited first by exposure and then by attention. When we attend to experiences, however, we do not just take them as they are. Rather, we arrange them to fit our frame of reference: this is known as *perceptual organization*. We next give them meaning in light of that frame of reference in what is called *perceptual interpretation*. Organization and interpretation are both necessary for us to respond to the stimuli. We can see how this works by applying it to a perceptual task.

Look at the four drawings in figure 5.2. Which do you like the most? Why? Compare your perceptions with those of others in the class. People will assign different meanings to what they see in the figure. Those who are attracted to a different drawing than you were will give reasons that reflect differences in the way they organized and interpreted the pictures. Sometimes they will have seen parts of a picture that you did not notice at all, but you may still prefer your original choice even after these hidden features are pointed out.

People may also select one picture over another because of its overall impression, which results from all of the prior experiences, norms, rules, and expectations that formed their individual frames of reference. As you compare your perceptions of figure 5.2 with those of others, you will notice that your own perception shifts a little to make their meanings valid in your own frame of reference. When you do this, you are accommodating their perceptions into your own evaluations.

Organization and interpretation are interrelated. We put data together to give it meaning. One way to view this part of the process is to think about what happens when we try to sketch a portrait of someone we know. We start with the general shape of the face and rough features—a basic organizational pattern. As we sketch, we organize the drawing to render an image of the subject.

● ● ●   ● ●   ● ● ●   ● ●

Nearness: Do you see four groups of dots?

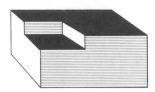

Likeness: The rectangles composed of Xs or circles, exclusively, are
easier to perceive than those composed of two circles and
two Xs.

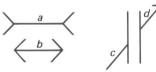
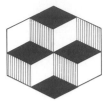

Part-whole relationships: The same set of
lines may be seen as forming a block
of wood or as outlining a recess in a
block of wood.

Shifting perception: The same figure may
be organized into different wholes or
patterns.

Perceiving parts as a whole: Lines a and b
are the same length. Lines c and d can
be connected to form a continuous
line. The illusion results from distorting
a part because of the larger whole in
which it is found.

Field-ground relationship

Old woman   Composite   Young woman

Just for fun

Past experience: We tend to see objects
that are familiar. In the picture at the
right, do you see the young woman
or the old woman?

Figure 5.2 Perceptual Organization and Interpretation

We do not create a face and then try to find someone who resembles it; that would put organizing ahead of interpreting. Instead, we organize and interpret together: We give the portrait meaning as we organize it and we organize it to give it meaning.

In conversations, the stress placed on particular words or phrases may affect our perception of the message. That is, once we have been exposed to and attended to a message, there are characteristics of the message that may influence our understanding of it. To explore this aspect of organizing and interpreting, try the following experiment. Repeat each of the phrases below, emphasizing a different word in the phrase each time. How does the meaning shift with the changes in emphasis?

I need that report tomorrow.
I think you're quite attractive.
Are you going to the game on Saturday?
I want to talk with you.

The way we organize and interpret information is very important for our relationships. What we hear others say influences our responses to them. For instance, when we asked you to change the emphasis in the statements above, did you think about how you might respond differently depending on where you heard the stress in a sentence? "I *think* you're quite attractive," produces a different response from, "I think you're *quite* attractive." Remember, there is both the emphasis placed by the speaker and the emphasis heard by the listener. If our perception skills are sharp enough, we will hear what was intended. If our skills are not very sharp, we make a mistaken response and thus add confusion to our relationships.

Organizing and Interpreting Through Closure

Very few of our perceptions are based on whole images. Rather, through the process called *closure,* we must create perceptions by putting together bits and pieces of data from our experiences. For example, consider the procedure of forming an impression of someone in an office. The objects you find in this person's space are the information from which you form whole impressions of this individual.

We are using closure when we add finishing touches to our perception of otherwise incomplete events by rearranging and filling in missing parts. We are also using closure when we draw inferences about an event from its bits and pieces, as when you finish another person's sentence or generalize about someone's character.

Figure 5.3

Georges Seurat, *Sunday Afternoon on the Island of La Grande Jatte,* 1884–86, oil on canvas, 81″ × 120⅜″, The Art of Institute of Chicago, Helen Birch Bartlett Memorial Collection.

Figure 5.4

Detail of Georges Seurat, *Sunday Afternoon on the Island of La Grande Jatte.*

Look closely at the reproduction of Georges Seurat's painting *Sunday Afternoon on the Island of Le Grand Jatte* (figure 5.3). What would you say is going on in this picture? Describe your perception of this painting. Now look carefully at figure 5.4, which is a small detail of the painting. As you can see, the painting is really just a mass of dots of various shades and densities. You used closure to bring these dots together into the picture you recognized in figure 5.3.

Closure affects perception in relationships also. Our general perception about a friend is really a summary of numerous discrete perceptions, smoothed into a consistent image. Also, in very close relationships, we often find ourselves able to understand the other's intentions with minimal expression. In well-developed relationships it is not unusual to find whole actions or ideas conveyed in just a word, phrase, or gesture. Because we know the other person well, closure enables us to communicate more efficiently.

Assimilation and Accommodation

Our ability to make sense of what we are observing, such as another person in a relationship, is affected by the way we use the frame of reference to act on it. Two aspects of perceptual organization, assimilation and accommodation, describe this process.[3] With *assimilation* we *change* what we perceive to fit our frame of reference. We may even use it to defend our beliefs, attitudes, and values. For example, we might see our partners in a relationship as loving and caring. When we observe the opposite, we may perceive the negative behavior as less intense as we weigh it through our frame of reference. With *accommodation,* on the other hand, we *adjust* what we perceive to fit the frame of reference, to make room for new information and experiences. It reflects an openness or willingness to be influenced.

Assimilation and accommodation always occur together; that is, a space is made for new information as the information is altered to fit that space. If our frames of reference offer us a generally positive feeling about a co-worker, for example, we are likely to use these processes to maintain this attitude. If, for instance, this individual acts sharply toward us, we might assimilate our observations, seeing the attack as less intense than if it had come from someone else. At the same time, we would accommodate the frame of reference about that relationship to include the new information.

The changes that information frequently undergoes during assimilation can contribute to inaccurate perceptions. The assimilation process may level, sharpen, or distort a perception to allow it to better fit our frames of reference. In *leveling,* details of a perception are lost, leaving only those parts that clearly fit the frame of reference. For instance, we may have a friend whose company we enjoy but with whom we've had our ups and downs. As we organize our perceptions about this person, we may retain the general positive feeling we get from several experiences rather than recall the particular high and low points that might contradict that overall attitude.

Frequently the details omitted are those that contribute to the uniqueness of an experience. That is what the term *leveling* implies—shaving off the peaks and filling in the valleys. An experience is easily assimilated if it looks like many others. If we find ourselves failing to see the uniqueness of people in our relationships, we may be leveling too much, and the relationships may suffer. We need to pay more attention to the individuality that various people bring to our relationships.

Sharpening is the editing of our perception by focusing on details that reinforce our frame of reference while discarding the rest. You can hear examples of sharpening when you listen to the conversation of old friends who are getting together after a long separation. Recalling the highs and lows of their experience serves as a ritualistic way of reminding ourselves of the importance of their relationship. The friends vividly sharpen their perceptions of their shared adventures and forget their more mundane activities to reinforce the feeling they have for one another quickly and strongly.

We change our experiences to fit our frames of reference.

Perceptual distortion is the outright changing of the content of our experiences to fit our frames of reference. You might alter your memory of the details of an evening if you had a particularly bad time with a friend whose company you normally enjoy. For example, you might come to admit that the service in a restaurant was not very prompt upon observing your friend's unfair criticism of it. The event can then be assimilated into the existing frame of reference because your friend's behavior was justified.

We also distort our perception of our own behavior. For example, to provide support for the relationship in the example above, you might remember that you too complained about the service. Perhaps when your friend spoke rudely to the waiter, you actually frowned at her. You might, however, distort your memory to recall frowning at the waiter instead. Too much distortion can lead to an unhealthy communication climate in our relationships because our partners may come to question the reliability of our perceptions.

Sometimes two people distort their perceptions of an event so that they can build their agreement into their relationship. This frequently happens with events that are not terribly important to either party. In the film *Annie Hall,* Woody Allen narrates a story about two lonely people sitting in a restaurant and talking. "This food is terrible," one says, and the other replies, "Yes, and the portions are so small." The contradiction between their points of view about the food is obvious. But, having agreement that something is wrong—whether or not it is the same thing—is perhaps more important than the content of their individual feelings. As a result of this distortion they built into their frames of reference the same feeling about dinner, but perhaps for different reasons. Although distortion does not always serve the best interests of our relationships, because perception is unconscious it may only be revealed after the fact. When we compare perceptions with our partners' and find too much of this kind of behavior, we must work to improve our perception. We can do this through careful attention to our perceptual and listening skills

Building Perceptual Skills

You can improve your perceptual skills by learning how to verify the accuracy of your perceptions and to sharpen your ability to take in and interpret information from your environment. But working on your perceptual abilities can be demanding and time consuming, so do not expect dramatic improvement overnight. And do not expect to retain any improvements without practice.

The basic tools of perception are your senses and your brain. The keys to developing your perceptual tools are attention, concentration, and time. You must pay attention to what your senses and your body are experiencing in different situations. Remember that improving your sensing ability is an ongoing, long-term process, so persistence is mandatory. Certain meditative techniques might help you concentrate on your senses.

Summary

Perception is the process by which we take in and give meaning to information around us. It is on the basis of our perceptions that we understand our relationships. All of our perceptions are filtered through our frame of reference, a collection of our attitudes, values, and beliefs. Perception is able to work as it does because it is active, inductive, and unconscious.

We select information from the wealth of data around us, paying attention to some while discarding most. Our frames of reference helps us to organize and interpret this information using closure, assimilation, and accommodation. Closure helps us feel that our pictures are complete. Assimilation and accommodation bring our perceptions and our frame of reference closer together. Sometimes this coming together of images occurs through leveling or sharpening, and other times through perceptual distortion. With practice, you can improve your ability to perceive and thereby improve your ability to communicate appropriately in your relationships.

Discussion Questions

1. Try to describe your frame of reference when you entered college. How did it affect your initial perceptions of the people you encountered? Did these perceptions in turn affect your frame of reference? If so, how?
2. Recall the details of your first image of your interpersonal communication professor. How have your impressions of this person changed since the course began? Has this altered your frame of reference? If so, why?
3. Have several class members explain the same important event in your community. How are the explanations different? Is there any evidence of selective exposure or selective attention? any leveling? any sharpening? any other distortion?
4. It seems that assimilation and accommodation might at times work against each other in ways that, at least temporarily, confuse your perceptions of a person or event. Describe an experience in which you were simultaneously shaping your perceptions to fit your frame of reference and adjusting your perceptions.

Endnotes

1. A. G. Athos and J. G. Gabarro, *Interpersonal Behavior: Communication and Understanding in Relationships* (Englewood Cliffs, NJ: Prentice-Hall, 1978), 137–48.
2. H. C. Triandis, *Interpersonal Behavior* (Monterey, CA: Brooks/Cole, 1977), 94–135.
3. J. Piaget, *The Construction of Reality in the Child* (New York: Basic Books, 1954).

≫|≪
UNIT 6
Perceiving Others Accurately

Preview

This unit explores the many ways that our perceptions of people influence communication in our relationships as well as the interpersonal attractions that lead to relationships and the roles we take in relationships. Our perceptions function together with our expectations for ourselves and others to create communication rules for our relationships and influence the relationship positions. These positions affect how we view ourselves in relation to the other person. Finally, both the nature of perception and the derivation of expectations can change. In this unit you will learn about how to improve your perception in relationships.

Key Terms

change
communication rules
expectations
inferential statements
interpersonal attraction
mutual perception
observational statements
perceptual filter
psychological aspects
relationship position
role
sociological aspects
stereotyping

Objectives

1. Explain what is meant by the mutual nature of perception.
2. Name two ways in which perception affects our attraction to others.
3. Give examples of sociological and psychological roles.
4. Recall an experience in which the mutual nature of role assignment posed a problem for a relationship.
5. Define expectation as a component of interpersonal communication.
6. Define communication rules. Explain the difference between the two ways communication rules are formed by giving an example of each from experience.
7. Create dialogues representing each of the four relationship positions.
8. Tell of an instance in which your perception in a relationship changed.
9. Distinguish between a statement of observation and a statement of inference.

Perceiving People

Perception of people is different from perception of things. Although the same basic processes are at work, two important distinctions separate these two kinds of perception.

First, interpersonal perception is *mutual.* As we take in and interpret information about someone, that person is doing the same with respect to us. This important characteristic of person perception has a significant effect. It leads us to be concerned about our self-images. For example, suppose you are interviewing for a job with a new company in your town. Assume you already have a job that you like, but someone you respect suggested that you look into this possibility as an interesting and stimulating change. Your interview will involve mutual perception—you are looking each other over. People of the company have an agenda: They want to decide whether or not to offer you a job. You also have an agenda: You want to decide whether or not to accept a job if offered. You try to respond in a way that will present yourself at your best. At the same time you evaluate them based on their questions and interviewing technique. This is a two-way process because perception of people is mutual.

Second, our expectations of people are less clear and more numerous than our expectations of objects. We have expectations about ourselves, about the roles we take into our relationships, about the role of our partners, and about the relationship itself. Objects are very consistent and provide for stable expectations.

The mutual nature of perception has a significant effect on our expectations in relationships, for both parties have expectations that, although they may differ, influence our perception of the relationship. We develop *communication rules* out of our perceptions about the expectations in a relationship. These are boundaries for the communication in our relationships. If we break the rules, perceptions are confused and expectations become unclear. When we observe the rules or change them through negotiation, expectations are reinforced and relational growth can occur.

> *We develop communication rules for our relationships. When we observe the rules or change them through negotiation, relational growth can occur.*

Finally, the expectations we bring to our communication with others come from a summary evaluation of our feelings about ourselves and those about our partners in the relationship. These summary evaluations are referred to as relationship positions. For example, if you take the position that both you and the other person are O.K. in the relationship, your communication will be healthy and contribute to the growth of the relationship. However, there are other positions you might take that could harm that growth. We will examine these ideas more closely later in the unit.

Mutual Experience Affects Interpersonal Relationships

Mutual experience affects the development of our relationships in two important ways: It influences interpersonal attraction—our willingness to establish relationships with particular persons—and it affects the roles we establish and maintain as the relationships develop.

Interpersonal Attraction

Interpersonal attraction describes our willingness to communicate and to develop a relationship with another person. We are attracted to those who are like us, those to whom we are physically close, and those whose physical attributes we admire.[1] Perception is crucial to this attraction because it provides the data we use to decide about whether to engage another person.

We begin to like people and to seek relationships with them in many ways that relate to the process of perception; two ways in particular stand out. First, we usually like people who like us. We perceive their behavior as positive and supporting. Consider, for example, the other students in your interpersonal communication class. There may be several whom you did not know before but have begun to like and talk with. Is there anyone among them who expressed a positive feeling about you before you really thought about a relationship with that person? If so, it was your perception of this event that attracted you to this person. Has this happened to you in other situations? Has it happened at your place of work?

Second, we usually like people who *are* like us. We think they are like us because our perceptions of them correspond to our perceptions of ourselves. These are people we may feel we understand and who seem to share a frame of reference similar to our own. Look around you. Perhaps you see people in your classes or at your job who seem to look or act as you do. Focus on those with whom you have begun relationships. Is it true that they are like you?

Occasionally, we are attracted to people because we are in frequent contact. The frequency of interactions may lead to the sharing of information and our learning to like someone. For instance, suppose you are new on the job and decide that having lunch in the company cafeteria might be a good way to get to know some of your co-workers. Few people notice you as you enter with your tray. However, one person does notice you and invites you to join him. If you do this daily you may learn much about this person and he may learn much about you. Perceptions are shaped in these contacts. They allow us to discover things about people that lead to our choices about liking them or not. We will maintain or increase contact, if we like each other, in order to allow the relationship to grow, or we may avoid or limit contact in order to terminate or limit the relationship if our perceptions are negative. Alternatively, an awareness that frequent encounters are inevitable may cause us to perceive positive information selectively. For instance, we might find something to like about a person because we wish to enjoy the time that we know we will be spending with him. The relationship might not grow very much, but it could develop sufficiently for our tasks to be done efficiently.

We also like and seek relationships with others because of physical attraction. Standards for physical beauty are tied very closely to one's individual frame of reference. And, like the frame of reference, these standards will change over time. Perception is very important in this aspect of attraction because we are making judgments about whether to communicate based on physical data that we take in through our senses. Consider the people in figure 6.1. Whom do you consider attractive? Whom do you find unattractive? Compare your preferences and the reasons for them with a friend and a classmate. How are your standards of beauty different? Are the standards of your friend closer to yours than those of your classmates? This kind of comparison will help you appreciate the personal nature of interpersonal attraction.

Role Assignment

A *role* is a pattern of behavior, a routine that we associate with a particular context. For example, in the classroom we would expect to find someone taking the role of teacher. This might include meeting and leading a class, stimulating the students' thinking, making assignments, and giving and grading tests. Roles have both sociological and psychological dimensions.[2]

Sociological aspects of roles are those patterns of behavior with social implications. In our various relationships, we may assume many of these roles, such as parent, teacher, student, and friend. The *psychological aspects* of roles are their placement in our frame of reference. This aspect personalizes roles and allows us to "own" them. You have noticed that most college professors have their unique ways of fulfilling their role, yet they all fulfill the sociological role of teacher. It is the psychological dimension of the role that provides the individuality of style. When we communicate in a relationship, we begin by assuming roles for ourselves and expecting certain roles of the other person. This establishes guidelines for the communication because roles represent patterns of behavior, many of which are understood socially.

Our perceptions as well as those of the others in a relationship are influenced by the roles we and the others assume. The act of assuming roles is mutual; we jointly work out our role relationships. We must be careful that the two of us are defining our roles appropriately for a given situation. For example, suppose you are accustomed to getting together with your co-workers for refreshments after work on Fridays. This Friday, your boss joins the group. You

Figure 6.1

identify her as your supervisor and assume your psychological version of that role for her. You may be surprised to see her if your understanding of her role did not include socializing with employees as an appropriate pattern of behavior.

Differences in role definitions can be negotiated when we discover them. In fact, successful negotiation is important if we are to function effectively in our relationships. Such differences are frequently encountered when we compare our psychological role definition with that of someone else. When this happens, we assume that the other person will behave in accordance with our definition of the role. Thus, our perception of the person's actual behavior will be filtered through our frame of reference; we do not allow for the other's frame of reference.

Consider how this perceptual filtering affects the interpretation of the following situation. Suppose you encounter one of your professors in the hall and he says, "Bring your term paper in and I'll take a look at it." If you see the professor as a disciplinarian, you might hear the statement differently than he spoke it: "*Bring* your term paper in so I can take a look at it!" In this case, the psychological aspect of your role definition and your relationship has influenced your perception of his message.

When we generalize role assignments in this way, we sometimes make mistakes that affect the capacity for our relationships to grow. The categories we use and the perceptions that result from them are inaccurate. Such errors are usually reflected in both language and action. For example, we know of patterns in marriage that lock spouses into "woman's work" or "man's work." Detecting these mistakes is a matter of comparing perceptions of the roles with the events we experience. To avoid this problem remember that both interpersonal attraction and role assignment are the parts of perception that are *mutual.* We enter relationships based on mutual interpersonal attraction and we develop those relationships through the mutual assignment and definition of roles. Our relationships continue to grow when we communicate in a way that acknowledges that the other person in the relationship is perceiving us just as we are perceiving our partner.

Expectations Influence Interpersonal Relationships

Expectations are an important part of the perception process. When we communicate, we do so at least in part by predicting the other person's responses.[3] We believe that we understand the person when our predictions prove accurate and that we do not understand the person when they prove incorrect. Sometimes, these expectations are based on our rigid impression of the group to which this individual belongs. This process is called *stereotyping.* Our expectations are stereotyped when they come from our knowledge of a group rather than of an individual. This becomes a problem when we fail to go beyond these general group expectations in our actions toward the person and fail to perceive the person as a unique individual. (Unit 13 examines stereotypes in detail and offers recommendations for dealing with them.)

Expectations relate to our perception of people and relationships in two important ways. First, they govern the establishment of communication rules. Second, our expectations of a given relationship are summarized as a *relationship position,* which guides communication with the other person.

Expectations and Rules

One way expectations influence perception is in the way we use rules to structure our interpersonal communication. Rules are patterns of behavior we use to form expectations about certain role relationships and certain situations. Here are some examples of communication rules in relationships:

"We don't talk about sex in front of the children."
"When we talk about the people at church, we never use their names."
"If you touch my elbow, I know you want to take me aside to talk privately."

Communication rules establish which topics are appropriate with various people and in various situations. For example, the rules governing communication in a relationship with a supervisor at work may not allow for the sharing of personal problems. If we break these rules, we might get an unexpected reaction. Similarly, it is probably permissible to discuss your finances with your spouse, but not at a dinner party. Following such rules builds our relationships and encourages others to have confidence in their perceptions of us. Violating the rules makes our partners unsure of their perceptions and thus hinders relational growth. Communication rules are about the appropriateness of messages for relationships and situations. We expect the partners in our relationships to play by the rules. Our expectations and perceptions depend on the use of these relational rules for communication. For example, suppose you and a close friend have agreed not to reveal the depth of your relationship to your co-workers until you both feel more certain about it. You would therefore not expect to find your partner talking about your friendship at an office party. If, however, that person did break this rule, your perception of him would certainly change, and you would have to renegotiate the rule before the relationship could continue to develop.

In their discussion of the formation of family communication rules, Kathleen Galvin and Bernard Brommel identified the basic process by which many communication rules are established.[4] These scholars pointed out that one way we create such rules is through direct, conscious negotiation. In the family, for example, certain topics may be forbidden at the dinner table. In the work place, you may have set a regular time for discussing your performance with your supervisor.

Similar rules emerge through the unspoken repetition of the responses in a relationship. For instance, in family communication, the good night kiss may be a long-established ritual. The kiss does not need to be requested; it is an act that we have always performed. When it does not happen, however, we notice, and assume that something is wrong. At work, you may know from experience that your supervisor is working and does not wish to be disturbed when you hear music coming from her office. Past experience tells you that she likes music when she is working hard, and only then. And she has learned that whenever she plays music while working, she will find herself undisturbed. Neither of you may have acknowledged this rule, but you both follow it.

The communication rules governing each relationship suggest mutual expectations about the topics we can discuss, the language we can use, and the people with whom we can talk about the relationship. They are directly related to our perceptions because we expect things to occur within the latitudes of acceptance prescribed by the rules. These rules provide us a predictable way of communicating that helps us avoid misunderstanding. When we find that they are not working, we perceive that the relationship must be renegotiated before further growth can occur. In short, our expectations and the communication rules that shape them clarify our perceptions in and of our relationships.

Expectations and Relationship Positions

Eric Berne developed a method of looking at relationships called *transactional analysis*.[5] His ideas are frequently used to explain the way people see themselves and how that vision influences their communication. Some of his concepts relate to our assertion of the importance of mutual perception. Transactional analysis suggests that we go through our lives acting out "scripts" that we write for ourselves or that others have written for us. These scripts

The Central Themes of Transactional Analysis

	You're O.K.	You're not O.K.
I'm O.K.	We're equal.	I'm one up on you.
I'm not O.K.	I'm one down on you.	We're both down.

have a central theme that establishes our basic attitude about ourselves in relation to others. There are four such central themes, each of which describes first how we see ourselves and then how we see others in relationships. The four positions are: (1) "I'm O.K., you're not O.K."; (2) "I'm not O.K., you're O.K."; (3) "I'm not O.K., you're not O.K."; and (4) "I'm O.K., you're O.K." Berne says that our actions toward one another are guided by these basic "life positions."

Berne's concepts can explain perception and communication in relationships. Rather than applying these "life positions" to whole personalities, we will look at them as differing from relationship to relationship. We want to suggest that the entire frame of reference for a relationship can generally be summarized in a basic "relationship position." We bring this position to our interactions with relational partners. These summaries guide our perceptions as we communicate in them. These basic relationship positions take the same form as those originally proposed by Berne:

1. "I'm not O.K. in this relationship, but you are."
2. "I'm O.K. in this relationship, but you're not."
3. "I'm not O.K. in this relationship, and neither are you."
4. "I'm O.K. in this relationship, and so are you."

The difference between our model and Berne's is that, rather than viewing everyone from a single perspective (for example, "I'm O.K., you're not"), we believe that the relationship influences the perspective. Thus we approach every person from a different perspective, picking up where we left off with that person and relationship. Three of these positions represent the beginning point for our

The child: "I'm not O.K. in this relationship, but you are."

expectations and perceptions in a relationship. We may find ourselves feeling that either we or the other person is not O.K. Only one of these themes ("I'm O.K., and so are you") promotes optimum growth in our relationships. The others tend to harm one or both persons and therefore stifle growth. Let's look at these positions and see how they affect expectations and perception.

"I'm Not O.K. in This Relationship, but You Are."

Our expectations are frequently dominated by a desire to give control of the relationship to the other person, whether that person wants it or not. This affects our communication when we find ourselves refusing to help make decisions that concern our relationships. This point of view also places all responsibility for making the relationship work on the other person. This is unfair and may be resented. We can help the relationship when we recognize that we have taken this position. The best way to do this is to communicate openly about our feelings about the relationship. We will probably find that the other person is more than willing to work with us to strengthen our relationship and our role in it.

"I'm O.K. in This Relationship, but You're Not."

We find ourselves blaming the other person for problems in our relationships when we approach it from this position. We may view situations with righteous indignation and expect that they will not work out because the other person will make a mistake. We may also be anticipating errors from the other person

The woman: "I'm O.K. in this relationship, but you're not."

and be difficult to please. This frame of reference creates a no-win situation for the other person; perhaps nothing that person might do will please us. Often, this results in the deterioration and termination of the relationship by the other person. The basic reason for such an attitude is our failure to acknowledge the other person's contribution to the relationship.

One way to resolve this problem is to review the relationship. Think back to its beginning and recall the other person's contributions. Then discuss those shared experiences to try to put the relationship in its proper perspective by reevaluating and perhaps redesigning the mutual expectations. Your relationship can grow in a positive direction once successful reevaluation and redesign have been accomplished.

"I'm Not O.K. in This Relationship, and Neither Are You."

This orientation suggests that the relationship is in considerable trouble, for we no longer have the motivation to want to control, nor do we believe the other person is capable of handling control. We blame both ourselves and the other person for the problems. We also expect to make mistakes and we expect the

The boy at left: "I'm not O.K. in this relationship, and neither are you."

other person to behave badly when we do so. At this point we must seriously consider our goals in the relationship—why we created it and what we want from it—and discuss them with the other person. Whether the relationship can be saved depends very much on the other person's perspective. For example, if the other person's perspective is, "I'm O.K. in this relationship, and so are you," then she will be willing to help us develop a more positive view of the relationship. Sometimes an outsider, either a friend or a professional, can help us examine our frame of reference.

"I'm O.K. in This Relationship, and So Are You."
This is the preferred point of view for healthy, growing relationships. With this attitude we acknowledge both our and the other's contributions to the success of the relationship. Our expectations tend to match the rules we have established and kept. We are not often confused by surprisingly negative behaviors. However, we do not deny that problems exist, but rather set a tone that will enable us to talk to the other person and do something about these problems. This frame of reference anticipates relational growth. We perceive the other in ways that promote effective communication.

Both people: "I'm O.K. in this relationship, and so are you."

The expectations that we bring to our relationships affect the way we perceive the other person and the relationship itself. The communication rules and our relationship position, which summarizes our view of the relationship and provides the basis for our actions toward the other person, are statements of these expectations. We maintain an appropriate perception of our expectations and those of our partner by clearly understanding the rules as well as our position, which facilitates interpersonal growth through communication.

Change and Perception in Relationships

Appropriate communication about our roles and expectations is critical to the development of our relationships. *Change* is one factor that influences our perception of interpersonal attraction, role assignment, the development of expectations, and the creation of relationship positions. We must be prepared to deal with change if we are to build long-lasting relationships. Changes in people may be physical, social, psychological, or professional. Of course, changes are not always readily visible—sometimes not even to the person who has changed. Still, changes interact with expectations in person perception.

The expectations we bring to a relationship may not be appropriate in light of changes in the other person. Similarly, the other's expectations may no longer work in light of our own changes. If both people have changed, all expectations may need adjustment, along with the roles in our relationship or our view of their importance.

Think about some of the physical changes you have undergone. How did your way of perceiving shift to accommodate them? Did the changes alter any of your relationships? If so, how? Next, think about an important social change in your life, such as your decision to start college, join a new social group, or find a new job. How did you perceive your new relationships? Did different rules emerge to control them? Did your new associations affect your perceptions of existing relationships? In what ways did your perceptions change? What changes have taken place in your career? If you have not yet begun working, you will find that when you do, your perceptions will shift again. New goals and values will develop around your professional roles, and your perceptions will change as you assimilate information into your new roles. If you already have a career, think about the last important change in your work role or responsibilities on the job. If you changed jobs recently, you may have much to say about the changes in perception that occur when you make a professional change.

Share some of the ways change has affected your perceptions of your relationships with your classmates. You may be surprised to learn that we have all gone through many transformations. Our relationships continue through these changes, and many of them grow along with us.

Building Interpretive Skills

We need to keep in mind two very important aspects of the perception process if we are to understand how to improve our perception of people in our relationships. First, perception occurs inductively. Our interpretations of stimuli represent inferences drawn from what we observe. Sometimes we lose sight of this fact and treat these inferences as though they are facts. This aspect of perception is important to remember because we can improve our ability to give meaning to our perceptions of people and relationships by learning to distinguish more clearly between our observations and inferences.

We must also remember that we perceive unconsciously. We cannot focus on perceiving but only on *what* is perceived. We can improve our powers of perception by learning to recognize inferences when we or others state them.

Herbert J. Hess and Charles O. Tucker have argued that statements of observation differ from statements of inference in three ways.[6] One difference is the extent of description in each. *Observational statements* are faithful descriptions of what was sensed: "I saw you pour the last of the coffee into your cup and then walk away with it." *Inferential statements,* on the other hand, go beyond description: "You poured the last cup of coffee and I'll bet you're not going to make a new pot."

A second difference is that statements of our observations make no judgments: "I smell something burning." Inferences, however, frequently involve judgments: "It stinks in here." Sometimes, a statement of inference goes beyond both observation and judgment: "That inconsiderate oaf must be smoking those disgusting little cigars again." If you assume that this last statement is a fact rather than an inference, you may be surprised when your friend reacts to it defensively.

The third difference lies in the way statements of observation and inference are limited. Observations are limited to a description of what the senses take in. Inferences, on the other hand, are limited only by the imagination of the perceivor. While observations can grow in depth and detail only as long as you concentrate on what you are perceiving, an infinite number of inferences can be generated from the most limited of observations.

Expectations are important aspects of our communication in relationships, for they represent statements of inference that we must make regularly. But as Hess and Tucker point out, it is useful to recognize guesses as guesses. The unrecognized inference is often the cause of misunderstanding and other relationship problems.

You can practice certain skills to develop your ability to perceive more accurately in your relationships. First, state your observations and then follow them with your inferences. For example,

"I see that you are shaking. You seem nervous to me."

"Your eyes are red. Are you tired?"
"I know you finished your paper. You must be happy."

Practice both alone and with others. When you are alone, remind yourself to clarify the observations that result in your expectations of others. When you are in conversation, actually state the observation and then your inference.

A second skill, and one that we introduced in unit 3, is that of checking out your *inferences*. You can check what is inferred on the basis of one sense against the evidence provided by other senses. For instance, a friend seems less talkative than usual. You may infer that she is tired. You can check this out by looking at her face. Does she look tired? Listen to her voice. Does it sound tired? Compare the data from several senses before drawing your inference. This technique works better at the moment of perception than it does after the fact. After all, remember that perceptual distortion can shape your memory of an event to support your inference about it.

Another way to check your inferences is to repeat your observation; that is, look again. You might repeat yourself or approach the subject from another angle. In the case of your tired friend, you might inquire indirectly by saying, "Have you been working many hours these days?" Then rephrase the question more directly, saying, "You seem tired to me." Find out if there is agreement between your first and second observations. Double checking your perceptions is sometimes time-consuming, but it can prevent the difficulties that arise from acting on an inaccurate perception. Sometimes it is necessary to ask a person to repeat what was said so that you can observe more carefully. The benefits in taking the time to do this are worth the effort.

The practice of these skills requires a conscious effort, especially at first. But you will soon see an improvement in your ability to express your perceptions of people and events in your relationships more clearly.

Summary

We have examined the process of perception as it operates directly on our communication in relationships. We began by discussing our perceptions of people. In doing this, we found that the mutual nature of such perceptions and the development of expectations are important.

We next explained how perception functions in the beginning stages of a relationship by looking at its effects on interpersonal attraction. But perception is also important as it relates to role assignment in the later stages of a relationship. One way to improve communication and perception in relationships is to clarify the communication rules, some of which are stated and some of which are assumed.

Certain expectations in relationships come from the general position we take on the relationship. "I'm O.K. in this relationship, and so are you" represents the most productive position because it enables us to communicate in a way that stimulates relational growth.

As we perceive others, we must also remember to account for relational changes and recognize observations and inferences. Three skills are crucial to the latter: We should first state our observations, then check them out, and finally repeat observations.

Discussion Questions

1. Call on the professor teaching a course you have considered taking to learn more about the course. Then answer the following questions.

   a. What tasting, smelling, hearing, seeing, and touching cues did you receive from the professor?
   b. Was the professor in good health? How do you know?
   c. Was the professor tired? How do you know?
   d. How old was the professor?
   e. Did you discover any evidence, either directly related to the person or to the environment, that would enable you to say whether this person is kindly? well read? involved in any extracurricular activity? involved with a family?
   f. Were you tired during this conversation? If so, how did this affect your performance?
   g. How do you think the professor reacted to you? What images did you leave?
   h. What perceptions of you do you believe would still be fresh and vivid in the professor's mind?
   i. Did you and the professor agree completely or even partially about the role expectations for the meeting? What were those role expectations? How do you know?

2. Identify three of your relationships in which the communication rules are very different. List some of the rules to show these differences. How is your perception of people and events guided by the rules in each case? Do you find yourself agreeing to things in one relationship that you might not in another? Is your communication style different?

3. Describe instances in which you assumed each of Eric Berne's relationship positions. How did the communication in these relationships occur? What was it like? What happened to each of these relationships? Did your position change? If so, how?

4. Go to a movie with several classmates and then discuss what you saw. Note the differences in inferences drawn from the same observed images.

Endnotes

1. M. Ruffner and M. Burgoon, *Interpersonal Communication* (New York: Holt, Rinehart and Winston, 1981), 179–94.

2. These ideas were introduced by G. R. Miller and M. Steinberg in *Between People: A New Analysis of Interpersonal Communication* (Chicago: Science Research Associates, 1975), 17–22; also see C. L. Book, ed., *Human Communication: Principles, Contexts and Skills* (New York: St. Martin's Press, 1980), 3–37, 108–38.
3. J. G. Gabarro, "The Development of Trust, Influence and Expectations" in *Interpersonal Behavior: Communication and Understanding in Relationships,* A. G. Athos and J. G. Gabarro (Englewood Cliffs, NJ: Prentice-Hall, 1978), 290–303.
4. K. Galvin and B. Brommel, *Family Communication: Cohesion and Change* (Glenview, IL: Scott, Foresman and Company, 1986), 64–93.
5. E. Berne, *Games People Play* (New York: Grove Press, 1964).
6. H. J. Hess and C. O. Tucker, *Talking About Relationships,* 2d ed. (Prospect Heights, IL: Waveland Press, 1980), 19–31.

>|<< Unit 7
Listening to Others

Preview

Most of what we know about other people
is based on what they say. The rest
results from guesses we make based not
only on what others say but also on how
they act. Listening to people—taking in
their messages plus making guesses
about the intent of those messages— is
very difficult. We can be effective listeners
if we understand how to do so. The aim of
this unit is to help you understand
listening and how to listen effectively in
your relationships.

Objectives

1. Construct a model of the listening
   process and explain each component.
2. Suggest the relational significance of
   saying "you aren't listening" when you
   mean "we aren't agreeing."
3. Explain why relational listening
   requires effort, withholding judgments,
   and empathy.
4. Demonstrate the skill of active
   listening.
5. Tell how active listening benefits an
   interpersonal relationship.

Key Terms
active listening
attending
critical listening
empathy
evaluative listening
forgetting curve
listening
message
paraphrasing
passive listening
remembering
sensing
understanding

Listening: What's Involved

"You're not hearing me" usually does not mean what it seems. Instead this statement usually means, "You're not listening to me *and* understanding me." *Listening* is much more complex than merely hearing. In fact, it has four components, each of which is critical to effective listening. We have placed these in a model to help you visualize the process (figure 7.1).

Listening involves sensing, attending, understanding, and remembering. You may hear and see when a friend comes to us with a problem, but did you really attend to what was said? Did you understand? Did you remember? To see this point more clearly, focus on the sounds around you. Perhaps you can hear the air conditioner or heater functioning. Perhaps you can hear people talking nearby. If you are indoors, perhaps you can hear sounds from outside

Figure 7.1 Components of the Listening Process

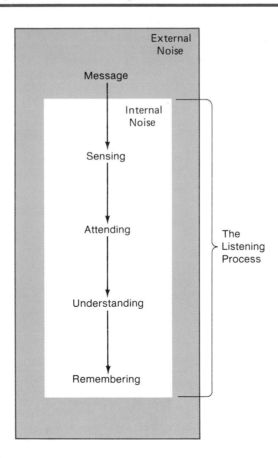

such as cars or birds. Locate, if possible, one of these sounds. Why didn't you sense this stimulus before? If it was there, you could have sensed it. However, you did not complete the listening process until we urged you to do so. Listening is thus more than sensing.

We are often not aware of the components of the process of listening because they blend into a nearly instantaneous act of listening. Our hope is that considering each component individually will help you increase your awareness of them.

A report two students gave of a simple listening assignment illustrates the complexity of the listening process and provides an illustration of its components. Elizabeth and Tim were to interview Ms. Phillips, a counselor at the University Psychology Clinic, about her view of what it takes to keep a relationship healthy. After the interview Elizabeth and Tim sat down to compare notes. They agreed in general about what Ms. Phillips had said, but there was also considerable difference on some points. Tim believed that he was right, and Elizabeth was just as certain that she was right.

"Tim, you always seem to think you're right. How can you say that you're right?" Elizabeth was a little upset and did not select her words carefully.

Tim's reply was not carefully worded either: "Come on, Elizabeth. If you would listen, we wouldn't have to fight."

"Wrong!" Elizabeth responded. "You aren't the greatest either! You're the one who should listen better. I can't wait until our class studies listening. You'll learn a thing or two, I'm sure!"

This was all Tim could take. He stormed off, muttering that he would show just who was listening. Later, he talked again to Ms. Phillips and found that he was wrong. He apologized to Elizabeth. She had cooled off a bit and was willing to forgive and forget. But surely some damage was done to their relationship, much of which could have been avoided had their listening been better.

Sensing

Sensing is receiving stimuli through the five senses. Generally, though, you concentrate on visual and auditory stimuli. You can hear a clock ticking and see its movement if there *is* a clock and if you have normal sensing capabilities. How is it, then, that you were not sensing it before it was pointed out to you? There was an intentional filter that kept you from listening.

Attending

If you were not aware of the clock, it may have been because you did not select its particular sound from the many of which you were conscious. Recall that thousands of stimuli are available for your attention. You select only those that seem relevant to the particular situation and ignore the others. This may be why you were able to sense but did not listen. You may have determined that the stimulus from the clock was not relevant, so you ignored it.

Selective attention helps you to concentrate on the message. It also allows you to block out what you choose to ignore. This selectivity contributes to poor listening when you ignore important aspects of the message. Just consider the mistakes Tim made when he filtered out important parts of Ms. Phillip's message.

Understanding

Understanding, the third component of the listening process, is the interpretation and evaluation of what you are able to sense. Understanding involves more than merely paying attention to what is heard; it implies that you assign a meaning that is close to what the speaker intended. Remember that meaning is related to more than the sensing. You get important data from your experience that helps you interpret the words you hear.

Remembering

Tim may have experienced a memory problem when he and Elizabeth interviewed the college counselor. *Remembering* is a difficult task for many people. Would you dare not to take notes if you wanted to remember what was said in a lecture? You might be reluctant to skip note taking for good reason; the *forgetting curve,* a graphic depiction of the retention rate, falls off rapidly. You lose a lot of what is said almost as soon as it has been said.

Just as you perceive and attend selectively, you remember selectively. You remember some ideas more easily than others because you have found them useful. Sometimes, you remember because you are particularly intrigued by the thought or see a potential "payoff." You encounter problems when you choose not to remember something that later turns out to be important.

Effective Listening Within a Relationship

Effective listening in a relationship has specific characteristics. Our goal is to help you develop a basic understanding of effectiveness.

Relational Listening Requires Effort

Listening requires us to exert varying degrees of effort, depending on the context. Listening requires fairly high energy. We must be active rather than passive participants. This does not mean that effective listening in all other contexts is necessarily passive. However, we wish to contrast relational listening with that done for recreation or amusement or escape.

Forgetting Curves. It's a lot easier to forget than to remember. We have to work hard at remembering.

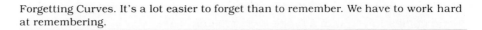

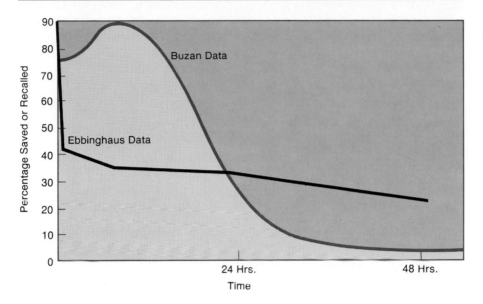

Listening actively demands that we be alert, with our attention focused on the speaker. This is a mutual process in which we try to tune into the other person's verbal and nonverbal *messages* to understand both the content of the message and the speaker's feeling about it. Listening actively suggests that the listener is thinking about—or is involved in understanding—what is being received. One way of achieving this kind of involvement is to ask yourself questions while listening, such as:

1. What observations are being reported?
2. What inferences are being made?
3. What feelings are being expressed?
4. What wants and expectations does this speaker seem to have?
5. What are the intended meanings of the message?
6. What degree of acceptance for the ideas and for the speaker personally are expected from you?

Passive listening, in contrast, suggests that the listener is not as involved with the speaker. Instead the listener is attending to what is being said without providing feedback. This may occur when we attend a lecture or watch television. We do not interrupt the speaker when we use this kind of listening, although we may provide subtle feedback in the form of nods, smiles, and eye contact.

Sometimes passive listening is appropriate in a relationship. Suppose a friend comes to you with a problem and merely wants you to hear what is on her mind. She does not want any input but wants only to tell someone about her frustration. The best way to help this person is to listen without interruption. Of course, you will find it difficult to convey understanding by using such limited feedback, but you will be able to show that you have listened by nonverbal cues such as eye contact and facial expressions, or an appropriate verbal response after your friend has finished talking.

"Don't confuse me with the facts. My mind is made up." **This is an unproductive attitude for a listener.**

Relational Listening Requires Withholding Judgments

We must make a special effort to keep an open mind if we really want to hear what another person is saying. This is easy advice to give, but often difficult to follow! We all have biases. It is often hard to spot them because we think of our biases as the correct view of a situation. Tim had this problem during the Phillips interview incident. He was unwilling to consider that Elizabeth's understanding of what had been said was correct. He was willing, however, to risk an argument with Elizabeth. He was also determined to spend the time to prove that Elizabeth was wrong, but in fact *he* was wrong. Perhaps if Tim had been less rigid, he could have heard Elizabeth's side of the situation. Perhaps hearing her may have prompted a difference in her response to him. Perhaps they may have gone together to talk to Ms. Phillips. Listening while withholding judgment can thus allow more effective and satisfying communication.

Judgment and closed mindedness cause us to filter what we hear through our attitudes and beliefs. Thus, the only way to set biases aside is to discover a way to identify them and take them into account as we listen. Bringing biases to a conscious level takes some effort, but the payoff is worth it. The question is how this is done. One particularly helpful technique is to ask this series of questions:

Position: What is the speaker's position on the topic?
Agreement: Do I agree or disagree with this position?
Strength: How strongly do I agree or disagree?
Importance: Do I consider this an important issue?

Such questions can help reveal not only our position but also the extent to which we may be closed minded. For example, if there is strong disagreement over an important issue, bias may be interfering with the listening.

There is also a place for *critical listening*—listening and then asking ourselves questions about what we have heard—in relational communication. It is often the second step in a listening task. First, we must listen with an open mind to be sure we get the whole message. Then, we can turn to critical listening as we discuss the message.

Relational Listening Requires Empathy

Empathy allows us to move from our perspective to the perspective of the other. There is a difference between understanding what has been said and understanding what a person has said *from the speaker's perspective*; the latter is a deeper and more reliable level of understanding that has a positive effect on relationships.

We can better understand the concept of empathic listening by contrasting it with the listening that Charles Kelley called *evaluative listening*.[1] Kelley said that empathic listening does not impose the listener's frame of reference on the situation, whereas evaluative listening does. Kelley expressed this distinction clearly:

> The difference between empathic listening and deliberative [evaluative] listening is primarily motivational. Both listeners seek the same objective: accurate understanding of communication from another. . . . The empathic listener lets his understanding of the speaker determine his modes of evaluation, which are automatic; the deliberative listener's understanding of the speaker is filtered through his predetermined modes of selective listening, and he actually spends less time as a communication receiver. The empathic listener is more apt to be a consistent listener, and is less prone to his own or other distractions.[2]

In other words, empathic listening requires us to withhold our evaluations— our personal views, not just our judgment—to hear the communication more clearly, understand it more fully, and respond more appropriately.

Consider the example of Elizabeth's and Tim's different understandings of the interview with Ms. Phillips. We might imagine that they each had previously disagreed with someone about what had happened in a certain event. This type of misunderstanding was not entirely new to them, yet neither could identify the problem facing the other. They chose, instead, to see only their own viewpoint. Imagine what a difference it would have made if they had understood the power of empathy in promoting understanding and cooperation. Empathic listening might also have helped them manage communication and their relationship more effectively.

Ability to empathize is enhanced when we fully understand the speaker. But sometimes the speaker does not give the kind of information we need. There are several response skills that will encourage a speaker to explain more fully.

1. *Tell of your interest in knowing more.* You can encourage the person to explain more fully by interjecting phrases and questions such as, ''What else happened?,'' ''Tell me more. What else were you feeling?,'' or ''Yes, I see.'' These probing statements and questions are illustrated in the following conversation.

Tim: I nearly got fired at work today!

Mary Ann: What happened?

Tim: You know I was just hired at the Soft Serve Ice Cream Shoppe. New employees are supposed to practice using the ice cream machine. There is a rule, though, about eating ice cream and not paying for it. I ate an ice cream cone that one of the other new people made. The boss really flew off the handle. I thought I was gone!

Mary Ann: What a shock! How were you feeling?

Tim: Sort of scared at first. It was like being a kid, caught with his hand in the cookie jar. Then I got really mad. I wasn't really doing anything wrong!

Mary Ann: Do you believe the boss wasn't being fair?

Tim: No, he was fair. I was warned. I just think it's petty!

Notice that the questions Mary Ann asked motivated Tim to say more.

2. *Be sure that your response is nonjudgmental.* Judgmental statements are those that reveal evaluation—good or bad, worthwhile or not. Often they convey disapproval, which sometimes arouses defensive behavior in the other person. Suppose Mary Ann had said to Tim, ''That was a really crazy thing to do,'' instead of, ''What a shock!'' This sort of response might have caused Tim to react defensively, which in turn could have led to his withholding of information.

3. *Recognize and affirm the other person's feelings.* Give a supportive response. Responding to aspects of the situation other than the speaker's feelings may not be received as well. For example, telling the other person, ''Don't worry. Things are not really that bad,'' might be seen as an insult that effectively says, ''You shouldn't be feeling and thinking what you are.'' Recognizing the other's feelings and empathizing with them avoids this problem. Here you must pay attention to the nonverbal cues you receive from the other person, as these often carry the feelings. In Mary Ann's dialogue with Tim, for example, she said, ''What a shock! How were you feeling?'' Such questions emotionally unite the speaker and the listener. By revealing the listener's interest in the speaker and the message, that person is likely to feel supported.

Active Listening

We have suggested that relational listening requires an active listening style. This is where the next technique gets the name *active listening*. Active listening is an important response skill for managing relationships productively.

The listener paraphrases to the speaker the content of the message. Often the active listener will also want to mention his own guesses about the feelings of the speaker.

When we paraphrase we give our version of what we heard the speaker say.

The act of translating what another person has said into our own words requires processing the information. What we present to the speaker is our understanding of what was said. Paraphrasing is thus far more than mere par- roting, which is the rote memory task of repeating what was said using the speaker's words.

To illustrate, some students can vividly recollect learning the Latin re- sponses in the Roman Catholic Mass years ago, although they may not have any notion of what the words mean. You must know the meaning of words to paraphrase them.

Suppose Cheryl engaged Elizabeth in this conversation as they left their work one day:

Cheryl: I met this really neat guy at Rick's last night. He seemed very interested.

Elizabeth: He's really super. It's great that you're so excited!

Cheryl: Excited doesn't really describe how I feel. I'd say I'm ecstatic. I've been waiting so long to meet someone like this. And I agree, he is really a super guy so far.

Elizabeth: I can really hear that sparkle in your voice. Tell more.

Elizabeth's use of active listening is clearly leading to her understanding of Cheryl's experience and feelings. This represents a deeper understanding than when we merely attempt to understand the idea being conveyed.

You must know the meaning of words to paraphrase them.

Benefits of Active Listening

Active listening offers four major benefits: First, we must listen more carefully so that we can repeat what we have heard. We will thus learn to manage lis- tening carefully and remembering, two of the most difficult parts of the process, more effectively. Second, we will know that we understand the other person. We usually *believe* we understand the other person, but generally we do not have much evidence that we do. Active listening provides that evidence. And, when we do not understand, we can discover the problem and correct it. Third, active listening allows us to show the other person that we understand. The other person will be able to verify our understanding of the message and dis- cover that we were sufficiently interested to pay close attention.

Active listening requires that attention is focused on the speaker.

This third benefit yields a fourth: A relationship may be nourished by the deeper understanding gained through active listening, as we listen to both the speaker's message and feelings. This deeper kind of listening occurs all too infrequently.

Active Listening Techniques

Active listening seems awkward to people who have never used it. The techniques described below are designed to help you understand how to use active listening most effectively.

1. *Give the speaker cues that you are listening.* These cues can be both verbal and nonverbal. Verbal cues can be comments such as, "Yes," "What else?", or "Tell me more." Be sure you use a variety of these cues. (Imagine how "Yes," "Yes," and "Yes" might be received by your listener.) Such comments invite the other person to give you the details necessary for better understanding and let the speaker know you are paying attention.

Nonverbal cues also show that you are listening. For example, maintain eye contact, nod, or lean forward slightly to display your interest. Finally, you may want to assume an open body posture by sitting or standing in a relatively direct position to your partner. Do not angle your body away from the speaker, and avoid crossing your arms or legs. Instead, establish a relaxed but alert posture so that you can directly observe your partner's verbal and nonverbal messages.

2. *Paraphrase both the content and feelings of the message.* The content is the easier part of the message for most people to understand. Thus, you may tend to focus mostly or perhaps entirely on this aspect. If there are clear feelings involved be sure to feed them back, too. This brief example illustrates this type of listening. Sue is responding to Mary:

> You have been talking for nearly a half-hour about whether or not to continue dating Peter. During that time the only reason you gave for continuing the relationship is that breaking up is such a hassle. From what you've said, I get the impression that you really don't think that you are that much in love with him. And beside this, you know that he will feel hurt and angry. Are you a little scared about the prospects of telling Peter you're through?

Listen to the message that does not have words—and bring that up to the level of talk, too.

Here is a second example of an active listening response. This time Charlie has been talking to John about work. John responds:

> You keep telling me that everything is fine at work, but every time you bring up the subject of your boss the tone changes. All of the enthusiasm leaves your voice. Is something bothering you?

3. *Clarify the areas of uncertainty.* Ask questions about what you have heard to ensure your understanding and receive additional relevant information. Such questions are not meant to probe deeply but rather to stimulate the speaker to express thoughts more fully. These questions should be viewed by our partners as stimulating and supporting. You can see now that asking questions can help to clarify a message in this dialogue between Annie and Russ. Russ was attracted to Annie. He had considered asking her to go to a movie, but decided against this because he knew she was busy studying. He thought she might be willing to spend some time getting to know him if he asked her for a "study" date. Annie heard him correctly when he asked her to study with him. Russ assumed that she understood that a study date would include a certain amount of horsing around. He was wrong:

Russ: Annie, I'm going to the library to study tonight. Would you like to go along with me?

Annie (with a note of skepticism): Well, I am really snowed with course work, but I guess I'd be willing to go study. In fact, that'd give us a chance to talk about our biology project. Do you understand that I really have to study?

Russ: What do you mean, 'really have to study'?

Annie: Russ, I'd be glad to study with you. And I'd be glad to spend some time just talking. But, tonight, if we go to the library to study, I need to study.

Russ: O.K. It's a deal. I'll pick you up at six.

Annie had avoided a misunderstanding and a potential problem by clarifying her uncertainty.

4. *Use active listening when the information is particularly important.* Active listening should not always be attempted but rather only when appropriate. You will need to decide what "appropriate," means for you. For us it means situations in which understanding is important. For example, a friend may want to tell of a problem or perhaps an exciting experience, we may be discussing a joint project, a child may need the answer to a critical question, or somebody may be explaining a complicated process.

5. *Learn a variety of ways to lead into paraphrasing.* Many people who use active listening for the first time will adopt a "lead-in" phrase such as, "What I heard you say is . . . ," and use it every time. This repetition can become annoying to that person's partners. Among the many lead-in phrases that you might learn are: "I think you just said . . . ," "Do you mean. . . ?," "Are you saying. . . ?," "In other words . . . ," "I'm wondering if you mean. . . ?," "Did you say. . . ?," and "So you think that. . . ?" Write down ten such phrases and learn to use them.

Summary

Listening is a process that involves sensing, attending, understanding, and remembering. Sensing is not listening; it is receiving stimuli through the senses. Listening, on the other hand, is more than receiving stimuli. It also includes attending (selecting one of the many stimuli and allowing it to register in the brain); understanding (interpreting and evaluating what is sensed); and remembering (recalling the understood message).

Because of this complexity, listening is a difficult process, especially in a relational context. Effective listening requires effort, withholding judgments, and empathy. We can learn to be more effective listeners by understanding and meeting these requirements. We can also use the technique of active listening to help us to focus on and remember the content and feelings of our partners.

Discussion Questions

1. Identify a person you would like to get to know better. Ask that person how his or her day is going. Engage in active listening as a part of this experience. Then report to your class:

   How did the person respond?
   How did you feel while actively listening?

What nonverbal cues did you get?
What were your images of the person?
What image do you think you projected?

2. Turn on the television and sit with your back to it. Listen for the cues, other than words, that are intended to help you interpret the program. These may include sound effects, a laugh track, or music. Identify as many of these auditory cues as possible, and report your findings in class. How did the inability to see the program influence your ability to understand?

3. It is reasonable to suppose that a person with a hearing impairment will have greater difficulty in listening than someone who is not impaired. How might a person with normal hearing impair her own ability to listen?

4. Suppose that you were to seek the advice of a counselor concerning some personal problem. How would you help yourself listen more effectively to receive the information you need? How would you help the counselor to understand your problem?

5. Suppose you receive a low grade on a midterm project. You believe the grade has been unfairly assigned, so you make an appointment to talk to the instructor about the problem. Identify attitudes and other factors that might make listening difficult for both you and the teacher in this context.

Endnotes

1. C. Kelley, "Empathic Listening," in *Small Group Communication,* ed. R. Cathcart and L. Samovar (Dubuque, IA: Wm. C. Brown Publishers, 1984), 297.
2. Ibid.

>>|<< UNIT 8

The Self-Concept and Relational Effectiveness

Preview

The images you have of yourself depend on your relational interactions, and these images control your communication. It is thus important to understand how your self-image has evolved and what you can do to change it. Moreover, it is valuable to learn how to help others develop more positive self-images.

Key Terms

attitudes
beliefs
derived beliefs
frame of reference
identity aspirations
labeling the dominant behavior pattern
material me
multiple selves
primitive beliefs
reflected appraisal
scanning the environment
self-concept
shared beliefs
significant others
social comparison
social me
spiritual me
surface beliefs
synthesis of beliefs
unshared central beliefs
values

Objectives

1. Define "self-concept."
2. Describe how beliefs, values, and attitudes shape your frame of reference.
3. Identify particular beliefs, values, and attitudes that are important to your self-concept.
4. Explain the processes that have contributed to the development of your self-concept.
5. Set goals for the further development of your self-concept and define the specific steps for the attainment of those goals.

Definition of the Self-Concept

We present ourselves to one another through our communication. And, naturally, we present ourselves differently from one encounter to another. However, certain aspects are repeated in many relationships. These flow from our *self-concepts*—the summary of the perceptions, ideas, and images we each have of ourselves. The very phrase "perceptions, ideas, and images," suggests that we have both a self *and* a concept of that self. A self-concept is a sense of who we are, that may or may not be close to the actual self.

The self-concept is the summary of the perceptions, ideas, and images we each have of ourselves.

A self-concept is not something we can see or touch but rather a useful idea that enables us to study the way we communicate in our relationships. Self-concept is comprised of the characteristics that we present about ourselves. We choose the aspects of self that we think are important to the relationship when we present these images.

Ideas About Who We Are

Interest in the self-concept is not new. In fact, twenty-three centuries ago, Aristotle argued that there were physical and nonphysical parts of the person. At the turn of this century, psychologist William James refined earlier ideas about the self. He suggested that there is a *material me*—my body, my home, and the physical objects around me; a *social me*—my awareness of how others see me; and a *spiritual me*—my awareness of myself as a thinking and feeling person.[1] Later, George Herbert Mead observed how people achieve self-identity through viewing those around them.[2] He suggested that the self has two dimensions—the *I* and the *Me*—which exist and function side by side, each controlling as well as stimulating the other. The *I* represents our private, unique aspects. It is this dimension of our self that provides our goals, creativity, and imagination. The *Me* represents our social side. It maintains an awareness of what is appropriate in certain situations. The *Me* understands how to get what the *I* wants in a socially acceptable way.

Components of the Self-Concept

The self-concept is a complex structure. This complexity is illustrated by the idea of *multiple selves*. We seem to be a different person in each of many different situations. An example may clarify this concept.

The self-concept includes many images of the self.

First, picture yourself at an athletic event. Now, contrast this image with one of yourself taking a final exam. Finally, imagine yourself at work on a very busy day. You would probably describe yourself differently in each setting. Which image is really you? Of course, all are. We have multiple selves, each dependent on a context. Together they form our self-concept. It is the context that makes certain aspects of our self-concept more important at a particular moment.

Self-concept is composed of our *beliefs, values,* and *attitudes.* Our beliefs give our self-concepts their substance, our values give them aspirations and standards, and our attitudes give them motivation. These three elements provide a structure in which we develop and build ourselves. Curiously, we make many assumptions about others on the basis of our own beliefs, values, and attitudes. We should thus look more closely at these components that determine our self-concept.

Beliefs, values, and attitudes reflect our assumptions about the world and our places in it. They differ, however, in their functions. Our beliefs represent the people, places, and things that exist for us. Our values appraise them, and our attitudes guide our behavior toward them.

These components of the self-concept also provide a *frame of reference,* a topic introduced in unit 5. We experience people, places, and things through this frame much as we look out through sunglasses or a window. In other words, a frame of reference is a set of interlocking facts, ideas, rules, and presuppositions that orient a person and give meaning to situations and experiences. Every combination of beliefs, values, and attitudes creates a different frame of reference. The particular frame through which we look at an event colors the way we interpret it. We will experience the event differently if we shift frames of reference; it is like changing the shade of your sunglasses. The differences caused by our frames of reference are central to our perceptions of people and messages, for they determine the self we present to the other person in a relationship. It is important to remember that the source of our frames of reference is the beliefs, values, and attitudes that make up the self-concept. Each frame of reference "represents" some idea about who we are.

We experience people, places, and things through a frame of reference.

Beliefs

At the core of our self-concept lie our *beliefs* about the existence and characteristics of people, places, and things. Any idea is a belief if it includes any form of the verb "to be." If you see one of your friends is acting in an unfamiliar way, you might say, "Are you okay? You're not normally like this." This is an expression of a belief that you hold about your friend. Other examples of beliefs are:

"I'm a tough but fair supervisor."
"I'm an educated person."
"You're attractive."
"My doctor knows what to do about my problem."
"My wife knows which tie will look best with this suit."

Some beliefs are more significant than others. In the examples above, if your wife says she does not know which tie will look best with your new suit, the belief is contradicted, but the results are not earth-shattering. On the other hand, if your doctor says she does not know what your problem is, the consequences are much more serious.

Beliefs may concern ourselves, others, or tangible objects. For example, when you are wondering about something you heard your professor say in class, you might conclude, "He's the teacher and so has a great deal of knowledge on the subject." The connecting of "teacher" and "knowledge" illustrates a belief statement.

Many beliefs are derived through *synthesis,* that is, they are developed from information outside our personal experience. Suppose, for example, you hear that your company is hiring a new Vice-President for Operations, a Mr. Schmidt. During the week before his arrival, you listen carefully to all the speculation about this new manager. You hear Tim say that he knows that four of the seven department heads were fired in Mr. Schmidt's last two years at his previous job. Marie says she overheard the president talking in the elevator about his concern for greater efficiency in the company. You know from your own experience that Mr. White, Mr. Schmidt's predecessor, was fired. You also know that he often missed meetings of department heads because he liked to take long lunches. When asked for your opinion, you might say, "Well, I think we're in for some tightening up around here. Mr. Schmidt must be some kind of efficiency expert that they're hiring to whip all the departments into shape." This statement represents a belief that comes from synthesis. You have had no contact with Mr. Schmidt, yet you believe him to be a taskmaster. This belief is based on your confidence in your friends' reports about Mr. Schmidt, information about his experience, and knowledge of the activities in the company.

Many beliefs are stated only occasionally yet underlie much of our communication. These are called *primitive beliefs.* Milton Rokeach suggests that beliefs are organized in a branching fashion from a central core of most primitive beliefs. He explains this concept of relative centrality in terms of four principles:

1. Beliefs about one's self, existence, and identity are much more central than other beliefs.
2. Shared beliefs about one's existence and self-identity are much less central than unshared beliefs (ones held by oneself).
3. Beliefs that are derived from other beliefs (rather then from contact with the object of the belief) are less central than derived beliefs.
4. Beliefs concerning matters of taste are less central than others. They are usually seen by the holder as arbitrary in nature and are thus relatively inconsequential in their impact on other beliefs.[3]

These interrelationships are shown in figure 8.1. At the outer ring of the figure are *surface beliefs,* or those that are least central. For example, have you noticed that you tend to sit in or near the same seat every time you come to class? This choice expresses your belief that there is something preferable about that location. This preference is probably flexible and has little impact on other beliefs. Your favorite flavor of ice cream and your favorite color are other examples of surface beliefs.

The next ring inward represents *derived beliefs,* or those we develop from indirect contact with an idea. Your assumption about Mr. Schmidt's character is such a belief.

Shared beliefs are shown in the next ring. These beliefs are held because of experiences that we are willing to discuss with others and often do. These beliefs provide a basis for our communication in interpersonal relationships. For

Figure 8.1 The Structure of Beliefs

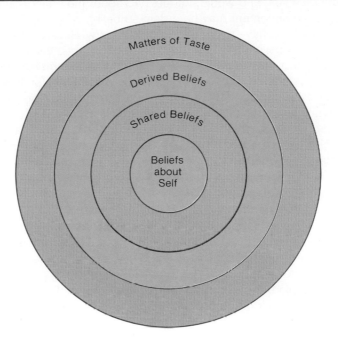

instance, you and your boss may share the belief that you usually speak up for yourself on matters affecting your role in the company.

Unshared central beliefs, in the center of the figure, are fundamental beliefs about ourselves that we rarely share with others. Thus they are not often directly challenged by others. This central core also includes our secret (and perhaps unconscious) hopes and fears, desires and delusions.

Beliefs are what we know about the world and our relationship to it. They exist as statements about what is. Beliefs about ourselves are the building blocks of the self-concept. In them we find the foundations for the images we present.

The nearer a belief is to the outside of the ring, the easier it is to change. Consider these statements, focusing on how difficult they might be to change. Ask yourself what number you would assign to each if 4 represented the hardest to change and 1 the easiest:

"I think I'll wear my gray suit to this job interview."
"This company appreciates a neat appearance."
"I pay attention to detail."
"I am proud of my careful nature."

The first statement represents a matter of taste—your idea about what looks good. You might have given it a 1 rating. You might easily be persuaded to wear your blue suit, and would not feel bad about the change at all.

The second statement may be a derived belief, which you may hold on the basis of what you have heard about the company. Because there is some basis for this belief, it would be more difficult to change than the first statement. You might assign it a 2 rating. It would take some information to cause a change—some other derived belief that would substitute for this one. Remember that what distinguishes a derived belief from other beliefs is that it comes from information and not direct experience.

The third statement might represent a shared belief or one that you intend to share, which suggests that it is more important than the less central beliefs. You might carefully choose your wardrobe for an interview to communicate this characteristic about yourself. You are involved personally with a shared belief, and only a direct experience can change it. You would probably find this belief more difficult to change than these first two, and rate it with a 3.

The last statement represents a central belief—one that you hold about yourself. These are the core of the self-concept because they are intensely held and are well protected; hence, you would give it a 4 rating. They provide stability for the self-concept.

You can explore these ideas about beliefs by completing the ''beliefs'' experience, at the back of the book. It should help you identify your self-concept building blocks.

Values

Values represent what is important in our lives. They include goals or standards of behavior and are evaluative in nature. Wealth, parenthood, inner peace, and a comfortable life are all values. Obviously, values involve beliefs. However, they move the self-concept one step beyond beliefs. Values sort beliefs into wants, goals, and guidelines that define the desirability of certain beliefs or combinations of beliefs. While beliefs represents what is, values suggest what *should* be. When we make a statement about what we ought to be or do, we are expressing a value. For example, you might believe that your professor in this course is tough but fair. You might apply the value that professors should be tough but fair when evaluating other teachers.

Frequently, a value serves as a means of summarizing several beliefs as a statement of goals. For instance, if you believe that children are the responsibility of both parents and that you are a responsible person, you might combine these beliefs into a value as follows:

Belief 1:   Children are the responsibility of both parents.
Belief 2:   I am a responsible person.
Value: When I have children, I should help take care of them.

Values represent what is important in our lives.

Figure 8.2 illustrates the relationship between beliefs and values.

Stewart Oskamp emphasized the significance of the value structure by stating that

> values are the most important element in the individual's system of attitudes and beliefs. They are ends rather than means; they are the goals a person strives for and which help to determine many of his other attitudes and beliefs.[4]

Values contribute much to the image we present to our partners in relationships. They also help us determine an image of others as we assign meaning to their behavior.

Sometimes these value systems come into conflict. Imagine, for example, that you are the sort of person who feels people should speak their minds, no matter what the consequences, and that your friend Elizabeth holds a different value. Perhaps she believes that people should retain a low profile in conflict situations. What might happen if you and Elizabeth had a conversation about an issue on which you disagree? Your emphasis on speaking openly contrasts with her desire to maintain a low profile. If you are to discuss the issue productively, you will likely need to be careful that you do not begin talking to

Figure 8.2 The Structure of Beliefs and Values

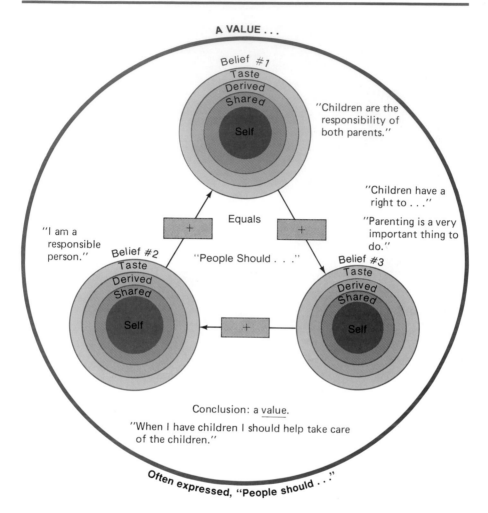

Elizabeth as though she holds the same values you do; she might react defensively since the value she places on speaking up and her belief about the
issue are different.

What do you value? Try the "values" experience at the back of the book
to explore your values.

Attitudes

Gordon Allport defined *attitude* in a way that is useful in a discussion of self-
concept.[5] He stated that attitude is a readiness of mind and body, organized
through experience, that directs our responses to all objects and situations to

which it is related. Our attitudes thus summarize and express our belief and value structures. In simpler terms, an attitude is always about something that we believe or value.

It is helpful to examine this definition in detail, because it covers all the components of our attitudes. Allport described an attitude as readiness; an attitude is our predisposition to act. Our action might take the form of words, a gesture or movement, or simply an expression, judgment, or thought.

An attitude exists in one's mind *and* body. Have you ever suddenly felt tension in your jaw at the mention of something you really disagree with? This illustrates the mental and physical nature of attitudes.

Our attitudes are organized through experience. This means that we learn these responses through the events and communication in our relationships. These learned responses become our natural responses, or attitudes, toward similar situations and relationships. For example, if we try to look good for a date and our date compliments us on our appearance, we may express gratitude that the person has noticed. We are ready to receive the praise, and in future dates, we will maintain this attitude.

Attitudes are also tied to the organization of beliefs and values. Just as values may summarize a set of related beliefs, attitudes may summarize a collection of values. Attitudes direct our beliefs and values toward action. This attitude structure, as it relates to beliefs and values, is shown in table 8.1.

To illustrate how this works, suppose you believe yourself to be an outspoken person. One of the values that helps you to select courses is that professors should encourage students to think for themselves, and to speak up for their beliefs. Among the course offerings for the next term is "Social Problems," taught by Professor Bettski. You took another course with this professor and enjoyed the experience. There were many opportunities to discuss, and you never felt ignored or overlooked. You also believe this teacher to be fair

Table 8.1 The Belief, Value, Attitude, System

	Belief	Value	Attitude
Essence	"Something is . . ."	"Should" and "good"	Personal intention
Example	"This course is about business ethics." "I'm interested in business ethics."	"A good course covers material that interests me."	"I am going to enroll in this course."
Example	"I am an honest person." "Bill did not tell me the truth about his actions last week."	"People should behave honestly. I expect my relationship partners to be honest with me."	"I want to discuss the issue of honesty in our relationship with Bill as soon as possible."

and competent. Your beliefs about yourself and your relationship with Professor Bettski, valued positively, result in an attitude that is illustrated by your willingness to sign up for the course.

A more general structure is revealed when you look more closely. You believe that you speak up for yourself. You value your assertiveness. You are even able to predict occasions when you are likely to speak up. Therefore, your attitudes are sometimes future oriented; that is, they involve expectations about what and how you will think and do.

The Development of the Self-Concept

Four processes are involved in the complex and ongoing formation of the self-concept: (1) labeling the dominant behavior pattern, (2) reflected appraisal, (3) social comparison, and (4) scanning the environment.[6] Not all of these apply directly to everyone, so ask yourself which apply to you. Keep in mind that these are not stages. Two or more can act at the same time in the development of self-concept.

Some of us observe our day-to-day activities and then *label the dominant behavior pattern.* For example, we may see ourselves constantly taking the initiative in both social relationships and business activities. If others reinforce this behavior by calling attention to it, we may come to think of ourselves as initiators—"take-charge" people. We will have developed an idea of ourselves that is based on a dominant behavior. Although this example accurately describes what happens in some situations, it may also simplify what is more often a very complex process.

A more thoroughly developed explanation of how the self-concept develops is found in the second process, known as *reflected appraisal,* that

An Example of Labeling

"I'm a pretty fair golfer."

An Example of *Reflected Appraisal*

An Example of *Social Comparison*

evolved from the work of George Herbert Mead[7] and Charles H. Cooley.[8] Mead wrote that our self-concepts are shaped early in our lives. The self-concept, he said, begins to emerge with the child's observation of the behavior of *significant others* (such as parents and peers).

Then, at play, the child begins to display this behavior. For example, a child may watch and listen to his father, as he cooks and talks about cooking dinner. After a while, the child will accompany the father into the kitchen. As the father prepares dinner, the child will get into the cabinets, play with the pots, pans, and utensils, and talk about cooking. Mead calls this "taking the role of the other."[9] The father may support this play by talking with the child about how "they" are cooking dinner. The child learns that it is permissible for the father to cook dinner and adds cooking as an aspect of self-concept. As the child grows, a concept of self is developed by other attitudes, values, and beliefs related to similar behaviors. Thus, the child's self-concept is a reflection of the appraisals of significant others.

The third process, *social comparison,* takes the idea of self-concept beyond the mere reflection of the attitudes of others. Here our self-concept evolves out of the comparison of the selves of others. Leon Festinger argued that we possess a basic need to have our beliefs and values confirmed by those around us.[10] We confirm some beliefs by checking facts. Others are confirmed by social comparison. Suppose, for example, you are asked to help hire a new director for a division at your company. Your task is to observe presentations given by each of the finalists and to offer a recommendation based on your preference. You notice that the other observers are comparing notes about the presentations as you leave one of these sessions. You might hear one say, "He really knows what this company is about," or "She understands our mission." While it is true that you are hearing the evaluations of the speakers, you are also hearing these people compare their own views of the company, its mission, and perhaps their part in it by comparing one another's reactions to the speakers' remarks.

Over time, we develop standards for comparison that we internalize and reinforce through other comparisons. That is, we have an idea about where someone *should* stand on an important issue if we are going to develop a relationship with that person. If he or she does not fit this standard, we may negotiate the standard. The growth of the relationship may be limited if we are not successful at negotiating or if we choose to live with the differences.

For instance, Peg and Sam were in the beginning stages of what both thought would be a lasting and healthy romantic relationship. They had much in common and seemed to get along well. One day, Peg was looking around Sam's house and discovered several guns in the closet. She was disturbed by this because she had very strong negative beliefs and values about keeping guns in one's home. When Sam came into the room, she said, "Sam, what are you doing with these guns? You're not the sort of person to keep guns around the house. You're going to have to get rid of these." Sam was surprised—and a little annoyed—by Peg's inquiry.

Before their relationship could continue to grow, they had to negotiate some agreement about this issue. Peg's belief about guns had become a standard for evaluating others. Sometimes, as in this case, the standards produce contradictory results. Several of Peg's standards for evaluating people indicated that Sam was someone like her—someone she should get to know better. However, this episode contradicted what she thought she knew about Sam. Sometimes we learn our standards for comparison so intensely that they may rule out the possibility of any later change due to social comparison.

Another way people shape their identities is by developing *identity aspirations:* They want to be recognized as a particular kind of person. This goal may cause them to behave in ways that will lead others to identify them as they would like to be identified. For example, a manager may want to be recognized as the best manager in her organization. To be the best of anything implies that someone else must agree that she has those qualities that are accepted as the "best." She may in fact be able to perform so that she feels good about herself as a manager and that those with whom she works acknowledge her efforts by calling her the "best." However, she may not be so capable in other areas. Suppose she also wishes to be identified as an athlete but lacks the skill. She might be able to achieve agreement about this view of herself by *scanning the environment* for incidents that will confirm this image. She could call attention to her memory experiences that emphasize her athletic ability on the basis of her ability to selectively perceive. She might also believe that she has to go up and down three flights of stairs in getting to and from her office to show that she is in good shape. The result may be an image of herself as an athlete. She is developing an identity aspiration through managing her perception.

Our relationships with others affect the process by which our self-concepts are shaped. We reflect on our communication with others, compare ourselves to others, and use others as models for our own behavior. Our perception of what others think of us and of how they react to our disclosures provides data that support aspects of our self-concepts. Cooley calls this the "looking-glass self," because in effect we use others as a mirror for seeing ourselves.[11]

Our relationships with others affect the process by which our self-concepts are shaped.

Guidelines for Self-Concept Development

Here are some suggestions to help you achieve your goals and develop your self-concept.

1. *Begin with a small change.* Recall that many of our beliefs, values, and attitudes were shaped gradually over a long period of time. Also remember that we have surrounded our more important characteristics with a protective layer of supportive information. Some people change themselves swiftly and easily, but most cannot. For the majority of us, self-change is most successful and long lasting when accomplished in manageable portions. Use your skills to predict how much change you can manage without interfering with your other

goals and priorities. Don't hesitate to slow your pace a little if you overestimate.

2. *Be specific about the changes you desire.* Wanting to be a "better" person is certainly a desirable goal, but how will you know when you have achieved it? A clearer statement might be, "I'm going to work with the local council the first Saturday morning of each month." The more specific you are, the better able you will be to visualize yourself effecting the changes and the easier it will be to measure your progress.

3. *Make agreements with yourself that will allow you to achieve.* Make agreements with yourself about what to expect. Sometimes it helps to include a reward for successfully carrying out desired changes. Encourage others to expect that of you as well, but take care not to hold them responsible for producing your change.

4. *Seek feedback about your presentation of self.* The concept of the looking-glass self tells you that the image you think others have of you is important. Find out if others are perceiving the changes that you are working toward. How do they feel about them? You may find that their encouragement and support will help you achieve your goals.

Changing the self-concept involves overcoming our natural inclination to resist change by using the proper techniques and attention. Although the self-concept does not change dramatically day-by-day, the complex process by which it is formed and developed is unending. We change gradually over time. As we express messages about who we are, we are guided by information acquired by our interaction with significant others, including family, peers, teachers, and media personalities.

It is valuable to consider certain aspects of ourselves as we see them and as they are seen by others. We must become aware of the characteristics that express who we are if we want to improve our interpersonal communication. To the extent that every message is, at least in part, about us, it is helpful to think and talk about our images.

Summary

Interpersonal communication involves the presentation of ideas about the people, places, and things in our world as well as information about ourselves. Our image of ourselves and our notions about what is appropriate for expression in a relationship determine the self-concept. The basic components of the self-concept are beliefs, values, and attitudes that together form a "window," known as the frame of reference, through which we view our relationships. Four processes operate in the evolution of the self-concept: (1) labeling the dominant behavior pattern, (2) reflected appraisal, (3) social comparison, and (4) scanning the environment. Maintaining and changing the self-concept requires attention and discipline.

Discussion Questions

1. Describe the frame of reference you would bring to a job interview. Consider the beliefs, values, and attitudes that would be involved.
2. List your significant others. Think about your communication and theirs, and identify instances of labeling the dominant behavior, reflected appraisal, social comparison, and scanning the environment.

Endnotes

1. W. James, *Psychology* (New York: Holt, 1910), 177 and following.
2. G. H. Mead, *Mind, Self and Society* (Chicago: University of Chicago Press, 1934).
3. M. Rokeach, *Beliefs, Attitudes, and Values: A Theory of Organization and Change* (San Francisco, CA: Jossey-Bass, 1968), 5.
4. S. Oskamp, *Attitudes and Opinions* (Englewood Cliffs, NJ: Prentice-Hall, Inc., 1977), 13.
5. G. W. Allport, "Attitudes," in *Handbook of Social Psychology,* ed. C. Murchison (Worcester, MA: Clark University Press, 1935), 810.
6. K. Gergen, *The Concept of Self* (New York: Holt, Rinehart and Winston, 1971).
7. Mead, *Mind, Self and Society,* 173.
8. C. H. Cooley, *Human Nature and Social Order* (New York: Scribner's, 1912).
9. Mead, *Mind, Self and Society,* 150–52.
10. L. Festinger, *A Theory of Cognitive Dissonance* (Stanford, CA: Stanford University Press, 1957).
11. Cooley, *Human Nature,* 152.

Self-Disclosure and Relational Effectiveness

Preview

We reveal ourselves to others through our communication. This uncovering of the self may not always be easy, but it is essential to relational growth. The information we reveal varies from one relationship to another, in some instances significantly.

We each develop a style of communicating about ourselves through the influence of significant others. To change our manner of self-expression, it helps to understand where we learned our particular method of self-expression. This unit will help you create more appropriate expressions of yourself.

Objectives

1. Define self-disclosure and recall examples of it in at least two relationships.
2. Identify the differences in your openness from one relationship to another.
3. Recall an instance in which bringing something about yourself into the open helped a relationship grow.
4. Trace the influence of family, peers, schools, and media on your style of self-disclosure.

Key Terms

blind self
hidden self
Johari Window
open self
overdisclosure
self-disclosure
underdisclosing
unknown self

Self-Disclosure and Relational Growth

One of the ways we know a relationship is growing is that the other person is able to make accurate predictions about what we would like, say, or do. For instance, suppose Helen knows that her husband John has had a hard day at work and she therefore has something special waiting for him at home—perhaps his favorite dinner or a book that he has wanted. This is her way of showing that there is understanding in their relationship. Perhaps on that same day friends call Helen to invite her and John to a party that night. Knowing that John would rather relax after such a hard day, Helen might decline the invitation without checking with him.

The key to correctly anticipating the wants and needs of others is the frequent communication of our own wants, needs, and expectations. The more our partners understand about how we see ourselves, the better their predictions will become and the more the relationship will grow. We call the process of revealing ourselves to others *self-disclosure*. Improving our ability to self-disclose and learning when and where to do this are important elements of relational development.

Relational growth is apparent when you correctly predict another person's behavior, needs, or wants.

Imagine that we keep all our personal information in a little box that we carry around with us. We select and present items from the box when we meet others. There is some information that we want most people to see and know, so we select these bits most frequently. There are other things that we reserve for only select individuals in special situations. There are still other things that we keep entirely to ourselves. Finally, there may be information tucked in the corners of the box that even we do not know exists. These are things we do not discover until we have spent some time and energy rummaging around in the box. Sometimes one of these unknown bits sticks to another bit that we are taking out of the box, and, without our knowledge, is presented to someone else. This is what Anthony Athos and John Gabarro call "a message sent unawares."[1]

The Johari Window

Two contemporary psychologists, Joseph Luft and Harrington Ingham, developed a model, known as the *Johari Window* (figure 9.1), to help people understand the relationship between the various ideas we present about ourselves.[2] The upper left block presents the information about us that is clear both to ourselves and to others. This information includes behaviors, attitudes,

Figure 9.1 The Johari Window

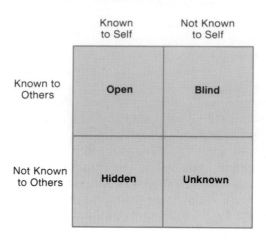

feelings, and desires, and makes up the *open self*. Consider for a moment what people in a particular situation—perhaps a club or organization—know about you. Name some of these things. How did they learn it? The things that you and others in the organization know are in the open area of the window.

The square at the upper right represents the *blind self*. This area contains things others know about us that are not evident. We may provide leadership in a club or organization, for example, yet not be aware of doing so. We learn about things that exist in the blind area through communication. Others bring these behaviors, attitudes, and bits of information into the open by telling us about them.

The hidden self and the unknown self are in the lower half of the window. The *hidden self* is that part of our private image we choose not to present to others. Almost everyone has information about themselves that they keep private. This may include information about ambitions, wants, desires, hopes, and fears. Can you think of anything you have *not* revealed to your supervisor at work or to your partner in a romantic relationship? You can see that the size of the hidden self varies from relationship to relationship. This is true for the other areas of the self as well.

Finally, Luft and Ingham reasoned that there is an *unknown self*. This area includes things about ourselves, perhaps talents or phobias—that even we do not know about, and have no reason to believe anybody else does either.

Openness is important to relational growth, but too much openness may be imprudent.

Self-disclosure is a matter of choice. We must choose wisely if relational growth is the goal.

How open are you in important relationships? The understanding that comes from shared openness helps each person perceive the other more accurately. Although it is easy to overstate the case for openness, in general, the more we know about someone, the fewer false assumptions we make about that person. It follows that openness is important to relational growth.

On the other hand, if the open self is too large, an opposite effect may result. A person who is too open is said to be imprudent, or not completely in control. Revealing information about ourselves that is not yet appropriate in a relationship is called *overdisclosing*. The motives of someone who overdiscloses are often suspect. We have all probably met a person with whom we feel uncomfortable because he is overdisclosing, that is, revealing either too intimate or too much information. In such a situation we would probably withdraw to avoid the overdiscloser. When this is not possible, we may subtly joke or tease about the situation. Generally, people do not come right out and tell the overdiscloser why they are uncomfortable. They hint about it instead.

Complete openness may also harm a relationship. Some things are better left unsaid. Private thoughts in a moment of anger, for example, may be hurtful to the other person, and not particularly important to the overall relationship.

We can learn much about ourselves and our style of disclosure by exploring the "blind" area of the Johari Window. Here is information that we are unable to perceive but that is known to others. Suppose, for example, we have a friend Bill who has certain annoying habits of which he is unaware. In this case, the unconscious behavior contributes to communication difficulties. Bill habitually stares off into space during conversations, looking past the person with whom he is talking and not really hearing what is being said. People frequently avoid Bill. They report feeling uncomfortable with him because he appears not to listen. Finally someone calls this habit to Bill's attention. At first he does not believe it, but when he pays attention to his communication, he sees that he does have the habits described.

Sometimes we are unwilling to share enough about ourselves to make a relationship work. This is represented by a hidden area that is too large or an open area that is too small. There are many reasons for not wanting to reveal things about ourselves, and sometimes we are right in keeping certain information or feelings hidden. Sometimes we are afraid to take the risk of self-disclosure. Because of this fear we do not allow the relationship to grow. Has this ever happened to you?

We can use the Johari Window to sort out the information that we impart to others. Select a relationship you would define as close and examine your open area in that relationship. Begin by writing down several of the major things you believe are known both to yourself and to the other person. Next, think about your hidden area in that relationship. Write down several of the major items you have kept private. Is there anything in your hidden area that you might be willing to disclose? Under what circumstances might you be willing to do this?

Learning about your blind and unknown areas in the relationship requires effort from you and cooperation from the other person. Review your lists of open and hidden items. What aspects of yourself were revealed to you as a result of examining the relationship? Finally, ask the other person to talk with you about the way she sees you, herself, and the relationship. Such a conversation may reveal even more about your blind and unknown areas.

By analyzing our self-disclosure, we learn how open we are and how to make more conscious choices about what to disclose. Thus, the Johari Window can be a powerful tool for examining interpersonal communication. It can help clarify the information we share with others and also help us understand ourselves better.

The key objective in self-disclosure is appropriateness: We wish to present an image that is correct for a relationship and its context. Two general rules will help you gauge appropriateness. First, remember that your window is not the only one present in a relationship. Both partners in the relationship must be willing to self-disclose for the relationship to work. Second, the level of disclosure must be balanced or even, rather than one-sided. If you have a very large open area and the other person has a very small one, you may find yourself overdisclosing or this person *underdisclosing*. Relationships in which disclosure is one-sided will not grow very much. When we disclose, we encourage equal disclosure by our partners. When the other person discloses, we feel encouraged to disclose more ourselves. Relationships grow as disclosures are made by both parties over time.

The Influence of Significant Others on Self-Disclosure

George Herbert Mead suggested that *significant others* enter the process of shaping the self-concept.[3] They also influence the amount and style of disclosure by their impact on our self-concept. Significant others are people we look to to discover what behavior is appropriate. As discussed in unit 8, these include family members, friends, religious leaders, teachers, and even media personalities. The role that each plays in development varies for each of us.

Family

Family members, particularly parents, provide the earliest stimuli in the development of our self-concept. In addition to satisfying physical needs, parents serve as a primary source of information, behavior, and attitude. They teach us what expressions will be appropriate in given contexts. Parents also play a major role in our development of definitions of our place in life. From them, we learn ways of expressing our feelings about what is going on around or inside us. Parents may exert a positive or a negative influence on our beliefs, values, and attitudes about such issues as achievement, education, religion, politics, love, and even bigotry.

Other family members are also a source of identification and mirroring in self-concept development. We may choose to emulate or avoid behavior we see. For example, you may have learned to communicate about conflict by watching family members resolve their conflicts. You may not notice that you have adopted their style of conflict management until you actually sit down and study it, comparing your behavior to what you recall of theirs. Mannerisms, gestures, and even language also may be copied in this way.

Even the birth order of brothers and sisters has been found to influence aspects of self-concept development. Research has determined, for instance, that first-born children gradually place great emphasis on achievement in life and are frequently expressive communicators. Middle-born children tend to value peer relationships and interactions more highly and usually see themselves as more independent than others, which they express in their communication. Researchers find last-born children consistently more dependent on others than older siblings, which may be reflected in their relationships.[4]

Look carefully for signs of these influences as you pay more attention to the way you express yourself. You may find that particular language, gestures, or even ways of talking about certain subjects (such as sexuality, money, or goals) come from family influences.

Peers

Peers are another set of significant others. They provide a general standard of social acceptability and a safe way to try out our social roles and styles of communication. Throughout adolescence, in particular, peer relationships nurture the development of the self-concept in terms of status, acceptance, leadership, sexuality, and romantic behavior.[5] If we look carefully, we will find that our language and other means of expression change as we move from one peer group to another. Many peer interactions occur within the context of a third important source of influence, the schools.

Schools

For much of our early lives, we spent our time observing and interacting with teachers. Children observe, for example, how teachers talk with others in school and may adopt some of these styles of expression. Some teachers display behavior patterns that children will not want to emulate. Perhaps a teacher has been particularly hostile in the way he disciplined a student. This may serve as a negative example of how to behave.

In addition to teachers, the school system itself influences the development of self-disclosure styles. Boyd McCandless and Richard Coop summarize the significance of this influence on our style of communicating about the self-concept by stating that "the school is a miniature social system in which the adolescent is expected to acquire basic cognitive, intellectual, and social skills, and which enables the student to earn primary or earned status."[6]

Children acquire the beliefs and a way of expressing them that will help them set and achieve goals in school. They also build the means to express their values and attitudes appropriately in an organized society. The impact of the school system on the self-concept is apparent throughout life. Even the selection of a college is made, at least in part, on the basis of the behavior style encouraged at that particular school.

Media Personalities

A fourth source of significant others is the mass media, particularly television. In 1987, Samuel Becker reported that the average American household had a television on for an average of seven hours each day. And children have always been a large audience. Becker found that children aged two through eleven watch an average of three and one-half hours of television every day. By the age of twelve, the average American child has been exposed to some 13,500 hours of television, an amount that is nearly double the time spent in school.[7]

Young people frequently nominate popular characters as people they want to be like when they grow up.

George Comstock detailed the influence television had on children in his 1978 essay "The Impact of Television on American Institutions." He summarizes this influence as follows:

> It captures children's attention for long periods, and presents them with information and portrayals not duplicated or readily tested in their real life environment. It is turned to by children for information not readily available to them in real life. It provides models of behavior children may emulate. It can alter the level of intensity of behavior through positive or negative reinforcement children receive. Viewing of violence increases the likelihood of aggressive behavior on the part of the young, but the larger implication is that television may influence other classes of behavior.[8]

Television provides role models. Frequently children nominate television characters as people they want to be like when they grow up. Children will even imitate the behavior of admired characters. Thus, television can exercise a pervasive influence on the development of our disclosure style. This influence can be positive or negative, of course, depending on the types of content to which we are exposed. You can test this idea out by listening carefully to the way people communicate. Sometimes you can hear them talking in ways that imitate popular television, radio, or film personalities.

It is often helpful to look for the source of the behavior or language when we discover an aspect of our style that we want to change. Knowing that our behavior originated somewhere can help us remember that it is neither permanent or unchangeable. We can control and use it or not, as we see fit, because we are able to see it as separate from us. Not knowing where a particular behavior came from can make us feel that we are forced to live with it and let it control us.

Summary

Self-disclosure is the act of revealing something about ourselves to another person. We do this to make our relationships grow. By using the Johari Window we can analyze our disclosure for various relationships and then decide whether our levels of disclosure are appropriate for these relationships.

Our style of disclosure comes from four main sources: family, peers, schools, and media personalities. If we want to change some aspect of our self-disclosure style, it can be helpful to think about the source of that aspect. Doing this separates the behavior from our self-concept sufficiently for us to work on changing it.

Discussion Questions

1. Can you recall an instance in which you found yourself overdisclosing and felt unable to stop yourself?
2. With all of the many factors operating in a relationship, how do you determine whether your partner is open?
3. Call to mind a child you know who is ten years old or younger. Can you evaluate that child's emerging self-concept? What are the contributing factors in this development?
4. Imagine that this same ten-year-old child has just brought home a report card with a very low mark in a major subject. In what ways might the child's self-concept influence her behavior? How will the parent's response affect the child's emerging self-concept?
5. List seven or eight of your significant others. Now rate the extent of openness you display in each relationship using a scale of 0 to 10, with 10 being the most open. How do you account for these different ratings? Are you satisfied with the differences? Share your thinking with a classmate.
6. Draw a time line for the past two years, marking important events in your relationships. Think of how you have self-disclosed about those events, focusing on the influences in your life that contributed to your

style of self-disclosing. You may wish to compare notes with a classmate.

Endnotes

1. A. G. Athos and J. J. Gabarro, *Interpersonal Behavior* (Englewood Cliffs, NJ: Prentice-Hall, 1978), 25.
2. The Johari Window was created by Joseph Luft and Harry Ingham during a summer laboratory in group development at UCLA in 1955. Their idea was later published by Luft. See J. Luft, *Group Processes: An Introduction to Group Dynamics,* 2d ed. (Palo Alto, CA: Mayfield Publishing Company, 1970), 11–20.
3. G. H. Mead, *Mind, Self and Society* (Chicago: University of Chicago Press, 1934).
4. B. R. McCandless and R. H. Coop, *Adolescents: Behavior and Development,* 2d ed. (New York: Holt, Rinehart and Winston, 1970), 223.
5. Ibid., 246.
6. Ibid., 333.
7. S. L. Becker, *Discovering Mass Communication* (Glenview, IL: Scott, Foresman and Company, 1987), 306–11.
8. G. A. Comstock, "The Impact of Television on American Institutions," *Journal of Communication* 28 (Spring 1978): 15.

Verbal Interaction

PART II

The Nature of Language

Preview

Language connects our ideas to the people in our relationships. Growth in relationships is difficult when our use of language is unskilled or inefficient. We use words to represent our ideas and to talk about the events in our lives. But we must remember that words only stand for those experiences and cannot take their place. This unit explores the nature of language and how it effects relational growth.

Objectives

1. Discuss the interrelationship among events, thoughts, and language using the Triangle of Meaning.
2. Explain abstraction as it applies to language.
3. Recall an example of how abstraction helped or hindered your communication in a relationship.

Key Terms
abstraction
combining
focusing
ignoring
language
levels of abstraction
rearranging
referent
symbol
thought
Triangle of Meaning

What Is Language?

Language is an important part of how we see our relationships and how they develop. As with other parts of the communication process, we must define language before we think about how it affects communication in our relationships.

Many people have studied language and offered definitions of it. We prefer the one offered by Howard Pollio, who said that language is a system of symbols governed by rules that describe which symbols are acceptable for use in communication.[1]

Language is a system of symbols governed by rules. It is our primary means of expressing ourselves to others.

Several important ideas about language are suggested in this definition. First, it tells us that language is made up of symbols—that is, words. Second, it implies that the words are abstract, that is not directly related to the objects and experiences they describe. For most of us there is some relationship, but

What one person experiences as frustration may not affect the other person at all.

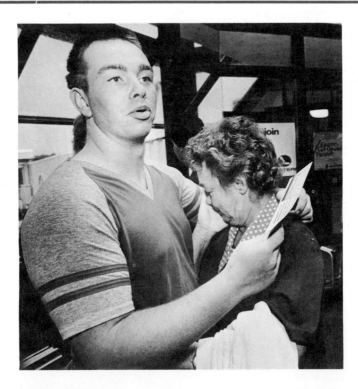

it may be somewhat different for each person who uses the word. Third, the use of language is governed by rules. We know a great deal about what those around us believe is appropriate language for each particular situation. Part of this knowledge comes from our culture and part from people with whom we communicate.

Language and Experience

Language is our primary means of telling others who we are and how we feel about them. We use language both to send and receive this information. We select words that we believe will convey our experience. As we come to understand the other person and his ideas, we attach to those perceptions language that describes what we are sensing. The other person is also using language—perhaps different from ours—to talk and think about his experience.

Many factors affect the information we take in and process. For example, our frame of reference includes the language we have acquired. We use this frame of reference and the language that is a part of it to filter the events we experience. If we have limited language to describe our feelings and emotions, that filtering process may not serve us as well as it might.

Suppose that a friend comes to you and talks in a tone that you perceive as anger. Perhaps the friend is actually experiencing and attempting to convey frustration. Suppose that "frustration" is not the word you use to label your observations. Instead, you select one that seems to fit your perceptions most closely, in this case, "anger." How do you suppose labeling frustration as anger might affect the relationship? How would this affect your response to your friend? How do you think your frustrated partner would react to being treated as though he were angry?

The Triangle of Meaning

Understanding the relationship between the words we use, what they refer to, and our ideas will help us become more aware of what is happening when we communicate our relationships. Charles K. Ogden and I. A. Richards depict this relationship as the *Triangle of Meaning* (figure 10.1).[2]

The *referent* at the lower right corner of the triangle is the subject of our communication. The referent may be a person, object, or event; it also may be a feeling, or want. The referent is the object of our perception and that to which the symbol refers.

The *thought* at the top of the triangle represents our perception and interpretation of the referent. Our feelings about the referent, past experiences related to it, and other perceptions may also be included. In other words, the thought is a mental image of the referent.

Figure 10.1 The Triangle of Meaning

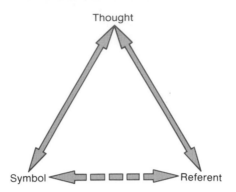

The lower left corner of the Triangle of Meaning is labeled *symbol.* A symbol stands for something else. In language, words, phrases, and sentences stand for thoughts. We cannot communicate our thoughts directly, so we translate them into language, which is a system of commonly shared symbols.

The arrows in figure 10.1 show the relationships among the elements of the Triangle of Meaning. A solid arrow connects the referent with the thought because the referent acts as a stimulus for the thought. One reason we have a thought is that we perceive a referent. Frequently, our thought is about the referent, but it may also involve something quite apart from what is taking place. For instance, you may be working hard on an assignment when your roommate asks if she can get you a cup of tea. She knows that you enjoy having tea while you work and that it is difficult for you to interrupt your work to make yourself a cup. Your response may be about the cup of tea—the referent in this inter- action. But you might also respond by saying something like, ''You know, I'm really lucky to have a friend like you.'' This represents a statement of your feel- ings about your roommate, stimulated by but only remotely connected to the referent.

The reason a relationship exists between the thought and the symbol we use to convey that thought is similar to the reason for the relationship between thought and referent. We use the symbol because we had the thought, and this symbol seems to represent it most conveniently. The symbol, however, does not represent all of the thought, nor does it necessarily represent the thought accurately. We select our symbols to communicate the intended idea as clearly as possible.

The broken arrow connecting the symbol with the referent suggests that these two elements need not correspond at all. There is no direct relationship between the word and the object; the word is not the object, and the symbol is not the referent.

You can understand the relationships illustrated in the triangle by listing your reasons for studying interpersonal communication. They must, inevitably, take the form of symbols. Here are possible answers:

"To get credits in an interesting subject."
"Because it's a required course."
"I heard the teacher was good."
"I want to improve my relationships."

None of these statements expresses all of your reasons for enrolling in the class. Thus language only *symbolizes* your reasons and puts them in a form others can understand.

The thought aspect of the Triangle of Meaning includes everything that occurs in our minds when we hear the question or perceive the referent. This includes assumptions, feelings, reflections about past experiences, physical sensations, and other mental activity. They relate to the answer to our question about taking this course because the answer is designed to represent some or all of them. Your thoughts also relate to the referent, which in this case is interpersonal communication. You have these thoughts because we gave you the topic to consider.

Remember that there is not necessarily a direct causal relationship between the symbol and the referent. Your reasons for studying interpersonal communication do not stem from interpersonal communication itself. Your words about it are not the same as your experience of it. The thought aspect of the Triangle of Meaning connects the symbol and referent.

Consider another example. If we show you the word "chair," you will think about it and then point to a referent chair. If we show you a chair, you will think about it and then utter the word "chair." You cannot move from symbol to referent or from referent to symbol without first passing through thought.

All these facts about symbols, thoughts, and referents are especially important in the language we use to describe our relationships. When we describe someone as a "friend," we have chosen this word to summarize our thoughts that might have developed over years. Consider the following example of how we use language to symbolize relationships.

George is an important person in Lisa's world. She uses words like "friend," "partner," and "colleague" to describe George. She also says he is "faithful, cares about me, helps when I'm down" and recalls their experiences together, elaborating that "he *visited* me in the hospital and cheered me up when my dog disappeared."

If George were your friend, you might use labels such as "best friend" in similar or different ways. You may also find interesting the various experiences from which these labels and explanations were derived. Note that how you use language to describe the relationship might influence your communication in it.

Figure 10.2 The Abstraction Process

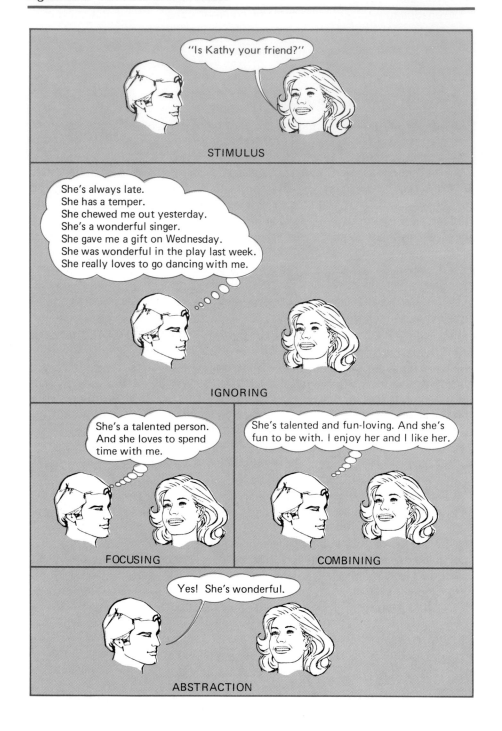

The Abstraction Process

The process of perceiving and making sense of language is called *abstraction*. We use abstraction to translate experience into thought and then into language. John C. Condon explained abstraction as an act of selection.[3] When we attempt to explain our experience of an event or a relationship, many images come to mind. For instance, when we think of "friend," many faces, images, and experiences are evoked. We must select those that will accomplish our purpose. Condon says that we choose by *ignoring* much of what is available to us, by *focusing* on a limited amount of it, and by *combining* or *rearranging* what is left into an expression of our intentions (see figure 10.2).

We can describe a relationship on many *levels of abstraction*. Higher levels of abstraction are more general. At these levels we ignore more of the specific information by focusing less on details. Lower levels of abstraction ignore less by focusing more on specific information.

Consider the example of Susan, who serves as a faculty advisor to the chess club, works on university committees, writes articles and papers about history, which is her field, and teaches classes. Our relationship with Susan can be described at a number of different levels of abstraction. When we refer to her as a "new history teacher," we are abstracting at a moderate level, ignoring much about her and focusing on a small amount of what we know about her. When we refer to her as a "faculty member," we have moved to a higher level of abstraction, ignoring more of the specifics. We combined much of our data into a single summary label that does not focus on any particular aspect of our experience of her. We might describe Susan at a very high level of abstraction by referring to her as a "state employee." This takes into account our data from our experience of Susan and is therefore accurate, but it also includes much that is not specifically about her. All sorts of people are state employees—tax collectors, clerks, and politicians. This high level of abstraction tells us less about Susan than the lower level abstractions. Abstraction is thus very important to communication in our relationships.

S. I. Hayakawa offered a useful explanation of how we abstract and how that abstraction relates to language.[4] He said that abstraction is like climbing a ladder. As we climb higher up the ladder our view of an event changes in several important ways. This affects the language we choose to describe the event. The higher we climb, the further we are from the ground, so we can see less detail but more of the surrounding territory. As we climb the abstraction ladder, our ability to relate experience through language is affected similarly. The more abstract our perception of the event, the farther we are from our direct experience of it. Our perception contains much less detail at higher levels. For instance, you might describe getting an A on a tough exam by saying, "That extra study time really paid off—I scored 97 out of 100, and got the highest grade in the class!" At a higher level of abstraction, you might say, "I did better than I usually do on exams." You can see that the lower level statement is

Abstraction Ladder. Start reading from the bottom up.

ABSTRACTION LADDER
Start reading from the bottom UP

8. "wealth"

8. The word "wealth" is at an extremely high level of abstraction, omitting *almost* all reference to the characteristics of Bessie.

7. "asset"

7. When Bessie is referred to as an "asset," still more of her characteristics are left out.

6. "farm assets"

6. When Bessie is included among "farm assets," reference is made only to what she has in common with all other salable items on the farm.

5. "livestock"

5. When Bessie is referred to as "livestock," only those characteristics she has in common with pigs, chickens, goats, etc., are referred to.

4. "cow"

4. The word "cow" stands for the characteristics we have abstracted as common to cow_1, cow_2, cow_3 . . . cow_n. Characteristics peculiar to specific cows are left out.

3. "Bessie"

3. The word "Bessie" (cow_1) is the *name* we give to the object of perception of level 2. The name *is not* the object; it merely *stands for* the object and omits reference to many of the characteristics of the object.

2.

2. The cow we perceive is not the word, but the object of experience, that which our nervous system abstracts (selects) from the totality that constitutes the process-cow. Many of the characteristics of the process-cow are left out.

1. The cow known to science ultimately consists of atoms, electrons, etc., according to present-day scientific inference. Characteristics (represented by circles) are infinite at this level and ever-changing. This is the *process level*.

closer to the direct experience of the event and the higher, more general level is much farther.

On the other hand, when we describe an experience from a higher level of abstraction, our perception includes more of the context surrounding the event. That is, it includes information that is not directly related to our experience of the event, but helps us understand it.

We select levels of abstraction based on how well we know another person—the depth of our experience in the relationship. To use the abstract "state employee" to describe Susan, we do not have to know her well at all. We can use this language and remain relatively far from our direct experience of her. The description "faculty member" is also rather abstract. Contrast this with our description of Susan as a "new history teacher."

Abstraction in Relationships

Levels of abstraction of language are important to relationships in three ways. First, the abstraction level identifies the characteristics of the relationship that we see. This includes not only ways of talking about the relationship, but also behaviors that are viewed as appropriate to some degree. For instance, when discussing details of your job with your new supervisor, you may find that your language takes on a very low level of abstraction. However, when talking about personal matters, the level of abstraction may be much higher. Your supervisor might, for example, ask, "How are things at home?" You might reply, "Everything's fine." It is important to use an appropriate level of abstraction in relationships. In the example above, it seems appropriate for the supervisor to inquire about your life at home. A detailed response that was either positive or negative would be inappropriate, given the level of the question. The nature of your relationship with your supervisor suggests a more abstract response.

Second, the abstractness of the language used in a relationship indicates our view of its depth and intensity. We tend to use less abstract terms of endearment, such as "dear" and "honey," with those to whom we are close. In less intense relationships, we tend to use more abstract, general terms, such as "sir," "ma'am," and "professor." When Dr. Stevens called the role for the first time in his class, he asked students to tell him if they had another name that they preferred, such as Fred instead of Frederick. One student, Tom, said that he preferred to be called "Studpuppy." Dr. Stevens and the other students in the class realized that this name was probably not appropriate to their relationship with Tom. After one embarrassing day of being called "Studpuppy" by both the teacher and his fellow students, Tom also realized this, and requested that everyone call him "Tom."

Third, the level of language abstraction used by one partner to talk about a relationship is similar to some degree to that used by the other partner. As relationships grow, partners may find themselves using similar language to describe their feelings. For example, when John is upset, he frequently says, "I have a problem, here," and then describes the situation. A little while after John started dating Sue, she was using similar language.

As a relationship grows, partners may find themselves using similar language to describe their feelings.

The more the two descriptions reflect similar levels of abstraction, the more the partners can sensibly talk with one another about their relationship. For example, Sue might say to John, "Are you happy with the way things are going in this relationship?" He might respond, "We go to the symphony together, and we talk about interesting things." Then Sue might say, "Yes, but are you happy with the relationship?" They are not communicating at similar levels of abstraction. Perhaps John should think about the relationship more abstractly, while Sue should lower her level of abstraction somewhat. Then they could both discuss their satisfaction with the same aspects of the relationship.

Language provides a set of symbols that we use to transmit our thoughts to others. Experiences of people, events, and objects are reconstructed in a symbolic form that becomes talk about those experiences. The words we choose to represent the idea we intend to communicate vary in terms of abstraction level. The more abstract our language, the farther we are from direct experience, the more territory our language covers, and the fewer specific details are included in our messages. Now compound the problem—as it is compounded in every relationship. While the complex process of abstracting is going on inside us, it is also going on inside the person with whom we are talking. Thus when we interact, we are truly living in a world of words. Figure 10.3 makes this problem clear. We have turned the abstraction ladders of two people sideways to show their interaction. Notice how far the talk of each individual is from their mutual experience.

Figure 10.3 Levels of Abstraction in a Relationship

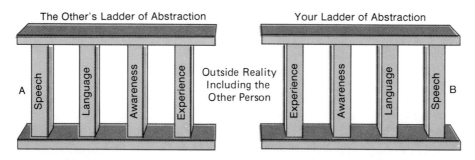

Summary

This unit focused on the interrelationships among events, thoughts, and language. The Triangle of Meaning shows that thoughts and language are tied to one another, but that words are not necessarily related to what they represent. Rather, words are abstractions that exist apart from experiences: they are created to assist in conveying those experiences to others. We describe our relationships using abstractions. The language we use indicates how we view the relationship and its intensity. It is important for partners in a relationship to view that relationship and talk about it at similar levels of abstraction. By doing this, they can work together to make the relationship grow.

Discussion Questions

1. Using the active listening skills you studied in unit 6, interview a friend or close acquaintance about something of personal importance to that individual. If possible, and if it is acceptable to the other person, tape the interview.

    a. What does the language used to talk about the situation tell you about this individual's self-concept?
    b. What does the language tell you about the way this person sees the situation?
    c. Do you find any patterns of language that suggest any consistent image of reality and frame of reference?

2. Secure permission from an elderly person to tape an interview in which the person recounts earlier experiences. Then report your answers to these questions to the class:

    a. Are there any language patterns that suggest an attitude or opinion about technology? progress? politics? religion?
    b. What is this person's image of you? What evidence in the language do you find for your conclusions?
    c. Can you identify variations in age, educational level, political affiliation, religious affiliation, or ethnic affiliation in the language people use? How so?

3. Bring an advertisement that includes words to class. How would you characterize the audience for whom it was designed, with regard to the following:

age	religious affiliation
sex	socioeconomic class
ethnic identification	geographical orientation
ecucational level	hobbies or interests
political affiliation	

    How did you decide?

Endnotes

1. H. R. Pollio, *The Psychology of Symbolic Activity* (Reading, MA: Addison-Wesley, 1974), p. 53.
2. C. K. Ogden and I. A. Richards, *The Meaning of Meaning,* 3d ed. rev. (New York: Harcourt Brace Jovanovich, 1959).
3. J. C. Condon, Jr., *Semantics and Communication* (New York: Macmillan, 1985).
4. S. I. Hayakawa, *Language in Thought and Action,* 3d ed. (New York: Harcourt Brace Jovanovich, 1972), 153.

>>I<< UNIT 11
Language and Relationships

Preview

Knowing how language affects relationships is important, because language provides a major tool for bringing about relational growth. We therefore must choose the language we use to talk about our relationships very carefully. Language has meaning in both common and personal terms. We use language to summarize our views of ourselves, other people, and even our relationships in ways that fit our frames of reference. We also hold opinions of the relative importance of people in our relationships that lead to different choices of language. This unit explores how language affects both the sending and receiving of messages and suggests means of improving the accuracy and meaningfulness of the communication in our relationships.

Objectives

1. Explain how relationships limit our choice of language.
2. Recall an example in which the nature of the relationship affected the language used in communicating an idea.
3. Define and give examples of denotative meaning.
4. Define and give examples of connotative meaning.
5. Explain how naming affects communication in relationships.
6. Explain how different views of a relationship affect the language used in it.

Key Terms
complementarity
connotative meanings
denotative meanings
language
naming
self-disclosure
symbols
symmetricality

The Language We Use

Our relationships are related to our *language* in three important ways: (1) The relationship limits our choice of symbols. (2) The nature of the relationship affects the meaning of certain symbols. (3) The language we chose reflects our view of the relationship.

Using Language in Relationships

Every time we communicate about a relationship we find ourselves faced with choices about what language to use. We select the language that seems appropriate to the particular relationship, which varies according to the roles we assign and take, our shared experiences, and the depth of intimacy.

The roles we and others take determine the language available for our use in a particular conversation. Consider the language we might use in describing a strong commitment in a romantic relationship. We might use the words "sharing," "love," "caring," and perhaps even "forever" when talking to another person. As we communicate our intentions to friends or parents, we may feel more comfortable with a different word, such as "serious," "comfortable," or even "compatible." We may be trying to convey similar feelings about our commitment in each case but we find that the role of lover demands a different menu of words than the role of friend or son or daughter.

What we and the other person have experienced in a relationship also affects our choice of symbols. For example, if you wanted to talk with a classmate about interpersonal communication, you would feel comfortable using terms learned in class. You might discuss "abstractions," "improving disclosure," or "the need to control." But in talking about interpersonal communication with someone who has not studied it—that is, a person who has not shared your experience—you would find your symbols more limited and more abstract.

Three aspects of our relationships influence the language we use in them: the roles we assign and take, the shared experiences, and the depth of intimacy.

The depth or intimacy of a relationship is a third aspect that affects the language availability for communication. In a more intimate relationship, we have more words for our ideas and are willing to share more fully. Suppose you have been trying to get to know your new boss for some time, but he has remained aloof, detached, and rather formal. Today you experienced a breakthrough and had a long discussion about the goals and expectations that you each hold of one another. You feel really good about this and cannot help smiling to yourself and others for the rest of the day. One of your co-workers notices your apparent satisfaction and inquires about your good mood. You might respond by saying, "I'm having a really good day . . . Things are really falling into place for me." When you return home at the end of the day and respond to a similar question from your spouse, you might say instead "George and I really got down to business today. We had a long talk, and I think we really understand one another better because of it!" In the first instance, the relatively low intensity of your relationship with your co-worker does not lead to an extended discussion of your happiness. The language available is thus smaller and more general. In the case of talking with your spouse, however, the greater intimacy of your relationship permits the use of language not only to describe the event but also to comment on its meaning and your feelings about it.

Denotative and Connotative Meanings in Relationships

Denotative meanings, or the common, dictionary meanings of words, are a part of all messages. These meanings usually do not include the context of the communication or information about the relationship between the communicators.

Sometimes we may want to stress the denotative meanings of words, as when we give instructions to a subordinate at work. We want to be as clear and specific as possible to assure that the task is properly done. Denotative meanings are also important when we are reporting an event because they allow the receiver of our message to judge its meaning or significance correctly without the cues that knowing us might provide about meaning. In both these

Table 11.1 Connotative Meanings

Speaker's Statement	Listener's Thoughts (Connotative Meaning)
Teacher: You know, a course in statistics might be really helpful for you, especially if you're planning to go on to graduate school.	*Student:* He wants to see me take a statistics course. He thinks everyone who goes to graduate school should have it.
Student: Well, I really hadn't thought about it, but now that you mention it, maybe I'll try it next term.	*Teacher:* He's interested. I should encourage him.
Teacher: I've been looking at your work, and it seems to me you'd do well at the graduate level. Do you have any interest in that?	*Student:* I'm surprised that a teacher would show this much interest in a student. It is flattering to hear this. I wonder if I really could handle graduate work.
Student: Do you really think so? I honestly don't know much about graduate school. How would I afford it?	*Teacher:* He is interested, but doesn't realize how talented he is.
Teacher: Why don't we go over to my office? I can show you some materials, and we can talk more about it.	*Student:* He wants to get to know me better. He wants to help me along. I like that.

instances, we want to be as clear as possible, so we use specific, unambiguous language. We describe the event at the lowest level of abstraction.

Another sort of meaning takes the listener beyond the denotational level. *Connotative meanings* are our personal meanings for words derived from our experience. They are influenced by the message, the person talking, the subject of the conversation, and even the environment in which it takes place.

Table 11.1 illustrates connotative meanings. The left column displays the conversation. The connotative meanings—what each individual might be thinking—are displayed in the right column. Of course, these are only some of the possible meanings that might have been assigned in this conversation. What judgments do you see implied here? What does each person seem to believe about the subject of the conversation? What are their views of each other? What difference could environment have made in their connotative meanings? For example, what if the conversation had taken place in the teacher's office? in a classroom after class? in the university center, in front of the student's friends?

People do not always say what they intend.

Because people do not always say what they intend in a way that we can understand, it is very important to be aware of the potential for misunderstanding connotative meaning. You can help yourself become better at listening for the intended meaning by practicing the listening skills presented in unit 6.

Our relationships play an important role in determining the connotations we find in conversations. Just as roles and the nature and intensity of the relationship influence our choice of language, these same factors affect our decisions about meaning.

Roles affect connotation quite directly. The same words might mean different things to various people, depending on their roles in a relationship, as the following example shows.

Margaret is a senior communication major taking her last few classes before graduation. The courses she needs are offered only at night, so she is out of the mainstream of activity that normally brings her together with other communication majors. One evening she is sitting in the lobby of a classroom building during a break, as are another student and her teacher, Dr. Grant. She sees Dr. Adams, one of her favorite professors from past terms, passing through the lobby. Margaret has often sought his advice and support. She exchanges greetings with him, and then Margaret says, "I have all my classes at night this term, and I never get a chance to see anyone anymore. It's like there's no one to talk with."

Now let's see how the roles of the people involved affect the connotative meaning in this situation. Margaret is in the role of student in a relationship with Dr. Grant, her new teacher. She also has a relationship with Dr. Adams, but

Roles influence the meanings we assign to the language we hear.

their roles might be better described as friends. Margaret also has a relationship with the other student, which is as a colleague or perhaps a co-worker. Now consider how the connotations might vary for each role. To Dr. Adams, Margaret might sound lonely, saying, "I miss you. Please spend some time with me." Dr. Grant might think she means, "I don't like night classes." The other student might hear her saying, "I don't feel I can talk with these people." On the other hand, Margaret's words might remind the student of a similar relationship. In this case, she might hear something like, "I like you, Dr. Adams," and then go on to think about how she likes working with her own advisor.

The response that Margaret gets from Dr. Adams will relate to the connotative meaning he associated with her message. Even though the message was intended for someone else, Dr. Grant's interpretation could influence his future interactions with Margaret. The same is true for the other student.

Roles influence the connotative, or personal, meanings we assign to language. We must consider roles and choose language that will address the range of connotations appropriate to the existing relationships.

Connotation also depends on the nature of the relationship. One way that our relationships grow is through our experiencing more and different kinds of situations. As we do this, we become accustomed to our partner's language and the intended connotations. You might have a friend, for example, who often compliments you, frequently using very affectionate language. The meaning you attribute to this person's language and intentions are connotative and depend somewhat on the breadth of your relationship. You might hear these remarks as romantic overtures if you have had only limited contact with the individual. On the other hand, with wider experience of this person, you might learn that such terms of endearment are only a way of expressing admiration and a desire for friendship. We must be careful about attributing connotative meanings based on limited experience.

Likewise, the depth of a relationship greatly affects connotative meaning. The better we get to know our partners, even in a single context, the better we can correctly understand their intentions. Sometimes people in relationships of great depth can talk with each other at a "relational level" about one issue while using language that is connotatively different in meaning to others who might be listening.

The case of Jim and his big celebration provides an example of this phenomenon. After a number of difficult years in his new advertising business, Jim had a very good year. He decided to give a huge champagne party for all his friends as a way of thanking them for their support through the hard times. One disaster after another occurred as the day of the party approached. Changes in the location, several caterers, and many other problems plagued the planning. Jim confided in his close friend Martha throughout, and she supported and encouraged him as he organized the event. When the day came and the party was in full swing, Martha arrived. She looked Jim over carefully and said, "Why Jim, you look wonderful . . . very relaxed. How are you?" Jim smiled, saying, "I'm fine, and thank you, Martha. Everything seems to be under control. I'm glad you could come." Martha responded, "I just knew this would turn out to be a lovely party. Do you think you can hold things together here? I want to mingle for a bit." Other party goers might hear connotations of affection in this exchange, but for Jim and Martha, this conversation was about the trials and tribulations leading up to this event. The connotative affection is there, and beyond that are expressions of caring, gratitude, and even teasing that only Jim and Martha can understand.

It is important to pay attention to the connotations that are unique to relationships, for otherwise much of the meaning in your interactions might be lost. The more involvement you have with another person, the more likely you are to share such relational connotations.

Language and Our View of Relationships

The third way language contributes to the growth of our relationships deals with our view of those relationships. This view includes our sense of self in the relationship, the way we see the other person, and our role expectations.

In examining our sense of self in relationships, we are talking about *self-disclosure*. In thinking about how we see others, we must consider *naming*. In studying role expectations in relationships, the concepts of *complementarity* and *symmetricality* must be discussed.

Language Expresses and Reveals the Self

Self-disclosure is the use of language to reveal information about ourselves to others. Our language reveals how we see ourselves and how we would like others to see us. Certain language clues are used intentionally. For instance, a child who is lonely may scream as though hurt to get our attention. Consider the following examples of the intentional self-expression:

"I can't do math."
"I like going out on the town."
"If I were you, I'd lay it on the line."

These are all direct statements about a person's view of herself. They may have been made to the self or to someone else. What images of this person do you get from these statements?

We use such statements to define what we are and are not willing to do. Sometimes we allow them to become rules that we feel obliged to defend.

However, we limit the possible range of our experiences and relationships when we do this. But even when this does happen, such statements still represent intentional messages about how we see ourselves and would like to be seen.

Some language reveals information about our self-concepts in more subtle ways. Listeners may draw conclusions about the way we see ourselves by noticing the frequency with which we talk about certain things or use certain metaphors in describing our experiences. Both these ways of communicating the self-concept are often conducted unintentionally.

We discuss certain ideas or subjects more frequently than others because they hold some special importance to us. Joseph, for example, tends to respond in conversations using monetary terms. On seeing a new car, he might try to guess its value. Once, after spending a good deal of time waiting to see a customer service representative at a local utility company, he conveyed his irritation by sending the company a bill for his time. If others want to be sure Joseph hears them, all they have to do is listen for a money-oriented response or phrase their message in financial language. Having an idea about what the person believes is important thus helps us select language that conveys our intended meaning.

Anthony Athos and John Gabarro suggest that the language we use in conversation reveals something about all aspects of our self-concept.[1] They encourage the use of active listening techniques as a way of seeking out information about the self-concepts of our partners in relationships. As we listen more to people talking about themselves—either implicitly or explicitly—we find it easier to bring growth to our relationships.

> ***Our language tells others about our self-concepts, attitudes, beliefs and values, and our feelings about our relationships.***

Listening carefully to the language we use to describe our experiences may reveal some consistency among the metaphors chosen and thus suggest what we consider important. If, for example, you place a high value on promptness, you may unconsciously include references to time in your conversations. As we saw when we examined the Johari Window in unit 9, we frequently use figurative language that is based in things that are important to us but that may be unknown to the people with whom we're talking.

The language we use in everyday conversation also reveals much about us. In fact, we sometimes intentionally choose language to create certain impressions about ourselves. For example, at job interviews we carefully select language that will clearly convey the contributions we believe we can make to a company.

Our goals, priorities, and assumptions can also be revealed by the style of our nonverbal communication, such as the loudness or softness that we give certain words, the rate at which we speak, and our facial and body expressions. For example, Bill graduated magna cum laude from a distinguished university, and he is very proud of this fact. When talking with his co-workers or friends and the subject of education or credentials comes up, he unknowingly communicates his pride by sitting more straightly and assuming a more authoritative tone. He does this even if his particular credentials are unknown and unmentioned in the group. People talking with Bill in this situation, though, leave believing he must know something about the subject.

Naming in Relationships

We communicate our view of the partners in our relationships through a process called *naming,* or the assignment of labels to these people. When we characterize a person as a friend, for example, we are naming. Examine the names you use when referring to people in your relationships and when talking directly to them. Thinking about how they are similar and different can help you understand how you see the other person and what you still need to know about him.

The names we use at a given moment convey our perception of the other person and also affect that perception. L. Carmichael, H. P. Hogan, and A. A.

Figure 11.1 Naming and Perception

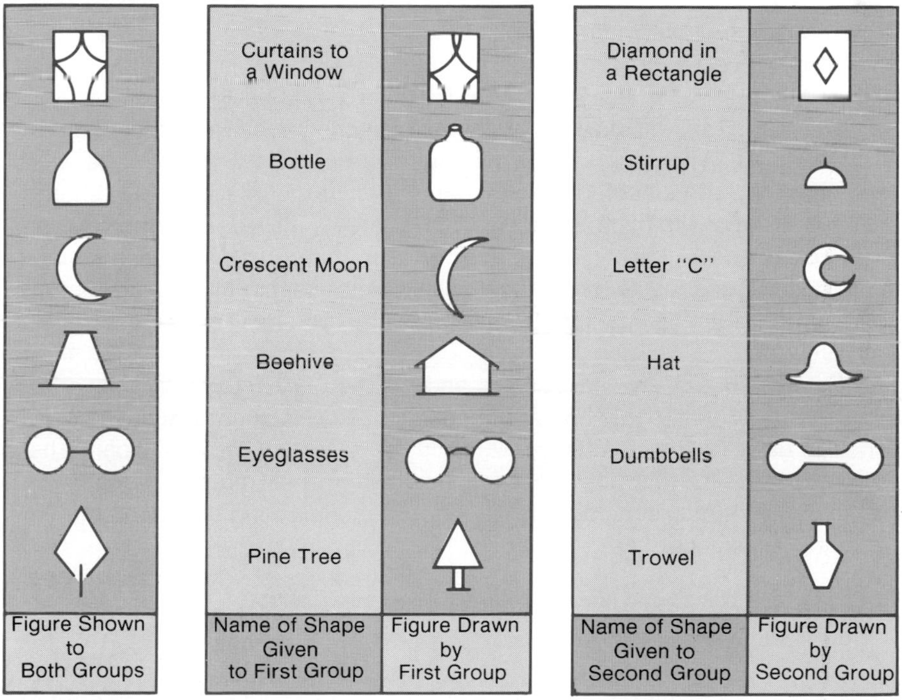

Figure Shown to Both Groups	Name of Shape Given to First Group	Figure Drawn by First Group	Name of Shape Given to Second Group	Figure Drawn by Second Group
	Curtains to a Window		Diamond in a Rectangle	
	Bottle		Stirrup	
	Crescent Moon		Letter "C"	
	Beehive		Hat	
	Eyeglasses		Dumbbells	
	Pine Tree		Trowel	

Walter conducted an experiment about the effect of naming on perception.[2] Two groups of people were shown the same set of drawings and were then asked to reproduce them. As the results depicted in figure 11.1 show, each group "improved" the drawings to make them more closely resemble their assigned names. In our relationships, we may "improve" our perception of our partner to more nearly match the name we have given that person.

John C. Condon observed that people tend to notice those things for which they have names.[3] They also tend not to see those things for which they have no names. Our relationships exemplify this principle. The names we have for people are part of our frame of reference, the filter through which we perceive others. We are naming when we assign language to describe our beliefs, values, and attitudes. We tend to notice, recognize, and acknowledge those people whose names we know more than those whose names we do not know. Likewise, we tend to notice those behaviors and characteristics that fit the names we have for people, while sometimes ignoring those actions that are inconsistent with those names. (For more on this process, see unit 4.)

Symmetry and Complementarity in Relationships

Our expectation of the roles in a relationship is also important to our selection of language. Dennis R. Smith and Keith Williamson explained that each of us has a view of every relationship that suggests the perceived status of the other person.[4] The view is *symmetrical* when we see ourselves as equal partners and is *complementary* when we see ourselves as in some way unequal to the other person (see figure 11.2). The complementary view is sometimes characterized as feeling "one up" or "one down" in a relationship.

Our language reflects our view of the relationship, either complementary or symmetrical. When our view is symmetrical, our language might be more "we" oriented, with clear indications that control of the relationship is shared. Our relationships with friends and classmates are typically symmetrical. Classmates usually have the same responsibilities in the course and thus share a common and equal basis for the relationship. A friendship might also be symmetrical when there is an expectation that each partner will contribute equally to its growth.

Relationships between parents and children are frequently viewed as complementary, as are teacher-student relationships. In such relationships, the language used in conversations will indicate that one of the participants has more responsibility than the other for determining their direction, goals, and growth. For instance, consider the language in the following dialogue that took place after class one day:

Dr. Penny: Jim, please stay for a minute. I'd like to talk with you.

Jim: Yes, Dr. Penny?

Figure 11.2 Symmetrical and Complementary Relationships

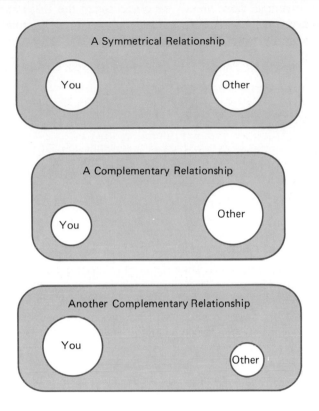

Dr. Penny: Jim, you're doing very well in this class. Are you doing equally well in your other classes?

Jim: Well, this is my best class, but I'm keeping up in the others also.

Dr. Penny: You may have heard that we're starting an honors program and a group of interested students are getting together in the seminar room to discuss it with me and the other participating faculty. You're welcome to join us.

In this conversation, Dr. Penny controls the goals and direction of the conversation and the relationship. He called Jim by his first name, but Jim referred to him more formally as Dr. Penny. When Dr. Penny asked about his other classes, Jim responded immediately with this private information. If the relationship were perceived by both as symmetrical, Jim might have said, "Why do you ask?" Dr. Penny asked Jim for what is, in effect, a closer relationship by inviting him to the honors meeting. The invitation carries with it more contact and an introduction to Dr. Penny's colleagues.

Problems can arise when our language reflects different views of a relationship.[5] For example, how would you characterize the following communication between two classmates, one of whom views the relationship as symmetrical while the other views it as complementary:

Beth: Hey, Joe, are you free tonight? I thought we might work on that proposal together.

Joe: Let me see . . . No, can't do it tonight, but I can give you Friday. Tell you what, you go ahead and get it roughed out, and then when we meet Friday we'll have something to work from.

Beth: I really think we should work on the basics together, Joe. We're going to have to share the outcome. We should each get in our ideas at the beginning.

Joe: Okay, fine, Beth, but you're going to have to type it up . . . I don't have the time for that kind of work.

In this conversation, Beth is struggling to maintain the equality that she perceives in the relationship. Joe, on the other hand, sees himself as "one up." He expects Beth to adjust to his schedule and to do what he considers the less important parts of the task. Their different perspectives of the relationship could bring them into conflict. Before they will get much work done, they are going to have to make some agreement about the nature of their relationship.

How do you think communication between a husband and wife might sound if both viewed the relationship as complementary but each saw the other person as "one down"?

In both these instances, as well as in other combinations of the two views, a third party listening to the conversation might get the impression that the two people talking do not know one another very well or that they do not like one another very much. To avoid this, we need to listen for language that tells us about the other's view of our relationship. We have a responsibility to talk with our partner if what we hear evokes images that are different from our own. We need to clarify our own view, to work for an understanding of the view of the other person, and to arrive at language that expresses some agreement about who we each are in the relationship.

Summary

Language is an important tool for achieving relational growth. Relationship roles, type, and depth limit our choice of language and contribute to the degree that our meanings are either connotative or denotative. Language reflects the way we see ourselves and our relationships. We express our intentions in a relationship by names we give it. We may view a relationship as symmetrical or complementary, and our language will reflect that view. Language can also reveal whether both people in the relationship share the same view and, if not, language can be used to correct the problem and help the relationship grow.

Discussion Questions

1. If connotative meaning is personal, how do we discover the connotative meanings others are using? What difficulties do we encounter in trying to learn them?
2. Are certain views more appropriate for particular relationships? If so, give examples.
3. Although naming places limits on our communication, it also serves important functions in helping relationships grow. At what point does naming cease to be helpful in the development of a relationship?

Endnotes

1. A. G. Athos and J. J. Gabarro, *Interpersonal Behavior* (Englewood Cliffs, NJ: Prentice-Hall, 1978), 398.
2. L. Carmichael, H. P. Hogan and A. A. Walter, "An Experimental Study of the Effect of Language on the Reproduction of Visually Perceived Form," *Journal of Experimental Psychology* 15 (1932): 73–86.
3. J. C. Condon, Jr., *Semantics and Communication* (New York: Macmillan, 1986).
4. D. R. Smith and L. K. Williamson, *Interpersonal Communication* (Dubuque, IA: Wm. C. Brown Publishers, 1985).
5. C. R. Berger and J. J. Bradac, *Language and Social Knowledge* (London: Edward Arnold, 1982)

>>I<< UNIT 12
Talking About Feelings, Wants, and Expectations

Preview

In our society we are taught, sometimes directly and sometimes subtly, that it is not acceptable to talk about feelings, wants, or expectations. These cultural and social norms work against better interpersonal communication. When our relationships are at risk there is a good chance that the problem revolves around such issues. The skills involved in talking about them include learning to separate feelings from emotions, learning more feeling words, learning to state what we want in terms of observable behavior, and learning to negotiate interpersonal contracts.

Objectives

1. Explain the differences between feelings and emotions and provide examples of each.
2. Describe and explain a three-step system for talking about feelings.
3. List the five most common categories of feelings and three levels of intensity into which these categories occur. Then give examples of words that occur in each category.
4. List and explain the steps for expressing wants and expectations clearly.
5. Explain how to help another person express feelings and wants clearly.

Key Terms
cognitive control
cognitive information
context
emotions
feelings
habits

We are in debt for many of the ideas in this unit to Charles O. Tucker and Herbert J. Hess, both of Northern Illinois University, De Kalb. It is difficult to know how much of the material in this unit came from them directly, and how much was assimilated during many hours of conversations on a hundred fishing and canoeing trips over many years. See their excellent and highly readable book, *Talking About Relationships*, 2d ed. (Prospect Heights, IL: Waveland Press, 1980).

In his wonderfully readable and helpful little book, *The Secret of Staying in Love,* John Powell makes a distinction between dialogue and discussion. Dialogue is communicating or sharing emotions or feelings; discussion is sharing thoughts, values, and decision making. Powell's argument is a pointed one:

> There must be an emotional clearance (dialogue) between two involved partners . . . before they can safely enter into a deliberation (discussion) about plans, choices, values. The assumption behind this distinction and the priority given to dialogue is that the breakdown in human love and communication is *always* due to *emotional* problems.[1]

Feelings, Wants, and Expectations Must Be Shared

We agree with Powell: A clear sharing of feelings and emotions must exist before meaningful discussion about plans, choices, and values can take place. You might assume, then, that our society would teach its children how to self-disclose. Unhappily, however, this is not easily done, for several reasons.

First, what we say cannot fully express what we experience. No matter how accurately we learn to report our experiences, our words can never *be* the experiences.[2] The words are important tools, of course, in communicating about an experience, but they are only a partial expression of it. What we experience is not at the verbal level but at an "unspeakable level."[3] The unspeakable level is the first of three orders of human experience; the second level is thought, and the third is language. (This idea was introduced in unit 10 as the Triangle of Meaning.)

Although we just cannot express much of what we know, we still must try. If we are going to enjoy and nurture ongoing relationships to which we are emotionally or physically committed, we must share our inner feelings, wants, intentions, and images so that others can know us and know themselves in us. In less committed relationships, we must also disclose ourselves and our feelings.

If talking about feelings, wants, and expectations is so important, why is it so difficult to do? First, although sharing our feelings and wants with others affects our relationships with those others, our society discourages clear talk about such personal issues in at least three ways.

1. *Our society teaches us that some emotions are bad and others are good.* To illustrate, most of us are taught from very early in life that it is good to feel grateful. "What do you say?" asks the grandmother when she hands her small grandchild a piece of candy. The answer, of course, is "Thank you." On the other hand, it is bad to feel angry. "Stop that this minute!" says a mother as she breaks up an angry squabble between her two young sons.

If you listen carefully on the rare occasions when people try to talk about their negative feelings, you will hear at least four ways that they punish each other for expressing such feelings:

Our society teaches us to suppress undesirable emotions.

The judge: You have no right to feel that way. She didn't mean any harm.

The optimist: Don't worry, everything will be all right.

The analyst: I know why you're feeling that way. You just want. . . .

The rip-off artist: I know exactly how you're feeling. Just the other day this happened to me.

In each of these cases the speaker may very well be trying to help. But what the person is communicating instead is, "I do not want you to talk about your negative feelings."

2. *Our society teaches us to suppress undesirable emotions.* In almost all families, children learn to feel comfortable with the expression and display of certain emotions and uncomfortable with others. For instance, a child who grows up in a large, loud, rough-and-tumble household may learn to be comfortable with expressions and shows of anger and uncomfortable with expressions of tenderness. In contrast, some children learn from their parents that displays of anger are simply not acceptable but that displays of affection and warmth are desirable.

3. *Our society teaches that some emotions conflict with basic values.* For example, young males are often taught that they should not cry because crying is not manly. If an emotional state conflicts with some deeply held value, that conflict will surely cause people to try to suppress the emotion.

The key words used to teach which emotions conflict with basic values and which do not are "ought," "should," and "right." For example, you might hear a parent saying to a child, "Don't cry. You should behave like a man." These terms harken to rules for behavior that exist only in the minds of the speakers. If you listen to yourself talk, you may be surprised to hear yourself using these words. Each time you do, you are referencing a rule for behavior. The rule is always inside you. Where do you think it came from?

A second problem involved in learning to talk about our feelings, wants, and expectations is that we tend to take our language for granted. We hardly notice the words we use—especially when we use them daily. Instead, we assume that the words we choose are an accurate reflection of our experience of ourselves and the world as well as the experience of others. We are not analytical about our word choice, preferring to use them automatically and without giving much thought to how they can limit and hurt ourselves and our relationships.

Thus, much of what we are taught by our society is contrary to relational effectiveness. We believe, however, that self disclosure is essential to effectiveness and interpersonal growth.

Units 8 and 9 examined our very powerful need for self-esteem—to love ourselves, to accept ourselves as we are, and to celebrate our existence. We cannot do this unless we receive many messages from others that we are lovable just as we are and that we are a joy to others. That is why those very early years full of affection, hugs, lullabies, and murmured approvals are so important. They answer the baby's questions, "Am I okay? Am I lovable?"

Throughout life we want to know, "Am I okay? Am I lovable?"

Later in life, the significant others on whom we depend for evidence of such positive regard begin to lay down conditions. We still want to know, "Am I okay? Am I lovable?" But now we hear answers like, "Yes, if you get good grades," and "Yes, if you follow the rules of appropriate behavior." Notice that getting "good" grades or following rules of "appropriate" behavior are difficult concepts. They actually translate to mean, "You are okay if you conform to the rules I have in my head about your behavior."

Then, if we are not confirmed by our significant others, we begin to adopt strategies that seem downright harmful to ourselves. For example, some people resort to becoming perfectionists. They hold themselves to meticulous standards of performance as the price of approval. Others wall themselves in with silence, which these shy people have come to believe is their only protection from disapproval. Still others develop anger. Not liking themselves and finding it easier to be angry than feel worthless or inadequate, they ventilate their pain with a show of temper.

However difficult it may be, learning to build a strong ego is clearly preferable to these damaging consequences that come from low self-esteem. Remember that self-disclosure is the most important part of that building process. In turn, learning to self-disclose means learning, first of all, to talk about our feelings, wants, and expectations.

Learning to Separate Feelings from Emotions

A definite distinction exists between feelings and emotions. *Feelings* are physical events of the human body experienced in the present tense. They are the body's response to physical stimulation. *Emotions* exist in the language you use to talk to yourself and to others about the feelings you are experiencing.

Feelings are physical. Emotions exist in language.

Of course, there are words that we use to talk about feelings separate from emotions, but not as many as you might imagine. Rather, when we try to talk about our feelings we tend to focus on the location of a feeling and then to label it using some combination of words that, *in that context,* suggest an emotional state. Or else we talk about the feeling in metaphorical terms: "It feels like. . . ."

What you feel is a physical experience. You feel the condition of parts of your body at some moment in time and space. The feelings exist as tiny firings in nerve endings in the tissues of your body. You feel tense muscles; you feel aching joints; you feel the lining of your stomach signaling you that you are hungry; you feel the sharp pain "behind the eyes" that sometimes occurs when you have eaten too much ice cream too fast. Feeling is a physical experience.

What you tell yourself about your feelings constitutes your emotions. While your feelings are physical, your emotions exist only in the world of words. To illustrate this difference, induce pain in your hand by slapping it against a table. Now try to describe the ongoing experience of the pain. Your description does not square with your experience.

Although your experience of pain is dynamic—constantly changing and continually in the present tense, a global experience of your entire hand—your language fails you. Language must flow in a single line. It must focus on one aspect of the dynamic experience at a time. Much of the experience is deleted. Much more is distorted. The rest is generalized. And, by the time you have described your experience, the description is already obsolete.

A second discovery is that while the experience is always in the present tense, the language you use to describe the feeling tends to be in the past tense. Students asked to do this exercise focus upon, say, the first joint of the right thumb. "It hurts," they say. "The experience is like a burning sensation.

Not liking themselves and finding it easier to be angry than to feel worthless or inadequate, some people ventilate their pain with a show of temper.

It was very hot, but now it's cooling off some. It was like someone was tapping a hot wire there at the joint."

Speakers use the past tense to "catch up" with experience in language. Notice that the students focused only upon the heat sensation of the first joint of the thumb. What of the rest of the experience? What was the rest of the hand expressing?

"It hurts" applies not only to the feeling, the experience of physical pain, but also to the emotions that surround your physical experience. For example, you might suddenly experience a loud noise while walking across the campus after dark. A barking dog jumps out from an azalea bush. You will have a physical experience—a sudden, electrochemical, very real, physical experience. The blood will rush away from your skin. Your endocrine system will instantly infuse your blood with certain chemicals. Your heartbeat will increase. Your muscles, now strengthened by the dramatically heightened adrenaline levels in your bloodstream, will tense. Your stomach will feel like it is knotting up. And, finally, the hair on the back of your neck will "stand up" and, chances are, you will begin to tremb   Under these circumstances—in that particular moment on the campus when confronted by a barking dog—you are experiencing a set of physical feelings. Notice that the *context* in which the event occurs contributes significantly to your experience. It's dark. You are walking across the campus. All the information in that event becomes part of the context. So does all the information that you carry with you into the event. You are sure you should not be walking alone. You are sure that it is late. You have read of people being attacked, and the thought frightens you.

With all of this context coming to bear on you at that moment, you experience your body responding to the sudden, loud appearance of the dog. Your feelings, again, are the physical events of your body that you experience in the present tense. They are your body's responses to physical stimulation.

What will you call them? Will you call them fear? Will you call them something more self-confirming? Will you call them startled? Would it be correct to say that you were surprised? And would it be correct to say that you experienced anger? at what? at the dog? at your own inability to control the fight-or-flight reaction? Will you call that experience cowardice? Will you call it embarrassment? What appropriately describes that physical condition in that moment in time and space? What you choose to call it is most important indeed, since so much depends on it! Your self-concept is at issue in your choice of words.

Your emotions exist not in physical feelings but in the words you select to label those feelings *in a particular context*. You *feel* your body, but you experience your emotions in quite a different way, with language.

Because you experience emotions with language, what you experience as emotions contains cognitive information. You take meanings directly from what you say to yourself about your feelings, based upon the context in which you experience them. Even the words you choose to talk about your feelings provide part of that context. The information you derive from that language controls your arousal. Although you may not realize it, and although you may not want to admit it, your emotions are under *cognitive control*.

We will soon argue that, if you will take the trouble to learn a broader vocabulary to talk about your feelings, you will experience a richer emotional range. But we're not quite ready for that idea.

When you think about the dog suddenly jumping out from behind a bush at you, you might suppose that the dog made you afraid. We tend to think of our emotional states as caused by events outside our bodies. We also tend to think that our emotional states themselves lead to behavior. So you may find nothing wrong with the following logic:

1. A dog barks while jumping out from behind a bush. This makes you afraid, so you jump back to get out of the way.
2. Someone you love dies. This makes you sad, so you grieve.
3. The car breaks down. This frustrates you, so you take out your frustrations on the car.

The context in which an event occurs contributes significantly to your experience.

In truth, we do not respond directly to an actual event. Rather, we take information from the event, give it meaning, and then respond to the cognitive structure of the event that we ourselves have created. Put another way, the event triggers a scanning of our experiences. We draw an inference about what is going on. We convert the inference into physical feelings. That is, we *interpret* the event, and then choose certain feelings and not others.

Because all this happens so fast that we are unaware of anything more than our experience of emotions, we act on the emotional state, assuming that it was caused directly by the event rather than the result of our own cognitive processes. Look again at the three examples of how emotions occur:

1. A dog barks while jumping out from a bush. You perceive the situation as threatening, immediate, and urgent. You also perceive it as dangerous. *You choose to jump away in fear.*
2. Someone you love dies. You perceive your loss. You understand that you will miss that person greatly. You realize that there were many things you did not say to the person, and regret that you did not work through some of the problems in your relationship. Facing all that, *you choose the emotional response of sharp distress or sorrow.*
3. The car breaks down. You see that you are going to be late. You begin to recall choices you made earlier to put off having the car repaired,

perhaps because you were too busy. You anticipate that dire consequences will result, both from being late and from having to expose your earlier, faulty choices. *You choose to respond emotionally.*

In each example, the response is not to the event per se but to your particular view of the event. You respond to the information you have drawn from the moment and the connections you have made between that information and your own prior experiences. These connections always exist as words. How you talk to yourself about the event shapes your responses. Could you have chosen other responses if you had chosen to talk about the event differently?

This fact—that people are responsible for choosing their emotional responses—is an important idea. You learn habitual responses to situations that seem to fall into similar categories. You seem to program yourself to respond to certain events in certain ways. Once the program is stabilized, you come to believe (at least, many people do) that you have little choice but to follow through with the programmed behaviors.

But it is possible to rewrite the program. It is possible to make alternative choices of behavior. The key lies deeply embedded in the language you use.

Emotions Are Under Cognitive Control

We have said that your emotions exist in the words you choose to talk about your body's physical feelings as you experience them in some particular context. We have also said that you choose those words out of habit and from a limited vocabulary. Our argument has been that your emotional range is restricted by these *habits* and limitations.

We often confuse our feelings with our thinking.

One way we limit ourselves is by too often confusing our feelings with our thinking. For instance, you might hear someone say, "I feel you spend too much time with the children." The sentence would be far more accurate, we believe, if it started with "I think" rather than "I feel": "I think you spend too much time with the children" makes it clear that the decision-making activity—the conclusion—is in the speaker's mind and that it is not a feeling. How does such a thing actually feel?

Here are a number of examples of how thinking is confused with feeling. We present them because we want you to see how often—and how subtly—we make this fundamental mistake.

1. *"I feel unloved."* How does "unloved" feel? sad? lonely? depressed? Who is involved when someone says they feel "unloved"? The speaker, of course—but might there also be another individual involved? We think so. In fact, we think that this speaker is wrongly taking personal responsibility for

someone else's nervous system by accepting "unloved" as his own doing rather than the other person's doing.

2. *"I feel put down."* "Put down" is an assumption (thought) about another person's *intention.* Notice too that intent is part of the agenda for talking about relationships.

3. *"I feel you have pulled away from me."* Here the speaker is making an inference based on some observed behavior. A more accurate statement might be, "I have observed that you have physically pulled away from me. Indeed, you haven't called in several days, and when we have been in the same places together you have stayed away from me. I am saddened, and I miss you very much."

4. *"I feel like a tramp when you look at me that way."* How does a tramp feel? The metaphor, in this case, is entirely a cognitive structure. It is an inference about the other person's *image,* triggered by someone looking "that way." You might ask what the speaker has observed. What does looking "that way" actually look like? In any case, you could change the sentence to make it more accurate by saying, "I see your look. What does it mean? Do you think I am a tramp?"

5. *"I feel used."* This statement is clearly a guess about another's intention or motive. It is not a statement of one's own feeling. Just how does "used" feel?

6. *"I feel tremendously involved."* This statement is also a substitution of thinking for feeling. Does the speaker feel excited? happy? What does "tremendous" feel like? What does "involved" feel like?

7. *"I feel as though you're lying to me."* This is obviously a guess about someone's intention, based on an observation. Perhaps the other person's statement seems inconsistent with known fact, or perhaps there is a question of trust inside the speaker. In any case, how does "you're lying to me" feel?

8. *"I feel real bad about that."* Here is a judgment about a feeling state that pushes the feeling into the speaker's head. What feelings are "real bad"? pain? sorrow?

> *You can learn new habits. You can learn to say "I think" when you mean "I think."*

9. *"I feel wonderful."* Wonder is also cognitive activity. How does "wonder" feel? These examples show that people habitually confuse feelings with thinking. But this is not necessary, for *you can learn new habits.* You can learn to interrupt the habitual choice of language. One way to do this is to replace "I feel" with "I think." *You can also learn new words* to express and experience a far richer emotional range. Obviously, learning these techniques will enhance your ability to manage your relationships.

Learning to Talk About Feelings

A simple, three-step sequence can help you learn to talk about feelings: (1) locate and name the feeling in your body, (2) describe the feeling state, and (3) name the emotional state.

1. *Locate and name the feeling in your body.* Remember that you feel your body and that your emotions exist in the words you use to talk about that physical feeling. To talk about the feeling more effectively, then, you need to identify where you are experiencing the feeling. Do a quick inventory of your major muscle groups. It may be convenient to work from your head downward.

Is the feeling in the muscles of your face? your forehead? your eyes? your mouth? Are your jaws clenched? Are the muscles of your throat or the back of your neck tense and hurting? Is the feeling in your shoulders? between your shoulder blades? in your lower back? in your abdominal cavity? Are the muscles in your chest constricted? Are you feeling the muscles in your pelvic girdle? Are your upper legs tight and hurting? Are you carrying something unpleasant in your knee joints? in your calves? in your ankles? Do your feet hurt? Name the feeling you are experiencing. You can use the feeling words found in table 12.2 to help you in this process.

2. *Describe the feeling with a metaphor.* Once you have located the feeling, try to describe it. How does it feel? What is it like? For example, if the feeling is painful, what does the pain feel like? fire? burning? Is it sharp? throbbing? Does it sting? feel like needles? cut like a knife? Is it a dull, heavy experience? Does it feel like something you may have felt before? like the result of a sudden blow? like someone punched you?

You might find it helpful to think in terms of *value, potency,* and *action* as you try to describe your feeling states. *Value* descriptions might include words along these continua:

good				bad
right				wrong
O.K.				not O.K.
ugly				beautiful

Potency descriptions might include words along these continua:

rough				smooth
hot				cold
bright				dull
hard				soft
sharp				blunt
high				low
strong				weak

Action descriptions might include words along these continua:

fast				slow
moving				still
running				standing
pushing				pulling
lifting				pressing

Another good way to describe your feelings is to try to give them a color. Is the feeling state blue? Is it yellow? Is it red? The color metaphors can be very potent in helping you understand and describe feeling states that may otherwise be difficult. The colors often bring to mind a metaphor that someone else can relate to. For example, one student, using our suggestions to describe a feeling in her arm, said:

> The feeling is . . . red and yellow, like . . . uh . . . like, something like an early summer day at the beach, when the sun is shining on you too hot. It is a deep, too hot feeling that seems to be standing still just about a quarter of an inch under my skin, and . . . uh . . . it's from just below my elbow all the way down the outside of my hand and into my little finger. But it's not sharp or jabbing.

Note that she started with a color combination, which brought to mind a metaphor that allowed her to describe the feeling. Then she gave it action and location, and finished with a statement of its potency and action. We think she did a good job of describing her feeling.

3. *Name the emotion you attach to the feeling.* After you have located and described the feeling, try to name the emotion that you associate with it.

To illustrate how you might use this three-step sequence, consider this student's effort to do it:

1. Locate: "I'm feeling something in the small of my back and between my shoulder blades. It's like. . . .
2. Describe: like someone was squeezing me in a vice. I mean, you know, like a heavy, tight, knotted-up feeling, as if some great pair of hands were holding on to my back and making a fist tighter and tighter.
3. Name: It's depressing, you know? Unhappy, and hurt, and very tiring."

You may find this three-step sequence more difficult than it appears. You will probably have to practice. We are not accustomed to locating our feelings, we are not very good at developing metaphors to describe those states, and we do not have much language to talk about our emotional experiences. If we did, we would experience a far richer emotional range.

Learning More Emotion and Feeling Words

One way to learn more emotion and feeling words is to work with your own experience to generate a greater vocabulary. You can do this by working through this simple experience. Begin by listing a set of emotion words. Recall that we have said that emotion words are the language you use to talk about feelings in a particular situation. If you were listing a set of emotion statements you might say, "I'm happy," "I'm sad," "I'm angry," "I'm afraid," and "I'm confused." The five words in each of these statements are emotional states. None of them suggest the feelings—the physical sensations that the body is experiencing—that are associated with the emotions.

   You can now generate a list of feeling words by considering what feelings go along with this set of emotional states. For example, think of a situation in which you might be happy. Then, make a statement like the following: "When I receive an 'A' in a class, I'm happy. When I'm happy I feel _____ , _____ , and _____ ." If you fill in the blanks with words that describe what your body is feeling, you will have feeling words. You might have included the words "bubbly," "buoyant," and "effervescent." Or perhaps you chose "electrified," "glowing," and "stimulated." You can list emotion words and use them to generate feeling words through this process.

   We asked our students to help us generate lists of emotions and feelings. They took the emotion words listed in table 12.1 and generated the one hundred feeling words listed in table 12.2. You might want to add to these lists. We think these lists can help you expand your vocabulary of emotion and feeling words. If your instructor asks you to practice writing or speaking about your emotions and feelings, use these lists as a reference to help you in the task.

Learning to State What You Want

In a relationship, sometimes we have a fairly clear idea of our feelings and those of the other person, but we may be uncertain about what either we or our partner wants. When this uncertainty takes form in talk, a message something like the following often results:

He: What do you want from me?

She: I just want you to love me more.

He: I *do* love you.

She: But I want you to love me *more.*

You can see that she is not giving him much help. How will she judge that he loves her more? Her only way is to observe his behavior and then interpret it to mean that he loves her more.

Table 12.1 Fifty Emotion Words That Name Emotional States

afraid	downcast	hostile	miserable	skeptical
angry	downhearted	impatient	overwhelmed	sleepy
anxious	embarrassed	indifferent	perplexed	sorrowful
apprehensive	embittered	infuriated	pessimistic	surprised
dejected	exasperated	irate	provoked	suspicious
despondent	fearful	jealous	puzzled	terrified
disgusted	frightened	lonely	repelled	troubled
dismayed	frustrated	mad	resentful	unhappy
dissatisfied	furious	mean	scared	withdrawn
distressed	horrified	melancholy	shocked	worried

Table 12.2 One Hundred Feeling Words

achey	edgy	jubulent	soft
agitated	effervescent	jumpy	sour
alert	elated	keyed up	spiritless
alive	electrified	lethargic	steaming
bitter	empty	light	stiff
boiling	energetic	limp	stiffled
breathless	expansive	listless	stimulated
bubbly	fast	loose	straight
buoyant	filled	low	stunned
calm	flat	numb	sweaty
churning	flushed	open	tense
closed	fluttering	out of control	tied-up
charged-up	free	paralyzed	tight
cold	fresh	placid	tingly
connected	frosty	pressed	together
constrained	full	puffed up	tranquil
consumed	glittering	racing	trembling
dazed	glowing	relaxed	twisted
detached	hard	restless	unnerved
disjointed	heavy	restrained	upside-down
dizzy	hollow	rigid	unsteady
down	hot	rushed	vibrant
drained	hurting	shaky	void
dry	icy	sharp	warm
dull	jittery	slow	wired

Consider a different situation, this time at work. Again, the vagueness comes from being unclear about what is wanted:

He: What do you want from me?

She: I want you to work better. I want you to increase your level of performance. I want you to be more professional.

He: But. . . .

Again, he isn't getting much help from his boss because she has expressed her wants and expectations in very vague and abstract terms. What does "increase your level of performance" mean? What does "be more professional" mean? And what constitutes "better work?"

In each case, the speaker can communicate more effectively by *expressing a want in terms of observable behaviors or measurable results that can be achieved within a specified time.* Here is how one student used this two-step sequence in an exercise in which he was pretending to be a professor:

She: What do you want from me?

He: I want you *to write* a term paper on the dragon ships of the Vikings, and submit it in draft form on the day of the midterm exam. I want it in final form on May 15, not later than 4:00 in the afternoon."

However, if many of our students had heard a professor make this request, they would still be frustrated. Surely they would want to know what standards they had to meet. Let's go further in the conversation—you might recognize yourself in it!

She: Do you want it typed? How many pages must it be?

He: Yes. Type it on high-rag content bond paper, not erasable bond. It probably should be about 15 pages long.

Distinguishing between the observable and the measurable appears to be the most difficult part of asking for what you want. In short, observable behaviors can be seen or heard, whereas measurable results can be counted. Table 12.3 offers help in this area.

Ask for Clarifications

Interpersonal communication events place you in both the sender and receiver positions. Thus you often must help others be clear about what they feel about and what they want from you. Your best recourse is, as always, to ask questions. You cannot correctly assume that you can read the other person's mind!

Table 12.3 Observable Behaviors and Measurable Results

Attitudes	Observable Behaviors	Measurable Results
to love	call me on the phone	at least once a day
to improve	arrive at work on time	every day
to be professional	research and write for publication	two essays in refereed journals each year
to care	say you care and show you care by making written and phone contact	three or four times a month
to help or participate	offer to sit with the children and to do the dishes and other household chores	a few times each week

Here is a three-step sequence that will help you get clarifications from someone else:

1. Talk about what you observe.
2. Talk about what you are inferring.
3. Ask what the other person wants.

This process is easy to learn and well worth the effort. Here is a sample of it in use:

1. (talk about your observations): "I can see your hands trembling, and I can hear your voice is strained, but I'm not sure what to make of it. . . .
2. (talk about your inferences): Are you angry? . . . Are you angry with me personally?
3. (ask what is wanted): What would you like me to do? . . . What does that mean? I have to guess?

Summary

Talking about feelings, wants, and expectations is difficult because of societal injunctions against doing so. But learning to talk about these things can contribute immensely to your ability to manage your relationships. The skills involved in talking about feelings include separating feelings from emotions and learning more feeling words. We described a method for achieving this goal. Learning to talk about wants and expectations means learning to specify observable behaviors, measurable results, and an appropriate time frame in which the desired results will be performed. It also means learning to help other people be clear about what they are feeling and what they want from you. We provided examples of talk that illustrate these concepts.

Discussion Questions

1. Differentiate between a feeling and an emotion. Have you ever confused them in a way that was damaging—or potentially damaging—to a relationship?
2. Working with two classmates, practice the three-step sequence for talking about feelings (locate, describe, and name) using these situations:
   a. Your response to a boss who is wrongly accusing you of an error someone else made.
   b. You are about to end a long-term romantic relationship. You do not want to hurt your partner, but you no longer want to be romantically involved.
   c. You are about to assert your right to adult status in your relationship with a parent who, even though you are over twenty, still treats you in a way that you think is "like a child." You are, in large measure, financially dependent upon your parent.
3. In the three situations above, what would you want from the other person? Work with two or three classmates to clarify those wants, and then role play the situation to practice the skills involved in expressing them.
4. Can you think of any situations in which our suggestions would not be helpful? If so, describe them, being as specific as possible. How might you assure clarity about your feelings and wants in those situations?

Endnotes

1. J. Powell, *The Secret of Staying in Love* (Niles, IL: Argus Communications, 1974), 73.
2. S. I. Hayakawa, ed., *Language, Meaning, and Maturity* (New York: Harper & Row, 1954), 27.
3. Alfred Korzybski, *Science and Sanity,* 4th ed. (Lakeville, CT: The International Non-Aristotelian Library Publishing Company, 1962), 34.

Assertive, Nonassertive, and Aggressive Communication

Preview

The language we use will contribute to growth in our relationships when it affirms the self-concepts of both partners. Our language must express our wants clearly and place responsibility for them on ourselves. Sometimes we make mistakes in our choices about language by giving up responsibility for our own choices or taking away another's right to choose. Often there is a pattern to this behavior. We may respond inappropriately to certain situations, personalities, topics, or behaviors. We can turn these habitual responses into opportunities for relational growth by learning to communicate assertively.

Key Terms

aggressive behavior
aggressive language
assertive behavior
assertive language
nonassertive behavior
nonassertive language
response to behavior
response to personalities
response to the situation
response to the topic

Objectives

1. Define nonassertive communication and relate a personal experience of it.
2. Define aggressive communication and relate a personal experience of it.
3. Define assertive communication and relate a personal experience of it.
4. Cite a personal experience that triggered nonassertive or aggressive behavior.
5. Practice an assertive response to the situation described in Objective 4.
6. Recall an experience that triggered your nonassertive or aggressive behavior.
7. Practice an assertive response to the topic described in Objective 6.
8. Recall a personality who triggered your nonassertive or aggressive behavior.
9. Practice an assertive response to the personality described in Objective 8.
10. Recall a behavior that triggered your nonassertive or aggressive behavior.
11. Practice an assertive response to the behavior described in Objective 10.

Appropriate Expression of Wants and Needs

Appropriate self-expression must include a consideration of the way language influences others' perceptions of our manner and style. The words we choose along with our manner of saying them may result in our being perceived as *assertive, nonassertive,* or *aggressive.* Look carefully at this situation and imagine what you might do if you were Mary Ann or Cheryl:

Cheryl and Mary Ann were sitting in the lounge in their place of employment talking about an assignment their boss had given them. Mary Ann, well underway on the project, was listening to Cheryl relate her difficulties in getting started on the assignment when Tim approached. Tim likes to talk and carry on about things, and is fun to have around when people want to socialize. However, he does not pay much attention to what others are doing and frequently interrupts his and others' work to chat. He is in the middle of doing that right now. As Tim was talking about his wonderful weekend, Mary Ann politely interrupted him, saying, "Excuse me, Tim. Cheryl and I are working on ideas for a project that Sam assigned to us. If you want to help us with some ideas, that's fine. If not, will you let us get back to it, please?"

Mary Ann dealt with Tim's interruption quickly and assertively. Notice that her response does not attack him but merely states what she wants in precise terms. She might have responded aggressively, saying, "Get lost, you jerk." Aggressive responses are frequently controlling and can be hurtful. With such a response, Mary Ann may get what she wants but at the probable expense of Tim's anger and a somewhat damaged relationship. She might also have given a nonassertive response, such as, "Gee, Tim, we're working, but you're not interrupting anything." This response is self-denying and completely gives control to another person. In this example, Mary Ann gives up what she wants but may resent Tim because of it.

Nonassertive behavior is generally anxiety based and involves giving up something.

Characteristics of Nonassertive, Aggressive, and Assertive Language and Behavior

Robert Alberti and Michael Emmons believe that *nonassertive behavior* is generally anxiety based.[1] *Nonassertive language* has the following characteristics:

It generally denies (or ignores) the self.
It can sound hurt, anxious, or inhibited.
It allows or encourages others to choose and receive what they want from
     the situation.

It usually does not achieve the desired goal.

Examine Anne's nonassertive responses below for evidence of these characteristics:

Richard: Anne, if I were you, I'd tell your boss that you have a right to have your vacation anytime you want it.

Anne: Maybe you're right, Richard, but I don't know what to say to him.

Richard: You've got to start sticking up for yourself. You let your supervisor push you around all the time.

Anne: I suppose so, but he is nice to me much of the time, and I could take my vacation later if he needs me. Maybe next month I'll sit down and have a talk with him.

Note that nonassertive behavior involves giving up something in our relationships. Anne is giving up taking her vacation when she wants it. She is denying herself and relying on Richard to solve her problems. Nonassertive behavior such as this can quickly lead to resentment, which compounds the difficulty of achieving relational growth. If Anne lets her dissatisfaction go unattended, she will eventually have an explosive confrontation with her boss, and he may not even understand why it is happening. Repairing a relationship after we have behaved nonassertively requires two steps. First, the built-up resentment must be overcome. Second, the issue that caused us to behave nonassertively must be resolved. Only then can the relationship resume its normal course. Anne is behaving nonassertively toward both her supervisor and Richard. She might respond assertively to Richard as follows:

Richard: Anne, if I were you, I'd tell your boss that you have a right to have your vacation anytime you want it.

Anne: But I'm not you, Richard. I have to approach my boss with respect if I want him to give me what I want.

Richard: You've got to start sticking up for yourself. You let your supervisor push you around all the time.

Anne: Excuse me, but I do stick up for myself when I think I need to. In fact, I'm going to meet with my supervisor tomorrow morning to discuss my vacation. He may or may not agree to let me have it when I want it, but at least he will know how I feel.

Aggressive behavior exists at the other end of the spectrum. It exhibits these characteristics:

It is self-enhancing but at the expense of another.
It is expressive, but belittles others.
It assumes control over the choices of others.
It usually achieves its desired goals, but does so by hurting others and
    damaging the relationship.

See if you can identify these characteristics in John's conversation with Pamela:

Aggressive Behavior

Pamela: John, I'm going to the movies Saturday. Would you like to go with me?

John: Are you going to one of those stupid, sappy relationship movies again? If you are, I don't want to go.

Pamela: Well, I haven't picked one out yet. Which one would you like to see?

     Aggressive behavior stifles growth in our relationships because it tends to cut off communication. Our partners will probably lower their esteem for us if we act this way too often. Eventually they may withdraw from the relationship. John's response to Pamela's invitation above puts her down and removes control of her evening from her. It implies that he knows what "good" movies are and she does not. Pamela will soon tire of this treatment and stop asking John out. Wouldn't you? However, John could have responded to Pamela's invitation assertively like this:

Pamela: John, I'm going to the movies Saturday. Would you like to go with me?

John: I'd like to go out with you, Pamela. What are you planning to see?

Pamela: I thought I'd like to see that new relationship movie, how about you?

John: Thanks, but I really don't think I'd enjoy it. Why don't you go and then we can meet somewhere afterwards?

Assertive behavior lies between the extremes of nonassertive and aggressive expression. It is usually the most appropriate and effective language for a given situation. *Assertive language* is characterized as follows:

It is self-enhancing.
It is expressive.
It indicates choices made by the self, for the self.
It may achieve the desired goals.
It does not achieve these goals by putting down the other person.

Assertive behavior and language help us express our ideas while preserving our own dignity and our partner's. Did you notice that in the assertive version of John and Pamela's conversation, he did not criticize her taste but was still able to disagree with her choice. This type of language permits openness in our relationships and provides the opportunity for them to grow through learning, agreeing, and disagreeing in a fair-minded fashion.

When and Why We Fail to Communicate Assertively

The major issue in communicating nonassertively or aggressively is one of control. We all have a need to feel in charge of ourselves and our relationships, and when we are communicating in ways that satisfy this need, we find ourselves in control. This feeling of control enables us to appropriately achieve the expression and satisfaction of our interpersonal needs for belonging and affection. We can lose this feeling of control in a number of ways. Certain situations, personalities, topics, or behaviors may trigger a nonassertive or aggressive response in us. We need to learn to recognize those that affect us this way so we can learn new assertive language to use in response.

Response to the Situation

Sometimes our choice to communicate nonassertively or aggressively is a *response to the situation.* In some situations we may act rather timid. For instance, we may feel shy and uncomfortable at large gatherings where we do not know anyone. Our language might reflect this discomfort in a number of ways. We might speak more politely than we usually do, we might choose language that reveals very little about ourselves, or we might remain very quiet, speaking only when spoken to. If our response to such situations is aggressive, we might talk loudly, intrude into the conversations of others, and dominate the conversations into which we are invited.

The assertive response requires that we give some thought to what we want from a situation.

The assertive response to a gathering where we do not know anybody requires that we first give some thought to what we want out of the situation. Do we want to meet people or participate in some particular aspect of the event? When we feel comfortable with our reason for being there, we may be able to act in such a way that we present ourselves and our wants clearly. We might, for example, begin by identifying someone we think is attractive or interesting. Then we would approach this person and introduce ourself. We should keep in mind that we are at the beginning stages of a relationship and must take care to disclose in appropriate amounts and depths.

Response to Personalities

Some of us are aggressive or nonassertive only in *response to certain personalities*. We might have difficulty, for instance, choosing language that accurately conveys our wants to our supervisor at work. In this circumstance, we might choose nonassertive expressions that seem to indicate that everything is fine, whether or not it really is. Or we might decide to hint about what we want. On the other hand, if we choose to respond aggressively, we might complain about every task we are assigned.

The assertive response in this situation is one of honesty. If we have concerns that a supervisor might be able to remedy, we must give that person the opportunity to do so. Such assertive communication is free of blame, and the time and place are appropriate to the subject we want to discuss. For instance, when our supervisor asks how things are going, we might say, "Most everything is fine, but I do have two concerns that you may be able to help me with. I'll be finished with this project at 3:00. Can we meet then to talk about them?"

Response to the Topic

We might also find ourselves behaving nonassertively or aggressively in *response to the topic*. For instance, we may have such strong feelings about the way our government should treat its veterans that when the topic comes up we find ourselves tongue-tied and either withdraw from the conversation or try to change the subject to avoid a confrontation. On the other hand, we might express our strong feelings aggressively by raising our voices to threaten those with differing opinions. This would likely end the conversation, so the goal would be achieved through intimidation.

The key to communicating about sensitive topics is mutual positive regard. We can express our views clearly if we remember that they represent a perspective that others may not have heard before or that they may disagree with.

The first step in learning to be assertive is understanding ourselves—who we are, how others see us, and what we want.

When dealing with sensitive topics, we can strive for an exchange of views. This means that we must use appropriate listening and feedback skills in addition to assertive language.

Response to Behavior

Sometimes we have to choose a way of communicating in *response to behavior* that we think is inappropriate. For example, suppose we are in a group working on a project. Susan, one of the group members, has missed several meetings. She arrives late for the current meeting and without the materials she had agreed to bring. You might respond nonassertively by saying, "Don't worry, Susan, I'll get the materials on my lunch hour tomorrow." Or you might respond aggressively, saying, "Susan, you have been lazy and irresponsible throughout this project! If you don't go and get the things right now and bring them back in an hour, we're going to exclude you from the project." The third alternative, the assertive response, might be, "Susan, would you go get the materials you were to bring now? We have set aside this time to work on our project and must have them before we can proceed." The assertive response is problem centered and present oriented. In responding this way you do not ask for excuses or explanations, only results.

Sharon and Gordon Bower summarized the importance of assertive behavior:

> Above all, as an assertive person you can learn to negotiate mutually satisfactory solutions to a variety of interpersonal problems—from dealing with your neighbor whose dog likes to march over your marigolds to adjusting an unsatisfactory relationship with a friend or relative.[2]

At times we may see the nonassertive alternative as most appropriate. For example, when someone who normally is quite pleasant is having a bad day and snaps at you, a nonassertive response may be best. You may want to overlook this action or put off discussion of it until a better time. Alberti and Emmons have said that there may be such times when, after examining the possible consequences of assertive behavior, you decide that another response is desirable.[3] They wrote:

> If an individual can act assertively under given conditions, but chooses not to, our purpose is accomplished. If he is unable to act assertively (i.e., cannot choose for himself how he will behave, but is cowed into nonassertiveness or triggered into aggressiveness), his life will be governed by others and his mental health will suffer.[4]

Generally, the assertive expression is the most productive. Using language to assert who we are and what we want can help us know ourselves better, present ourselves in a better light, and contribute to the growth of our relationships.

Improving Assertive Communication Skills

There are several keys to improving assertive expression. First, we must understand ourselves—who we are, how others see us, and what we want. Unit 8 suggested ways to clarify the self-concept. Second, we must observe our own actions in relationships. For example, you might keep a diary for several weeks in which you note instances of nonassertive, aggressive, and assertive behavior. Finally, we can analyze our behavior using the information we have collected. The following questions and suggestions can help us achieve insights:

1. Is there any pattern to your behavior? That is, are there certain situations, people, or topics that cause you to behave in a way that you would like to improve?
2. Are you pleased with any examples of your assertive behavior? Compare the details of these events with those you identified above.
3. Which factors or people in a situation help you to remain in control of

your expression? Which trigger nonassertive or aggressive communication?

4. Examine those situations in which you would like to see some improvement and choose *one* to work on.
5. Recall how you communicated in that situation and consider alternative responses.
6. Plan for your next encounter with the situation, person, or topic that caused you a problem by rehearsing your response. You might get some feedback from a friend. Bower and Bower suggest that you actually write out the sort of message you might want to deliver.[5]

Plan for your next encounter with a situation, person, or topic that caused you to behave in a way you would like to improve.

7. Face the situation, person, or topic assertively, taking care not to get carried away. Remember your goals for the relationship. When we work to change our behavior, the greatest problem we face is that we sometimes go too far in the opposite direction. For instance, we may move from an aggressive expression to a nonassertive one or vice versa. This overcompensation can be avoided through careful thought before *and* during your encounter.
8. Apply the same procedures to another encounter. Remember, each situation may pose a different set of circumstances for you to face. Some of your areas of needed improvement are more stressful than others, while some are more complicated. Treat each encounter individually, giving full consideration to the relationship and your goals in it.

You will find that assertive behavior is, in many instances, easier to achieve than you thought. One reason for this is that such behavior is self-rewarding, for when you behave assertively you accomplish what you set out to do. You may not always get what you want, but you will have the satisfaction of knowing that you communicated your wants in a way that helped you express yourself accurately, that fairly considered the other person, and that contributed to the growth and development of your relationship.

Summary

We have described assertive, nonassertive, and aggressive behavior and language. Nonassertive language denies the self and results in our giving up what we want. Aggressive language is the opposite: We get what we want at the expense of others, often putting ourselves above them. Assertive language enables us to preserve our own dignity and that of our partner while expressing what we need to say. We fail to communicate assertively when we give up control of our language to automatic responses triggered by situations, topics, personalities, or behaviors. We can improve our assertive communication by developing a firm sense of our self-concept and observing our own behavior as we communicate. If we can learn to identify what triggers nonassertive or aggressive communication, we can work to change those habits. Doing this will open the door to greater relational growth.

Discussion Questions

1. Why should we worry about being assertive or improving our communication styles? Can't people just accept us as we are? What would you tell the generally aggressive person who says, "I am what I am, take me or leave me."
2. Explain how you might help a relational partner overcome nonassertive behaviors in all four of the areas we discussed—situation, topic, personality, and behavior.

Endnotes

1. R. E. Alberti and M. L. Emmons, *Your Perfect Right: A Guide to Assertive Behavior* (San Luis Obispo, CA: Impact Publishers, 1974).
2. S. A. Bower and G. A. Bower, *Asserting Yourself: A Practical Guide for Positive Change* (Reading, MA: Addison-Wesley Publishing Company, 1976).
3. Alberti and Emmons, *Your Perfect Right,* 11.
4. Ibid., 47–48.
5. Bower and Bower, *Asserting Yourself,* 87–104.

>>I<< UNIT 14

Problems with Language in Relationships

Preview
Quite often the evidence of problems in our relationships comes from the language we use. Sometimes the words we choose to express our ideas do not account for the uniqueness of the other person. At other times, we forget that we are in control of the language we use and instead allow our words to control us. We also create difficulties when the language we use to name ourselves, our partners, or our relationships does not change as our relationships grow. Likewise, masking reality by using words and symbols as substitutes for reality can create problems. Finally, we sometimes use language that expresses extreme points of view rather than our experience. This unit will help you recognize and deal with these problems by helping you find language that will more effectively promote nourishment and growth in your relationships.

Objectives
1. Recall an instance of language stereotyping that resulted in interpersonal problems. Explain how this occurred.
2. Explain "self-fulfilling prophesy." Provide an example from personal experience.
3. Provide a personal example in which rigidity of language posed a problem for a relationship.
4. Discuss the way reification contributes to problems in relationships.
5. Recall an experience in which polarization, or the two-valued orientation, interfered with communication in a relationship.

Key Terms
confusing the map of a relationship with
   its territory
multivalued orientation
polarization
possessing the symbol
reification
rigidity in naming
self-fulfilling prophesy
stereotyping
stress
two-valued orientation

Language is our principal tool for achieving relational growth. It is so important that the correct use of language has been associated with our basic well-being: We feel better about ourselves and our relationships when we are using language appropriately. In unit 13, Robert Alberti and Michael Emmons were quoted as saying that assertive language and behavior relate directly to our mental health.[1] This is also true for other aspects of language, including the level and flexibility of the words we choose. Alfred Korzybski said that attention to these and other aspects of language can provide a measure of sanity.[2] The noted language scholar S. I. Hayakawa summarized Korzybski's definition of "sanity" as follows:

> The sane individual, he said, does not confuse levels of abstraction; he does not treat the map as if it were the territory; he does not copy animals in their reactions, and therefore is not a dogmatist, or a categorist (the pun is Korzybski's, not mine); he does not treat as identical all things that have the same name; he does not exhibit a two-valued orientation in which absolute good is pitted against absolute evil. . . .[3]

This definition clearly identifies several language skills that Hayakawa and Korzybski believe are important. Problems with these areas of language use include treating all things with the same name as though they are the same, confusing words and the things they represent, and thinking of and describing our experiences in terms of opposites. When we have difficulty using language, relationship problems inevitably result. And as long as such problems persist, growth is hindered. This unit will help you learn to use language effectively by adopting techniques that allow you to avoid many of these difficulties.

Stereotyping and Self-Fulfilling Prophesies

Wendell Johnson is often quoted as saying, "To a mouse, cheese is cheese, that's why mousetraps work."[4] He was saying that because expectations are often not questioned, the uniqueness of a situation is frequently missed. You may have heard this same idea applied to people or relationships:

"What did you expect? Women are like that."
"Hey, what can I do? Business is business."
"You men are all alike. You never pay any attention to the details."
"I'll have to turn down your offer to introduce the guest of honor. I'd get up and make a fool of myself."

We frequently create traps for ourselves when we choose language carelessly. We react to people as representing a class rather than themselves. We ignore their individuality and miss the opportunity for genuine communication. This is damaging to relationships because we think of our partner as a category

Stereotyping begins early and may create a self-fulfilling prophesy.

of person rather than a unique person. We limit opportunities for new contacts, new experiences, and new or improved relationships when we talk in these ways.

People and relationships are unique. Communication difficulties can result when the uniqueness is ignored. These problems affect not only the person who starts the conversation, but also the other person involved and the relationship between them. Ignoring the uniqueness of people, including yourself, is called *stereotyping*. When stereotyping is taken too far, it can result in a *self-fulfilling prophesy*, which means that our expectations work to help bring about what we think will happen.

Stereotyping is the act of taking ideas about a group and applying them to a member of that group without seeing whether they actually describe that person. You are probably aware of ethnic or racial stereotyping. You may even have witnessed sexual and age stereotyping. When actions based on stereotyping are widespread, as in these cases, the resulting problems are both interpersonal and societal.

We will consider stereotyping in more personal terms. A relationship is most meaningful when we can really know and deal with someone as an individual. However, it is difficult to appreciate the person fully when your frame of reference is based on a stereotype. Sometimes the stereotype will not be evident in our language but will influence our responses. Consider the following example.

John holds certain ideas about heavy people that affect his expectations of them in conversation. "Fat people are jovial," he says, "always in a good mood. They must not take things very seriously, or they wouldn't be able to treat life so lightly." Judy, who is overweight, sits at her desk working on a quarterly report for her department. She has had some trouble getting started on the report and thus is worried that she may not get it to her boss on time. When John wanders in to pick up some papers, he sees Judy working and he goes over to her to talk. "Hey Judy," he said, "what are you doing in here on a Saturday?"

"I'm trying to make some headway on this report," she said, distracted. "I'm behind schedule, and have to really get going to finish by Tuesday."

John didn't seem to notice her distress, saying, "I can't believe you're worried about it, Judy. You aren't the type to take a thing like this too seriously. Are you going to the concert tonight?"

Judy looked up in disbelief. "No John, I'm sure I'll have to put in more time on this report."

John smiled at Judy, continuing, "Right, Judy, we'll see you there. And smile, you don't even look like yourself with that frown on your face."

As John walked off, Judy tried to get back into her work. Their communication had done nothing to help her feel better about herself or her task. Further, their conversation contributed nothing to the growth of their relationship. John did not pay attention to Judy's experience of the moment because he allowed his stereotype to govern his communication. Had he looked at Judy as unique, instead of as a representative of his stereotype of heavy people, he might have chosen language that offered support, encouragement, and relational growth.

Stereotyping is common and even beneficial in the early stages of a relationship. It is useful in finding things to talk about with people we would like to know better. We can draw inferences about them, based on stereotypes that give us topics to explore. We then check out these inferences as we communicate and, based on our findings, build a relationship by comparing and contrasting the person's uniqueness with those stereotypes.

If, for example, we meet a university student, we might guess that the person is interested in the music that students generally enjoy. We test this inference and then expand on it by being more concrete in our talk as we learn about the particular tastes of our partner and share our own. The stereotype thus served as a basis for engaging the other person.

Stereotyping influences our relationships in another, more indirect way.

Sometimes we form an image of a person based on a stereotype and then select language to predict who that person is and what will happen to us. That image may be so real to us that we respond to our predictions rather than to the events themselves. In other words, we act to make our predictions come true. We have created a self-fulfilling prophesy by which we ignore our own individuality as well as the uniqueness of others. Telling ourselves, for example, that we cannot speak before a group of people may lead us to turn down opportunities that might benefit us. By giving a talk, we might allow others to learn something about us and our subject as we improve our public speaking ability. None of this is likely to happen if we allow our prediction of failure to keep us from trying.

Self-fulfilling prophesies also may interfere with the way we act. Telling ourselves, for example, that we are not good at solving problems may lead us to put more energy into rationalizing a poor job instead of carefully analyzing the problem. This self-deception can reinforce the label "not good at solving problems" because we frequently do not notice that we devoted much of our time to creating language that explains our failure. We may believe that we are spending that time trying to solve the problem. Thus the next time we have to solve a problem, we still have a negative label, and even worse, we have had a recent experience that supports it. As we communicate this to others, we teach them stereotypes of ourselves that contribute to their view of us and may affect their relationships with us. In this instance, when a group problem-solving assignment is given, we may not be sought out by those with whom we would like to work, for they have heard and believed the stereotype that we have promoted through language choices.

The solution to the self-fulfilling prophesy begins with understanding its nature. A self-fulfilling prophesy can only involve something over which we have some control. Remember, we write the prediction and make the events happen as we communicate about that prediction. If you say, "It will snow Friday," your prediction may or may not come true. There is nothing you can do to influence the outcome. If, on the other hand, you say, "Boy, you're going to be angry with me," you can do a good deal to make this happen or prevent it.

A self-fulfilling prophesy can only involve something over which we have some control.

Once we understand that we control how we describe the state of our relationships, we can choose to not participate in negative fantasies. We then have to create language that presents ourselves and our relationships in new, positive, and realistic ways and work to carry out the behaviors suggested. In the case of the problem-solving example above, we must say something like, "I know I did not do well on my last assignment, but I'm not going to let that get in the way. I know what I did wrong, and I'm going to be careful to avoid making those same mistakes. I'm going to use my last decision making assignment to improve myself, not as an excuse for another failure. And if I don't do well this time it will be because of what I did this time, not because of who I am."

Rigidity in Naming

As our relationships grow, our definitions of them must keep pace. Hayakawa pointed out that problems can result when this does not happen.[5] The names that we choose for ourselves and our relationships may "harden" or become fixed. As a result, we come to believe that (1) other definitions must be wrong, and (2) we need to protect ourselves and our relationships from experiences that challenge these names. This *rigidity in naming* seriously affects the health of our relationships and our own mental health. Hayakawa explained this problem as it relates to the language we use to describe ourselves:

> When the self-concept is thus rigidified, it may remain unchanged for a while. Trouble arises from the fact that the self will not stay put. The self slips away from the self-concept; the individual's ideas about himself become less and less real as time goes on. In other words, it may originally have been true that the man was the best salesman in the company, but as time goes on and the facts of life change, it will require more and more self-delusion on his part to maintain his self-concept.[6]

Rigidity also occurs in relationships, as this example of Bart and Tina illustrates. Throughout their twenty-year marriage, Bart's view of their relationship has been dominated by a traditional stereotype about the place of women. About six years ago, Tina decided she wanted to go to college. Bart encouraged her because he viewed "the wife taking classes" as a way for her to get out of the house, a diversion. Tina was very good in school and managed to complete her degree in six years, while juggling housekeeping and child care. She increasingly called on Bart to manage some of the household affairs as she became involved in her studies. Bart helped but grumbled about it, saying that if his help would allow Tina to finish school and get back into the home sooner, it was worth the effort. He did not alter his view of their relationship, even though its realities were changing. Tina is now talking about graduate school. Bart is flabbergasted: "How can she do this?" He does not recognize what has happened. If they are to be happy, they need to communicate in ways that more accurately convey how they and their relationship are changing and how they can channel these new goals and events into something positive for them both.

The consequences can be very unpleasant when both parties hold outdated definitions of the relationship. One couple we know remained married for at least five years after the relationship was actually over. Their need to hold an unchanging definition of the relationship led them to pretend that it was working and to communicate as though things were fine. They might have been able to salvage their marriage if they had recognized the problem earlier and, perhaps with professional help, addressed it. The relationship met a tragic end because they recognized only one definition and failed to see that they might have used other, more appropriate definitions.

To keep pace with the constant changes in a relationship, seek new language to describe it and talk about it often.

We must realize that we, our partners, and our relationships all grow and change. We must work to find ways to describe what is really happening even if we do not like the direction of this growth. Remaining anchored in past views of a relationship will diminish our effectiveness in it. The way to achieve definitions that keep pace with growth is to seek new language to describe our relationship and to communicate frequently about how each partner sees it and its future.

Confusing the Map of a Relationship with Its Territory

A very basic rule of language is that a word only represents the thing, event, or person it symbolizes. In other words, language provides a map that describes the territory of experience but is detached from our true experience of the relationship. When we respond to our symbols for a relationship as though they were the relationship itself, we are *confusing the map of a relationship with its territory.* We are substituting language for experience.

An extreme form of this is called *reification,* or treating a symbol as if it were a real thing—an object we can manipulate. Ideas like democracy, friendship, and love have many associations, but do not exist in and of themselves. They become reified when we try to find things which correspond to them. We are fooling ourselves when we manipulate the objects associated with these ideas and think that we are changing the ideas. For example, Mary recently had an idea about the way her company could offer adequate day care for the children of its employees. She expressed her ideas as a written proposal, which she showed to her co-workers. At this point reification took over. As her co-workers made suggestions about how her idea might be improved, Mary viewed their efforts as denials of her idea and to some extent of herself. She had taken an idea, determined that her plan defined that idea, and decided that any change in her plan was a change in the goal. Her stubbornness resulted in a lack of support for the proposal, even though it was a good idea.

When we reify something, we treat the symbol as if it were a real thing—an object we can manipulate. The boy vents his anger on the empty carton.

    We also do this in relationships. Bart, in the case above, decided that they no longer had a real marriage when Tina began behaving in ways that did not fit that definition. The ideal marriage was reified by Bart. John Condon clarified this problem when he wrote, ''The problems of reification are especially common when the terms are preceded by adjectives such as *real* or *pure* or *true* or *essential.* There is no such thing as true love, there is only love. There is no essential man, there are only men, and so on.''[7]
    Another aspect of reification is *possessing the symbol.* We sometimes come to believe that by owning something that symbolizes an idea, we become that idea. Phil, for example, wanted to be recognized as a jogger. He believed that the way to do this was to acquire all the things joggers have—special shoes and clothing, timing devices, and volumes of information on the subject. But he will not *be* a jogger until he starts running. We frequently use things to symbolize relationships. This is all right if the purpose of the things is to remind us of the relationship and how we value it. The problem occurs when we come to believe that the fate of the things is the fate of the relationship. We understood Karen's reluctance to part with her dead husband's possessions. However, when we went to dinner at her house and found a place set at the table for him, we began to suspect that the things were serving as more than a reminder: Karen refused to acknowledge her husband's death. She was keeping

him by keeping his things. This extreme situation shows just how unhealthy this problem can become. Karen is now fine after much counseling, but her reification of the symbols held her down for quite some time.

Such concepts as power, love, and sensuality do not result from our owning the objects that sometime represent them. These artifacts do have communicative significance, but we must constantly remind ourselves that symbols *are not the things they represent* and that *possession of the thing is not the same as possessing the quality for which it stands.*

Polarization encourages a way of thinking in which there are only two possibilities.

Polarization and the Two-Valued Orientation

The term *polarization* describes our tendency to use language that occurs in pairs of opposites. We describe our experiences as good or bad, old or new, black or white, and so on. When we rely too heavily on such language, we encourage a way of thinking in which there are only two options. This *two-valued orientation* limits our ability to see the options that may exist. For example, you may enjoy seeing very friendly relationships among your subordinates but do not know what to think of George. George does his job but *never* socializes with his co-workers. He does not come to company-sponsored social events or parties given by his colleagues. When work is slow, he does not join with co-workers as they relax; he keeps to himself. Some of your employees have begun to complain about George, calling him "stiff" and "difficult to get along with." In the meantime, George has become even more withdrawn. One two-valued orientation might suggest that you fire George. After all, either you get along on the job or not, and George does not. Another two-valued orientation would have you tell your employees to leave him alone and do their jobs. After all, you either do the job or not, and George does.

The two-valued orientation surfaces in polarized language. We talk about problems, relationships, and feelings about ourselves in extreme terms. We limit the kinds of relationships we can have when we use this language to define them, since our two-valued orientation dictates that the other person *must* be wrong when we disagree.

The alternative to the two valued orientation is a *multivalued orientation.* This use of language assumes from the start that it is possible to have relationships in which both parties get what they want. It leads us to look between the extremes for language that will describe our wants, feelings, and experiences.

A multivalued orientation might prove useful in creating a satisfying solution to the problem between George and his co-workers. Many values operate as people communicate in the workplace. In this case, two are productivity and a positive atmosphere. If your goal as a manager is to maintain both values, you cannot take a rigid "either/or" position on the problem. You must take a multivalued approach. George needs to see that getting along with co-workers can help him do an even better job, and his co-workers need to see that while getting along is important, so is doing the job well. Conversations with all the employees about the importance and interrelatedness of both issues would help. In these, it will be important to define the problem clearly as *ours*, as opposed to *yours, mine,* or *George's.* You might state that "we want to get the job done well here, and an important part of that is everyone getting along. That doesn't seem to be happening these days. I want to find out what we can do to make it happen." Perhaps restructuring the work hours or rearranging the space would increase communication between George and the other workers. Can you think of other multivalued approaches to this problem?

Stress has a significant effect on the problem of two-valued orientation, language, and relationships. Condon reported that as the stress of a situation increases, the people in that situation increasingly see and describe it in a two-valued orientation.[8] In an earlier example, we described Judy's problems writing her report. If this occurs often, she might fall into the trap we are describing. The stress surrounding the assignment might mount to where she sees only two options—to come up with an idea immediately or to admit to her boss that the report will be late. This unrealistic limiting of options is characteristic of the two-valued orientation. The multivalued approach, on the other hand, acknowledges the problem ("I am having a hard time with this assignment") but also keeps it in perspective ("and it is only one part of my job—I'm doing fine in the rest of it."). The two-valued orientation encourages stress by leading us to focus on extremes. The multi-valued perspective helps us relax by adopting a more productive outlook.

Control is also important in the multivalued orientation. We can easily lose control of our relationships when we communicate from a two-valued orientation because this position has built-in ultimatums. We are either "for them or against them," "in or out," or "up or down." Such language launches the relationship toward an inevitable outcome. In the case of Bart and Tina, a multivalued orientation eventually won, although Bart had initially taken the two-valued position. But he began to see that there was more to his relationship with Tina than simply her presence in the home. When they looked for other ways to view their relationship, Bart and Tina found much that they still shared and were able to redefine their marriage and take control of it once again.

You may find that stress has been a factor in your interpersonal conflicts. Perhaps your language in such situations reflected a two-valued orientation. As emotions heightened, you may have increasingly viewed the issue in terms of having or not having the relationship rather than in terms of the source of the conflict. This is a particularly unpleasant aspect of the two-valued orientation. When you find yourself in such a situation, you must take hold of your language and work very consciously to describe the conflict in a multivalued way. Unit 24, which discusses conflict management, can help you with this.

Summary

Stereotyping and the self-fulfilling prophesy, rigidity in naming, confusing the map of a relationship with its territory, and polarization and the two-valued orientation—can damage our important relationships. These problems, however, can be managed if we remain aware that we use symbols to express ideas, not to substitute for them. Remember also that usually more than two definitions and options are available as you approach relational problems. Work to adopt and maintain language that expresses and supports a multivalued frame of reference.

Discussion Questions

1. What stereotypes have people applied to you? In what instances were these helpful to your relationship? In what instances did these hinder the growth of the relationship?
2. Think about the people in your relationships. Is anyone living a destructive self-fulfilling prophesy? What can you do to help this person break this cycle?
3. What topics are you more likely to address through a two-valued orientation? Why do you think this is so?
4. Recall a relationship that was stressful. Describe the relationship. What role did the language used play in your description? What was the language like? What did you do to alleviate the stress?

Endnotes

1. R. E. Alberti and M. L. Emmons, *Your Perfect Right: A Guide to Assertive Behavior* (San Luis Obispo, CA: Impact Publishers, 1974), 47, 48.
2. A. Korzybski, *Science and Sanity: An Introduction to Non-Aristotelian Systems and General Semantics* (Lancaster, PA: Science Press Printing Company, 1983).
3. S. I. Hayakawa, *Symbol, Status and Personality* (New York: Harcourt, Brace and World, 1963).
4. W. Johnson, *People in Quandaries* (New York: Harper and Row Publishers, 1946).
5. Hayakawa, *Symbol, Status and Personality.*
6. Ibid., 41.
7. J. C. Condon, Jr., *Semantics and Communication* (New York: Macmillan, 1985), 53.
8. Ibid., 76.

Nonverbal Interaction

PART III

Body Communication and Relational Effectiveness

Preview

In this unit we examine the communication potency of general and particular body cues, such as body movement and gestures and face and eye behavior. These cues influence how others interpret our talk and how we interpret theirs. The unit ends with specific suggestions about how to apply the information presented to our relationship communication.

Key Terms

adapter
affect display
artifacts
body movement
clothing
emblem
face and eye behavior
gestures
illustrator
kinesics
posture
regulator

Objectives

1. Identify, explain, and provide examples of how behavior in each of these broad categories can communicate:
   a. clothing
   b. artifacts
   c. body movement and gestures
   d. face and eye behavior
2. Discuss what the literature about body cues suggests about your choices of behavior.
3. Identify and analyze your own specific nonverbal body cues.

People use a large number of *cues* to send signals to one another. Five of these are especially important: clothing choices, artifact choices, body movements (the way of walking, for example), habitual and cultural gestures, and face and eye behavior. Although we may not always be aware of choosing our nonverbal messages, we *can* send such messages more intentionally if we wish. Moreover, we can become more sensitive to our nonverbal behavior, to how others receive it, and to how they interpret it.

Our point is clear. If messages that we send are not interpreted as we intended, we may be causing communication problems for ourselves and those who matter to us. Similarly, if we interpret another's message wrongly or do not pick it up at all, our faulty receiving skills may be causing problems in our relationships. We thus need to understand the nonverbal message systems we share with other people and to heighten our awareness of their use.

Clothing

The *clothing* we wear may be used to say something about us. For example, we do not hesitate to "dress up" when the occasion dictates. We have a clear sense of when this is appropriate. Likewise, we do not hesitate to "dress down" under the correct circumstances. And, if we are like most people at times we have not been sure about what to wear for an occasion. Should we dress up? How much? Should we dress down? How much?

These questions and concerns suggest that we are frequently aware of the messages that are sent by our clothes. Figure 15.1 says a lot about the people in it. Look at the photo very carefully and consider the dress. Do you think the people have selected clothes that say something about how they see themselves? Can you infer anything about their socioeconomic levels? about their educational levels? What specifically tells you this?

If you could not see the faces, would you be able to tell anything about the ages of the people in the picture? Could you infer anything about the sex of the individuals in the photo? What signals are you picking up on?

Nearly all research on the relationship between what people wear and the people themselves has focused upon personality and such characteristics as age, sex, socioeconomic status, and educational level. These demographic variables constitute stereotypes, and you probably are fairly sensitive to them. Some of this research is over twenty-five years old. For example, M. L. Rosencranz conducted a fairly intensive study about clothes-conscious people in 1962.[1] He found that there was a relationship between married women who were clothes-conscious and their social status. They were usually in the upper social classes; they were usually joiners—that is, they belonged to many organizations, and they usually were rather well educated and more comfortable in intellectual conversations than were married women who didn't care much

Figure 15.1 Differences in clothing communicate about the people and their relationships.

about clothes. Clothes-conscious women also tended to have fairly high incomes and to be married to white-collar workers.

None of this is surprising, of course. Common experience tells us that dress is a leading indicator of status. But if we look at the phenomenon from a somewhat different perspective as Aiken did in 1963, we discover some interesting additional information.[2] Aiken wanted to know what kind of woman had an interest in clothing. He found that clothes-conscious women tended to be a bit insecure, quite conscientious, and stereotypical in their ways of thinking. They were also persistent and conventional, given to compliance in the face of authority, and rather tense and "uptight."

Aiken also found that women who are interested in and concerned about economy in relation to clothing were responsible, alert, efficient, precise, intelligent, conscientious, and controlled. They would probably spend time shopping for bargains, purchase quality clothing, and be concerned about the clothing budget. Aiken inferred that such care about clothing, reflected in what a women wears, speaks about the personality of the woman herself.

Aiken asked a third question: What kind of woman prefers elaborately detailed clothing and lots of jewelry—much more than normal? He found that these women were not intellectual but rather conventional and stereotyped.

They were also sympathetic, sociable, and conscientious. Moreover, they tended to be somewhat submissive.

On the other hand, women who conformed to popular norms of dress were found to be socially conscientious and traditional. They were moral women, quite sociable, and they, too, were submissive. They tended to focus upon economic, social, and religious values, but not so much upon the more aesthetic values of the culture.

Consider the clothes you are wearing now. What are you saying about yourself?

Finally, Aiken wanted to know what kind of women dressed primarily for comfort. Not surprisingly, such women were self-possessed and self-controlled, socially cooperative, and very sociable. Somewhat surprisingly, however, they were considered to be thorough and deferential to authority.

In a later study, Rosenfeld and Plax discovered that clothes-conscious men were guarded, they deferred to authority, and believed that people were easy to manipulate.[3] On the other hand, men who were not very clothes-conscious were fairly independent and aggressive. They did not think people were easy to manipulate. Interestingly, men who were more interested in clothing for such practical reasons as warmth rather than for aesthetic reasons were somewhat inhibited and rebellious. Women in this category were clever and confident. Conversely, men who were interested in the aesthetics of dress were generally more success-oriented. They were seen as mature. Women in this category, however, were self-centered and detached.

Other research[4] leaves no doubt that clothes communicate a lot about the wearer. William Thourlby[5] has suggested that clothing is the basis upon which people judge each other in at least ten categories:

1. economic level
2. educational level
3. trustworthiness
4. social position
5. level of sophistication
6. economic background
7. social background
8. educational background
9. level of success
10. moral character

Employment interviewers know the importance of dressing correctly. There has even evolved a "dress code" for interviewing, and interviewers representing the Fortune 500 companies listed correct clothing choices high on their list of characteristics they were looking for in a candidate.[6] Mark Hickson and

Figure 15.2 What do the artifacts tell about the relationship?

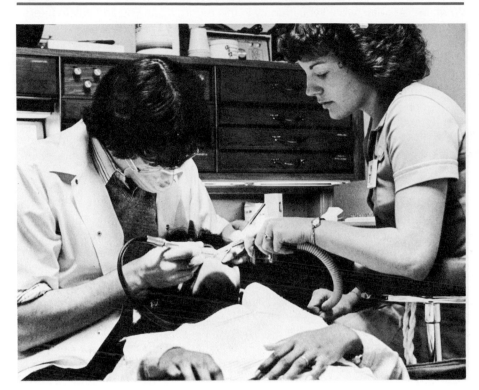

Don Stacks[7] concluded from their review of the literature on clothing that interviewers tend to hire their own images. To succeed in the interview situation, you should dress much like the interviewer. The interviewer will be dressed in close conformity to the suggestions that John T. Molloy[8] made as a result of his investigation.

Clearly, then, on the basis of common sense and these examples, our clothing choices communicate a great deal about us. Clothes tell about our place of work (formal and informal dress codes), influence the social impression we make, tell people if we are likable or sexy, and say something about our age and social status.

Artifacts

Look at figure 15.2, another picture of people. This time, though, do not concentrate on their clothing (although that too is sending messages), but look at the *artifacts,* the things people "collect" around themselves. What do the individuals do for a living? Where were they at the moment that the photo was taken? Do the artifacts tell you anything about the nature of their relationship? What, in particular, would you identify in this regard? Can you find any markers, or artifacts that suggest that one of the individuals is claiming a territory? Who? What territory? How do you know? Now look more closely. Do any artifacts suggest relative wealth? If so, which ones? Do any suggest the personality of the individuals? Is there evidence of private life? family? hobbies? What do you know about the individual whose space this is? How do you know it?

Such personal artifacts as glasses, jewelry, and make-up and such environmental and property artifacts as art objects, books, and desk tools provide a good deal of information to a perceptive observer. Interestingly, the early studies in nonverbal message exchange that focused on these particular artifacts could not explicitly determine the communication! For example, near the end of World War II, people with glasses were perceived as more intelligent, more industrious, and more honest than those without.[9] By 1968, women who wore glasses were seen as religious, conventional, and unimaginative.[10] By 1972,[11] however, women with glasses and no make-up were generally perceived as conservative and low in individuality by their male colleagues. Women with glasses and make-up were perceived by their male counterparts as artistic, intelligent, self-confident, and sophisticated, but they were perceived as low in seriousness. Other women found them to be intelligent but conceited and cold.[12] Whether these women actually had these characteristics is unknown. But this is how they were perceived.

It has been known for thirty-five years that a woman's lipstick can have an important bearing on how she is perceived. A 1952 study examined the effects of lipstick on the perceptions men had of women.[13] In that study, a small group of men saw women as more frivolous and more interested in males if they wore lipstick. Interestingly, the men were not able to identify the basis upon which they made their judgments!

The results of this thirty-five-year-old study are probably not surprising. Casual observation on any college campus suggests that women believe their facial appearance, including the decision to wear lipstick, can have an impact on how they are perceived. Moreover, advertisements in women's magazines throughout the past three and a half decades reveal that lipstick and other make-up merchandisers have very consistently played to that perception.

Molloy also studied the effects of make-up on the perceptions that men have of women. He used six women, aged 18 to 40 as models. He asked them to apply a minimum of makeup, and then took pictures. Next he asked professional make-up artists to apply make-up to these same models and photographed the results. Then he asked men under the age of 25 to judge the photos. Of one hundred men, 92 picked the minimum make-up pictures as the most appealing. Of 100 respondents between 25 and 35, 67 percent found the minimum make-up photographs most appealing, as did 62 percent of respondents between 35 and 45.[14]

Clearly, such artifacts as cigars and cigarettes, make-up, briefcases and purses, and tools can contribute to the impression you make on others. The question you must ask is whether you are creating the impression you would like. This impression does not have to occur by chance, for you can control the message value of artifacts.

Body Movement and Gestures

Body movement and *gestures* fall within the broad field of nonverbal study called *kinesics.* Gross body movement and gestures, not the subtleties of facial expression, can have an enormous communicative impact, whether this is intended. Of course, common sense makes this statement obvious, since our language is full of references to the communicative potential of gross body movement and gestures such as the following:

"You really look down."
"Mary Ann is really wound up tight today."
"He's so troubled that he looks like he's carrying the weight of the entire
     company on his back."
"Perk up, Phil."

Have you thought about the messages you send just by the way you walk? Suppose for instance, that you are in the city—perhaps Chicago, Los Angeles, New York, or Atlanta. You are walking alone down the street. After about six seconds of observation, a mugger could determine whether you were an easy mark! Could you make the same determination?

In a study based on this question, Rubenstein videotaped sixty people walking alone in the late morning hours, then asked a panel of convicts to rate whether they would be easy to mug.[15] The convicts were asked to rate each subject on a scale of one to ten: one meant "a very easy rip off," and ten meant "would avoid it, too big a situation, too heavy." Each videotaped sequence lasted from six to eight seconds. The expert judges had no difficulty in agreeing about which of the pedestrians would be easy marks: Their movements were awkward. They walked as though in a daze. They seemed oblivious to what was going on around them. They appeared to be in conflict with themselves. On the other hand, pedestrians who were seen as "too heavy" walked in evenly paced, determined steps that rocked from heel to toe. They appeared goal-oriented, determined, and confident about where they were going.

The study of body movement and gestures as communication is a relatively new discipline. Among the first individuals investigating the body's communication independent of voice was Ray Birdwhistle, whose most important work appeared in 1970.[16] Of course, you have heard about or read such books as *Body Language,* by Julius Fast. This book, a popularization of some of the research conducted in the early 1970s, was copyrighted in 1977.[17]

Even though this is a relatively new area of study, we know a surprising amount. For instance, there does not appear to be a nonverbal vocabulary composed of discrete units. In contrast, English includes an alphabet having twenty-six letters and a much more subtle set of base units, called *allophones,* which, when combined, make words. There are standard dictionaries of the English language, but not of nonverbal language.

Paul Ekman and Wallace Friesen categorized gross bodily movements into *emblems, illustrators, regulators, affect displays,* and *adaptors.*[18] The definition and an illustration of each term are shown in figure 15.3.

Posture

Perhaps even more subtle than gestures, *posture* communicates an enormous amount of information about you. Even so, except for a few moments when you are conscious of posture, you do not think very carefully about how you stand, sit, slump, or slouch.

Researchers have been able to develop an interesting and simple categorization for observing and recording body posture. There are basically only three categories: standing, bent-knee (including sitting), and lying.[19] These postures occur along a continuum with *gesture* at one end and *spatial behavior* at the other. Thus it is possible to observe posture as an extension of gesture. Likewise, it is possible to judge if a person's posture cues involve increasing or decreasing distance. This categorization is simple, yet very powerful, for it can record as many as a thousand possibilities.

Posture offers information about your attitudes, status, and self-image. It communicates your sex, and whether you conform to the stereotypical gender cues of the American culture. Along with how you move from one place to another, posture reveals your personal and interpersonal style and image. And finally, posture communicates your emotions. Because these cues are so very important, it is surprising that people appear to be so unconcerned about the posture messages they send.

Imagine, if you can, that you are sitting on the beach in late afternoon. It is autumn, so there is a crispness in the air, and not many people on the beach are wearing swimsuits. Instead, the costume of the day is blue jeans and t-shirt, a sweater or light jacket, and bare feet. Some blue jeans are rolled up slightly so the walkers can wade along the shoreline. As these people walk in front of you, they are silhouetted against the sun path on the water. What can you tell about them? Can you tell if they are male or female? Can you determine their approximate ages? Can you tell if they are attached somehow? Are they intimate? Can you tell if they have known each other for quite a while, or if their relationship is relatively new? Is one dominant? Is one person "showing off" for another? Can you tell how anyone is feeling? And perhaps more importantly, *how* can you tell? For if it is true that you can draw inferences just from the

Figure 15.3 Categories of Gross Body Movements and Gestures

Term	Definition	Examples
Emblem	Deliberate movements that can be directly translated into words; discrete, categorical behaviors that are generally known and accepted. Familiar *emblems* are the "O.K." sign, the "come here" sign, and the hitchhiker's sign.	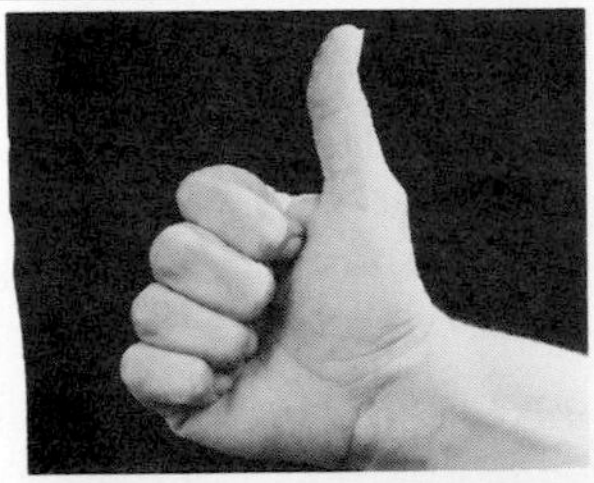
Illustrator	Deliberate movements used to reinforce and enrich verbal message. The up-and-down movement of the head while saying "yes" and the reaching out and drawing back of the palm while saying "Let's go" are *illustrators*.	
Regulator	Body movements that help us to interact; a gesture system that controls turn-taking in the flow of communication. *Regulators* include nodding our heads, adjusting the focus of our eyes away from the speaker, and raising our hands.	
Affect display	Any movement or gesture that reflects the intensity of our feelings. *Affect displays* may show fear, anger, tiredness, or even surprise.	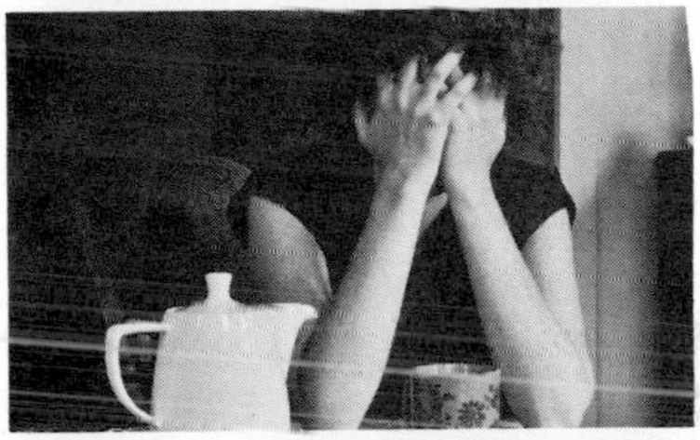
Adaptor	Any movement or gesture that is displayed to alleviate psychological tension. Adaptors include biting our nails, wringing our hands, and hiding our face.	

data available in the silhouettes of people who are paying no attention to you, it is reasonable to suppose that other people can draw such inferences about you from the way you present your body, too.[20]

Imagine again the people on the beach. Suppose that one woman leans forward toward a man. She allows herself to brush against him as she smiles into his face. He turns to face her, about eighteen inches apart, and smiles. He touches her eyebrow with his index finger and traces the line of her nose down to her mouth. She nibbles, then kisses, his finger. They clasp hands and amble down the beach, bumping and brushing into each other as they go. Shortly they stop and face each other again, now holding both hands.

These postural and touching cues suggest that these two individuals are nurturing a relationship. They apparently are attracted to each other. Each welcomes the other's proximity and touching behavior. To each other and to you, they have communicated an enormous amount of information. You and they could interpret the behaviors because each of you understands the norms of such behavior in the American culture. Such behavior is called *immediacy behavior,* one of two categories of behavior by which postural and other gross body cues can communicate attitudes, style, status, and emotions. The other category is *relaxation,*[21] which deals with the degree, or extent, to which you are agitated or excited.

If you lean toward someone, smile, reach out, and open yourself to that person, you are expressing immediacy. If you lean away, pull back, withdraw from touch, and never touch; if you frown, glance away, avoid eye contact, and keep your distance, you are also expressing a dimension of immediacy. Thus, immediacy behavior exists along a continuum in context with degrees of relaxation. Don't be confused; the terms are not opposites. Immediacy exists in degrees. Nonverbal behavior that decreases or increases the closeness between us and another, or that inhibits or improves visibility between us and another is an important means of relationship communication.

We observe these behaviors and base our guesses about the components of our relationships upon them. Unfortunately, we rarely talk about them. Instead, we believe that we "know" what they "mean." So we tend to fall into the dangerous habit of pretending that we can read others' minds by looking at their behavior.

Face and Eye Behavior

Just as gross body control and movement can communicate, so can particular body cues, such as face and eye behavior. Indeed, the face and eyes are probably the most powerful generators of nonverbal messages. So powerful are they that for centuries, they have been the subject of poetry and song, and the cause of very dramatic interpersonal and international episodes.

Research shows that women engage in more eye contact than men,[22] and that eye contact has both positive and negative aspects. We demand public speakers to establish and maintain eye contact with the audience. We learn early in life that it is not polite to stare,[23] and we especially dislike being stared at when the other person's eyes can not be seen.[24] Eye contact is important in regulating our conversations, especially turn-taking.[25]

Studies have shown that even pupil size can send an important non-verbal message.[26] Larger pupils are perceived as more attractive, so much so that photographers often attempt to enlarge the pupils of their models.[27] There even appears to be a correlation between pupil size and lying.[28] The act of lying actually causes fluctuations in pupil size. Conjuring up the lie is accompanied by smaller pupil diameter. Actually telling the lie appears to increase pupil size.[29]

Even eye direction communicates. Gur and Gur[30] wanted to know if there was a relationship between eye direction and defensive mechanisms. They discovered that people who tend to look to the right also tend to project and turn against others as a defense mechanism, whereas those who tend to look to the left also tend to repress and deny things as a defense mechanism.

Clearly, face and eye behavior does communicate. But this behavior tends to be so subtle and habitual that we have a very difficult time controlling it. Even so, it bears directly on your relationships. To make our important point again, if you feel that you are in trouble in a relationship, or if you become aware of some facial or eye behavior that seems significant, be willing to talk about it. Ask about it. Check your inferences against the actual experiences of the other person. Otherwise you risk acting on a guess that may very well be wrong.

People sometimes manage facial expressions to *neutralize* or *mask* emotions. You neutralize a facial expression of emotion when you try to eliminate it altogether. Perhaps you have heard of someone displaying a "poker face." This expression refers to the generally accepted wisdom that, if you are playing cards, you should maintain rigid control of the facial and eye muscles to avoid telegraphing your hand.

Similarly, in American culture, growing up male means, among other things, that it is not acceptable to express your strongest emotions— especially sentimental ones—with your face and eyes. Because of this, many young men have been embarrassed because they were moved to tears by a scene in a movie. The embarrassment undoubtedly arises from a conflict between experiencing and displaying an emotion. Men are not supposed to display visual expressions of fear and sadness except under extreme circumstances because these are considered feminine emotions.

Neutralizing emotions can be very risky and dangerous. Your entire nervous system could be damaged if you train yourself not to accept and express such emotions as fear and sadness.

Emotions are masked when you attempt to present a facial expression that is different from your experience. People often try to conceal strong or socially unacceptable feelings. For example, even though you may be feeling enraged, you will surely try to mask that emotion in public since it is unacceptable in most companies to "make a scene." And an employee would surely be unwilling to display public disapproval of the boss's decision, although a conference might be held in private.

Controlling Face and Eye Behavior

Interestingly, the range of emotions your eyes and face are capable of expressing is very great, but your ability to control and manage such expressions is limited. When you are being fluent—when you are thinking about your ideas or emotions, but not your facial muscles—your facial expressions may not be under conscious control. When you are trying to manage the impressions you are making, you tend to use one of a very limited number of techniques for controlling facial and eye behavior.[31]

Sometimes we manage facial expressions *to intensify or minimize* the emotion we are experiencing. Can you remember attending a surprise party, perhaps one thrown in your honor? Was the guest of honor truly surprised? Or was the guest of honor intensifying the emotion? How do you know? *Intensifying,* in this sense, is nothing more than doing what is expected for the purpose of pleasing friends and maintaining relationships with them. If a friend tries to surprise us and we like her, we will register surprise with a facial expression (or, at least, will try to do so), whether or not we are truly surprised. If a friend is experiencing sorrow, we will register our empathy in a facial expression because we care about him and about our relationship with him. If we reveal our emotions to someone, and it seems appropriate or necessary in that context for this person to reinforce our emotions, this will be done so by intensifying.

But, of course, there are times when a facial expression of emotion is unwarranted and unacceptable. We then try to minimize our facial expression. Everyone does this. For example, we have performed well on an exam. But, knowing that our friend did poorly, we make an attempt to control our natural sense of excitement.

In all of this work, researchers have only been able to put together a general taxonomy that will allow accurate understanding of the general and particular body cues as they occur in context with each other. Still, we do know that they are important in our day-to-day conversations and especially in our important relationships. Since our grasp of these nonverbal messages is tenuous, it is important to remember that *we cannot read another individual's mind.* If we observe nonverbal messages and then assume that we know what they mean, we may well be doing just that—pretending to read the other person's mind. It is far better to talk about what we have observed and to tell the other individual what we are guessing, for this allows our partner to confirm or deny our inferences. Our relationship then will be better able to grow.

Researchers have only been able to put together a general taxonomy of body cues. We must thus learn to talk about the inferences we draw from nonverbal messages.

Using Nonverbal Skills Effectively

The ideas presented above about our nonverbal body messages strongly argue for some common sense and care in our interactions with other people. Try to dress appropriately and conservatively. In addition, research the dress expectations that people are likely to have. All that is required is a phone call, visit, or direct observation.

Recall that nonverbal communication is two-way, and that both we and the other people in our relationships send off and receive messages on purpose and by accident. As a receiver we should try to become more aware of our own biases and receiving behavior habits. Are we responding to some behavior of our partner that has no message value? That is, are we responding to some unintentional behavior that really does not reflect how that person is actually thinking and feeling? Or are we assigning meaning based on our own standards and assumptions? For example, our personal dress code may cause us to believe that a person means one thing by his clothing when he actually does not.

Try to become more sensitive to your use and interpretation of others' body movements and gestures. At the first moment that you feel confusion or uncertainty about someone's intention, ask about that intention. Say, for example, "I'm aware that you just pulled away, but I'm not sure why. Will you tell me?" The person may be able to help you understand the behavior. Sometimes, however, she may not know why she pulled away. Even when this is the case, talking about the behavior can make the initiator aware of it. Remember to listen carefully to what the other person says, to inquire about her interpretation without defensiveness, and to accept or explain yourself calmly.

Remember also that the face is an important indicator of emotions and feelings. It is also a method of nonverbal expression that is difficult to control. Try to remember to smile when it is appropriate to do so. Smiling and raising the eyebrows are positive, responsive behaviors that are generally encouraging. Of course, if the subject is a very serious one, smiling too much may be an inappropriate response. Also remember to look—not stare—at your partners during conversation. Try to focus your gaze at the speaker. Lack of eye contact often suggests lack of interest, a message that may be far from the one you wish to send.

Think also in terms of what the image you wish to project may mean about your face and eye behavior. Think, too, about your assumptions as you perceive the other person's face and eye behavior. More careful attention to these subtle cues can contribute to your success in managing your relationship.

Especially in important and tense moments, slow things down, and bring your observations and inferences to the level of talk. If you are responding to another's eye shifts, that person may need to know that—especially if these messages are unintentional. If the other person is responding to some facial mannerism of yours, you need to be aware of that. Candor and direct talk are the best means of remedying a misunderstanding. Practice the skills of talking about relationships. Practice the skills of active listening. In times of conflict, slow down, calm down, and work hard to get and give feedback often.

Summary

Messages that we send with our body are directly related to our effectiveness in relationships. Our clothing, artifacts, and body movement and gestures all convey information about us. Especially significant in relationships, facial and eye behavior communicates our intentions and feelings. People even use pupil size as a measure of interpersonal attractiveness.

Since we cannot read another person's mind, the inferences we draw from someone's body messages may be in error. Further, our own bodily messages may be inconsistent with our words. These facts argue strongly for learning to talk about our observations and the inferences based on them so that errors can be corrected. Similarly, it is important to learn to solicit feedback about how other people are interpreting our body communication.

Discussion Questions

1. What are some of the general body cues that you and others in your classroom are using right now? Working with one or two classmates, try to identify what messages are being sent, either intentionally or unintentionally. List them under the headings: "clothing," "artifacts," "body movement and gestures," and "face and eye behavior."
2. To what extent do you believe your images of others are based on nonverbal messages you are not aware of receiving? Describe instances in which your nonverbal behavior unintentionally influenced others. Compare and contrast these with those of your class members. What are the similarities and differences?
3. Is it possible to learn to control general and particular body cues as we interact with others? What would be the effect if the other person realized that you were trying to control your nonverbal messages?
4. Is it possible to learn to give and get feedback during a conversation? How might you help yourself and the other persons in a relationship (someone who has not had this course) increase both the quality and quantity of the feedback you give and receive?

Endnotes

1. M. L. Rosencranz, "Clothing Symbolism," *Journal of Home Economics* 54 (1962): 18–22.

2. L. Aiken, "Relationship of Dress to Selected Measures of Personality in Undergraduate Women," *Journal of Social Psychology* 59 (1963): 121.

3. Reported in L. B. Rosenfeld and T. G. Plax, "Clothing as Communication," *Journal of Communication* 27 (1977): 23–31.

4. J. Kelly, "Dress as Non-Verbal Communication," paper presented to the annual conference of the American Association for Public Opinion Research, May 1969, and cited in M. L. Hickson III and Don W. Stacks, *NVC: Nonverbal Communication Studies and Applications* (Dubuque, IA: Wm. C. Brown Publishers, 1985), 74.

5. W. Thourlby, *You Are What You Wear* (New York: New American Library, 1978), 1.

6. K. W. Watson and L. R. Smeltzer, "Perceptions of Nonverbal Communication During the Selection Interview," *The ABCA Bulletin* (June 1982): 30–34.

7. Hickson and Stacks, *NVC*, 77.

8. See J. T. Molloy, *Dress for Success* (New York: Warner Books, 1975); and Molloy, *The Woman's Dress for Success Book* (New York: Warner Books, 1978).

9. G. Thornton, "The Effects of Wearing Glasses upon Judgments and Persons Seen Briefly," *Journal of Applied Psychology* 28 (1944): 203–7.

10. P. N. Hamid, "Style of Dress as a Perceptual Cue in Impression Formation," *Perceptual and Motor Skills* 20 (1068): 904–6.

11. P. N. Hamid, "Some Effects of Dress Cues on Observational Accuracy, A Perceptual Estimate, and Impression Formation," *Journal of Social Psychology* 86 (1972): 279–89.

12. Ibid.

13. W. McKeachie, "Lipstick as a Determiner of First Impressions of Personality: An Experiment for the General Psychology Course," *Journal of Social Psychology* 36 (1952): 241–44.

14. Molloy, *Women's Dress for Success Book*, 85–86.

15. C. Rubenstein, "Body Language that Speaks to Muggers," *Psychology Today* (August 1980): 20.

16. R. L. Birdwhistle, *Kinesics and Context: Essays on Body Motion Communication* (Philadelphia: University of Pennsylvania Press, 1970).

17. J. Fast, *The Body Language of Sex, Power, and Aggression* (New York: M. Evans and Company, Inc., 1977).

18. P. Ekman and W. Friesen, "The Repertoire of Nonverbal Behavior: Categories, Origins, Usage, and Coding," *Semiotica* 1 (1969): 49–98.

19. M. Argyle, *Bodily Communication* (New York: International Universities Press, 1975).

20. We are assuming that the individuals in our examples and discussions are from the same culture. There is some evidence that both the culture and general body configuration of an individual influence how the body is used and posed and under what circumstances. For example, the ancient Romans ate lying down. This position must have seemed as comfortable to them as sitting at a table seems to us. Both are culture-bound examples of posture control.

21. See A. Mehrabian, "Inference of Attitudes from Posture, Orientation, and Distance of a Communicator," *Journal of Consulting and Clinical Psychology* 32 (1968): 296–308.

22. R. Exline, "Exploration in the Process of Person Perception: Visual Interaction in Relation to Competition, Sex, and the Need for Affiliation," *Journal of Personality* 31 (1963): 1–20.

23. N. M. Henley, *Body Politics: Power, Sex and Nonverbal Communication* (Englewood Cliffs, NJ: Prentice-Hall, Inc. 1972), 151.

24. Ibid., 152.

25. S. Duncan, "Some Signals and Rules for Taking Speaking Turns in Conversations," *Journal of Personality and Social Psychology* 23 (1972): 283–92.

26. For an excellent overview of this literature, see Hickson and Stacks, *NVC,* 104–6.

27. A. S. King, "The Eye in Advertising," *Journal of Applied Communication Research* 1 (1973): 1–12.

28. B. Ambler, "Information Reduction, Internal Transformation, and Task Difficulty," *Bulletin of Psychonomic Science* 10 (1977): 43–46.

29. I. Heilville, "Deception and Pupil Size," *Journal of Clinical Psychology* 32 (1976): 675–76.

30. R. Gur and R. Gur, "Defense Mechanisms, Psychosomatic Symptomatology and Conjugate Lateral Eye Movements," *Journal of Consulting and Clinical Psychology* 43 (1945): 416–20.

31. P. Eckman and W. V. Friesen, *Unmasking the Face* (Englewood Cliffs, NJ: Prentice-Hall, 1957).

Touching, Environmental Messages, Space, and Relational Effectiveness

Preview

Touching is extremely important to our relationships and our personal health. How and when we touch is a function of conscious choice. Beyond interpersonal contact, we are also affected by the environment. The size, arrangement, and treatment of space, including lighting, color, texture, and distance, can influence how we perceive and respond to other people and experience ourselves. Out of these raw materials we evolve our own territorial prerogatives and infer those of others. Even the angle of interaction and the personal distances we choose to put between ourselves and others can strongly affect our relationships.

Key Terms

angle of interaction
coactive
competitive
cooperative
cooptive
environmental cues
friendship/warmth touching
functional/professional touching
intimate distance
love/intimacy touching
personal distance
personal-causal distance
public distance
sexual/arousal touching
social-consultive distance
social/polite touching
space
territoriality
touching behavior

Objectives

1. Explain the importance of touching to physical health, and suggest the implications of this explanation for interpersonal relationship growth.
2. Describe Heslin's five categories of touching behavior.
3. Explain how perceived attractiveness and color can influence human interaction.
4. Define "territoriality," and review the four types of territories described by Lyman and Scott.
5. Review Sommer's and Cook's studies of the angle of interaction and suggest the significance of their research for your own relationship management.
6. Identify and explain Hall's categories of personal distancing and suggest their implications for your own relationship management.

Touching Behavior

There is little doubt that everyone needs and wants physical contact with others. If someone is deprived of this contact, the deprivation can be damaging. As you mature, much of what you know about conducting your affairs and managing your relationships is a function of the touching behavior you have experienced. Each of these statements has been developed and supported by research. But what do they mean to you, as a student of interpersonal communication?

Touching behavior is generally completely a matter of choice. We can usually choose to touch or to withhold touch. We can choose to respond positively when touched or to withdraw from the touching. Our choices have a very powerful effect on ourselves and the others in our relationships. As you will see, touching can communicate strong messages about attitudes, developmental needs, body contact needs, status, and images about the relationship with the person touched. Touching even has a direct bearing on our personal health and growth.

How does touch affect your relationships?

To illustrate the potency of interpersonal touch—and of touch deprivation—we can turn to a very large literature. For example, in 1972, Ashley Montagu published a study involving 173 breast-fed and nonbreast-fed children. Children who had not been breast-fed had four times the number of respiratory infections, twenty times more diarrhea, eight times as much eczema, more hay fever, more asthma, and more of a variety of other diseases than did the breast-fed children.[1] Although it is likely that other factors contributed to these problems, Montagu concluded that touch was in part responsible. He strengthened his argument by citing cases in which adults suffering from a variety of psychological problems were successfully treated by therapy that employed extensive physical contact. Tactile deprivation has also been shown to be a causal factor in problems involving speech, symbol recognition, and lack of trust and confidence.[2]

Some very dramatic findings in research with animals have also shown the powerful effects of touch deprivation. A very famous early study was published in 1958 by Harry Harlow and R. R. Zimmermann.[3] Laboratory-raised baby monkeys had become so attached to the cloth pads in their cages that they threw temper tantrums when the researchers attempted to replace the pads. So Harlow built a terry-cloth surrogate mother with a light bulb inside to radiate "body heat." He built a second surrogate mother of wire mesh. These "mothers" were placed in cubicles next to the infant monkey's cage. In half the cases the wire mother provided milk, but the terry-cloth mother did not; in the other half, the terry-cloth mother provided milk, but the wire mother did not. The baby monkeys were allowed to spend time with the mothers on demand, for as long as they wished. The finding was that the infant monkeys spent dramatically more time with the terry-cloth mother, whether or not the mother provided milk. This conclusion makes a powerful statement about touching.

Touching is the first form of communication that an infant knows and is an important aspect of communication throughout life.[4] Among adults, most touching conveys some greeting or symbolic gesture, which differs from culture to culture.[5] For example, psychologist Sidney Jourard found striking differences in the number of body contacts per hour from society to society. He studied touching behavior in cafés in San Juan, Puerto Rico, in Paris, in Gainesville, Florida, and in London. The Puerto Ricans were the most frequent touchers, with up to 180 contacts in an hour. The French touched each other 110 times per hour. The Americans, in contrast, were not very frequent touchers. Jourard counted only 2 contacts per hour in the Gainesville café. But the British were the most reserved. Jourard did not record a single case of physical touching in the London café.[6]

Richard Heslin and his colleagues have been studying touching behavior for ten years, and have developed a category system that conveniently organizes the discussion of such behavior.[7] (The category system is Heslin's; we provided the definitions and examples presented in this table.) Of course, we

Table 16.1 Heslin's Categories for Touching Behavior

Category	Definition	Example
Functional/professional	Touching that delivers some professional service	Example relationships: physician/patient; barber/client; swimming instructor/student; make-up artist/actor
Social/polite touching	Ritual touching that acknowledges someone's personhood or essential humanity, and/or acknowledges or neutralizes status differences	Examples: handshake, the kiss on the hand, the kiss on a cardinal's ring; ritual greeting hugs
Friendship/warmth touching	Casual and spontaneous touching that signals mutual acceptance and positive regard, but excluding love or sexual touching	Examples: asexual greeting hugs or kisses among friends or family; congratulatory shoulder- or back-patting; mock-violent behavior such as the playful shoulder punch
Love/intimacy touching	Touching behavior that signals a special, or bonded, relationship, or that assumes or confirms intimate access to be appropriate to that relationship	Examples: hand holding, whether the couple is stationary or moving; mutual hand-on-hip postures; lap-sitting
Sexual/arousal touching	Touching that conveys sexual meaning or produces sexual stimulation	Examples: prolonged kissing; petting; sexual foreplay; sexual intercourse

would add the category of *antisocial touching:* touching that violates a person's sense of propriety. Examples here would be unwelcomed sexual advances or a punch in the nose.

While this system is convenient, it cannot be very comfortably used to identify distinct sets of behaviors because communication events always occur within some context. It is the individual communicator's understanding of the context and the relationship within that context that govern the judgment about the appropriateness or inappropriateness of a touch. Moreover, touching behavior can rarely be isolated in just one category. Human relationships are more complex than this. Thus, two simple but very powerful conclusions can be drawn:

1. Touching behavior suggests a bond between the people who touch and are touched.
2. People respond to touching behavior according to their estimate of its appropriateness within that relationship and within that context.

Based upon these conclusions, it is reasonable to point out, once again, that a person who is concerned about improving interpersonal communication must become sensitive to human touching behavior and to the cues that people send about their estimates of touching appropriateness. We will undoubtedly feel tense and uncomfortable in response to touching that seems inappropriate in its context. However, we only *infer* what the other person means by the touch unless we are willing and able to talk about the experience when it seems fitting to do so.

Touch only *suggests* a relationship—a bond—between the toucher and the touched. It does not explicitly tell us what only the other person can about her feelings, wants and expectations, intentions, latitude of acceptance, and the images of us, herself, and the context. If we want to know these things and want the other person to know these things about us, we must bring them up to the level of talk.

Environmental Cues

Can you imagine yourself in the environment pictured in figure 16.1? You could probably draw many inferences about the people who occupy this space—about their personalities, relative socioeconomic status, and style of life. You can also get a good sense of your own ability to be comfortable in such an environment from the *environmental cues:* light and color, sound control, the physical layout, decor, and dimensions. Where would you be most likely to sit if you were a visitor in this space? Where would you be likely to sit if you were in the room by yourself for a fairly long time? Would these seating decisions change if you owned this space? Would you rearrange the furniture? What image do you have of the status, warmth, stability, and privacy of the individuals who

Figure 16.1

own this space? Are they friendly? personable? formal? casual? Do they have social clout?

Now look at the environment shown in figure 16.2. Would you find yourself comfortable in these rooms? Do you find the textures and the layout appealing? What about the light and shadow—do they contribute to the way you feel about this space? What can you infer about the people who own the space?

The use, arrangement, and the treatments of space communicate a great deal about you. Indeed, there is a large and growing body of research collected from a broad variety of academic disciplines that focuses upon the impact of environmental factors upon the human condition and upon the transformation of spaces into reflections of the self.

We judge that a space is somewhere along a continuum from attractive to ugly. This judgment tends to generalize to all our related experiences. So, for example, if someone were put into a truly ugly room, the individual would be more likely to make negative judgments about the individuals whose photographs he viewed while in the room than he would if the experiment were

Figure 16.2

conducted in a beautiful room.[8] Similarly, color, texture, lighting, and decoration effects can all make an important difference on those people who occupy space and upon their perceptions of each other.

For example, colors are often termed "warm" or "cool" and are very carefully used to suggest such feelings as affection, vitality, calm, cheerfulness, sadness, or anxiety. Beyond this hesitation, you pick up on the moods that colors generate. Thus, if you paint your workroom with bright red and yellow hues, before long you would find that your mood improved, but later became somewhat disturbed. You would likely be more productive and energetic in such a room than in one having walls painted in deep shades of blue and violet, a black floor and ceiling, and black velvet tapestry hangings.

A. H. Maslow and N. L. Mintz were interested in the attractiveness of space and its impact on human behavior when they conducted their now classic study of the impact of three different rooms.[9] The three rooms included a "beautiful" room, an "average" room (a professor's office), and an "ugly" room. For this latter room they simulated a janitor's storeroom.

People were placed in one of these rooms and asked to judge and rate the negatives of photographs of faces. The photographs were rated higher in the ''beautiful'' room. Both the experimenters and the respondents reported that they were more fatigued in and more eager to escape the ''ugly'' room.

Kitchens and others[10] studied the influence of the aesthetics of rooms by using live communicators rather than photographs. They developed an ''unattractive'' room with dull green walls, unshaded light bulbs, paint-splattered furniture, and a green couch with a broken leg and torn cushions. Their ''attractive'' room was freshly painted and decorated by a professional interior designer. A regular classroom was used as a control to measure the impact of the ''unattractive'' and ''attractive'' environments. Their results were very much like those of Maslow and Mintz.

Color is another aspect of aesthetics that has been studied. Wexner[11] and then Burgoon and Saine[12] attempted to relate color to certain moods and meanings. You can use table 16.2 as a reference in selecting color schemes that will have the effect on mood that you wish!

Table 16.2 Color in the Environment: Moods Created and Symbolic Messages

Color	Moods	Symbolic Meanings
Red	Hot, affectionate, angry, defiant, contrary, hostile, full of vitality, calm, tender	Happiness, lust, intimacy, love, restlessness, agitation, royalty, rage, sin, blood
Blue	Cool, pleasant, leisurely, distant, infinite, secure, transcendent, calm, tender	Dignity, sadness, tenderness, truth
Yellow	Unpleasant, exciting, hostile, cheerful, joyful, jovial	Superficial glamor, sun, light, wisdom, masculinity, royalty (in China), age (in Greece), prostitution (in Italy), famine (in Egypt)
Orange	Unpleasant, exciting, disturbed, distressed, upset, defiant, contrary, hostile, stimulating	Sun, fruitfulness, harvest, thoughtfulness
Purple	Depressed, sad, dignified, stately	Wisdom, victory, pomp, wealth, humility, tragedy
Green	Cool, pleasant, leisurely, in control	Security, peace, jealousy, hate, aggressiveness, calm
Black	Sad, intense, anxiety, fear, despondent, dejected, melancholy, unhappy	Darkness, power, mastery, protection, decay, mystery, wisdom, death, atonement
Brown	Sad, not tender, despondent, dejected, melancholy, unhappy	Melancholy, protection, autumn, decay, humility, atonement
White	Joy, lightness, neutral, cold	Solemnity, purity, femininity, humility, joy, light, innocence, fidelity, cowardice

Source: J. K. Burgoon and T. J. Saine, *The Unspoken Dialogue: An Introduction to Nonverbal Communication* (Boston: Houghton Mifflin, 1978), 110. Reprinted with permission.

Now look again at figure 16.1. Notice how its designers contrasted light and dark. The room seems pleasant, calm, and relaxing. It is dignified but welcoming. What feeling do you get from figure 16.2?

Space

People use *space* in a direct way. For example, there is some evidence that human beings are territorial creatures, and that the person-to-space ratio, or *density,* has an important bearing on interpersonal perception and communication. In addition, there appears to be a fairly well-tuned set of cultural norms about the appropriate interpersonal distance that guides individuals in their actions with others. Even the angle of interaction appears to be related to the quality and amount of interaction. Obviously, then, the dimensions of space can operate as communication.

Territoriality

If we "own" space, it gives us a number of behavioral prerogatives that another individual cannot assume with that space. *Territoriality* is this tendency for individuals to claim and "own" space, and then use it as an extension of their own personal space. Perhaps you have noticed that at the beginning of a new term, you and other students select the desk or chair in which you will sit and then "claim" that space. We have noticed that our students sometimes will develop such a solid claim on a chair that other students begin to refer to it as "Tim's" or "Elizabeth's chair." We have seen students express, both nonverbally and verbally, their irritation when, after a couple of weeks, someone else sits in a chair that they had claimed.

After a person has staked out, claimed, and begun to own a territory, that claim is very precisely defined—but not only by the individual. It is also defined by the culture. The amount of space that any individual can "own" in this fashion varies from culture to culture.

Finally, it appears that the amount of space anyone can legitimately "own" is dependent upon cultural status. To illustrate, a secretary in the trust department of a local bank "owns" her desk and chair. She also "owns" the typewriter at her desk. But her desk and chair are placed in a large room with similar desks and chairs. This room also provides corridor space through which the trust officers and clients pass to get to the officers' enclosed spaces. The head of the department also "owns" space. His office is in the corner of the building and is about three times the size of any of the trust officers' smaller cubicles. Thus depending upon their status, these people own differing amounts of space.

But what does this phenomenon of territoriality have to do with interpersonal communication? In superior-subordinate relationships, such as those between physician and patients, boss and employees, judge and citizens, professor and students, and dean and professors, territoriality can work to the advantage or disadvantage of each participant, depending upon the goals each has for the interaction.

The territoriality issues that bear directly on relationships evolve out of a complex mix of context and norm. That is, we have learned to occupy the same established spaces according to a powerful, but usually unspoken, set of rules and assumptions. To violate them would be to impose oneself on another and perhaps to risk the relationship.

Lyman and Scott believe that there are four types of territories, which they base on accessibility.[13] *Public territory* is an area that individuals may enter freely. Parks and public playgrounds are both examples of such space, as are certain parts of government buildings, the lobby of a public library, and the common area of a shopping mall. About the only rule for using public territory is that you have a legitimate purpose.

The second category in the Lyman and Scott model is *interactional space.* This territory is mobile. When and where people congregate informally, as well as the consent of the people, mark its boundaries. The boundaries may be larger or smaller and more or less irregular depending upon the people, the context, and the nature of their interrelationships. For example, you and your friends may go to a restaurant to have lunch and to enjoy each other's conversations. The interactional territory will depend in part on the number of people in the group. If the restaurant has only tables and chairs and if the tables all have four chairs, you might very well decide to draw a second table to the first, thus establishing an interactional territory of a different shape and size than the planned seating arrangement in the restaurant. Similarly, your group may decide to stand on a sidewalk waiting for the restaurant to open for lunch. As you stand there, the group's nature, size, loudness, power relationships, and the like, will define a space that you will temporarily "own." To experiment with this kind of interactional territory, imagine what would happen if some stranger walked up to your group and stood within its boundaries!

Lyman and Scott's third classification is *home territory.* This is the private space that you occupy with legal sanction, such as your house or apartment. Outsiders must gain permission to enter home territory, or else they are in violation of law. In some cases, the law is so strongly written that the owner of home territory may legally shoot and kill an intruder who is forcibly entering.

The last category in the Lyman and Scott system is *body territory,* or *personal space*—the area immediately surrounding your physical person. It changes size and shape depending upon the nature of your relationships with others and the context. For example, a close relative may actually touch and kiss you, but only within certain unwritten rules and limitations. A close friend may have different prerogatives for entering your body space.

We are bound by the rules and assumptions that govern the use of space, and we must discover ways to communicate about them.

Within each of these categories of territory, we are bound by the rules and assumptions that constantly shift and change according to such variables as the overall size of the space, the number of people, the nature of their relationships, and the clothing they are wearing. We must navigate through these various territories within the rules that are operating or risk our relationships. And, since those rules are entirely in the minds of the people applying them, we often make mistakes. Clearly, a concept such as territoriality can have an important bearing on the success of a relationship. For relationships to grow, people must find a way to communicate about the rules and assumptions they are applying.

Angle of Interaction

Robert Sommer[14] has attempted to relate people's seating choices, or *angle of interaction,* to their perceptions of each other and of the situation. He was especially interested in whether the two-person subject groups of his study would perceive themselves as cooperating, competing, and coacting. Sommer asked people to report how they would seat themselves under the circumstances he wanted to study. His findings were replicated by Mark Cook in the United Kingdom. Their findings are very useful (fig. 16.3 and tables 16.3 and 16.4).

When Sommer asked his subjects to show how they would locate themselves if they were going to compete with each other, they typically took positions opposite each other. The large majority preferred *competitive* positions across a table, face-to-face.

When he asked the subjects to seat themselves in a *cooperative* situation, he found that they assumed closer positions. One of the most common seating choices for this situation was diagonal seating across the corner of the table. Such an arrangement provides some security (the corner of the table intervenes between the participants) while at the same time allows them to make close visual and tactile contact. They can work with each other at more intimate distances. This position also permits the individuals to exchange personal and intimate information while maintaining their integrity and dignity, and without violating the personal and private space of the other.

Sommer next asked his subjects to show where they would sit if they were in a situation in which they were working on the same task and trying to show mutual support. He called this arrangement *cooptive.* Most agreed that they would sit side-by-side. This allows the participants to work together, to touch, to maintain personal distances, or choose intimate distances. And at the same time, the position makes it possible for one subject to control—or

Figure 16.3 The Four Most Popular Seating Arrangements (Sommer)

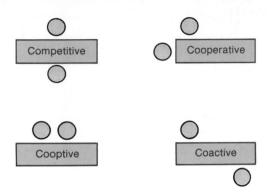

"co-opt"—the other. Interestingly, his subjects also found this position to be fairly satisfying for cooperation.

Finally, Sommer wanted to know where his subjects would sit if they wanted to work privately but on essentially the same task, so they could make contact and exchange views only now and again. In what he called the *coactive* position, the subjects chose to arrange themselves as far away from each other as they could at the table.

Recall that nonverbal communication can be related to the person's culture. Sommer's study was repeated with British subjects by Mark Cook,[15] who found some differences between the American and British arrangements. Tables 16.3 and 16.4 show Cook's findings.

Personal Distancing

The angle of interaction is closely related to the patterns of *personal distances* of a culture. Personal space is used as a communication medium. Special space around you is reserved as private, and you do not let many people invade this private space.

You may have felt uncomfortable when someone came too close to you. At other times, you were very pleased to have people get so close that actual contact was made. Thus, the private bubble of space is very flexible, shrinking and expanding according to your relationships. The prominent anthropologist Edward T. Hall[16] explored this use of private and personal space. He discovered that most Americans have what he called *intimate distance,* which extends from their skin to about eighteen inches. People reserve intimate distances for very close relationships or for telling secrets.

Table 16.3 Seating Preferences at Rectangular Tables (Cook)

	1	2	3	4	5	6
Conversation						
U.S. sample (151 responses)	42%	46%	11%	0%	1%	0%
U.K. (univ.) sample (102 responses)	51	21	15	0	6	7
U.K. (nonuniv.) sample (42 responses)	42	42	9	2	5	0
Cooperation						
U.S. sample	19	25	51	0	5	0
U.K. (univ.) sample	11	11	23	20	22	13
U.K. (nonuniv.) sample	40	2	50	5	2	0
Coaction						
U.S. sample	3	3	7	13	43	33
U.K. (univ.) sample	9	8	10	31	28	14
U.K. (nonuniv.) sample	12	14	12	19	31	12
Competition						
U.S. sample	7	41	8	18	20	5
U.K (univ.) sample	7	10	10	50	16	7
U.K. (nonuniv.) sample	4	13	3	53	20	7

Source: M. Cook, "Experimentation on Orientation and Proxemics," *Human Relations* 1970, Vol. 23, pp. 61–76.

For normal, informal conversations Americans use what Hall called *personal-causal distance,* or from about eighteen inches to about four feet from the skin. However, business transactions and less personal business are conducted at a distance from four feet to about twelve feet, which Hall termed *social-consultive distance.* The closer ranges in this bracket are typically used to present a more personal image in formal or business situations. The more distant space is typically used to keep people of lower power at a distance. If you went to a professor's office, for example, you might find that she has placed her desk between herself and her visitors.

Hall also identified a *public distance,* which extends from about twelve to about twenty-five feet in the near phase, and beyond twenty-five feet in the far phase. This distance characterizes public address and other communication situations outside of buildings. Figure 16.4 illustrates Hall's categories for the use of space.

If you study the figures and apply the research, you will discover that you can use the information to help you attain your goals. Occasions in which seating arrangements and standing distance can be important include:

Table 16.4 Seating Preferences at Round Tables (Cook)

	x x ⊙	x ⊙	⊙ x
Conversation			
U.S. sample			
(116 responses)	63%	17%	20%
U.K. (univ.) sample			
(102 responses)	58	37	5
U.K. (nonuniv.) sample			
(42 responses)	58	27	15
Cooperation			
U.S. sample	83	7	10
U.K. (univ.) sample	25	31	44
U.K. (nonuniv.) sample	97	0	3
Coaction			
U.S. sample	13	36	51
U.K. (univ.) sample	16	34	50
U.K. (nonuniv.) sample	24	26	50
Competition			
U.S. sample	2	25	63
U.K. (univ.) sample	15	22	63
U.K. (nonuniv.) sample	9	21	70

Source: M. Cook, "Experimentation on Orientation and Proxemics," *Human Relations* 1970, Vol. 23, pp. 61–76.

a business luncheon

a dinner date

a one-to-one conference with a superior on a joint task

a one-to-one conference with a colleague on the division of tasks on a joint project

a one-to-one conference with a subordinate in which you are assigning an important task

an informal social gathering

an employment interview

an appraisal interview about your work performance

an appraisal interview about your employee's working performance

Summary

Touching and the use and treatment of space can have an important effect on our perceptions of other people and of ourselves and on how others perceive and interact with us. These matters are thus directly related to interpersonal effectiveness.

Figure 16.4 Hall's Categories for the Use of Space in American Culture

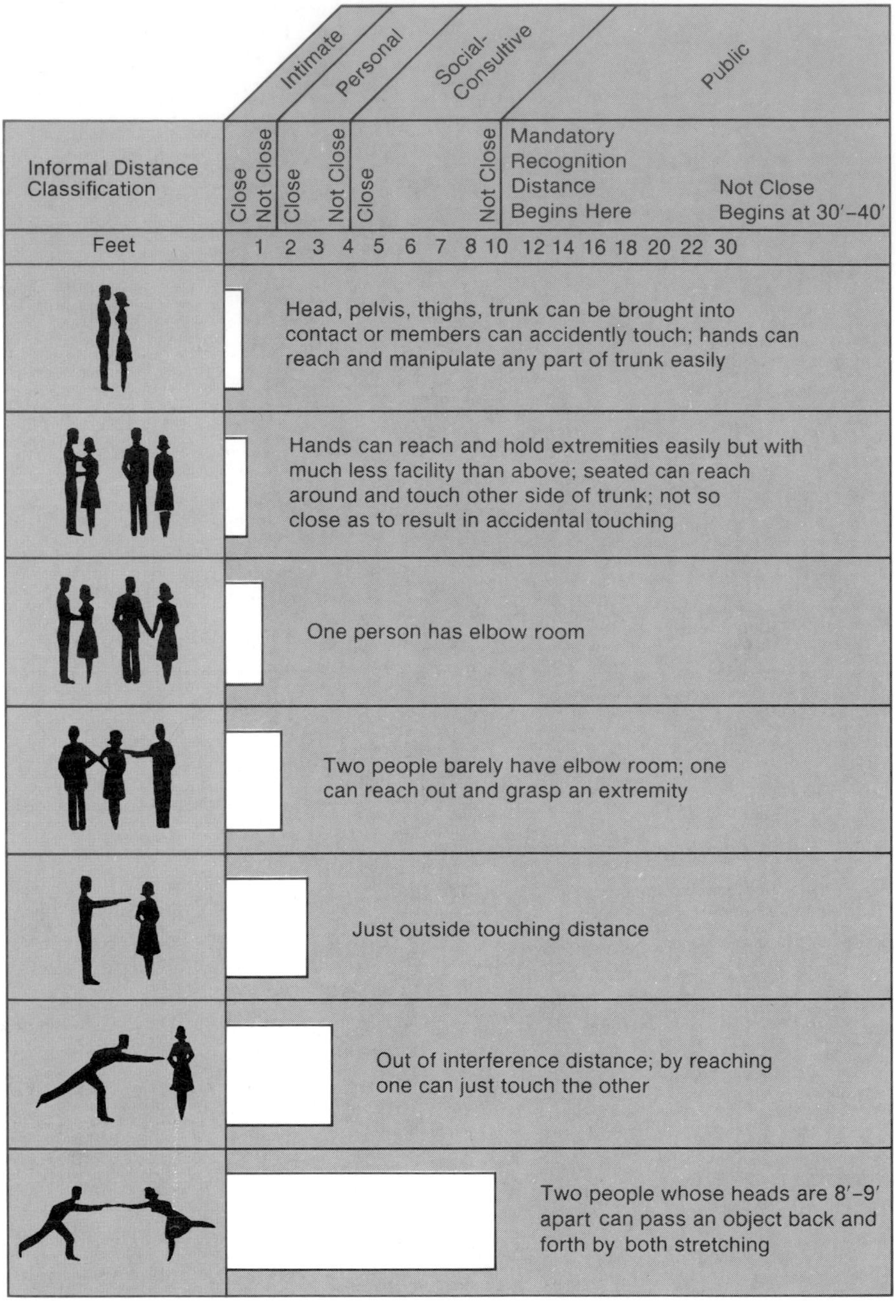

Informal Distance Classification	Intimate — Close	Intimate — Not Close	Personal — Close	Personal — Not Close	Personal — Close	Social-Consultive — Not Close	Mandatory Recognition Distance Begins Here	Public — Not Close Begins at 30′–40′
Feet	1	2 3	4	5 6 7	8 10	12 14 16 18 20 22 30		
		Head, pelvis, thighs, trunk can be brought into contact or members can accidently touch; hands can reach and manipulate any part of trunk easily						
		Hands can reach and hold extremities easily but with much less facility than above; seated can reach around and touch other side of trunk; not so close as to result in accidental touching						
		One person has elbow room						
		Two people barely have elbow room; one can reach out and grasp an extremity						
		Just outside touching distance						
		Out of interference distance; by reaching one can just touch the other						
		Two people whose heads are 8′–9′ apart can pass an object back and forth by both stretching						

Our personal health, our sense of interpersonal attractiveness, our "ownership" of territory, and our understanding of appropriate distances are all a part of the nonverbal message system that we use to interpret another person's spoken language and interpretation of our own. These messages do not have to be left to chance, and our effectiveness in our relationships may depend upon a more conscious and intelligent selection of such communication.

Discussion Questions

1. Do you believe that touching is important to the health of people who are touched? Why or why not? Discuss touching in the context of your relationship with:

   a. your parents
   b. your brothers and sisters
   c. your closest same-sex friends
   d. your closest opposite-sex friends
   e. your relationships with powerful others, such as your professors, and your employers

   How is touching actually done in these relationships? Would you recommend any changes in your touching behavior or that of others?

2. Examine the room you are now in. With one or two classmates, try to discover the impact of each of the following environmental features on the interactions it was designed for.

   a. color
   b. texture
   c. light
   d. space
   e. artifacts and decoration
   f. furniture arrangement and style
   g. temperature
   h. sound control

3. Can you find any evidence of "territoriality" in the room you now occupy? On what basis do you draw your conclusions? Is there any evidence that the "territoriality" assumptions of the people in the room are affecting their interactions?

4. To what extent, if any, does Hall's system of interpersonal distance categories hold true in your own life or in the lives of one or two of your classmates? What are the implications, if any, of this informal research on your conscious use of distance in managing your relationships? In particular, discover any implications from your informal discussion on how you will use distance in relationship to your:

   a. parent
   b. sibling

    c. employer
    d. professor
    e. favorite aunt or uncle

Endnotes

1. A. Montagu, *Touching: The Human Significance of the Skin* (New York: Perennial Library, 1971), 82.
2. J. L. Despert, "Emotional Aspects of Speech and Language Development," *International Journal of Psychiatry and Neurology* 105 (1941): 193–222. See also J. Bowlby, *Maternal Care and Mental Health* (Geneva: W.H.O., 1961).
3. H. H. Harlow and R. R. Zimmermann, "The Development of Affectional Responses in Infant Monkeys," *Proceedings, American Philosophical Society* 102 (1958): 501–9.
4. D. Morris, *Intimate Behaviour* (New York: Random House, 1971), 31.
5. M. H. Krout, *Introduction to Social Psychology* (New York: Harper and Brothers, 1942).
6. S. M. Jourard, "An Exploratory Study of Body-Accessibility," *British Journal of Social and Clinical Psychology* 5 (1966): 221–31.
7. N. R. Heslin and T. Alper, "Touch: A Bonding Gesture," in *Nonverbal Interaction 2*, J. M. Wiemann and R. P. Harrison eds. (Beverly Hills, CA: Sage Publications, 1983), 47–75.
8. A. H. Maslow and N. L. Mintz, "Effects of Esthetic Surroundings: I. Initial Effects of Three Esthetic Conditions upon Perceiving Energy and Well-Being in Faces," *Journal of Psychology* 41 (1956): 247–54.
9. Ibid. See also N. L. Mintz, "Effects of Esthetic Surroundings: II. Prolonged and Repeated Experience in a 'Beautiful' and 'Ugly' Room," *Journal of Psychology* 41 (1956): 459–66.
10. J. T. Kitchens, T. P. Herron, R. R. Behnke, and M. J. Beatty, "Environmental Esthetics and Interpersonal Attraction," *Western Journal of Speech Communication* 41 (1977): 126–30.
11. L. B. Wexner, "The Degree to Which Colors (Hues) Are Associated with Mood-Tones," *Journal of Applied Psychology* 38 (1954): 432–35. See also D. C. Murray and H. L. Deabler, "Colors and Mood-Tones," *Journal of Applied Psychology* 41 (1957): 279–83.
12. J. K. Burgoon and T. J. Saine, *The Unspoken Dialogue: An Introduction to Nonverbal Communication* (Boston: Houghton Mifflin, 1978), 110.
13. S. M. Lyman and M. B. Scott, "Territoriality: A Neglected Sociological Dimension," *Social Problems* 15 (1967): 237–41.
14. R. Sommer, *Personal Space: The Behavioral Basis of Design* (Englewood Cliffs, NJ: Prentice-Hall, 1969).
15. M. Cook, "Experimentation on Orientation and Proxemics," *Human Relations* 23 (1970): 61–76.
16. E. T. Hall, *The Silent Language* (Garden City, NY: Doubleday, 1959).

>>I<< UNIT 17
Silence, Time, and Vocalics

Preview

Our use of silence, time, and a very complex system of vocalic cues constitutes an especially important nonverbal message system. We base our interpretations of our partner's feelings, wants, and intentions on it. Similarly, the other person in our relationship is continually comparing what we say against how we say it to infer our meaning.

Some of these nonverbal cues, such as what we mean by silence in our relationships, may be unique to an individual. Others are characteristic of our culture. For example, our culture understands time as a series of clicks, sixty to a minute, sixty to an hour. Others think of time differently. Clearly, the personal or cultural assumptions that we make—and that others make—about these matters can affect our relationships.

Key Terms

connotative
denotative
formal time
informal time
interactive silence
interpretation
maintaining
monochronic culture
polychronic culture
psycholinguistic silence
refusing
requesting
silence
sociocultural silence
time
turn-taking
yielding
vocalics

Objectives

1. Explain and provide examples of how silence can:
   a. convey the inadequacy of language
   b. link words and people
   c. enhance emotion
   d. persuade
2. Identify and describe Bruneau's three forms of silence.
3. Explain how time and how people use it can communicate important relational messages.
4. Compare and contrast a monochronic and a polychronic culture.
5. Explain the differences between formal and informal time, and suggest the importance of these differences to relationship management.
6. Identify and describe features of the vocalic message system, including some of the subcategories of vocalization and vocal quality.
7. Name at least nine types of interpretation that people draw from the vocalic message system.

Begin your study of this unit by playing a child's game. Here your task is to discover the "secret message" below by filling in a letter for each blank:

Non___ ___ ___b___ ___   m___ ___ ___ages
c___ ___ ___ ___ ___cate.*

How were you able to complete the statement? We think you did it easily because of the information carried in the spaces and blanks, in context with the letters.

Silence

The process you used to decipher the message is similar to the one you used to understand spoken words. The space between the words tells you a great deal about how to interpret them, for *silence* is the background upon which all spoken language is structured. Silence can exist without language, but language cannot exist without silence.[1] The sounds and the silence that surround language constitute an enormously complex set of nonverbal cues. We use silence to communicate threat or to show respect; to demonstrate the inadequacy of language and to enrich spoken messages;[2] to link words and people; to enhance emotion; to communicate judgments; and to spur people into action.[3]

What are you saying when you remain silent?

Silence can have both positive and negative impact on our relationships. For example, especially in early stages of a relationship, silences can be very embarrassing—so much so that the participants in an awkward silence will resort to such behaviors as coughing, throat clearing, singing, whistling, and drumming the fingertips, to mask the silence.[4] On the other hand, silence can actually communicate intimacy.[5]

To illustrate the complexity of this one phenomenon as a part of our communication system, Thomas Bruneau[6] identified three forms of silence that are important to communication. *Psycholinguistic silence* is the silence that is part of the temporal sequence of speech in encoding and decoding. *Interactive silence* is a pause, or interruption, in interpersonal interactions that are used for making decisions, drawing inferences, exercising control and power, and adjusting interpersonal distances between the talkers. *Sociocultural silence* includes cultural assumptions and such formally sanctioned silence as the silence

*Nonverbal messages communicate.

we observe in churches or has been imposed by some authority. This category also includes the silences that people in our society use for deliberate rhetorical or persuasive effect, such as the "silent treatment" that a teen-age girl sometimes applies to her boyfriend.

Rollo May pointed out that even infinitesimally small pauses can have enormous communicative significance. A pause is the "locus of the speaker's freedom," he says.[7] That is, the pause, whether short or long, that we fill with vocalizations allows us to stop to think or to listen to others, to "mold" our conversation this way or that, to tell a joke, or even to capture a new idea that is forming. By giving us the freedom to carry out a number of important communication activities, a pause thus helps us shape the uniqueness of a comment or a response, and consider and create the next utterance.

What does all this mean to us as we manage our relationships? It means, clearly, that we will do well to become much more sensitive to silences and that we must remember we cannot read another person's mind. *Silences carry important relational messages. Since we cannot read them we must learn to bring our interpretations of them up to the level of talk and to ask about them if they are troublesome.*

Time

Edward T. Hall was concerned about more than space-related messages (see unit 16). He also was very interested in *time* as a communication system, noting a number of cultural differences in the way people use time.[8] For instance, Hall described the Navajo Indians' belief that the time to start a ceremony is when all the necessary preparations are made. Such an understanding would defy the expectations of certain North American industrialists for whom time is money. Time is spent; time is made; time is bought and sold as a commodity in advertising; time is saved and managed. Time is never approached casually unless special rules of some subculture allow it.

For example, a group of people who clock their workday activities with great precision may go on a weekend canoe trip with the understanding that all watches and clocks must be left at home. "There's no time on the river," says one. This statement verbalizes the subcultural rule that gives the group permission not to manage time.

Occasionally, we run into an individual whose notions about time are quite different from ours. For most Americans, time runs itself out in a line of predictable measure: 60 seconds to a minute, 60 minutes to an hour, 24 hours to a day, 365 days to a year. "Time marches on." But for Cheryl, time stops! In her lexicon of time, the key is not the relentless ticking of a clock. For her, time is a process of preparations and completions. She begins a project, such as writing a term paper, and time stops until she has finished that task or some identifiable portion of that task. Time then resumes its cultural rhythm until she

five minutes before the appointed moment." He felt so strongly about this orientation that he would, for example, leave home at least an hour before an appointment just in case his car had a flat tire.

In contrast, his wife experienced time as process. For her, time was a series of activities connected by transitions. She might decide to bake a pie, for example, and then do it. While she was in the process of baking that pie, time did not click by. Rather, it stopped. It had no significance. When the pie was done, she could make a transition to the next activity.

These conflicting views of time created problems for the couple. He found it easy to criticize her because she was "always late" and "dawdled." She often criticized her husband because he was "so compulsive and uptight" and because he "never gives me time to do anything."

A young couple also reported having problems over time orientations. She was concerned about the future, and he was oriented to the present. She wanted to make plans for a family, careers, and the purchase of a house and a car. He preferred to stay in the present, to concentrate on his studies. "I'll get a job when it's time," he would say. "Right now I want to get an A on that exam tomorrow." "What good is the A if you don't know what you will do with your education?" she would ask. "Don't you have any ambitions or hopes or dreams? And don't they include me?" These differences in focus—present versus future—made communication and coordination difficult.

In sum, time talks.[12] We use time to manipulate others, to exercise power, to invest special meaning in our utterances, and to serve as a frame of reference through which we interpret other people's behaviors.

Vocalics

So far we have explored some of the body and environmental cues that can have an important impact upon interpersonal relationships. Even so, those messages-without-words have not received nearly as much study over the years as *vocalics*. Indeed, vocalics may constitute the most important nonverbal message system. Certainly it is vitally important for *what* we say cannot exist independent of *how* we say it, which is called *vocalics*. Variations in rate, pitch, and force and such particulars as how we articulate the suprasegmental elements of language are included in this category. Also included are our particular ways of phrasing and pausing. Figure 17.1 illustrates the complexity of this message system. The figure shows that features of vocalization and voice quality directly affect language interpretation and that these elements all work together to produce our unique vocal styles. Each variable is important to your interpersonal communication, and each is one that you can learn to control.

There is a massive body of literature related to vocalics, including the entire study of speech pathology and audiology, oral interpretation, and a good part of the actor's art.

Figure 17.1 The Complexity of Vocalics as a Nonverbal Message System

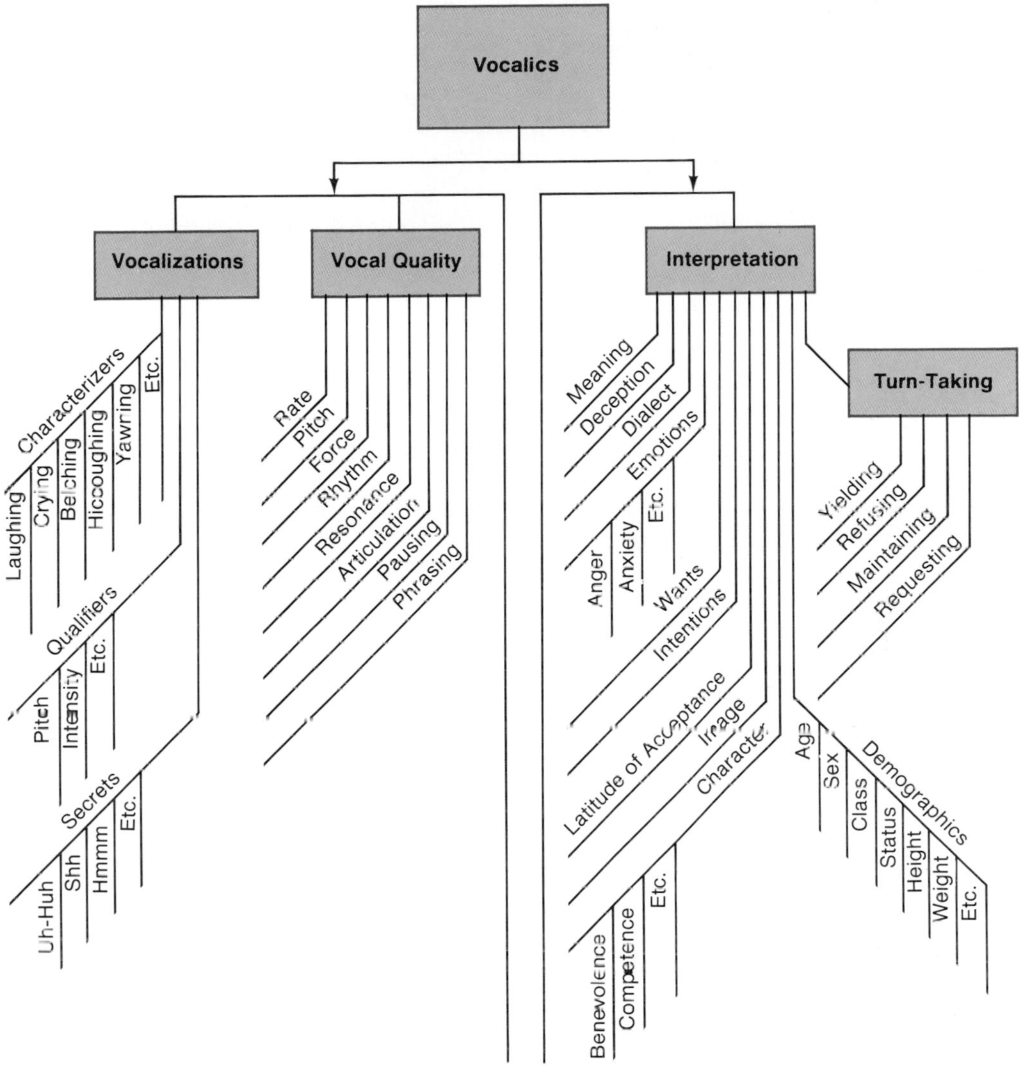

Vocal Quality and Vocalizations

Think of the range of interpretations possible from vocal quality. We suspect that you could expand figure 17.1 under the heading "interpretation" with a little thought and effort. Even so, we have suggested some of the more obvious possibilities. We determine that someone is lying, for example, partly by the

"tone of voice." We make guesses about her emotional state, wants and expectations, intentions, latitude of acceptance, character, and her image of us.
We can also tell the age and sex of that individual and something about her
social class and status by listening to her vocal quality and vocalizations. We
can even try to judge a person's height and weight based upon the sound of
her voice. But if we can make these guesses, so can she.

As mentioned before, guessing introduces the risk of error. If we act upon
our interpretations as though they were true, but they turn out to be wrong,
we may very well place our relationships at risk. That is why it is so important
to learn to be sensitive to our processing of the nonverbal messages we send
and receive and to learn to bring our observations and guesses up to the level
of talk when it seems appropriate. Since we cannot read another's mind, we
must be told what is happening.. Since our culture does not teach us to tell
each other these things, we use nonverbal message systems instead. But we
can choose and sometimes should discuss them.

Interpretation

Recall that meaning can be either *denotative* (the dictionary meaning), *connotative* (the personal meaning), or both. This lesson can be made more subtle
and more significant by saying that our understanding of the world *is* our world.
We live in a world of words, not of things. This lesson is important when considering a third variable: *interpretation*. Figure 17.1 shows that we interpret
vocalics cues as we make guesses about such things as character, emotion,
and deception. It is primarily by such cues that we learn to understand what
others are telling us, although these cues never exist in isolation from the other
nonverbal message systems. Was that sentence an insult? Did she intend her
sentence to be an invitation? Is she playing it cool? Or did she mean it when
she said she wasn't interested? Did Mother's "no" mean "no"? Or, did it mean
"maybe"?

How do vocalics affect a message? What does an insult sound like?

Turn-Taking

Another important variable is turn-taking. During a conversation, how do we
know when it is time for us to talk and when it is time for the other to talk? How
do we know whose turn it is when the talk turns into a fight or a squabble?
Could we be making judgments about others, and they about us, because of
turn-taking behavior?

You may know someone who sometimes seems rude. Perhaps this individual monopolizes the conversation; seems insensitive to your position in a
conflict; runs over your sentences with his own, and doesn't appear to know

how to put a period on his remarks. This individual is sometimes called a bore, and is rarely welcomed into groups. However, he could choose to change this situation merely by becoming sensitive to the turn-taking behavior of others and by learning to signal his interest in turns. As you see from figure 17.1, there are at least four categories of signals for taking turns in a conversation: *yielding, refusing, maintaining,* and *requesting.*

Applying Nonverbal Concepts to Relationships

Silence, time, and a complex set of paraverbal cues work together to provide the texture and color of spoken language. It is on these bases, primarily, that we know how to interpret the meaning of a sentence. What are the implications of these ideas for you in managing your relationships?

For a sender of messages, these ideas strongly argue for clarity in language choice, for directness in expressing feelings and wants, and for candor in responding to others. The solution to vagueness and uncertainty is clarity. But beyond this, you must become much more aware of the messages we send. Remember that you may be sending more messages unintentionally than you are sending on purpose. Take time to assure that your nonverbal messages are consistent with your intention and to ask for and to understand feedback from others.

For a receiver of messages, these ideas strongly argue for oral feedback. Become aware of the nonverbal messages you are picking up. Remember that

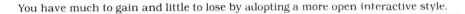

You have much to gain and little to lose by adopting a more open interactive style.

you are not consciously aware of many of the nonverbal cues you are interpreting. Again, the solution to vagueness and uncertainty is specificity and
clarity. Ask many questions about the other person's intentions and inferences.
Verify your own guesses about what the other person means. If you find yourself uncomfortable, bring that discomfort to light. Say, for example, "I'm uncomfortable, confused. And I'm frustrated by the apparent contradiction
between what you are saying and how you are saying it. Am I right to understand that you mean . . . ?"

Talk about your habitual uses of time, and your wants and intentions regarding your own and the other person's habitual uses of time. Set some ground
rules for your relationship by working through your assumptions with your
partner. You both need to know how to predict the other's thinking in this matter
so that you can identify a true deviation from expected behavior.

Encourage other people to give you feedback often about how they are
experiencing your talk. Set your natural defensiveness aside, even if the others
are not skillful in giving feedback. Listen carefully to what they say, and reward
them for being clear with you. You have much to gain and little to lose by
adopting a more open interactive style.

Especially when you are in conflict, try to slow and calm things down.
Both you and the other party will tend to exaggerate the nonverbal and vocalic
messages. You will talk louder and faster. You will undoubtedly change the
pitch and pause patterns of your normal speech. However, you can choose to
avoid this behavior.

First, express your intention to calm the situation. Do not hesitate to ask
for help in this matter from the other person and to try to work out an agreement
about how you will accomplish this important goal. One obvious way is to agree
to practice the skills of active listening—to paraphrase what the other is saying
and to talk about the inferences you are drawing from each other's nonverbal
and vocalic messages. Finally, keep in mind that there is always time to go
back and try again. You cannot reverse what happened yesterday, but you
certainly can talk about it and make new contracts for the future. These interpersonal contracts, after all, are the foundation of every healthy relationship.

Summary

How we use silence bears directly on our relationships. Bruneau identified three
kinds of silence: psycholinguistic, interactive, and sociocultural. Silence forms
one of the most important bases on which people draw inferences about their
relationships.

Silence is closely related to time and how we use time. Monochronic cultures use time in an arbitrary way, understanding it as a regulating phenomenon over which they have no control. A clock provides a good example of our
own culture's monochronic use of time. Polychronic cultures, on the other hand,
are more tolerant of individual differences in the use of time because they place

more importance on interactions and on people. There are also differences between formal and informal time that may bear importantly on relationships. How we orient toward time may be the most important factor in our perceptions of the behaviors of others, and our interpretations of what those perceptions mean.

In addition to silence and time, other features of the vocalic message system include features of vocal quality and such vocalizations as laughing and the vocalized pause. From these data we infer meaning, emotions, and sincerity. We also use these tiny elements of vocalics to judge such things as competence, sex, and age.

Clearly, this complex nonverbal message system is somewhat beyond our control most of the time. We must learn to bring our inferences about it up to the level of talk if we are going to manage our relationships skillfully.

Discussion Questions

1. Working with a few classmates, list ways that silence can communicate language inadequacy.
2. In what ways do you use language to link yourself to your friends? Do you also use silence as part of this linking process? If so, how?
3. How can silence enhance emotions? How can it persuade? With one or two classmates, provide two examples of each use of silence from your experiences.
4. Do you use time differently from people you know? If so, in what ways? Have the differences influenced your relationships with these people? If so, how?
5. How are formal time and informal time different? Give three examples of each. How might these differences affect your ability to develop a new relationship?
6. Using figure 17.1 as a guide, try to explore as many ways as possible to change the meaning of this sentence: "Did John say that again?" How do you think the variety of its potential meanings could influence your ability to manage your relationships? Explain.

Endnotes

1. M. Pickard, *The World of Silence* (Chicago: Regnery, 1952), 1–15. See also S. N. Ganguly, "Culture, Communication, and Silence," *Philosophy and Phenomenological Research* 29 (December 1968): 200.
2. R. L. Scott, "Rhetoric and Silence," *Western Speech* 36 (Summer, 1972): 146–58.
3. V. Jenson, "Communicative Functions of Silence," *ETC: A Review of General Semantics* 30 (September 1973): 259–63.
4. M. L. McLaughlin and M. J. Cody, "Awkward Silences: Behavioral

Antecedents and Consequences of the Conversational Lapse" *Human Communication Research* 8 (Summer 1982): 299–316.

5. E. G. Beier, "Nonverbal Communication: How We Send Emotional Messages," *Psychology Today* 8 (1974): 53–56.

6. T. J. Bruneau, "Communicative Silences: Forms and Functions," *Journal of Communication* 23 (March 1973): 17–46.

7. R. May, "The Significance of the Pause," in *Freedom and Destiny,* 1981, and excerpted in J. Stewart, *Bridges Not Walls: A Book About Interpersonal Communication,* Fourth Edition (New York: Random House, 1986), pp. 86–91.

8. E. T. Hall, *Beyond Culture* (Garden City, NY: Doubleday, 1976).

9. E. T. Hall, *The Silent Language* (Garden City, NY: Doubleday, 1959). See also J. K. Burgoon and T. J. Saine, *The Unspoken Dialogue: An Introduction to Nonverbal Communication* (Boston: Houghton Mifflin, 1978), 101–4.

10. J. Meerloo, "The Time Sense in Psychiatry," in *The Voice of Time,* ed. J. T. Fraser (New York: Braziller, 1966).

11. T. J. Cottle, *Perceiving Time: A Psychological Investigation with Men and Women* (New York: John Wiley and Sons, 1976).

12. Bruneau, *Communicative Silences,* 32–39.

Managing
Relationships
Effectively

PART IV

>|<< UNIT 18
Initiating Relationships

Preview

Growing, healthy relationships are a great source of pleasure. This unit addresses the beginning of such relationships. It introduces ideas about the reasons we engage others in relationships, the engagement process, and the role of definition and rules in relationships.

Key Terms

engagement process
interpersonal attraction
interpersonal needs
physical attraction
prediction
proximity
relational definition
relational rules
relational stability
similarity
social attraction
task attraction

Objectives

1. Discuss why people initiate the engagement process.
2. Explain some of the fundamentals of attraction.
3. Suggest how the basic interpersonal needs of inclusion, control, and affection affect the decision to engage in a relationship.
4. Describe the engagement process.
5. Identify the function of definition and rules in relationship development.

The desire to interact with others and to develop meaningful relationships with others is strong in all of us. In fact, there is probably nothing more important to us. This unit begins our focus on relational development and managing relationships by answering the question "Why do we engage?" Then it addresses the engagement process itself and lays the groundwork for understanding relational development.

Why We Engage

Physical, Social, and Task Attractiveness

Interpersonal attraction is the most obvious response for engaging others in conversations that lead to relationships. This attraction might be physical, social, or task-related.

Physical attraction is clearly an important factor in initiating communication. We are more likely to start a conversation with a person we find physically attractive. But defining physical attractiveness is a difficult assignment. Everyone has some ideal image of an attractive person—usually of someone who resembles themselves. We may know that we don't fit an ideal image perfectly, but we usually think of ourselves as *within the range* of what we consider attractive.

Other than mere attractiveness, we might want to engage in conversation because of an attribute we believe is related to attractiveness. Researchers find that certain inferences are drawn regarding attractive people. They are thought to be more sexual, personable, persuasive, popular, happy, kind, interesting, confident, sociable, serious, and outgoing.[1] We might engage an attractive person in conversation because we suppose the person possesses some of these attributes.

In our culture, physical attractiveness is an especially important factor for women, for we have been taught to think of women in terms of attractiveness and men in terms of ability. Table 18.1 summarizes the results of a study that shows how qualities were judged to be important in a potential relational partner and how they differ for men and women.

Social attraction, like physical attraction, is highly dependent upon the individual's frame of reference. Socially attractive people seem to draw others into engagement. You might feel attracted to a person with a sense of humor, a storyteller who can carry the conversation. On the other hand, someone else might feel attracted to a person who is direct but less forward and who can talk about woodworking. Generally, if we look around our social circle, we will discover something about our definition of "socially attractive." We are drawn to a socially attractive person because her behavior meets our needs for social stimulation, which are particular to the persons involved.

Table 18.1 Physical, Social, and Task Qualities Rated as Important for a Partner by Both Men and Women

For Men	For Women
1. achievement	1. physical attractiveness
2. leadership	2. erotic ability
3. occupational ability	3. affectional ability
4. economic ability	4. social ability
5. entertaining ability	5. domestic ability
6. intellectual ability	6. sartorial ability
7. observational ability	7. interpersonal understanding
8. common sense	8. art appreciation
9. athletic ability	9. moral and spiritual understanding
10. theoretical ability	10. art and creative ability

Source: R. Centers, "The Completion Hypothesis and the Compensatory Dynamic in Intersexual Attraction and Love," *Journal of Psychology* 82 (1971):117.

A person is *task attractive* if we enjoy working with him. When we appreciate the way people work on a project, whether in a club, social organization, or on the job, we seek more contact with them. Working with them brings enjoyment as well as productivity. Both of these elements, enjoyment and productivity, are important parts in task attraction. So, if we believe that the person is efficient and productive but also boring, we are not likely to engage in conversation with that individual.

Proximity

We have a tendency to be attracted to those who are in *proximity* to us, the people who live and work close to us. Leon Festinger, Stanley Schacter, and Kurt Back conducted a famous study of how friendships formed among residents of a student housing development. They found that they were based on the distance people lived from each other and whether the unit faced onto the courtyard.[2] The closer a student's room was to another's, the more likely it was that they would form a friendship. In addition, those who faced the courtyard formed more friendships than those who faced the street. Their physical closeness thus provided the opportunity to talk and form friendships. This same principle holds for residents of apartment buildings. People most often form friendships with those who live near them on their floor.

Physical distance is very important in the initiation of relationships. We have the greatest opportunity to talk to those that are near us. Thus where we sit on the first day of class or when we attend church will largely determine who we will be able to engage. As time passes, we may move beyond those

Proximity is important to our relationships. It is difficult to nourish a relationship from a distance.

who are physically close to us, but proximity will remain a factor in how our relationships develop.

It is not the mere closeness that creates attraction but also that we have the opportunity to interact with these people. We seem to be able to find things that attract us in a variety of persons. As we get to know someone we gain information about her. We find that we have some interests and come to know how the person thinks and acts. This allows us to be able to predict her behavior. All of this causes us to feel comfortable around the person and to develop attraction. Of course, on the other hand, if the initial exposure is unpleasant, repeated exposure may decrease attraction.

Similarity

We often like people who are similar to us in physical characteristics, intelligence, attitudes, abilities, race, and nationality. We are attracted to such people because they validate us. The similarity between their personal characteristics and beliefs and ours confirms that we find them attractive and believe that we are also.

We find that there is a difference between those to whom we say we would be attracted and those with whom we form friendships. We associate with people who are similar to us in attractiveness.

Attitude similarity is especially important. If we believe in God, we may be uncomfortable with a person who does not. This extends not only to what we like but also to what we dislike. Such similarity is particularly important when the attitude is a significant one. Core values fall into this category. Matters of taste, such as a preference for a certain color, usually do not. As relationships move beyond initial engagement, the salience of attitudes might change. This explains some divorces. Attitudes toward children and spending money, for example, might be neither similar nor very important prior to marriage. Once they become salient, however, they can drive people apart.

We are attracted to people with similar attitudes for two basic reasons. First, their agreement with us reinforces our self-concept and feeling of being O.K. It is rewarding to be reinforced in this way. Second, these people are more likely to act in ways we can predict, which makes us feel more comfortable around them. This predictability extends to our ability to predict how we will be received. We are especially attracted to people we think will like us and treat us well.

There are, of course, cases in which opposites attract. If a person likes to control, then he might be attracted to someone who wants to be controlled. In fact, Theodore Reik argues that we seek mates who have a characteristic we do not have but envy.[3] He would say that when we see a couple in which one partner is an extrovert and the other is shy, we can explain their attraction in part by these complementary traits.

Basic Interpersonal Needs

We experience three basic *interpersonal needs* that affect our decision to engage: inclusion, control, and affection. Each may be present in a degree range of high to low. Moreover, we both give and receive these needs. For example, we have a need to include others and a need to be included; we have a need to control others and a need to be controlled; we have a need to love and a need to be loved. Table 18.2 gives examples of how basic interpersonal needs can affect the likelihood of engagement.

Expectations of Relational Benefits

Murray S. Davis suggests that there are four motivations for interpersonal engagement:

1. the impulse to receive stimulation
2. the impulse to express experiences
3. the impulse to assert oneself—to test ideas
4. the impulse to enhance enjoyment of certain activities.[4]

Table 18.2 Interpersonal Needs and Initiating Relationships

Need	Intensity	Impact on Initiating
to include	high	may give parties and include new acquaintances
	low	may stick to own circle of friends; may avoid initiating
to be included	high	may seek opportunities to initiate; may "push" self on strangers
	low	may avoid contact; may enjoy being alone
to control	high	may initiate contact with those who appear to be easily controlled
	low	may initiate contact with those who appear to be equal or able to hold their own in a relationship
to be controlled	high	may initiate contact with those who appear to dominate others
	low	may initiate contact with those who do not control others; may avoid contact with those who appear to control
to love	high	may initiate contact with those who need "warmth"; may avoid contact with those who appear to be "cold" and uncaring
	low	may initiate contact with those who appear to need little affection; may avoid initiating contact
to be loved	high	may initiate contact with those who appear to give "warmth"; may avoid contact with those who appear to be "cold" and uncaring
	low	may initiate contact with those who appear not to give too much affection; may avoid initiating contact

Because of their importance, these require individual discussion.

The Impulse to Receive Stimulation

We often experience this impulse when Saturday evening comes along and we have no plans to share the evening. The impulse is also strongly felt when a dating relationship ends and we feel alone.

Sometimes this impulse for stimulation is generated by a relationship that has become too routine; the people become bored and this boredom gives them the initiative to begin new relationships.

The Impulse to Express Experiences

To visualize this impulse, suppose you have been looking for a car to buy and have just found the right one at the right price. Your immediate impulse is probably to share the news with someone. Everyone has had a similar experience. You feel frustrated and perhaps even a little cheated if nobody is available to share your news, for the joy of sharing such an experience is important.

The same is true about bad news. If the boss has been grumpy and you received the brunt of it, you will want to share this experience. This sharing is an opportunity for you to receive empathy and encouragement from another. It may even prompt the other person to share a similar experience. This reciprocal sharing provides a basis for comparing your experiences to those of others.

Can you recall a time when you felt that you did not do well on a test? It probably did not take you long to seek out others in the class with whom you could commiserate! "That was some kind of a test," you said. "Yeah," your friend answered. "I think it was the hardest one yet. What did you think of that essay question?" You both shudder at the thought of the question before you add, "I'll study harder next time."

The Impulse to Assert Oneself—to Test Ideas

This impulse is not related, as you might suspect, to assertiveness. Rather, it refers to the expression of an idea that needs testing. People have impulses to express ideas of which they are unsure and for which they need feedback. This expression and its related feedback undoubtedly serve to develop an individual's identity and self-concept. We may not be particularly interested in confirming our ideas, but we want to discover how others react to them. We are acting on an impulse for both social contact and comparison when we seek people out for this purpose.

The Impulse to Enhance Enjoyment of Certain Activities

Finally, we are motivated to engage others because being together enhances our enjoyment of an activity. We join together to play games and to engage in other recreational activities. We also join together to celebrate our important events. Imagine celebrating your birthday by yourself. Or perhaps you can picture yourself trying to celebrate Independence Day, July 4th, by yourself. Being together allows us to share our joy, our excitement, and our thoughts so that we gain more enjoyment from the activity.

Engaging Another Person

Mere talk is not necessarily interpersonal communication. Interpersonal communication moves beyond the impersonal application of societal rules. Impersonal talk is important, of course, but it relates only minimally to engagement. William and Judith Pfeiffer suggested that the important last step in the *engagement process* is *contact*.[5] They illustrated the engagement process in four steps, as shown in figure 18.1.

Figure 18.1 The Engagement Process

Awareness – – – – – – →Excitement – – – – – – – → Action – – – – – – –→Contact

Very simply, this process progresses from becoming aware of the person to being excited by the prospect of the conversation, to acting on that excitement, and finally to making contact. Real contact is never made if there is an intent to remain impersonal. Only an intent to get to know the person psychologically moves us to make interpersonal contact.

The initial engagement is an important step in establishing a relationship and therefore deserves special attention. We have said a good deal about interpersonal skills. Here we want to summarize some of the skills and behaviors for you to use as you meet new people:

1. Try to establish appropriate eye contact. This usually means relatively direct contact to signal that the communication channel is open. Experiment with what seems comfortable for you. It is important that you maintain eye contact without staring. You will usually find that too steady a gaze will make the other person uneasy.
2. Experiment to find an appropriate interpersonal distance. Approach the person to the point that you feel comfortable and close. Check your posture. You may want to avoid closed positions, such as standing with your arms crossed or folded in front of you.
3. See if a direct approach to meeting the person works well for you. You might say something like, "Hi, my name is Jerry," rather than the usual game playing such as "Didn't I see you at Soloman's last Friday?"
4. Try having the person talk about herself. This gives you a chance to respond positively to what the person says. Also, most people seem to enjoy talking about themselves, so this may help them feel at ease.
5. Remember that the face is an important conveyer of feelings. Consider ways to use your face to tell the other that you are enjoying meeting her. One of the simplest ways to do this is to remember to smile. Head nodding can also be effective if used in moderation.
6. Search for similarities between you and the other. Maybe you share classes, hobbies, or other interests. Have you lived in the same cities? An awareness of your similarity is an important source of attraction.
7. Consider how you react to a positive person versus a negative person. We think maintaining a positive demeanor is very important. Sometimes we slip into negative behavior unknowingly, which should be avoided.
8. Be careful not to engage in too intimate self-disclosure. Sometimes we find ourselves enjoying someone so much that we say more about ourselves than we should. Initial engagements are not nourished by too intimate or too negative self-disclosure.

Relational Definition and Rules

Underlying our developmental view of communication in interpersonal relationships are two fundamental elements—*definition* and *rules*—which have their beginning in the engagement process. The extent of our agreement on these elements with those with whom we have formed a relationship becomes an important measure of a relationship's stability as it moves through the various stages.

Relational Definition

We have a definition of our relationship at every point in its development. A typical definition is "We enjoy each other, but we are mere acquaintances." Another couple might define their relationship by saying, "We are best friends." An eighteen-year-old said, "You'd have to say we're friends—special friends— but just friends."

A *relational definition* indicates the *relational stability*. A *stable relationship* is one in which there is agreement about its kind and nature, as when both say that they are "best friends."

William W. Wilmot presented three aspects of relational stability:

1. Relationships stabilize because the participants reach some minimal agreement (usually implicitly) of what they want (relationally and otherwise) from the relationship.
2. Relationships stabilize at different levels of intimacy.
3. A stabilized relationship still has areas of change.[6]

Outsiders may not understand why the relationship is stable, as, for example, when parents evaluate the relationships their offspring have with others. Outsiders may believe some aspect of a relationship is crucial, while the participants see it as unimportant. For example, consider the marriage that is stable because the participants value the financial resources they can give each other. For them this security is important. The fact that they hold few interests in common may not matter. (Of course, some of us may wonder about how satisfactory such a relationship actually is.)

People will not be satisfied unless they can achieve a minimal positive agreement about what they want from their relationship. For example, mere acquaintances may want to receive a happy greeting when they meet each other. They may not need any particularly meaningful conversation.

Relational stability depends upon agreement by both partners about the kind and nature of the relationship.

Wilmot's second aspect of stability is that individuals fix the relationship at a particular level of intimacy that they find satisfying. When they agree on this, they stabilize the relationship at that level. Such agreement is important if the relationship is to be satisfying. Suppose you meet a professor who shares your particular academic interests. You think that it would be nice to get to know him as a friend. He, however, thinks that the acquaintance level is enough for a student-teacher relationship. You have a definitional problem that could generate some awkward moments, as you try to be a friend and he brushes you off as an acquaintance.

Finally, Wilmot's third point suggests that stability does not mean stagnation. There is always some change in a relationship that requires negotiation. As time passes, people want different things from a relationship. If these wants are met, a new definition is struck and the relationship takes on new stability. If they are not, the resulting instability might lead to relational deterioration.

Relational Rules

People behave according to their cultural, societal, and psychological experience. For example, our culture helps us define an appropriate distance between those engaged in a conversation. Our social contacts will give us a sense of what it means to be polite. The way we see ourselves in relationships—based on how others react to us—and the way we see others will give us rules for behaving. Our behavior is thus governed by a set of *relational rules* that evolve from these three sources.

Behavior is governed by relational rules that evolve from cultural assumptions, social experience, and psychological need.

But how do we discover these rules? The answer lies in the concept of *prediction*. We predict how the other person might act based on cultural, social, and psychological data we get from the person and her verbal and nonverbal behavior. The relationship can be thought of as primarily *impersonal* when the data are cultural and social,[7] and *interpersonal* when the data are psychological.

Psychological data become available as partners in a relationship become acquainted through self-disclosure. They become aware of each other's personalities. This gives them an additional basis for predicting behavior that may be more reliable since it takes into account the uniqueness of the person. Now the relationship has moved from the impersonal level to the interpersonal level. This allows the partners to set rules based upon their respective preferences. Among a group of friends, for example, it might be permissible for Tim to tease Cheryl about her weight. And the group might permit Tim to express his temper when he is angry. They may also establish the informal relational rule that allows Mary Ann to dominate all the others during a crisis. Each rule is based upon a knowledge of the members' peculiarities and an agreement on rules that will allow the group to succeed. The more often the group members adopt rules based on their relationships, the more predictable, interpersonal, and intimate they become.

Summary

The desire to interact with others and to develop meaningful relationships is strong in all of us. Our decision to engage a person, or to begin a relationship, rests upon a number of factors. Attractiveness—physical, social, or task-related—may influence the decision. Our willingness to make the contact is also influenced by the proximity of the other person. We are more likely to engage those who are physically close to us. Similarity is another key factor in our decision to engage. We are attracted to people who share our interests and beliefs. Those we like often possess similar physical characteristics, intelligence, attitudes, abilities, race, and nationality. Of these factors, attitude similarity is especially important. We even want our partner to share our dislikes. Similar attitudes attract because this congruency reinforces our self-concept and increases our ability to predict how our partner will act.

We also engage to fulfill our needs. We need to receive stimulation, to express experiences, to assert ourselves—to test ideas, and to enhance our enjoyment of activities. In addition, we seek fulfillment of our needs to include and be included, to control and be controlled, and to love and be loved.

Finally, we addressed the issue of initial engagement. The process involves awareness that leads to excitement. This is followed by action and contact. We offered some advice about how to carry out engagement. Be sure to establish eye contact and maintain a comfortably close distance. Introduce yourself and perhaps say something about who you are. Try to be active, positive, and involved. Remember that the face conveys feelings, so smile some of the time. Look for commonalities, as these will help you and your partner see your similarities. Regulate your self-disclosure so that it is appropriately intimate for an intial contact. Relational definitions and rules will begin to form from this first contact as we develop definitions of the relationship and appropriate behavior for us and the other person in the relationship.

Discussion Questions

1. As a group, consider why people engage in relationships. Generate a list of answers and compare them with those offered in this unit. Are there differences? Do motivations relate to people's age or place in life?
2. It has been suggested that the ideal person to whom we think we would be attracted and those who actually are our friends are different. In practice, is this true? If so, why?
3. Do similar or different characteristics attract others?
4. Consider someone you would describe as an acquaintance. How would you define this kind of relationship? Would the definition differ if the relationship is male/female rather than between people of the same sex? Now think about rules that might be shared in such a relationship. List as many as possible.
5. Consider someone you would describe as a friend. Suggest a definition of this kind of relationship. What rules might people in this relationship adopt? Would the violation of these rules be more or less important than between acquaintances?

Endnotes

1. See Keith Gibbins, "Communication Aspects of Women's Clothes and Their Relationship to Fashionability," *British Journal of Social and Clinical Psychology* 8 (1964): 301–12; E. Berscheid and E. Walster, "Physical Attractiveness," in *Advances in Experimental Social Psychology* 7, ed. L. Berkowitz (New York: Academic Press, 1974); C. L. Kleinke, *First Impressions: The Psychology of Encountering Others* (Englewood Cliffs, NJ: Prentice-Hall, 1975); R. C. Bailey and T. S. Schreiber, "Congruency of Physical Attractiveness Perception and Liking," *Journal of Social Psychology* 115 (1981): 285–86; and E. D. Tanke, "Dimensions of the Physical Attractiveness Stereotype: A Factor/Analytic Study," *Journal of Psychology* 110 (1982): 63–64.
2. L. Festinger, S. Schacter, and K. Back, *Social Pressures in Informal Groups: A Study of Human Factors in Housing* (New York: Harper and Row, 1950).

3. T. Reik, *A Psychologist Looks at Love* (New York: Farrar & Rinehart, 1945).
4. M. S. Davis, *Intimate Relations* (New York: The Free Press, 1973).
5. W. Pfeiffer and J. Pfeiffer, "A Gestalt Primer," in *The 1975 Annual Handbook for Group Facilitators,* eds. J. W. Pfeiffer and J. E. Jones (La Jolla, CA: University Associates, 1975), 183.
6. W. W. Wilmot, *Dyadic Communication,* 2d ed. (Reading, MA: Addison-Wesley, 1979), 152.
7. G. R. Miller and M. Steinberg, *Between People* (Chicago: Science Research Associates, 1975), 22–25.

>>|<< UNIT 19
Relational Development

Preview

This unit begins our consideration of the factors that influence the development and growth of relationships. Here we will discuss how relationships grow and are maintained, with an emphasis on the development of relational competence.

Key Terms

attraction
bonding
"coming together" process
experimenting
initiating
integrating
intensifying
inviting
relational growth
renegotiating
revising communication
self-disclosure
trust

Objectives

1. Describe the initiating stage in relational development, including the factors that promote relational growth.
2. List the characteristics of the experimenting stage in relational development, including suggestions for promoting relational growth.
3. Explain the process of intensifying in relational development, including the signs of intensifying and suggestions for promoting relational growth.
4. Explain how relationships integrate. What are the signs of integrating and how can relational growth be promoted?
5. Discuss the role of renegotiating in relationships. What are some of the possible outcomes of this process?
6. Explain what bonding means in a relationship and why a relationship moves to that stage.

One of the most frustrating experiences is a relationship that fails. In fact, we insulate ourselves from this disappointment by expecting that relationships might not grow, mature, and prosper. Yet in spite of our emotional preparation, we are surprised and even saddened when we discover that relationships we value are failing.

We believe the ability to care for a relationship is a skill that is central to happiness. But the alarming rate of divorce in America attests to the difficulty of maintaining healthy, growing relationships. In fact, in 1988, one of every two marriages will end in divorce.[1] If we assume that people do not enter marriage expecting failure, why does this happen? There is no simple answer to such a complicated question, but we believe that skill in caring for a relationship contributes significantly to its success or failure. In this unit we focus on *relational growth*—the *"coming together"* process.

The concept of developmental stages in interpersonal relationships has been investigated by a number of scholars.[2] One of the clearest explanations was presented by Mark Knapp,[3] who says that the "coming together" process occurs in five stages: (1) initiating, (2) experimenting, (3) intensifying, (4) integrating, and (5) bonding. Table 19.1 presents these stages and representative conversation for each category.

Initiating

Initiating occurs when we make decisions about a person's attractiveness. We observe the person from afar, and decide whether we will invite the person to interact. This decision is based on at least two factors: the situation and our attraction to the person.

Table 19.1 Stages of the "Coming Together" Process

Stage	Representative Dialogue
Initiating	"Hi, how you doin?" "Fine. You?"
Experimenting	"Oh, so you like to ski? So do I." "You do? Great! Where do you go?"
Intensifying	"I . . . think I love you." "I love you, too."
Integrating	"I feel so much a part of you." "Yeah, we are like one person. What happens to you happens to me."
Bonding	"I want to be with you always." "Let's get married."

Source: M. L. Knapp, *Social Intercourse: From Greeting to Goodbye* (Boston: Allyn and Bacon, 1978), 13.

Situation

The situation may encourage or inhibit communication. Social situations such as parties, for example, give us permission to mingle and involve others in conversation. The odds that we will talk to people we have never met increase because of the situation.

Likewise, we are more likely to initiate a conversation when the situation gives us something in common with the other person. If you are interested in sailing and attend a boat show, you would be likely to talk about sailing with someone there.

On the other hand, the situation might detract from our willingness to engage another person. As a freshman college student at orientation, it may have been difficult for you just to walk right up to people and talk to them. The newness of the situation and doubts about appropriate behavior may have acted as constraints. But suppose that during orientation, you shared a dormitory room with another student. The fact that you were living in such close proximity increased the likelihood that you initiated a relationship with your roommate.

Attraction

Attraction is the second factor that may invite or keep us from initiating communication. When we consider what we know about people without talking to them, it is easy to understand why attraction is a key ingredient. For example, we can observe physical appearance and compare it to our likes and dislikes. Perhaps we like people who are close to our age, who smile frequently, or who have medium-length hair. It would be a safe guess that many of the characteristics we like are very similar to our images of ourselves.

Sometimes, however, we are intrigued by someone who is very different from us. Although our attention and imagination may be excited by the person, we will usually pass up the opportunity to develop a relationship. The person represents too many unknowns. And does not appear to share our background, values, and beliefs.

Usually such a decision is influenced by what we want from the situation. If we are looking for someone we would like to date, we apply one set of standards; if we are looking for advice about sailboats, we are likely to apply quite different standards. Although there is very little concrete data available on which to base a decision at this early stage, we still make decisions about continuing or breaking off the relationship.

Inviting

Once our decision is made, we search for an appropriate way of *inviting* communication. The message we send may be, "I'm a nice person, and I'm fun, too. Let's talk." We may then make a friendly inquiry about the situation, such

We are much more likely to meet people when we share an interest.

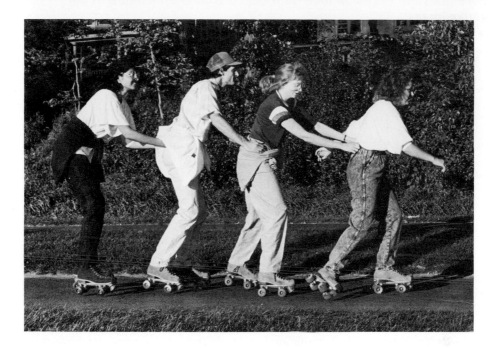

as, "I see you are taking interpersonal communication, too," or, "What kind of boat do you like to sail?" With such statements, we suggest that the communication channel is open, and that we want to discover a topic for conversation.

This inviting process takes only about fifteen seconds, but the outcome is crucial to further relational development. At this point, we decide to: (1) disengage, (2) keep the relationship at a superficial level, or (3) move to the next developmental stage.

The decision to disengage usually results when we discover that our schedules and situations do not coincide and thus would make a continued relationship difficult. Or, we may decide that we share so little that even casual acquaintance would not be worth the effort.

The decision to keep the relationship at a superficial level is a common one. Usually one person decides there is not enough in common to warrant a more meaningful relationship. A number of other reasons may provoke such a decision. For example, we might not see ourselves as having time to develop a new relationship. Or perhaps we want to wait to see how the other person responds before we decide to intensify our contact. We expect to continue to see the person and make small talk when we choose to remain at this level.

Willingness to set aside time for a relationship is a measure of our commitment.

A decision to move the relationship to the next stage represents a willingness to make an investment. We want more than mere small talk. We want to get to know the other person. We set aside time to be together. We extend our contact with the other, which clearly represents a deeper commitment to the relationship.

Experimenting

Exploration of the unknown characterizes the *experimenting* stage in relationship development. The focus in this stage is on exploring the possibilities for a relationship. The data collected here help us decide whether to keep our relationships on a relatively superficial level or to move on to greater commitment. We usually decide to maintain fairly casual relationships. If a relationship is to grow, we must collect more information about the other person.

Collecting Information

Strangers often begin experimenting by collecting standard information—names, hometowns, and places of employment. Students often exchange their major, year in school, and perhaps social organizations to which they belong.

Which of these bits of information do you ask for when you are beginning a relationship?

names	*year in school*
hometown	*social organizations*
place of work	*church affiliation*
academic major	*marital status*
kind of work	*sexual preference*
academic minor	*hobbies*

Since talking about such standard information quickly becomes superficial, we search for some common interest or experience to which we can shift. This moves us to a new depth of *self-disclosure* and to more meaningful and slightly more personal topics. As we share values as well as information, we begin to develop relational norms. This even more personal, more revealing conversation becomes the basis for decisions about the future of the relationship.

In this stage of relational development we begin to risk disclosing our private selves. Initially, of course, we will be cautious and tentative about what we say. We wait to see if the other person also discloses. Most of us will not take on this risk unless we wish the relationship to grow.

The experimenting stage varies in length. Sometimes we discover a significant difference between us and our partner almost immediately. This might cause us to retreat instantly to talk that is more characteristic of the initiating stage. At other times, we are intrigued by a person but wish to pursue a gradual exploration process. Perhaps we have several other significant relationships and assume a "wait and see" attitude. Of course, we may decide very quickly that we have so much in common with our partner that we have no difficulty visualizing a more serious and committed relationship.

Promoting Relational Growth

Relationships are not sustained and do not grow if they are fed only by small talk. We must discover significant areas of common interest as well as cognitive similarity if our relationships are to prosper. Research has shown that common interests and especially similar attitudes, values, and beliefs are most important for maintaining interpersonal attraction.[4]

For example, if you believe that doing well in classes is important, you may want your relational partners to feel the same way. If you place great value on a particular religious belief, you will want the other person to value it as well. We experiment with and explore more and more topics as we work through this experimenting stage. We are disclosing ourselves, demonstrating trust, and making decisions about the other person's compatibility.

During all this checking and double-checking, the commitment remains at the acquaintance level. And, as is true of the initiating stage, there are several possible relational choices throughout the experimenting stage. We might end the relationship because there is not enough commonality to sustain interest. Or we might decide to remain at the acquaintance level. In fact, this is the fate of most of our relationships; the contact remains occasional and the talk is not particularly intimate. Work relationships are frequently maintained at this level. The third possibility, of course, is for us to intensify a relationship if we find it satisfying and see that there is the basis for building a deeper and more significant relationship. Of course, if we are to do this, the other person in the relationship must make a similar decision.

Intensifying

Intensifying signifies a change in our relationship; we move from acquaintance-ship to friendship. Because intimacy and trust increase as we commit more fully, this represents a major step in relational development. This stage gets its name from the fact that communication actually becomes more intense. We are enjoying the relationship, and so we talk more often and for longer periods. We may also spend more time together, which also suggests increased commitment.

During this stage we show more and more of our private selves. We are willing to risk more because of the intimacy of the relationship and the *trust* we are developing in each other. We also may learn about some of our partner's secret fears. This sharing helps us understand each other as unique individuals. We begin to understand our partner's perspective on the world.

Signs of Intensifying

Knapp identifies numerous verbal cues that indicate that a relationship is intensifying,[5] including:

1. Forms of address become more informal: first name, nickname, or some term of endearment.
2. Use of the first-person plural becomes more common: "*We* should do this," or "*Let's* do this."
3. Private symbols begin to develop, sometimes in the form of a special slang or jargon, sometimes using conventional language forms that have understood, private meanings.
4. Verbal shortcuts built on a backlog of accumulated and shared assumptions, expectations, interests, knowledge, interactions, and experiences appear more often: one partner may request that a newspaper be passed by simply saying, "Paper."
5. More direct expressions of commitment appear: "We really have a good thing going" or "I don't know who I'd talk to if you weren't around." Sometimes such expressions have an echo: "I really like you a lot," or "I really like you, too, Elmer."
6. Increasingly, a partner acts as a helper in the daily process of understanding the other person: "In other words, you mean you're . . . ," or "But yesterday, you said you were. . . ."

Nonverbal behavior also changes. More touching and closer interpersonal distances occur at the intensifying level. Sometimes attempts are made to coordinate clothing styles and more time is consumed in interactions.

Promoting Relational Growth

Relational growth at this stage is enhanced through increasing the amount of self-disclosure. You begin to share information that is generally withheld from acquaintances. You may talk about your problems in other relationships, or reveal your fears and even your personal failures. This willingness to make yourself vulnerable is a sign of trust. Increased trust and self-disclosure allow you to know more about each other, to discover areas of commonality, and to increase liking.

Integrating

We may move beyond viewing ourselves as separate and begin *integrating* when the intensification of self-disclosure in our relationship has been satisfying. It is at this stage that we move closer together. Knapp suggests that "two individual personalities almost seem to fuse or coalesce, certainly more than any other previous stage."[6] Relational partners spend more time talking to each other and may even share a house or apartment, which allows them to increase their contact.

Partners enjoy their relationship so much that they often distort their perceptions of each other. Frequently, the distortions can be heard in their talk about each other. One might say, for example, "This is the most wonderful person I've ever met," "He is so nice; I'm so lucky," or "We never fight because we see everything the same way." Such overly positive statements are gross generalizations and frequently distortions of reality.

Signs of Integrating

The verbal and nonverbal behaviors that characterize the integrating stage can be described as intensifying, sharing, and minimizing differences. You share where possible, and minimize differences between you and the other person in your relationship. Knapp found that this sharing and minimizing process has several forms:[7]

1. Attitudes, opinions, interests, and tastes that clearly distinguish the pair from others are vigorously cultivated: "We have something special; we are unique."
2. Social circles merge, and others begin to treat the two individuals as a common package. They send one present, one letter, and one invitation.
3. Intimacy "trophies" such as pictures, pins, and rings are exchanged so that each can "wear" the other's identity.
4. Similarities in manner, dress, and verbal behavior develop that accentuate the oneness.
5. Actual physical penetration of various body parts contributes to the perceived unification.
6. Sometimes common property is designated: "our song," a joint bank account, or joint authorship of a book.
7. Empathic processes seem to peak so that explanation and prediction of behavior are much easier.

8. Body rhythms and routines become closely attuned.
9. Sometimes the love of a third person or object will serve as glue for the relationship: "Love me, love my dog."

Knapp stated that these behaviors (or at least some) do not characterize only male/female relationships. Any relationship in the integrating stage will exhibit some of them.

Interaction in this stage is characterized by self-disclosure that increases in both scope and intimacy as partners come to know each other in new ways. They are able to share their worlds and even create a new, common world in the process. This leads to deeper trust, which then enables people to risk sharing themselves even more.[8] Frank Dance has illustrated this process as a spiral (figure 19.1).[9] The act of sharing reflects the commitment that has developed during the integrating stage of the relationship.

Language patterns change during the integrating stage, too. You will hear more use of "we," "us," and "our," instead of "I," "me," and "mine."[10] Integrating partners develop their own language to describe recurring events. For

Figure 19.1 Characterization of the Trust–Self-Disclosure Spiral

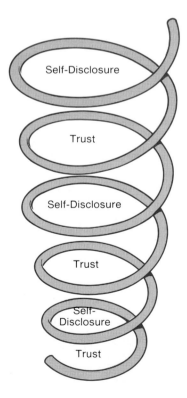

example, in a work situation, one partner might say, "Let's go fishing." What he really means is, "Let's quit work early and go play." Nicknames may also be developed for one another.

Integrating partners develop their own language to talk about recurring events in their lives.

Talk about the relationship also develops. You hear signs of both integration and optimism if you listen carefully. Two sisters might say, "It's so wonderful the way we are able to talk to each other. I can't imagine it being any better for us." Or two lovers might say, "I can't believe the way I feel when I'm away from you. We just seem to fit together. I can't imagine not being together forever." These statements reflect the decision to examine the relationship more closely. This moves the pair to the next stage.

Promoting Relational Growth

Relational growth can be enhanced by being aware that several significant relational behaviors and skills are forming during the integrating stage. Definitions of roles and rules for behavior may develop that either enhance or hinder the relationship. You can influence the adoption of effective roles and rules.

People in this stage develop unique roles, rules, and definitions. For instance, one person may generally have the last word in arguments. These people may have begun to define their relationship as superior/subordinate. On the other hand, they may share in the decision making and hear each other out. Equality defines this relationship.

Characteristic conflict management techniques may also emerge during this stage. If the persons in this relationship start to "manage" conflict by yelling at each other, this style of conflict management may be accepted as appropriate. But if problem solving is adopted instead, they will develop certain rules related to this style. They have an opportunity to promote relational growth if they are able to create a productive conflict management style.

Activities and hobbies are integrated into the relationship during this period as well. If, for example, you like to go fishing and your partner does not; he probably will not define that activity as part of your relationship. But usually friends do not mind giving things up and adopting particular interaction patterns that they would not generally display. People sometimes do this just because they find each other attractive. They feel excited about each other. Sometimes they perceive the relationship and their activities within it selectively, changing, for them, the nature of that activity. A young woman in our department reported that her boyfriend loves to sail, but that she is afraid of the water. Nevertheless, she goes sailing with him almost every weekend. We asked her to account for this apparent inconsistency in her behavior. "I just feel so safe when I am with Charlie," she answered.

Julia T. Wood suggests that such distortion presents a special irony. Individuals are less attentive to the communication patterns and rules at a time when many important understandings and rules are developing. For example, they begin to form unsatisfying methods for handling conflict that could lead to deterioration later in the relationship when the incompatibilities in managing conflict are discovered. Wood suggests that "the critical process of generating rules and roles for the relationship, thus, proceeds almost without partners' awareness."[11]

Renegotiating

Questioning the relationship is a natural part of the development process. The intensity that represents the previous stage, which is characterized by an idealism, cannot go on forever. At some point we take a more careful look at our relationship as we begin to wonder where it is going. We consider if a more formal, lasting commitment ought to be the next step. We are ready to think seriously about our relationship, its value, its problems, and its future. We feel a need to make a decision to keep the relationship as it is, to scale it down, or to make a deeper, more public commitment to it. Wood has termed this stage *revising communication.*[12]

Although Knapp does not include this stage in his relational development scheme, we think that it should be considered so that the bonding stage makes sense. Bonding represents public and perhaps legal commitment. Before we take such a step, we frequently will want to examine the relationship more carefully than we did during the integration stage. Furthermore, we may attempt to negotiate changes in things we do not like. If this is not possible, we may begin the disengagement process.

Examining the Relationship

The first step in *renegotiating,* then, involves a private examination of the relationship. Many questions and thoughts are raised: "Can I tolerate this person who wants to take a dominant role?" "I wish she didn't argue so negatively." "Can this relationship really last?" "Do we really have enough in common?" Such examination is vital to the decision to make a public commitment.

We base this examination process on a cost-benefits analysis. Costs might include the pain involved in putting up with some irritating behavior, the time involved in a deeper commitment, and restrictions associated with adhering to the other person's schedule. Beyond these usual costs might be giving up your self-identity. For example, you may have a vision of a person wanting to control you in ways that seem alien to you. On the benefit side, we consider the satisfaction we get from sharing with someone we enjoy. We think of the fun involved in our joint activities. We see a good deal of confirmation of ourselves.

Figure 19.2 The Renegotiation Process

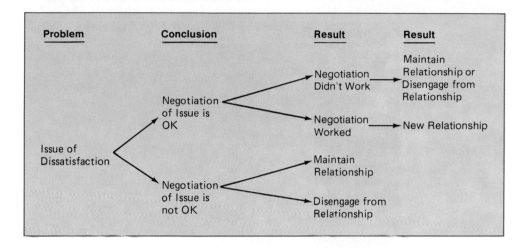

These and many other positive aspects of our relationship are weighed against potential costs. This analysis process is not likely to be as straightforward as simply listing all of these costs and benefits. We are usually aware that we have questions about our relationships that we must answer. We are likely to compare our experiences to those we have had with others.

The answers and conclusions from this examination may generate dissatisfaction with some aspect of the relationship. We have listed some options for renegotiating a relationship (figure 19.2).

The Renegotiation Process

The renegotiation process begins with the discovery of the pain created by dissatisfaction with some aspect of the relationship. Suppose you begin to weigh alternatives: "Should I ask her to try to change her ways? Should I offer to change my ways? Should we both give up a little in order to smooth things out?" We will decide to negotiate if we believe that there is good chance of success and that the effort is worth the potential pain involved: "She's certainly the best woman I've ever known. So what if she doesn't do this the way I'd like. Her compromise makes sense, and my own part of the bargain may be better than what I was doing before." When we think that there is not much chance of success or that the pain is too great, we may put the relationship on hold or begin the disengagement process: "She'll probably never change. Anyway, she says she won't change, and I believe her. Hum. That leaves me with no alternative, because I just can't stand to be around that behavior."

Irwin Taylor and Dalmas Altman have described this process as a movie

Bonding is a public or private ritual that signifies a contract and formal commitment.

shown in reverse.[13] The relationship may move backward through the successive stages. This means less disclosure and less contact. If you and the person in your relationship decide that negotiation is reasonable, you may begin to discuss differences but fail to come to agreement. This might then result in either a "holding pattern" or disengagement. But if you and your partner successfully renegotiate your differences, you are ready for the final developmental stage—bonding.

Bonding

Bonding is different from the stages already discussed because all the others are part of a process rather than an event in themselves. This process is relationship evolution. Bonding, however, is different. It is a special kind of commitment, but not necessarily sexual intimacy—although this is true with lovers. Bonding is a voluntary, ongoing commitment to the renegotiated relationship.

There is some disagreement about the public nature of the commitment represented by bonding. Knapp suggests that it is "a public ritual which announces that commitments have been formally contracted."[14] In contrast, Wood says that "bonding may occur privately between partners or it may be public, as in a ceremony."[15]

Public bonding can create a different kind of relationship than private bonding. Private bonding must rely more on the strength of the relationship to keep it intact. The fact that outsiders have witnessed a public bonding can help to preserve the relationship.

The central features of bonding are its voluntary nature, its indefinite length of commitment, and the special rules attached to it. Its voluntary nature and indefinite length are symbolically important. They signify a powerful force that changes the nature of the relationship.[16] Bonding permits you and your partner to deal with each other with new freedom because you no longer need to be concerned that minor infractions will destroy your relationship. You can be yourself in ways that were previously impossible because of your commitment to the future. Thus, new rules of behavior are generated based on the new definition of the relationship.

Summary

Sometimes relationships do not seem to work very well, but you can increase your chances by knowing how to care for them. This involves understanding how relationships grow and come apart and being able to promote relational growth.

Relationships move through stages of growth. The pattern usually appears as follows:

Initiating → Experimenting → Intensifying → Integrating → Renegotiating → Bonding

Initiating involves making a decision to engage another person in conversation based on the situation and on your attraction. If the situation seems right and there is sufficient attraction, initiation is likely. Since there is still much that is unknown at this stage, you move to the next level, *experimenting*. Here you exchange information to discover common interests. Generally, this talk moves from superficial to more meaningful disclosure. The disclosure allows comparisons that are useful in deciding about the future of the relationship.

Intensifying signals a change in the relationship from acquaintance to friend. Self-disclosure increases dramatically as you and your partner are willing to make yourselves vulnerable by discussing personal problems and failures. Nonverbal behavior becomes intensified in this stage as more touching and closer interpersonal distances are desired.

Integrating suggests coming together in ways that create increased contact. This could be living together or just more frequent contact. Activities that your partner does not enjoy may be dropped, as the emphasis is on doing things together. There is an infatuation with the other person.

Renegotiating takes place as you try to decide if you want to make this friendship more permanent and committed. At this stage, you and your partner are conducting a private examination of your relationship. When attempts to negotiate the dissatisfactions fail, disengagement may begin. Successful negotiation leads to a new relationship and bonding.

Bonding signals a special kind of commitment to intimacy, a voluntary commitment to your partner for an indefinite period, with new rules. These rules are the result of successful renegotiation of the relationship.

Discussion Questions

1. Trace one of your long-term relationships through the stages of development outlined in this chapter. Discuss how closely it mirrored these stages. Did it skip any? Did it backtrack? Were there stages in your relationship that we did not mention? If there were differences, how do you account for them?
2. What happens to a relationship if bonding occurs before renegotiation?
3. Can you make a relationship work? If so, how? Can you renegotiate a relationship more than once? If so, how?
4. More than half of the marriages in America end in divorce. Where do these relationships go wrong? What information in this chapter will help you to identify the pitfalls in such relationships?
5. Are working relationships in business any different from working relationships at home? Why or why not?
6. Can a person make you love him or her? Can you make someone love you? Does this have anything to do with attraction? Does attraction have anything to do with loving?
7. Can you disclose yourself too much in a relationship? How much is "too much"?

Endnotes

1. Source: National Center for Health Statistics, Public Health Service, Washington, D.C.
2. See C. R. Berger and R. J. Calabrese, "Some Explorations in Initial Interaction and Beyond: Toward a Developmental Theory of Interpersonal Communication," *Human Communication Research* 1 (1975): 99–112; S. W. Duck, *Personal Relationships and Personal Constructs: A Study of Friendship Formation* (New York: The Free Press, 1973); T. M. Newcomb, *The Acquaintance Process* (New York: Holt, Rinehart and Winston, 1961); and Julia T. Wood, "Communication and Relational Culture: Bases for the Study of Human Relationships," *Communication Quarterly* 30 (Spring 1982): 75–83.

3. M. L. Knapp, *Social Intercourse: From Greeting to Goodbye* (Boston: Allyn and Bacon, 1978), 17–28.

4. Newcomb, *The Acquaintance Process*; W. Griffitt and R. Veitch, "Preacquaintance Attitude Similarity and Attraction Revisited," *Sociometry* 37 (1974): 163–73.

5. Knapp, *Social Intercourse,* 20.

6. M. L. Knapp, *Interpersonal Communication and Human Relationships* (Boston: Allyn and Bacon, 1984), 38.

7. Knapp, *Social Intercourse,* 21.

8. G. L. Wilson, "Trusting and Self-Disclosure in Dyads" (Ph.D. diss., University of Wisconsin, 1979).

9. F. E. X. Dance, "Toward a Theory of Human Communication" in *Human Communication Theory: Original Essays,* ed. F. E. X. Dance (New York: Holt, Rinehart and Winston, 1967), 288–309.

10. M. S. Davis, *Intimate Relations* (New York: The Free Press, 1973), 56–91.

11. J. T. Wood, *Human Communication: A Symbolic Interactionist Perspective* (New York: Holt, Rinehart and Winston, 1982), 177.

12. Ibid., 178–80.

13. I. Altman and D. A. Taylor, *Social Penetration: The Development of Interpersonal Relationships* (New York: Holt, Rinehart and Winston, 1973), 174.

14. Knapp, *Social Intercourse,* 21.

15. Wood, *Human Communication,* 180.

16. Knapp, *Social Intercourse,* 21–22.

>>I<< UNIT 20
Defensiveness in Relationships

Preview

The old saying, "We always hurt the ones we love," means that when we argue with those who are close to us, the arguments often end in hurtful behavior because there seems to be no way to deal with communication that creates defensiveness.

Key Terms

certainty
control
defensive behavior
evaluation
neutrality
reflexive behavior
strategy
superiority
supportive behavior

Objectives

1. Discuss the major reasons people defend themselves in interpersonal communication situations.
2. Specify and explain the two basic strategies people use to defend themselves.
3. Identify the characteristics of a defensive interpersonal communication climate.
4. Discuss the consequences of defensive communication behavior.

A group of college students decided to go out after class one Thursday night to relax after a particularly tiring week. Midterm exams were finally over, and this was an opportunity to have fun. After they had settled in and ordered their second round of drinks, Susan noticed that something seemed to be bothering Phyllis. She had chosen to ignore Phyllis's sullenness, but finally decided that Phyllis was spoiling the good time they all had hoped to have. Susan confronted her. "Phyllis," she said, "you're being pretty hard to get along with. What's your problem?"

Phyllis was experiencing a problem, but she was doing her best to keep it to herself and did not think she was bothering anyone—she certainly was *not* being hard to get along with. Instead of responding directly to Susan, Phyllis picked up her drink and moved to another table. Apparently she was more upset than anyone had imagined, because in a few minutes she came back long enough to say, "Susan, you think you know everything. Well, you aren't so much fun to be around either! I'm leaving and don't expect me to come back!" She then turned and left before Susan could speak.

Susan began to say something, and Tim ran to try to stop Phyllis. Phyllis would not come back, so he returned. Susan was really angry and continued to make negative statements about Phyllis. It was not long before the group left the restaurant.

What about Susan's communication had so angered Phyllis? After all, Susan seemed to sense that she was experiencing some kind of problem. It appears that she was even struggling to remain involved with the group in spite of the situation. The problem seems to lie in the language Susan used to talk to Phyllis. Her statement, "You're being pretty hard to get along with," is not only a negative evaluation of Phyllis but also an implication that Susan thinks she has some right to evaluate Phyllis's behavior. Susan was also labeling her behavior as a "problem," which likewise assumes she has a right to do so.

Both Phyllis and Susan regretted their behavior after they had had time to reflect. They talked about the event and were able to be supportive and show that they cared. We frequently regret our defensive behavior.

It seems that just living life exposes us to conflict. We communicate in ways that trigger unexpected emotional responses from the other. Of course, sometimes the response is not unexpected. We could have predicted the response if we had paid close attention to the language used. Evaluative statements almost always will yield an urge to defend.

> **We can often predict a defensive response just by listening to the language we use.**

This unit will explore *defensive behavior.* We begin with a discussion of why we defend ourselves. Next, we present a detailed explanation of when and how we defend ourselves. We conclude with suggestions for responding differently to defensive communication behavior.

Why We Defend Ourselves

Carl Rogers, a therapist who has studied how to create a supportive climate, and Fritz Roethlisberger have suggested that we have a natural tendency to evaluate and judge others. They believe that a "major barrier to mutual inter-personal communication is our very natural tendency to judge, to evaluate, to approve (or disapprove) the statement of the other person or the other group."[1] Rogers and others that share his concern provide suggestions for counter-acting this natural tendency. These will be the topic of unit 21.

But why do we have this natural tendency? Perhaps we disapprove of someone's behavior that does not match our expectations, and thus we judge that person. Then, if the issue is important, we tell the other how we think he or she should think or behave.

But why do we react in this way? Why was Phyllis so anxious to counter— or at least stop—Susan's judgment of her? The answer might be quite simple. Her judgment, or definition, of Phyllis was quite different from Phyllis's image of herself. This threatened her self-concept. If she had not perceived Susan's judgment as threatening, she might have ignored her, or perhaps acknowl-edged the problem and asked Susan for help. But instead she chose a dra-matic way of saying, "I disagree with your evaluation."

This defense of self-concept specifically involves two areas. First, we defend our view of the outside world. We want our view of correct behavior and thinking to be confirmed. But, even more importantly, our defense of our self-concept involves our defense of our worth as a person. We want to be respected, listened to, and understood. This was Susan's goal when she said, "Phyllis, you're being pretty hard to get along with. What's your problem?"

Worth as a person is at the heart of our defensiveness. We believe that we cannot always be right and are willing to tolerate being wrong some of the time. Yet, we find it intolerable to be denied our worth as a person *and* to be wrong, too. We cannot listen to talk that says that we do not count, that we are inferior, that we do not have the right to have an opinion. When another person evaluates us, we are likely to defend ourselves unless we make a con-scious decision not to.

When and How We Defend Ourselves

There are two basic strategies we use to defend ourselves. We can *avoid* or we can *confront.* There are a number of circumstances in which we decide to ignore or avoid, but two seem especially important. One occurs when we decide the opinion of the other person does not count. In order to care about an eval-uation, we must think the other person's view matters. We can decide that for ourselves, or we can decide that because other people, people we value, think the opinion does not count. If you do not care about the other's evaluation, we can ignore it.

A second reason to ignore another person's evaluation is because we do not want to hear it. Leaving allows us to avoid the evaluation altogether. Can you think of anyone you avoid because you believe that they will say things you do not want to hear?

People also engage in direct confrontation when they feel and believe that they are being attacked. These people—especially those who behave aggressively toward others—take the offensive to defend their self-concepts. They believe the best defense is to counter directly the other person's attack. This kind of confrontation can be carried out supportively if we are willing to utilize assertive and supportive communication behaviors. But often people engage in aggressive communication behavior that generally creates further defensiveness.

Defensive Behavior

In a classic essay, Jack Gibb described the behaviors he observed while listening to groups engaged in defensive communication.[2] He noted that six such behaviors appear regularly: evaluation, superiority, certainty, control, neutrality, and strategy.[3]

Evaluation

Defensive communication involves *evaluation*. We voice a judgment about the other person. We might say, "You are stupid," if we are sufficiently angry. Or we make some assessment of the other person's behavior, such as: "You're not doing your best." Sometimes we question the other person's viewpoint or motives: "I know what you are trying to do. You are trying to manipulate me." Evaluations of this kind are almost always seen as challenges to self-concept and produce an urge to defend ourselves.

Susan's remark, "you're pretty hard to get along with," judges Phyllis. It says that there is something defective in her. The statement is not a challenge to one of Phyllis's ideas about the world but rather to her ideas about her self. It in effect is saying, "You are not a fun person to be around." This negative definition affects the relationship between Susan and Phyllis.

Superiority

Superiority is behavior that implies that you are better than another person, that you are somehow wiser, and that you can make judgments that overrule the other person's sense of self. The question, "How can you say that?" provides an example. The implication of this statement is "I can't imagine any right-thinking person saying what you said. Explain yourself." This suggests that we have some superior knowledge that qualifies us to question the other person's statement. This superiority is often enhanced by avoiding the intonation of a question and using the intonation of a statement.

Evaluation and superiority are closely linked. When a person is in the position to evaluate, that person is assumed to have some superior knowledge or insight. To judge another person, to offer suggestions as to how that person should behave, implies superiority. It implies that we have set ourselves above someone else. Thus, the superior attitude is often a direct attack on the other's self-concept. Susan implied superiority when she judged Phyllis.

Certainty

Certainty is represented by rigidity in view. It suggests confidence in our interpretation of the facts of a particular situation. It often establishes a win-lose situation—if we are right, the other person must be wrong, and proven wrong. This attitude has great potential to harm a relationship. Once we become rigid in our position, we often believe we must put the other person down to "win." When this person resists our attempt, we escalate our effort and risk further damage to our relationship.

Certainty has great potential to harm a relationship.

There is a clear relationship among evaluation, superiority, and certainty. Superiority and certainty are often necessary if our evaluation of another person is to have its intended impact. In other words, evaluation requires superiority, which in turn requires certainty. Consider how Susan spoke to Phyllis. There was no hesitation or sense of doubt in Susan's judgment. She did not say that Phyllis *might* be hard to get along with or that she *might* be experiencing a problem. She said, with confidence and certainty, that Phyllis was hard to get along with, and that she had a problem. This was a direct affront to Phyllis's self-concept, one that she could not let go unchallenged.

The use of language that indicates certainty of judgment will, in all probability, cause negative reactions. Since views frequently differ, and since there seems to be no room for negotiation when certainty exists, the most likely response is confrontation and challenge.

Control

Control means creating messages that either intimidate or suggest inadequacy in an attempt to get what we want from the other person. You may try to impose an attitude or viewpoint because you want someone else to believe as you do. Control may also come in the form of a threat in an attempt to keep the other person from doing something. For example, you might say, "If you do not spend more time with me, I'll start seeing other people."

Attempts to control imply that the other person is somehow inadequate. This implies a judgment and superiority. We often imply, "I am right and you are wrong. Adopt this way of doing it. Think this about yourself. Do what I want." Most people will feel hurt when the other person in the relationship wants to exercise excessive control. The result may be an attempt to make a defense, and perhaps to withdraw from the relationship.

Neutrality

A defensive climate is also created by *neutrality*. Neutrality suggests that we have little concern for the other person's viewpoint. When we attempt to control the other person, we often display neutrality. It is as if we are saying, "I know that you have a view, but I am right and I don't care if you have a different view. Agree with me." Not wanting to hear and understand the other person's view communicates that she does not count; that her view is not worth considering. This neutrality will surely result in an attempt at self-defense.

Neutrality also indicates that we do not care about the other person's feelings. Imagine a fight with someone who is crying and showing other signs of being deeply hurt. You are so angry that you say, "Cry if you like. This is the way it is going to be!" This verbal disregard of the other's feelings, usually accompanied by nonverbal displays of disregard, often causes the other person to lash out in an effort to hurt and show disregard.

Strategy

The final behavior that produces defensiveness is the application of a *strategy* designed to trick another person into making the decision or thinking the way we want.

This strategy may be overt or covert. An overt strategy might be to employ some or all of the behaviors that cause defensiveness. For example, if you show that you are not interested in someone's opinion and indicate that you want that person to believe that your opinion is the only one that counts, you are deliberately planning to gain an advantage over her. If the other realizes you are using a strategy of manipulation, she may then resent you. She will object and do what she can to defend herself, most likely by attacking you in the same ways that you've attacked her. A covert strategy, on the other hand, might be to cause her to believe that you are interested in her viewpoint while subtly trying to cause her to accept your own. You may be successful, but resentment and hostility will result if you are found out!

Strategy is acceptable in a chess game because it is a game of attack and defense.
Strategy is not a wise tactic in a relationship.

Table 20.1 lists the characteristics of each of the six behaviors that create
defensiveness. You can use it to analyze communication in your relationships.
Careful analysis may uncover some surprises. You may find, as many have,
that you are not as conscious of your behavior toward the other person as you
might be. You may also discover that you want to change your communication
behavior.

Consequences of Defensive Behavior

When we become involved in defensive communication, we begin to focus on
ourselves. We plan messages to use in self-defense. We stop listening, so we
are not likely to hear the other person's position. The other person might be
making some important points and even trying to accommodate our position,
but all in vain. We find that being firm in our position often keeps us from losing,
so we become even more rigid. Often we repeat the position as a response to
whatever the other person says. We get absorbed in our own thoughts and

Table 20.1 Characteristics of Defensive Climates

Evaluation   To make a judgment about another person; to make an assessment of the other to raise questions about the other's viewpoint or motives

Superiority   To communicate that you are superior; to suggest that the other person is inadequate in comparison

Certainty   To be rigid in your viewpoint; to try to correct the other; to assume a win-lose position

Control   To try to manipulate the other; to attempt to impose an attitude or viewpoint on another; to try to keep the other from doing something; to imply that another person is inadequate

Neutrality   To show little or no concern for the other or his problems and viewpoint; to treat the other as an object rather than a person

Strategy   To plan what you want and then trick the other into thinking he is making the decision; to cause the other to feel that you have an interest in her when you do not

Source: J. R. Gibb, "Defensive Communication," *The Journal of Communication* 11:3 (September 1961): 142–45. Adapted by permission.

become less sensitive to nonverbal cues. Our perception becomes distorted. Finally, if the other person persists—and this is likely because the other person has also stopped listening and becomes rigid—we try to lash out and hurt that person. It is as if by hurting the other, we win despite what that person does. But have we really won?

Regret

Perhaps you can remember a time when you lashed out. But did you actually win much of anything? More likely, you regretted the event. Especially in close interpersonal situations, in which you really do have a stake in the outcome, the result is usually *regret*. We wish that we had had more control and that we had not hurt the other. Susan's willingness to talk with Phyllis about their difficulty may well have been motivated by regret.

Hostility

Defensive behavior also often leads to hostility because both the aggressor and the defender are manipulating. Their strategies are calculated to achieve their personal ends. This is not to say that people should not achieve their own goals. Rather, when manipulation is used to achieve personal ends at the expense of another, hostility often follows. The outcome of hostile behavior appears to be neutrality, the "I don't care" attitude. What often follows is "I want to hurt you."

Damage to the Relationship

Defensive behavior does serve the function of defending oneself, but seldom does it achieve any lasting or satisfying results. When people become rigid in their positions and stop listening, there is no way to resolve their differences. At least there is no way that is likely to be satisfying to all involved. Certain strategies are often employed by a given individual, but the results are generally damaging. For example, you might lash out—hurt the other person so badly that she lets you have your way. This is winning only in the sense that you got your way. However, you lose in the sense that you may have damaged the relationship.

Another strategy is pulling rank. This involves imposing your viewpoint on the other person because you are in a position of power. Resentment is generated, and the relationship is probably damaged. In the work place, this means that the damaged worker is likely to be less productive and may even sabotage the work effort. Even though the boss "won," she also lost.

Reflexive Behavior

Is it necessary to engage in defensive behavior? We believe that it generally is not. You can select an alternative and then have more control of your own behavior. You can decide not to use defensive behaviors once you understand what they and the alternatives are. Knowing the general outcomes of defensive behavior may be helpful in persuading you to remain supportive. If you know that "winning" usually also means losing, you will be more likely to choose behaviors that have a greater "winning" potential.

At a second level, many interpersonal transactions are *reflexive behaviors.* This means that what we do affects what others are likely to do. This principle operates when we decide to become defensive. But we can decide *not* to become defensive. In this case, the other person will find it more difficult to continue the attack. Thus, the other is encouraged to adopt more reasonable and perhaps supportive behavior.

Refusal to accept the definition of the situation as defensive can have a profound effect on the other person's ability to define it. It is difficult to fight with someone who will not fight! But in addition to not fighting, you also counter the wrong definition of a situation with your own definition. Remaining supportive (instead of defensive) is saying to the other person, "I want to talk about the situation. I want to talk in a way that won't damage our relationship. I want us both to be satisfied with the outcome. Let's cooperate in deciding."

Many interpersonal transactions are reflexive, especially when the parties involved have some commitment to the relationship. Commitment may spring from liking and affection, or it may spring from interdependency. Interdependency means that each person needs the other for some reason. For example, the boss needs you to get the work done, and you need the boss—or at least you need a job. Commitment makes a difference in how the other person is treated. If one person ignores the other's attempts at fairness, the commitment is damaged. If both parties behave badly, both have ignored the commitment. Then, to the degree that they understand the commitment, remaining supportive should have an influence on the outcome.

This was essentially what happened with Susan and Phyllis when their communication broke down. Both behaved defensively. This damaged their relationship. Because the group had a stake in the relationship (even though the other members did not participate in the exchange), other group members could legitimately demand that an attempt be made to restore the relationship.

Summary

This unit focused on the behavior displayed when you are engaged in supportive and defensive communication. Rogers argued that people engage in defensive behavior because there is a natural tendency to evaluate others. He concluded that this is a major barrier to effective interpersonal communication. This tendency to evaluate is often met with defensiveness. Evaluation suggests some defect in the other person, who may feel a need to defend his self-concept—to say that his view counts and that he has a right to his perspective.

Sometimes you defend yourself by ignoring or avoiding the other person altogether. But if these choices are unavailable, you may attack. American culture teaches that "the best defense is a good offense."

Defensive behavior involves six categories of communication: evaluation, superiority, certainly, control, neutrality, and strategy. The consequences of defensive communication behavior are numerous. Perhaps the most damaging are:

1. Defensive communication may signal rejection or disconfirmation. Rejection is an outright denial of the other person's definition of self. Disconfirmation suggests that the person or person's opinion does not exist.
2. Defensive communication may lead a person to stop listening, become rigid in her position, and perhaps lash out at the attacker.
3. Defensive communication may lead to hostility. When others do not seem to care and do not seem to take you into account, you become hostile.

Discussion Questions

1. In what social contexts are you likely to behave defensively? What behavior in particular do you use to express defensiveness? Given what you have learned in this unit, how will you work to alleviate defensiveness?

2. Identify three people you know well. What causes them to behave defensively? Does your behavior produce this?
3. Using Gibb's six categories to analyze defensive situations in which you have been involved, do you think he is right or wrong? Are your behaviors consistent with what he says will produce defensiveness?

Endnotes

1. C. R. Rogers and F. J. Roethlisberger, "Barriers and Gateways to Communication," *Harvard Business Review* (July–August 1952): 28–34.
2. J. R. Gibb, "Defensive Communication," *The Journal of Communication* 11:3 (September 1961): 141–48.
3. Gibb's theory has received considerable support from textbook authors because it makes sense and is easily applied. Some empirical support for the theory is beginning to appear. See J. V. Civikly, R. W. Pace, and R. M. Krause, "Interviewer and Client Behaviors in Supportive and Defensive Interviews," *Communication Yearbook I,* ed. B. D. Ruben (New Brunswick, NJ: Transition Books, 1977), 347–62; and W. F. Eadie, "Defensive Communication Revisited: A Critical Examination of Gibb's Theory," *The Southern Speech Communication Journal* 47 (Winter 1982): 163–77.

⫸|⫷
UNIT 21
Supportiveness in Relationships

Preview
Relationships can be enhanced if you
know how to create and maintain a
supportive climate. This unit offers
suggestions on how and when to be more
supportive. Supportive behavior has many
benefits for the relationship.

Objectives
1. Identify the characteristics of
   supportive communication behavior.
2. Explain the benefits of supportive
   communication behavior.
3. Specify how you can help remain
   supportive when you have a difference
   with a partner in a relationship.

Key Terms
description
empathy
equality
inference
problem orientation
provisionalism
spontaneity
supportive communication

Supportive communication behavior reflects an attitude toward the other person in the relationship. What you do is related to your experience with that person. In other words, you have developed ways of managing the situations that produce defensiveness from a particular person. And even if those methods are not particularly productive, you are likely to continue to use them unless you make an effort to change. Change is most easily accomplished by working with the person to initiate the change. You might decide to work toward a more supportive relationship. *Supportive communication* is talk that affirms the other person and the relationship; defensive communication disconfirms the other person and the relationship.

We can decide to work toward more supportive relationships.

Carl Rogers captured the essence of the supportive attitude with his term "unconditional positive regard." He explained the attitude and its effects on the other person:

> [A supportive attitude] . . . means that he prizes the client in a total, rather than a conditional way. I mean that he does not simply accept the client when he is behaving in certain ways and disapprove of him when he behaves in other ways. He experiences an outgoing, positive feeling, without reservations, without *evaluations*. The term we have come to use for this attitude is "unconditional positive regard," and we believe that, the more this attitude is experienced by the therapist and perceived by his client, the more likelihood there is that therapy will be successful and that change and development will take place.[1]

Rogers was referring to the therapeutic setting and the healing that takes place when the supportive attitude of a therapist is perceived by the client. This principle is also important in our day-to-day communication. A supportive communication climate allows for *change* and *development*. It enhances the relationship by enabling the participants to understand and adjust their viewpoints in a nonthreatening environment.

Characteristics of Supportive Climates

Consider this short dialogue that took place when Jean was trying to help her friend, Ryan, overcome a difference he had with a group to which they both belong. Jean tried to be supportive. "Ryan," she said, "I wonder if we can talk about what was going on last night at Stan's? I can see that you are pretty upset with Phil, and perhaps the group, too. I wonder if you're willing to talk about what we did to cause you to feel so frustrated and angry. The group asked me to talk to you. We like you and want you to come back." "Well, Jean," Ryan answered, "Phil was being absolutely impossible. He's always on my case and I'm not going to take any more of it. If he'd change his attitude about people, he'd be decent. I'm through with him—and those other people, too!''

Jean was being generally supportive, and Ryan sensed this. Her supportive behavior set an atmosphere for potential understanding. Her communication defined how she saw their relationship, and Ryan was willing to accept that definition. We will use her language to illustrate some of what we have to say about supportive communication.

Jack Gibb identified six categories of supportive communication behavior: description, equality, provisionalism, problem orientation, empathy, and spontaneity.[2] We will present each of these and illustrate how the communication might be carried out within a relationship. Then we will discuss the benefits that supportive communication can have for a relationship. Finally, we will present some ideas that will help you be supportive.

Supportive Communication Behavior

Description

Description is nonjudgmental communication that presents factual information about perceptions regarding what was happening in a situation. It may be about feelings, actions, or events. The communication does not imply or ask that the other person change his behavior. It also includes straightforward requests for factual information.

You can avoid the defensive communication called evaluation by using descriptive behavior instead. To do this, you must be able to recognize an *inference*. An inference is a conclusion based on your interpretation of what you observe. An interpretation of many events involves your subjective evaluation. In this case, it is close to what Gibb called evaluation: It is an opinion about what *you* observed. Thus, an inference is not a description; it's an evaluation.

There is really very little description in the conversation between Jean and Ryan but neither is there any evaluation. Jean made only one inference: ''I can see that you are pretty upset with Phil. . . .'' Her use of the word ''are'' made the inference sound like a judgment. She could have made it sound like an inference saying, ''you seem to be.''

Equality

Equality is the presentation of ideas in such a way that the other person sees us as like them in status. It has nothing to do with the actual status of the person or the definition of status within the relationship. It is rather a statement about how we are viewing the other person in relation to us for the immediate communication event. We display equality by not ''pulling rank''; minimizing

What is this person doing? Your answer is an *inference*—a conclusion based on your interpretation of what you observe.

differences in ability, status, and power; treating the other person's views with the same respect that we give to our own views.

Notice also that Jean did not "pull rank." She was careful not to put herself in a superior position by either her verbal or nonverbal communication. She picked a time and place when she could talk to Ryan on his own ground. She went to him even though she could have called him and asked him to come to her place to talk. She also did not offer him advice or give her interpretation of what had happened at Stan's. She tried to remain an equal by minimizing any differences in status and position. Remaining equal helps a person feel supported.

Provisionalism

Provisionalism is behavior that suggests tentativeness in presenting ideas. The word "seems" conveys tentativeness; the word "is" conveys certainty. Provisional language suggests that if more data were presented, you might be willing to change our attitudes and views. It allows for the possibility that the other person could have a view that is different from yours that you would be willing to consider.

Jean also tempered her approach with provisionalism. She included several tentative statements in her dialogue. For example, she said, "I wonder *if* we can talk about what was going on last night at Stan's?" The use of "if" allows Ryan to choose not to talk. In the second part of the sentence, Jean avoids certainty by suggesting that she is open to interpretations other than her own.

Jean also said, "I *can see that you are* pretty upset. . . ." No provisionalism exists in this statement. Instead, she exhibited certainty, one of the communication behaviors most likely to yield defensiveness. She could not *see* that Ryan was upset. She could perhaps see his facial expressions, body posture, and tension and hear his tone of voice, phrasing, and pausing. But Jean could not *see* that Ryan was upset. She had to *guess* that her observations meant something, and she called that something "upset." Jean's guess was correct—Ryan *was* upset.

But what if it had been incorrect? Suppose your interpersonal communication instructor meets you outside the classroom. She knows that your mark on the midterm examination was low. She also believes that you will not like the mark because she has an image of you as an achievement-motivated individual who takes pride in a consistently high grade-point average. So she hands you your paper before class begins and says, "I know you'll be upset with the grade. Would you like to talk about it?" What does her guess do to your relationship? It puts you on the defensive.

You now have to process the low grade in her presence and, perhaps, in the presence of other students. You also have to do so on very short notice, and moreover, you have to deal with your emotional condition using language she has placed upon it—"upset." She has *seen* that you are upset, so, clearly, you *are* upset. You are not allowed any other options, such as, for example, surprise, relief (if you didn't get the F you expected), or confusion. Or suppose the paper she handed you was not your paper. Does this mean that in all other interactions, she did not know who you were?

To defend yourself, you may do a number of things. You might, for example, play the passive role. That is, play it cool. Do not let anyone know what you are experiencing. Above all, do not involve yourself with the teacher, since that individual carries all the power in the teacher-student relationship.

You might also defend yourself by attacking her. You might use strong language. For instance, you might judge the quality of the test, complaining about the vagueness of the questions and the unfairness of including certain subjects. If she buys into your game, your low mark would be her fault, and you would have successfully defended yourself.

Problem Orientation

Gibb defines a *problem orientation* as an approach to talking about differences that conveys "a desire to collaborate in defining a mutual problem and seeking its solution."[3] We are saying by our words and actions that we have no solution, viewpoint, or behavior that we plan to impose on the other person. The problem orientation requires that both people present their ideas and goals by using provisional communication so that they can jointly evaluate the situation and come to a decision.

A problem orientation suggests to the other person that we are willing to share in the problem-solving process. The exchange between Jean and Ryan also exhibits this. Jean's question, "I wonder if *we* can talk about what was going on last night at Stan's?," suggests a problem orientation. She seems to be saying, "Let's work together so that we can understand this and agree on how you can rejoin the group." She makes no attempt to control Ryan by either interpreting what was going on or giving him a preconceived solution to the conflict. She makes it clear that she expects to engage in joint problem solving with Ryan.

Empathy

Gibb recommended a fifth supportive behavior, *empathy,* which we can show by listening carefully, perhaps using active listening, and telling the person that we understand how they feel and why. You might say, "Sue, I understand that you felt really devastated when you did not get that job. I think that I might understand how you felt. I had a similar experience a couple of years ago." Genuine empathy can also be demonstrated by showing respect for the other person's value system and affirming that person's worth. Language such as "I think I can understand how you would see it that way" can achieve this.

Showing empathy is an important factor in promoting relational growth. Genuine empathy is very powerful because it represents an attempt to understand the other person's position and possibly even to identify with the problem. Empathy requires effort from the listener. Empathy is usually valued and viewed as supportive. For example, Jean attempted to empathize with Ryan by saying, "I have had some frustration myself, so I can *understand* how you might have that kind of experience with the group." Ryan recognized her effort. Thus, by establishing a caring atmosphere, she reduced his sense of threat to his self-concept.

An empathic attitude is also communicated nonverbally. Your face and body can signal that you do care about the other person. False concern can produce mixed messages; you can say you care with your words but that you don't care with your actions. When messages are mixed, the nonverbal behavior is usually that which is believed.

A display of empathy, if it is to be effective, must flow from a sensitivity to the other person. Gerald Miller and Mark Steinberg said that it must be a transactional process.[4] By this they meant that we receive information from a person about his or her experience. Then we must read these messages accurately and decide to respond empathically. Sometimes it is difficult to read these messages because they may take the form of subtle nonverbal cues. At

Empathy must flow from sensitivity to the other person.

other times, the verbal and nonverbal messages might contradict each other. We must thus carefully and skillfully analyze what the other person is telling us. Finally, we must make a decision about the effect of empathy. Miller and Steinberg suggest that we ask, "Would an empathic response be rewarding to this person?" It might be that the person is having a bad day and would rather not be reminded of the fact.

Spontaneity

Finally, Gibb identified *spontaneity* as a quality of supportive communication. Spontaneity is direct, honest, and straightforward behavior and communication. It suggests that we present our views openly while using other kinds of supportive behavior. When spontaneity does not involve description, equality, and provisionalism, the straightforwardness can be hurtful.

Sometimes circumstances are such that being open about our feelings would be destructive to the communication. If you are feeling very angry, you have thoughts that you would not have if you were in a different frame of mind. Perhaps you should wait to talk about the differences you are having. There are things in every relationship that might be better left unsaid. Spontaneous communication behavior must be tempered with good judgment if it is to promote relational growth.

''Spontaneous behavior'' is not planned. What this means in practice is that we have not carefully selected the words we use to express our ideas. Sometimes you may want to select carefully the precise words you will use. But consider how such careful selection might be interpreted. Your nonverbal behavior might suggest that you have something to hide or that you are trying to manipulate. Spontaneous behavior is often the better choice.

Jean was being straightforward when she spoke to Ryan about the problem. She stated exactly why she wanted to talk and what she wanted from the communication.

Table 21.1 summarizes and compares defensive and supportive behavior. The two types are presented in column form so that you can compare them.

Benefits of Supportive Communication

Supportiveness can have a positive effect on the communication providing two requirements are met. First, the behavior must be perceived as genuine. For example, if you are being so frank that it is out of character or beyond the bounds of normal behavior, the spontaneity may be seen as a manipulative strategy to gain the other's trust and is apt to produce defensiveness.

Second, the quality of the relationship may affect the success of an attempt to be supportive. Some caring, or at least some dependency, must exist if the attempt is to matter to the other person. If you do not care what a friend thinks about you, you can treat him in almost any way you want. You can, for example, try to hurt him without worrying about the effect.

Providing these two requirements are met, four important benefits are possible from supportive communication: encouragement, acceptance, dialogue and understanding, and relational growth.

Supportive Behavior Provides Encouragement

It is easy to be discouraged about our ability to handle our interpersonal relationships. Supportive behavior counters these sources of discouragement. Instead of discouraging, supportive behavior improves interpersonal relationships and affirms the other person in an encouraging way. It also provides a greater chance of achieving interpersonal goals because it encourages us to talk through our differences without feeling threatened.

Table 21.1 Defensive and Supportive Behavior

Defensive	Supportive
Evaluation	*Description*
To make a judgment about another person; to make an assessment of the other, to raise questions about the other's viewpoint or motives	To be nonjudgmental, to ask straightforward questions, to request factual information, to present descriptions that do not force the other person to change behavior or attitude
Superiority	*Equality*
To communicate that you are superior; to suggest that the other person is inadequate in comparison	To avoid pulling rank; to show the other respect; to minimize differences in ability, status, and power
Certainty	*Provisionalism*
To be rigid in your viewpoint; to try to correct the other; to take on a win-lose position	To be tentative with your behavior, attitudes, and views; to convey the attitude that more data might change your mind; to solve problems with the other rather than to impose your own view; to share data and work jointly on a task give-and-take fashion
Control	*Problem Orientation*
To try to manipulate the other; to attempt to impose an attitude or viewpoint on another; to try to keep the other from doing something	To want to engage in mutual problem solving; to suggest by your words and actions that you have no solution, viewpoint, or behavior to impose on the other
Neutrality	*Empathy*
To show little or no concern for the other or his problems and viewpoint; to treat the other as an object rather than a person	To identify with the other person's problems and feelings; to show respect for the other's value system; to affirm the other's worth as a person
Strategy	*Spontaneity*
To plan what you want and then trick the other into thinking he is making the decision; to cause the other to feel that you have an interest in her when you do not	To express straightforward behavior; to avoid deceiving; to have unhidden, uncomplicated viewpoints and motives; to be honest

Source: J. R. Gibb, "Defensive Communication," *The Journal of Communication* 11:3 (September 1961): 142–45. Adapted by permission.

Supportive Behavior Enhances the Possibility of Acceptance

The person who causes another to "give in" wins the argument but does not gain real acceptance of either the outcome *or* himself. But supportiveness can produce acceptance in both areas. When you convey acceptance of the other person and the other's ideas, you are likely to create a feeling of trust and confidence. Even if the final decision is not to the other's liking, such a feeling is beneficial to the relationship.

Supportive Behavior Encourages Dialogue and Understanding

Supportive behavior encourages us to listen. When we listen, we are more likely to understand the other. If we are both listening and trying to understand, genuine dialogue can take place. In contrast, defensive behavior often leads to ineffective listening and rigidity. Obviously, defensiveness does not encourage productive communication.

Supportive behavior offers a far greater chance of success and growth in our relationship because it encourages us to approach others as equals, to engage in joint problem solving, and to listen carefully in order to express empathy. The result is honest, straightforward communication.

Supportive Behavior Encourages Relational Growth

Supportive communication promotes self-esteem, self-disclosure, and growth in our relationships. Supportive behavior allows us to feel more confident. Trust develops, which in turn promotes sharing. Sharing helps us understand ourselves more fully, to be confident, to try new things, and to grow as people. If we engage in defensive communication, we risk potentially negative conse-

Supportive behavior encourages relational growth.

quences for both ourselves and our relationships. The attack on another person's self-concept and the lashing out that often accompanies such defensive communication can lead to a disengagement process.[5] Obviously, there is no growth in the relationship when this occurs.

Growth and engagement result from sharing made possible by the trust we develop in each other. We are able to decrease risk because we believe that there is greater likelihood of support. Trust allows self-disclosure. The opportunity to get to know another person in a nonthreatening environment, even when there is disagreement, provides an opportunity to find what we have in common. This, in turn, can promote liking and attraction. Thus, supportive behavior is a key to a growth-promoting atmosphere in our interpersonal relationships.

Remaining Supportive

Supportive communication sounds simple, but is very difficult. Because it is not as easy as it seems, we want to offer some pointers on remaining supportive.

You Can Disagree and Remain Supportive

You do not have to suppress your viewpoint and accept the other person's to be supportive. Supportiveness is not a matter of right and wrong. You can disagree and still work out an understanding without attacking the other person. For example, you might say, "I disagree with your position, but I do understand how you can believe as you do. Can we work out a cooperative position?" A statement like this says that, while you disagree, you know the other person has a legitimate viewpoint and that you are willing to cooperate in coming to a decision. This kind of relational affirmation will make it easier for you and the other person to talk about your disagreement.

Understanding the Need for Interdependency

Try to figure out if there is some sort of caring or mutual need in your relationship. Every relationship has some degree of interdependence. Understand the strength of this interdependence. If it is strong, there is a chance that a particular need will cause the person to be concerned about how she treats you. Interdependency helps check the other's tendency to treat you badly in the face of your supportive behavior. Sometimes it helps to affirm the other as a way of beginning a talk. One young person started a difficult conversation with her parents by saying, "I need to talk with you about a decision I've made. I first want to say that I care a great deal for you and your opinion. But as I am growing up, I need to make some decisions for myself." Then she talked to them about a young man she had agreed to marry.

Look for the Best Time to Talk

Sometimes people get caught in an emotional rage and are unable to respond to supportiveness. Under such circumstances it is better to postpone the talk. The other is probably incapable of listening. Withdraw from such an unproductive moment without damaging the relationship but make a commitment to talk later. Be sure to carry through with your stated intentions; approach the person at a more appropriate time.

Practice the Supportive Skills, Especially Empathy and Equality

Incorporating supportive communication skills into your routine behavior may be a slow task. Try being supportive at the very next opportunity. Practice the skills aloud. For example, how many ways can you think of to say or suggest:

1. The behavior in question may be described as. . . ."
2. We share this problem. Let's work at solving it cooperatively.
3. "I understand and can relate to your problems and feelings."
4. "You and I have equal status, power, and ability. We're both O.K. just the way we are."
5. "Your position is legitimate. You have a point of view. I am willing to discuss this issue with an open mind. I am not certain. . . ."

Remember that the habitual tendency to be critical is difficult to overcome. As you increase your skill with language and nonverbal communication, practice in more difficult relational settings. You will discover that you can be supportive, that it does make a difference, and that this gives you a new and welcome freedom.

Focus on empathy and equality. If you are empathic, you will listen more carefully. If you avoid "pulling rank," you will avoid the notion of superiority. These two attitudes generate a definition of the relationship that promotes the other supportive behaviors.

Summary

The alternative to defensiveness is supportiveness. Supportive communication is characterized as descriptive, equal, provisional, problem oriented, empathic, and spontaneous behavior. Supportiveness produces many important benefits for both the person and the person's relationships: It gives encouragement, enhances the possibility of acceptance, encourages dialogue and understanding, and promotes interpersonal growth.

There are four ways to improve supportive communication. Tell yourself that you can disagree and still remain supportive. Understand the need for interdependency. Look for the best time to talk. Practice the supportive skills that Gibb suggests. If you learn to communicate supportively, your relationships will be better, more satisfying, and more productive. These benefits seem worth the effort necessary to obtain them.

Discussion Questions

1. Using Gibb's six categories of supportive communication, analyze a situation in which you successfully managed a difference. Were your behaviors consistent with what Gibb said would produce a supportive climate? Give examples of your supportive behaviors.
2. How can you help yourself remain supportive when you have a difference in opinion with another person? How can you help the other person remain supportive?

Endnotes

1. C. R. Rogers, "The Therapeutic Relationship: Recent Theory and Research," in *The Human Dialogue: Perspectives on Communication*, ed. F. W. Matson and A. Montagu (New York: The Free Press, 1967).
2. J. R. Gibb, "Defensive Communication," *The Journal of Communication* 11:3 (September 1961): 141–48.
3. Ibid., 143.
4. G. R. Miller and M. Steinberg, *Between People: A New Analysis of Interpersonal Communication* (Chicago: Science Research Associates, 1975), 174–76.
5. I. Altman and D. A. Taylor, *Social Penetration: The Development of Interpersonal Relationships* (New York: Holt, Rinehart and Winston, 1973), 173–80.

≫|≪ UNIT 22
Managing Power in Relationships

Preview

All relationships involve needs and dependency. We have a great deal of power because of these factors. We can learn to use power more effectively when we understand the types that are available. Part of any analysis of power use should be its costs and benefits. This unit is designed to help you understand power and use it effectively in interpersonal relationships.

Objectives

1. Define the concept of power.
2. Tell how power is relational and how relational factors affect it.
3. Describe and illustrate the various power bases.
4. Describe power games, including strategies for managing them.

Key Terms

coercive power
expert power
importance
legitimate power
power
referent power
reward power

It is difficult to imagine a relationship in which power does not play an important role.[1] There is a power dynamic in family, work, and social relationships. That power is a part of life seems so obvious that we will not take the time to present our evidence. You must understand power if you are to manage your relationships effectively.

We begin this unit by defining power and showing how it is relational. Then we examine the types that are available for use. Finally, we present some common power games with representative language that might be appropriate for managing them.

Power Defined

Power has been defined as the ability or potential to influence others.[2] But what exactly is this "potential to influence"? Wally Jacobson suggests that it involves two factors—needs and dependency:

> If we want or need certain things, material or nonmaterial, that another person possesses, we are dependent upon that person in proportion to the strength of our desire for these things. Further, our dependence upon another is simultaneously related to whether we can get those same things from sources other than the person on whom we are originally dependent.[3]

Power, then, is perceived influence that one person has over another and is based on the other's dependency. To the extent that the other person is dependent upon us and perceives that dependency, we have power over him. Further, this person's dependency is reduced by the degree that he believes that these needs can be fulfilled elsewhere.

Power Is Relational

One of the important facts about power is that it is relational. It is generally not an attribute of the power user. Instead, it belongs to the social relationship. Thus, power is only effective if someone allows us to use it. If the other person does not wish us to use power, she might choose to ignore us, to withdraw from the relationship, or to otherwise prevent us from exercising it.

Endorsement Factors

Willingness to allow a power attempt depends, in part, on the appropriateness of the source of power. One of the appropriateness factors is the relational definition. Every relationship is based upon some definition of how the partners stand in relation to each other. A number of terms might help you think about power in relationships. One set is "equal/equal" versus "superior/subordinate." Imagine how one of these definitions might affect your willingness to allow someone to use power. The use of *coercive power*—power that is based upon threat of punishment—provides an example. If a relationship has been defined as equal/equal (perhaps a friendship), one of the friends may reject the other's attempt to exercise coercion. On the other hand, in a superior/subordinate relationship (perhaps in the work place), the subordinate may be willing to accept coercive power even though he does not particularly like it.

A second factor (one that may override the definitional factor) is *importance*. Two aspects of importance may have an effect. First, you may endorse a power attempt because the relationship is more important than the issue. Suppose, for example, that a friend wants to borrow ten dollars. You have a strong aversion to lending money to anyone, yet your friend says, "I can't understand why you won't lend me ten dollars. What are friends for? I guess we aren't as good friends as I thought!" Perhaps you sense that this issue is going to threaten your relationship and thus lend your friend the money.

The second aspect of importance is the value assigned to some issue. You may go along with power use because you realize the issue is more important to the power holder than the relationship. Suppose you have a significant dating relationship with a person who is not as serious about religion as you are. This person says to you, "Quit bugging me about going to church with you. When you do this, I don't think you love me. You know I don't want to go to church. If you don't stop, it is going to affect the way I feel about you." You reply, "My church is very important to me. You will go with me if you want to date me." If your strategy worked, it did because you figured correctly that the relationship was more important than the issue of going to church. In such a situation, both kinds of importance are operating to allow coercion in an equal/equal relationship. So the two factors that control the exercise of power are (1) how we define the relationship, and (2) importance.

Commitment to the Relationship

Compliance to a power attempt is related to the commitment each person has to the relationship. We can imagine situations in which we are equally committed and thus equally dependent on each other. In these cases, neither person has more power.

Many relationships, however, are not evenly balanced. When one person is less committed to the relationship, she has more power because she may be willing to risk the relationship to get what she wants. The person who cares more may go along with a power play rather than risk the relationship.

The relationship itself is not always the issue. Instead, the rewards that are available in the relationship may be at stake. Imbalance in the need to be rewarded can be a source of power. For example, if I need your love and affection very much, I may do what you want in order to keep receiving them. You would have a great deal of power under these circumstances.

Power Bases

One of the best descriptions of power is by John French and Bertran Raven and their associates,[4] who identified five bases or categories of power: referent, expert, legitimate, reward, and coercive.

Referent Power

Referent power is available when someone identifies with you because that person likes you and values several of your attributes. The more this is true, the more that person will want to please you. Thus the referent power increases.

One of the clearest examples of referent power is the emulation a younger sibling attempts because of the attraction to an older sibling. A seven-year-old girl we know does all she can to emulate her eleven-year-old brother. She wears clothes like his, refusing to wear dresses. She asks for toys that are like his, rejecting dolls. She asks to enroll in karate because she admires his involvement. He has power because he serves as her referent. He can get her to do many things for him.

Referent power is based on liking.

The use of referent power may or may not be conscious. For example, if you are attracted to someone, you may do things without being told. A teacher may hear from former students who, years after they have left the university, report on how influential the teacher was—much to the surprise of the teacher! In this case the teacher exerted unconscious influence on the student. The same kind of influence occurs in other relationships. Parents, for example, often exert referent power that guides their childrens' behavior when they are not present.

Expert Power

Sometimes we are able to exert *expert power* over others because we have knowledge that they do not possess. A physician, for example, can influence you in matters of health but may not be able to help you remodel your house. You might follow an accountant's recommendations on tax matters but not on managing a relationship conflict. In fact, you may consider an influence attempt outside an area of expertise to be a matter of poor judgment.[5]

We are sometimes influenced by the comments of a well-respected person because we think that the person's superior intelligence in one area may be representative of a more general expertise. Thus we may think that an accountant or even a physician may know something about investing money, or that clergy are able to comment on interpersonal relations.

We are also more apt to be influenced if the source of power seems to be unbiased. The fact that an expert does not have anything to gain by what she says may give her greater power.

Legitimate Power

Legitimate power usually comes with position; a belief that people in certain positions have a right to direct and influence the activities of others. Those who exercise leadership in our society—clergy, political officials, industrialists—may have influence because of their accomplishments and positions. A parent is also in this position in relation to young children. A supervisor is in this position in relation to employees. Legitimate power is a result of the role and has little to do with the person occupying the role. Legitimate power is not limited to formal role relationships. Our culture extends legitimate rights to exercise power to certain people. We can sometimes be influenced by an older person, for example.

Reward Power

Reward power, sometimes called reinforcement power, comes from control of something that is valued by the other person. This may be tangible (perhaps money or material goods) or intangible (love or faithfulness). Of course, the

Legitimate Power

significance of the possession is an important factor in the amount of power we have to exercise. If the person values the fact that you do little favors, he might do a great deal to please you so that you continue to do them.

A relationship usually implies some kind of reward power. We maintain relationships because they are rewarding in some way. The more rewarding the relationship, the greater the reward power. Rewards may include affection, stimulation, meaningfulness, material goods, security, and confirmation of the other person. Their significance can vary according to the nature of the relationship. In a friendship, for example, you might emphasize affection; in a work situation, you might emphasize material rewards.

Coercive Power

Coercive power is generally associated with force: We threaten in some way. You might threaten to do something (perhaps dissolve the relationship) or to withhold something (perhaps our affection). Teachers might reward with high grades and punish with low grades. Parents might reward by increasing allowance and punish by withholding allowance.

Coercive power is only effective when the person toward whom it is directed actually believes that it may be used. For example, parents who threaten but rarely follow through find that their threats do not seem to have much power. In a dating relationship, if someone threatens to withhold affection, but only withdraws it temporarily and then "kisses and makes up," he may find attempt to use coercive power ineffective.

The strength of coercive power depends upon how the other person views the punishment. If it seems mild, we may decide that we will do as we please to see if the other is really willing to carry through. Coercive power is strongest when the punishment seems severe and highly likely to be administered.

Costs and Benefits of Power Use

Some power attempts are costly. Coercive power may be the most costly. It is most effective when the power agent does not have to carry out the threat. The primary method of convincing a person that we might carry out a threat is to have done so in the past. Punishment yields negative feelings that are difficult to overcome. Thus, coercion is costly because it decreases attractiveness. In addition, a power agent must be prepared to receive hostile and angry feelings from the other.

Coercive power affects the recipient's ability to perform and learn. A study by K. Sheley and Marvin Shaw showed that use of coercive power caused people working in a group to *decrease* their performance following their leader's plea for *greater* effort.[6] In a classroom setting, Virginia Richmond and her associates found that coercive power decreased both cognitive and affective learning.[7] These same findings seem also to apply to excessive use of legitimate power.

The use of power may be costly for the user.

The use of coercive power can also backfire. Coercion can create a martyr of the recipient of a power attempt. In this case the person may become angry and gain increased satisfaction by not complying. The noncompliance may then create anger in the power user that may reward the target of the coercion.[8]

There can also be an unexpected cost associated with the use of expert power. When information is shared, the other person is no longer dependent on the expert for the information. This is why in work contexts, some managers carefully guard certain knowledge. A manager may fix a machine rather than teach the employee how to repair it. The administrator of a medical clinic shared her information about the budget with a group of physicians. Once they knew how much money was available and who was getting it, they could exert power over her with respect to spending on their own projects. By giving up information she had allowed each of them to gain expert power.

The main benefit in exercising power is that we can gain greater control over the various contexts in which we find ourselves. We can gain more power and control if we understand and exercise power to our advantage because we are seen as someone who is in control.

The use of power can offer other benefits to a relationship. When we use reward power to gain compliance, for example, the other person is more likely to be positive and happy. He is also more likely to comply. Reward power also seems to increase attractiveness. People like those who have rewarded them. Finally, reward power seems to increase the effectiveness of most other bases of power. Legitimacy is less likely to be questioned. Referent power increases because of liking, and others are more open to our persuasive attempts.

Managing Power Games

Game playing often involves some attempt to exercise power. Three such games are discussed here.

Ignoring the Partner

One power play is a game that ignores the partner. One person pretends that the other is not there, or in some way does not count.

This game can take one of several forms. One is to ignore the person completely—the "cold shoulder" treatment; remain silent when being addressed. Another form of this game is not taking "no" for an answer. Someone may also choose to ignore another's rights by breaking the rules of common courtesy (for example, by standing too close, using the person's personal property, or talking too loudly). When such behavior is confronted, the usual response is to plead ignorance to the rules of social behavior.

One way to combat game playing is to confront the person directly and assertively. Describe the behavior specifically and ask what it means. Then, tell the person that you do not appreciate the power game and that you mean what you say. Say, for example, "I notice that you have been picking up papers from my desk and reading them. Why are you doing that?" Pause here to hear an answer. Then say, "I don't want you to pick up papers that are on my desk and read them. I want you to stop doing that, and *I mean what I say.*" If the person is ignoring you, you might say, "I notice that you are being quiet when I am around. Is something going on?" If the person says nothing is happening, you might respond, "I'm really glad to hear that. I'd like to talk about. . . ." Here you believe the person and get on with your agenda. If the person says that there is a problem, you can engage in mutual problem solving.

Creating an Obligation

Another power game uses the principle of fair treatment. The game player deliberately does something to create an obligation. The essence of the game is embodied in the words, "You owe me one." We all engage in this kind of exchange, but it becomes a power game when it becomes deliberate.

This game sometimes occurs between grown children and their parents. The parents have sacrificed a great deal, as most parents do. In this case, however, the sacrifice was made with the expectation that some day the children would be able to repay the effort. For example, a parent may say to their grown child, "Why can't you be here for Christmas? You know how much this means to me. After all we've done for you, can't you take a little time to be with us?" Or consider this example: "How can you do so poorly in your classes? We are sacrificing and spending money that we need for other things just to get you to college. Show us you appreciate our effort by making good grades!"

This kind of game is played in dating relationships, too. Perhaps the man spends a great deal of money on a present so that the woman will be obligated to grant him sexual favors that she may be otherwise reluctant to give. This same game can be played the other way. Perhaps the woman gives sexual favors and, in return, demands a marriage promise. A less extreme example of this game might be to help a person do a term paper and then demand an evening out.

Again, the best way to stop this game is to confront it directly. You might say, "I'm surprised you are suggesting that you want something because you helped me with my term paper. I would enjoy taking you out for a good time, but I resent these conditions. I'd like you to stop doing things for me if you are going to ask for something in return. I want you to do things for me because you want to do them. And, I want to do things for you because I want to do them—not because I feel obligated."

A good way to stop power games is to call attention to them.

Name Calling

A final power game has its basis in name calling. The person playing this game exercises power by seizing the opportunity to define the circumstances by calling a name. For example, a man might say to his male friend who is dating a woman he does not like, "How can you date that *dog?*" The strongly negative language is used as a power play. The man is assuming the right to label this situation in a way that will influence his friend. Or consider how you might feel if a colleague would say of your proposal: "How could you do that! That is a worthless, bankrupt plan!"

Counter this kind of power play by redefining the situation. Call attention to the overstatement of the issue and then present your view. You might say, "That's pretty strong language—'dog.' I'd say 'that nice, enjoyable sophomore' is more accurate. You might not like her, but I do." Or, you might make a stronger statement: "I am amazed that you would see my plan that way. I resent such strong, negative language. If you want to talk about this, O.K. But you don't have a right to treat me this way."

Summary

Power is the influence one person has over another and is based upon dependency. Power is relational because of this dependency. This means that the other person in a relationship must endorse—that is, submit to—your attempts to exercise power. Willingness to endorse power attempts depends on how the relationship is defined and how important the issue is. Commitment to maintaining the relationship also has a significant impact on power. Generally, the person who cares the least has the most power because that person is more likely to exit the relationship if wishes are not granted.

Power has five bases or sources. It may come because we admire a person and are therefore trying to please—referent power. It may be a function of some superior knowledge—expert power. Sometimes, someone's office or position gives that person a recognized right to control the other person—legitimate power. Finally, power can come from being able to reward or punish—reward or coercive power.

The exercise of power has both costs and benefits. Generally the use of power connected with arousal of negative feelings leads to undesirable side effects. Coercion can lead to decreased effort, martyrdom, and increased antagonism and hostility. Costs can also be incurred when expert power is used. We make others experts in the particular area when we give information. Sometimes the given information is used as a basis of power by the receiver. The exercise of power also has its benefits. It provides greater control. In addition, reward power can produce a happier and more positive partner in our relationship. It also enhances the ability to use other kinds of power.

Finally, we described three kinds of power games. The first, ignoring the other person, involves pretending that the person does not exist, pretending not to hear what was said, or ignoring common courtesy and rights. Direct confrontation is the best way of countering this behavior. The second game, creating an obligation, is played when one person deliberately does something nice to obligate the other. Direct confrontation, along with saying you will not respond to this behavior, is the best response. Name calling is the third power game. To counter it, reject the other person's definition of the situation and suggest our own.

Discussion Questions

1. How does viewing power as relational affect your use of it?
2. Several endorsement factors that affect the willingness of a person to accept an influence attempt have been suggested. Can you think of others?
3. What effect does the exercise of power from each of the five bases have on a relationship?
4. Consider the three power games discussed in this unit. What strategies

would you suggest for managing them? Have you experienced other power games? How could they be managed?

Endnotes

1. An appreciation for the many relational contexts in which power is a concern can be gained from M. S. Hanna and G. L. Wilson, *Communication in Business and Professional Settings,* 2d ed. (New York: Random House, Inc., 1988); and K. M. Galvin and B. J. Brommel, *Family Communication: Cohesion and Change,* 2d ed. (Glenview, IL: Scott, Foresman, 1986).
2. C. C. Manz and D. A. Gioia, "The Interrelations of Power and Control," *Human Relations* 36 (1983): 461.
3. W. D. Jacobson, *Power and Interpersonal Relations* (Belmont, CA: Wadsworth, 1979), 4.
4. J. R. P. French and B. H. Raven, "The Bases of Social Power," in *Studies in Social Power,* ed. D. Cartwright (Ann Arbor, MI: Institute for Social Research, 1959), 150–67; B. H. Raven, C. Centers, and A. Rodrigues, "The Bases of Conjugal Power," in *Power in Families,* ed. R. E. Cromwell and D. H. Olson (New York: Halsted Press, 1975), 217–34.
5. French and Raven, "Bases of Social Power," 164.
6. K. Sheley and M. E. Shaw, "Social Power to Use or Not to Use," *Bulletin of the Psychonomic Society* 13 (1979): 257–60.
7. V. P. Richmond and J. C. McCrosky, "Power in the Classroom II: Power and Learning," *Communication Education* 33 (April 1984): 125–36; V. P. Richmond, L. M. Davis, K. Saylor, and J. C. McCrosky, "Power Strategies in Organizations: Communication Techniques and Messages," *Human Communication Research* 11 (Fall 1984): 85–108.
8. N. Miller, D. C. Butler, and J. A. McMartin, "The Ineffectiveness of Punishment Power in Group Interaction," *Sociometry* 32 (1969): 24–42.

Managing Intrapersonal Conflict

Preview

Intrapersonal conflict suggests that we are having difficulty making decisions. We have trouble choosing between two competing ideas. Intrapersonal conflict is often a prelude to interpersonal conflict. Thus, our ability to manage this competition affects how we view ourselves and our relationships. This unit helps you understand the nature of intrapersonal conflict and to select a strategy to manage it.

Objectives

1. Distinguish among the various locations of conflict.
2. Identify and illustrate three kinds of intrapersonal conflict you have experienced.
3. Suggest several intrapersonal conflict intervention techniques.

Key Terms

approach-approach conflict
approach-avoidance conflict
avoidance-avoidance conflict
displacement
frustration
interpersonal conflict
intrapersonal conflict
role conflict
substitution

Phil believes that conflict is beneficial, so he tries to work through it without being overly nervous about the outcome. He serves as leader of a group at work in which one member, Mark, is chronically absent. This absence is making the group less productive. Phil knows that his boss will hold him accountable for the group's work. He also knows that Mark will be very angry when he raises the issue of his absence from so many meetings. He does not want to look bad before his boss, nor does he want to confront Mark. There is a conflict going on in Phil as he tries to make a decision about two undesirable options. He is experiencing intrapersonal conflict.

This unit will help you understand the various kinds of intrapersonal conflict and how to manage them. We begin by differentiating between intrapersonal and interpersonal conflict. Then we discuss the types of such conflict. Finally, we present techniques for managing this conflict.

Conflict Locations

The *intrapersonal conflict* that Phil is experiencing is the most common and perhaps the most difficult kind of conflict to handle. It is rooted in how an individual perceives and talks to himself about situations. There are three categories of intrapersonal conflict: (1) approach-avoidance conflict; (2) avoidance-avoidance conflict; and (3) approach-approach conflict. Each describes what occurs within an individual during particular conflict episodes.

Sometimes intrapersonal conflict produces a decision to confront another person about the difference. This moves internal conflict to an interpersonal, relationship context. All of the needs and motivations of the other person affect the communication. *Interpersonal conflict* may be very complex, since it may stem from any one or more of five possible causes: differences in goals, competition for scarce resources, differences in status, differences in perception, or games played for some particular result.

Although some conflict is dysfunctional, or not useful, other conflict serves a purpose. Where the conflict is dysfunctional, you need a method for identifying and changing the useless behaviors. (These intervention skills are detailed later in the unit.) You also need a method for identifying and encouraging the useful behaviors.

Intrapersonal Conflict

If Mary Ann decides to go to a movie and drives to the theater only to discover that the movie is no longer playing, she will experience frustration. If you have to decide between going to a movie with one friend and attending a party with another, you will experience frustration. If Phil comes to a meeting expecting

Figure 23.1 Intrapersonal Conflict

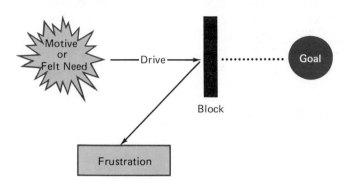

all to go well only to find Cheryl raising a question about Mark's continual absences, Phil will experience frustration.

Each of these situations is similar. In each there is a felt need, followed by some drive toward a goal. And in each case there has been a barrier. But look at the three examples carefully. You will see that there is a fundamental difference between the frustration Mary Ann and Phil experience and the one you feel. The source of the blockage you encounter is internal, whereas that felt by Mary Ann, Phil is not. Only you experienced intrapersonal conflict (see figure 23.1).

Approach-Avoidance Conflict

Approach-avoidance conflict occurs when a single object, idea, or activity is both attractive and unattractive at the same time (figure 23.2). You would like your relationship to grow and you know that you have a difference with the other person, but you want to avoid the conflict that you know must be managed if your relationship is to grow. Approach-avoidance conflict is very common, and is also the most difficult to manage.

Consider another example of approach-avoidance conflict. If you are offered an opportunity to move up in your company (something you want very much) but can only do so at the expense of your best friend, what will you do? If you have ever experienced anything like this, pause to consider the ethical bind. Then you know what approach-avoidance conflict can mean.

Still another example, a very common one, is the fear of sexual contact instilled in the young. American culture labels such contact as "bad" or immoral. But a youngster cannot avoid or escape the factors that make sexual contact attractive. The resulting conflict sometimes becomes so severe that it causes personal anxiety.

Figure 23.2 Approach-Avoidance Conflict

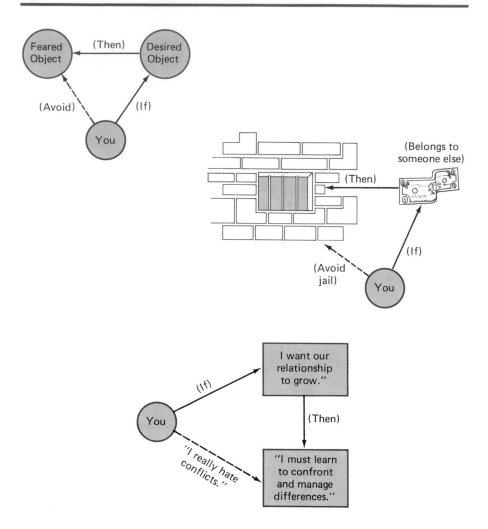

Avoidance-Avoidance Conflict

Avoidance-avoidance conflict (figure 23.3) is produced when we must choose between two objects, ideas, or activities that are both undesirable alternatives. If you find yourself in deep water at the sea and cannot swim, you have no difficulty expressing your fear. If you can, you move quickly toward shore. But if you are afraid to enter the water again and are asked by the person you date to go swimming, you hesitate may to express your fear because you do not want to encounter disapproval. This is a case of avoidance-avoidance conflict, in which both alternatives are repulsive.

Figure 23.3 Avoidance-Avoidance Conflict

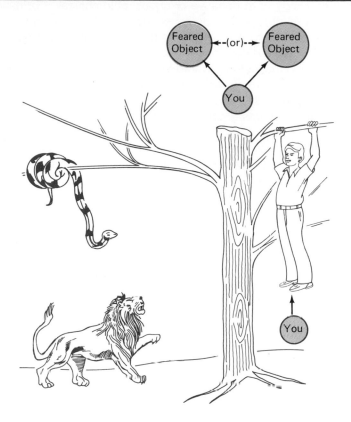

A soldier, wishing to avoid the danger of combat, might resist his desire to run because he also wishes to avoid the consequences of deserting. His buddies would call him a coward. His officers might actually shoot him. At the very least, he would be court-martialed.

An employee who has made an error might experience this double avoidance conflict, too. She might hesitate to report her error to her superior because she fears the superior's disapproval. At the same time, she knows that she must report it because the consequences of not sharing this information will cost the company a good deal of money and inconvenience.

Individuals working in groups often experience the same dilemma in the form of *role conflict,* which is the result of the inconsistent expectations of two or more persons or groups. For example, a line manager will want more resources for his work unit—and indeed his subordinates may expect this—while upper management expects him to implement the latest cost-cutting plan.

In each of these cases, the double avoidance conflict derives from the need to choose. Frequently, an individual resolves such conflict by moving in a direction that avoids both negative or undesirable choices. For example, a youngster who does not want to do his schoolwork, but also wants to avoid the punishment that this implies, may elect merely to stay away from school— to "play hooky." Soldiers have done the same thing: Hundreds of young men fled to Canada during the Vietnam War to escape the alternatives of their double avoidance conflict. This can be viewed as *delinquent behavior,* or behavior that is not socially approved, and so is considered inappropriate. Yet, for some of the persons involved, it was a carefully planned strategy of "not playing the game."

By understanding avoidance-avoidance conflict, you will be able to recognize it and, perhaps, to make intelligent decisions about it. You may even be able to avoid it, or at least know what to expect.

Figure 23.4 Approach-Approach Conflict

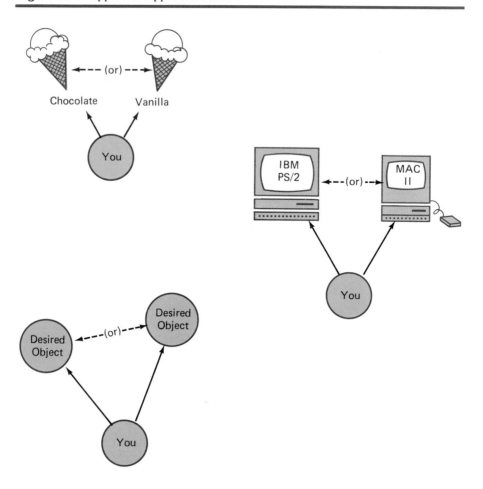

Approach-Approach Conflict

Approach-approach conflict is generated when a person is faced with choosing between two objects, ideas, or activities that are equally attractive. The individual is thus torn between two appealing goals. For example, a small boy at the movies may have to choose between spending his money for a candy bar or a soft drink (figure 23.4). Approach-approach conflict is the easiest of the intrapersonal conflicts to resolve.

Individuals often do not have great difficulty making a priority decision in an approach-approach conflict situation. Sometimes, people resolve it by discovering a larger goal that is achieved by either choice. The young man, for instance, might realize that his real goal is to have fun on Saturday afternoon. Indeed, the approach-approach conflict might be considered personally serious only if the individual wants to avoid the loss of one of the alternatives. This would mean that the situation has developed into an approach-avoidance conflict.

The problem with approach-approach conflict is the impact of the person's choice on others. Suppose you ask your supervisor to purchase a piece of equipment for your work, perhaps a typewriter with a memory bank; you would then have a vested interest in his choice. Suppose another employee asks him to spend about the same amount of money for a television camera and recorder. She, too, would have a vested interest in the boss's choice. The boss is attracted by the idea of getting a memory bank typewriter *and* a television camera and recorder, but does not have enough money to buy both items. He is faced with an approach-approach conflict. You or the other employee, however, will be dissatisfied by his choice.

Intervention Techniques

Intrapersonal conflict, as you recall, occurs when an individual must choose from among alternatives that imply unpleasant consequences. Because intrapersonal conflict exists inside your head, it follows that it exists in your world of words. Thus an effective way to manage intrapersonal conflict is to work on your use of language. But how do you do that?

Social learning theorists have suggested one possibility. Briefly, the theorists emphasize the importance of imitation in learning. This kind of behavior shaping has been called *modeling,* or *observational learning,* and sometimes, merely, *imitation.*[1] For example, children learn table manners by observing the behavior of their parents and "significant others." Occasionally they will try some alternative behavior, only to find that it is not accepted. Behaviors are reinforced positively if they resemble those they are imitating. "Jane, you are a very nice little girl—and your manners are very nice." Behaviors that are not like those being imitated are reinforced negatively: "Mind your manners, girl!"

We can learn a lot about managing intrapersonal conflict by taking a closer look at the concept of modeling in childhood. Suppose, using the illustration

Figure 23.5 Frustration

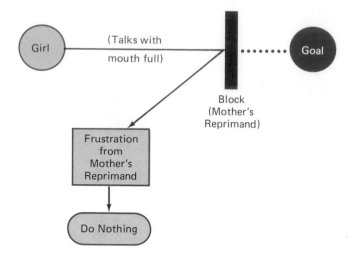

of table manners, that a child begins to speak to her parent with her mouth full of food. She knows she is not supposed to do this, but she also has heard a knock at the door and believes that no one else at the table has heard it. For the child, this may present approach-avoidance conflict. She obviously wants to talk, but she wants to avoid mother's disapproval. So she chooses to speak. Mother says, "Mind your manners. Chew with your mouth closed. Don't talk with food in your mouth."

We can see at least four possibilities here. First, the child may experience *frustration,* and choose to do nothing. She is silenced by her own conflict. We would say that this is a dysfunctional adaptation to the situation and to her conflict. Her goal, after all, is to get someone to answer the door. Figure 23.5 illustrates this option.

A second possibility is that the child will find an alternative means to her goal. This is called *displacement,* and is illustrated in figure 23.6. The girl knocks on the table while pointing and gesturing toward the door. This behavior causes the other people at the table to direct their attention to the knocking the child heard in the first place. We believe that this choice would be beneficial to both the child and the family.

A third possibility, called *substitution,* exists. In this case the child would substitute a new goal for the one she could not achieve. This new goal could be anything, of course, but a common one among children, because of their egocentrism, is to call attention to themselves. So, it is possible that the child might do something she knows is naughty. Perhaps, in response to her mother's reprimand, she will stick her tongue out. This would be a high-risk strategy, however, and almost certainly dysfunctional. Figure 23.7 illustrates this alternative.

Figure 23.6 Displacement

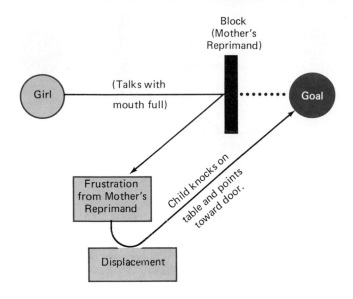

Figure 23.7 Substitution

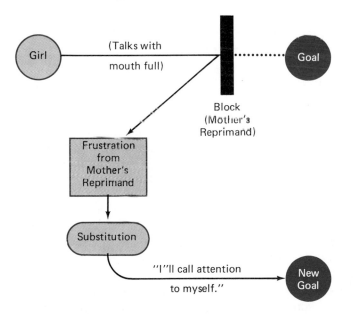

Figure 23.8 Rationalization

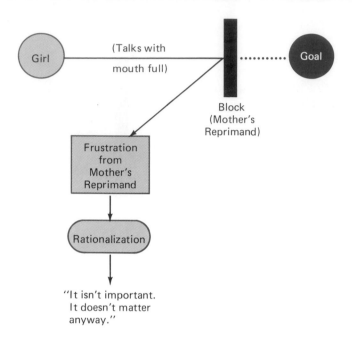

"It isn't important.
It doesn't matter
anyway."

Finally, the child could choose *rationalization* as a solution to her situation. In this case she might decide that the knocking at the door was not important. As represented in Figure 23.8, the rationalization is that the goal wasn't worth achieving. Such adaptive behavior might be either functional or dysfunctional.

Regardless of the approach taken, the point is that the child *tries* some behavior. If it is reinforced, that behavior is likely to be repeated. Each positive reinforcement increases the likelihood of the behavior being tried until, ultimately, the behavior becomes a "learned" response.

For adults, who no longer have a mother to tell them what to do, the key to modeling as a means of learning is the human capacity to represent observed behavior symbolically. There may be no parent to provide the reinforcement, but you can still draw reinforcement from the behavior and its consequences.

Put a different way, modeling can shape adult behavior because you can talk to yourself about the behaviors you want.to shape. This key returns conscious control of your internal conflicts directly to you. *You can choose to manage intrapersonal conflict by working with your personal habits of language choice.* Here are some suggestions:

1. *Use tentative and moderate language as you consider a conflict.* This may keep you from developing the conflict as a fixed and unbending phenom-

enon. This advice will not be easy for individuals who are accustomed to using language extravagantly. You may have to work hard to keep your language habits in mind, but it can be done!

To illustrate, instead of saying to yourself, "This outcome will be *awful*," you might say, "This outcome will be unpleasant and even difficult, but I can manage it."

2. *Look for positive ways to express the conflict.* We have often asked students to write down the first things that pop into their heads when they think of conflict. They almost always use terms like "a battle," "awful," or "unpleasant." But no one *has* to choose such language. There are almost always positive ways to express intrapersonal conflicts.

Instead of saying, "I hate having to miss the Boston conference, but I can't get out of this commitment," you might try something more positive: "I don't want to miss the Boston conference, but this commitment is important."

3. *Temper negative consequences by manipulating the factors that bear on them.* Suppose you are experiencing a conflict because you want to buy a sporty, late-model car but do not want to assume as large a debt as the purchase would require. You resolve your conflict by selecting an older, less stylish

Negative consequences can be tempered by manipulating the factors that bear on them. If the woman buys a less expensive coat, she can use the savings for other things she wants.

car that costs much less. You might temper the negative consequence (you are frustrated because you do not have the sporty car) by looking at the benefits of your wise economic choice: ''I have saved about $5,000. My monthly payments will be only about $90 instead of $200. There is a lot I can do with that $100 difference.''

4. *Talk to a friend who may be able to help you problem solve.* Sometimes we get locked into a particular way of looking at a situation. If we are willing to share the frustration with a trusted friend, that person can help us gain insights. Once we gain an additional understanding of the situation, we find it easier to make a decision.

5. *Look for alternative understandings of a situation.* Has this ever happened to you? You have been home from college for spring recess for less than two hours when your mother starts scolding you for not doing your laundry while at school. Now she wants you to do your own wash and to run a couple of loads for your brother and sister, too. You would rather read one of your assignments because you want to finish your schoolwork so you can enjoy your vacation. Your mother's behavior seems like nagging, and you feel like telling her so, packing your bags, and going back to campus.

You don't want to do the laundry, you don't want to speak disrespectfully to your mother, you don't want to hear the nagging, and you don't want to feel resentful. In sum, you are experiencing intrapersonal conflict.

Instead of meeting your mother's aggressive behavior with your own aggression, you ask yourself what the cause of the trouble might be. Her behavior is atypical of your mother, and seems unreasonable. So you go to the kitchen and say, ''Mom, this isn't like you. You are usually so glad to see me when I get home—and you usually want me to get my schoolwork done as soon as I can. You only talk like this when something is wrong. What's going on?''

We believe that intrapersonal conflict cannot be avoided. But we also believe that it is possible for you to intervene—if you are careful about how you talk about the conflict. It may also be helpful for you to seek a trusted friend with whom to share some of your concerns. The friend's fresh perspective can help you to consider alternatives that might not otherwise occur to you.

Summary

Intrapersonal conflict is a struggle going on in your head that you are trying to resolve. Interpersonal conflict represents some differences between two or more people. Interpersonal conflict is often more complex than intrapersonal conflict.

Intrapersonal conflict may fall into the category of approach-avoidance. That is, we may want to do something positive, but something negative is also likely to result. Avoidance-avoidance conflict involves a situation in which we must act but know that whatever choice we make will have negative consequences. Approach-approach conflict is characterized by equally appealing choices.

We can help ourselves manage intrapersonal conflict by examining our definitions of the situations. We can talk to ourselves in tentative language about our inferences. This helps us avoid becoming locked into rigid thinking. We can look for positive ways to express the conflict. We can temper the negative consequences by manipulating factors that bear on them. We can also talk with a friend who might be able to problem solve with us. Often another person can give us a unique perspective that we have not seen. We might also speculate on the consequences of an alternate approach. Intrapersonal conflict is often a function of feeling chained to a set of circumstances. Whatever we can do to broaden our perspective can help us deal more effectively with those circumstances.

Discussion Questions

1. Do you believe that conflict can be located? If so, where does it reside? Working with one or two classmates, try to list the locations of conflict. Why would it be useful for a student of conflict management and interpersonal communication to be familiar with such a list? How might such a list be helpful in developing intervention strategies when conflict arises?
2. We have said that there are three kinds of intrapersonal conflict: approach-approach, approach-avoidance, and avoidance-avoidance. Do you believe it is possible for these to coexist in an individual? If so, give an example.
3. Working with one or two classmates, offer at least three examples of each type of intrapersonal conflict.
4. Suppose that some friend has asked you for help in managing a conflict. Working with a small group of classmates, develop suggestions for intervening in each type of conflict. Be sure that your suggestions *clearly state what to do.*

Endnote

1. See S. W. Littlejohn, *Theories of Human Communication,* 2d ed. (Belmont, CA: Wadsworth, 1983), 147–48, for more on modeling.

>>|<< UNIT 24
Managing Interpersonal Conflict

Preview

American society defines most conflicts as either winning or losing situations; there must thus be a winner and a loser. Conflict situations can, in fact, present creative opportunities for cooperation in overcoming differences. In this unit, we propose a set of skills and a plan for learning to manage conflict more productively. Effective conflict management can enhance the growth and development of your relationships.

Objectives

1. Define interpersonal conflict.
2. Explain when conflict may be dysfunctional.
3. Identify each interpersonal intervention technique and classify it as to its win-lose potential.
4. Discuss how partners typically manage conflict in close relationships.
5. Develop a plan for managing interpersonal conflict that uses the confrontation and problem-solving technique.

Key Terms

compromise
control
confrontation or problem solving
dysfunctional conflict
emotional appeal
empathic understanding
expressed struggle
forcing
functional conflict
incompatible goals
interdependent parties
interpersonal conflict
lose-lose techniques
manipulation
non-negotiation
personal rejection
scarce rewards
smoothing
win-lose techniques
win-win technique
withdrawal

Because Phil believes that conflict is harmful, he tries to avoid conflict in the group as much as possible. Tim had been showing up late for group meetings, and Phil could tell that something was going to happen soon. Cheryl was saying in private that she "had had about all of this lateness that she was willing to take." Phil dared to suggest that she needed to keep her feelings to herself for the good of the group. He said, "After all, Cheryl, you know that if you tell him off and make a big deal out of his being late, he might get mad and not come to the meetings at all. He might even cause trouble. Let's just plan to start fifteen minutes late."

You can imagine how Cheryl reacted to this suggestion since she never holds back. She addressed Phil directly: "What do you mean? Start the meeting fifteen minutes late? How can you suggest such a thing? I'm not going to let him mess up our project just because he can't get here on time. Next time you get an opportunity, ask him to start getting to the meetings on time."

Phil said no more. All he was trying to do was to make things run smoothly. Now he was going to have to talk to Tim. He knew that Tim would be upset and that he would be right in the middle. Now he was even more anxious than he was before he had tried to help. He could feel the anxiety in the pit of his stomach. When he left the meeting, he thought that maybe he would be sick.

Phil's experience is not unusual for those who believe that conflict ought to be avoided. Phil tried to smooth over the conflict in the hope that it would go away. Cheryl, on the other hand, realized that the conflict resulting from Tim's lateness and the group's need to have him there on time was necessary to discover some reasonable way for the group to proceed. When Phil tried to smooth over the conflict, Cheryl would not let him do so. Thus, conflict broke out over the attempted cover-up.

Phil did not talk to Tim. At the next meeting, Cheryl brought up the difficulty. She had considerable experience managing conflict and knew of several options for talking with Tim. She had found that confronting the problem directly and problem solving with the person involved worked best for her. She was thus able to manage this conflict without damaging her relationship with Tim or his relationship with the group. Phil was both amazed and relieved.

This unit will examine options for managing conflict. We begin by defining conflict and then move to a discussion of general intervention techniques and their likely outcomes. Next, we discuss how to use two general strategies for managing conflict. Finally, we present a plan for working through conflict.

Interpersonal Conflict Defined

Joyce Hocker and William Wilmot have defined *interpersonal conflict* as an *expressed struggle* between *interdependent parties*.[1] This definition has several implications. In particular, the word "struggle" implies that the parties understand that they have incompatible goals, that the rewards are scarce, and that the other person (or persons) involved is keeping them from achieving their goals. The aim of each party is to prevail or to gain the rewards. Opponents in intense conflict may even attempt to damage, neutralize, or eliminate each other.

Expressed struggle

Interdependent parties

The important terms in the definition are "perceived" and "*incompatible goals.*" There must be perceived differences between the individuals as well as striving for goals or *scarce rewards.* If there is no striving, there is no motivating force for the conflict. Note that sometimes the differences between people are real; other times they are merely imagined. Yet, in one sense it does not matter if a difference is imagined, for if the persons involved *believe* that there is a difference, real or imagined, they will act on what they think is true.

Incompatible goals

Scarce rewards

Functional and Dysfunctional Conflict

There can be both positive and negative outcomes from conflict. Morton Deutsch pointed out that destructive conflict exists when we believe we have lost as a result of the conflict and so are dissatisfied with the outcome.[2] But if we are satisfied, *functional conflict* has occurred. Although most conflict management does not result in either of these extremes, the goal is to make the outcome as functional as possible.

In *dysfunctional conflict,* we expand the conflict step-by-step even though there are other options. In fact, we often lose sight of the initiating causes altogether. This expansion in conflict often includes an increase in the size and number of issues, the number of participants, negative attitudes, and our willingness to bear costs. Reliance upon control, threats, force, and deception increases dramatically. There is also a movement toward uniformity in position. Pressure is applied on members of a side who might listen to the other point of view. This reliance on control, threats, force, and deception is destructive to relationships and therefore dysfunctional.

Functional conflict is managed so that some satisfaction is achieved and the relationship is not seriously damaged. It is usually controlled, whereas dysfunctional conflict is usually out of control. *Control* is the careful management of both the relationship and a decision about the basic difference you have with the other person. It is functional conflict if: (1) some personal and/or organizational goals are accomplished by some of the participants, and (2) the relationship is not permanently injured.

Furthermore, dysfunctional conflict is fostered by what Alan C. Filley calls the "Good Loser Ethic."[3] He describes the good loser ethic as embodied in this logic:

> In a disagreement, there must be a winner and a loser.
> The loser is not going to be me.
> So you will have to lose.
> But losers can make trouble.
> So I'll tell you that you are bad (or evil) if you complain about your loss.

Filley concludes his discussion of this ethic by pointing out its evil and the problem in resisting it:

> The argument against the Good Loser Ethic may be made on economic as well as moral grounds. If the result of the Good Loser Ethic is a reduced self-esteem on the part of the recipient, then the cost may well be reduced energy, reduced creativity, and lower levels of measured intelligence. The lower self-esteem results in less motivation and less personal resources for those affected. On the other hand, where individuals resist the Good Loser Ethic in power-oriented systems, preserving their self-esteem, the alternative consequences may be less cooperation and greater conflict in the social unit.[4]

So Filley presents a two-sided problem. He suggests that the good loser ethic is evil, but that resisting it may lead to greater conflict and less cooperation. If cooperation is important, and it is, some kind of conflict management scheme is needed to preserve energy, creativity, and intelligence, *and* to enhance cooperation.

Intervention Techniques

Research has produced a list of general methods used in managing conflict: forcing, withdrawal, smoothing, compromise, and confrontation or problem solving.[5] Briefly, they involve the following:

1. *Forcing*—using power to cause the other person to accept a position; each party tries to figure out how to get the upper hand and cause the other person to lose
2. *Withdrawal*—retreating from the argument
3. *Smoothing*—playing down the conflict (differences) and emphasizing

the positive (common interests), or avoiding issues that might cause hard feelings

4. *Compromise*—looking for a position in which each gives and gets a little, splitting the difference if possible; no winners and no losers

5. *Confrontation* or *problem solving*—directing energies toward defeating the problem and not the other person; encouraging the open exchange of information; best solution for all: the situation is defined, the parties try to reach a mutually beneficial solution, and the situation is defined as win-win

Each of these strategies for managing conflict has a likely outcome. Filley has provided us a useful way to classify these techniques according to their outcomes.[6] Some are win-lose methods, in that one person seems to win and the other seems to lose. Others are lose-lose methods, and one is win-win. Let's see how these strategies are classified when we look at them based on the most likely outcome.

Outcomes of Intervention Techniques

Win-Lose Techniques

Two methods are classified as *win-lose techniques,* that is, one person will win, and the other person will lose.

Forcing is usually a win-lose strategy. It uses power (or perhaps majority rule, in the case of a group) to cause the other person to accept a goal. The loser is forced to abandon her goal. Often the mechanism for keeping the other person in line is the "good loser ethic" described previously. For example, it is not nice to complain when the majority votes against you.

Most of us are willing to accept forcing to manage conflict in such a situation when a majority vote is the result of deliberation. We are even willing to accept the decision of our boss if it seems equitable. However, we generally do not feel comfortable with forcing in an interpersonal relationship in which we view the other person as an equal. Forcing strategies under these circumstances can damage the relationship.

Withdrawal may not seem like it involves conflict at all since this method does not necessarily involve direct communication. But in most cases of withdrawal, there is some nonverbal communication, maybe some interpersonal communication, and certainly intrapersonal conflict on the part of the person who retreats. The winner wins because the loser, by withdrawing, is giving permission for the other person to proceed.

Often the loser resents the winner because the loser believes she was

Withdrawal

forced into withdrawal. The force that brought about the retreat may have been a fear of the consequences of voicing a difference. Thus to avoid an uncomfortable feeling or perhaps potentially significant damage to the relationship, one person withdraws and allows the other to have what she wants. In either case, damage may have been done to the relationship. The damage arises if resentment is caused in this process. Resentment causes dissatisfaction that might lead us to look for and emphasize the differences between us and the other person. This emphasis can produce further dissatisfaction as we begin to think that we do not have as much in common with this person as we once had.

Lose-Lose Techniques

With *lose-lose techniques,* both people give up something. Two such methods are frequently applied to manage conflict in interpersonal relationships.

Smoothing falls into the lose-lose category because we usually settle nothing when we use it. Sometimes we can "bury the hatchet," but this is not often the case. More frequently, one or both parties continues to suffer intrapersonal conflict. Sometimes the intrapersonal conflict becomes so intense that we decide to bring up the difference again.

Buried, unresolved issues generally do not promote relational health. The resulting tension is often hard to ignore. Resentment can build when we be-lieve that we cannot talk about certain things with another person. For those who feel this tension due to smoothing, a more productive strategy for man-aging conflict may be available.

Sometimes a person in a relationship will get greater satisfaction from a conflict-free relationship than from a resolution of a difference and the release of tension associated with managing it. Smoothing is a viable option for this person.

Compromise is a lose-lose method because both parties have to give up something. They may not manage the issue to either person's satisfaction. We do not often think of this method as a lose-lose strategy because each party voluntarily agrees to give up something. If each gives up a fair share, they may feel they have reached an equitable agreement. This is often satisfying.

Genuine compromise can promote growth in our interpersonal relation-ships. Most of us realize that we will have differences that cannot be resolved so that the goals of both people can be met. However, it is satisfying to know that the other cares enough about the relationship to be willing to compromise. See if a win-win strategy might work before deciding that compromise is nec-essary.

Win-Win Techniques

The alternative to these win-lose and lose-lose conflict management strategies is the *win-win technique* of confrontation and problem solving.

Confrontation and *problem solving* is practiced when we bring a problem out in the open and try to use a joint problem-solving approach. This problem solving may take one of two forms. If the parties are not too far apart in their positions, they may merely need to focus on the goals and sort through the information each of them has about the problem. In such cases, it may be rel-atively easy to reach an agreement. If, however, they are far apart on an issue, they may need to go through a more careful, step-by-step, decision-making process. The important consideration here is to focus on the goals that each partner hopes to achieve, to reach an agreement, and then to work toward fulfilling the goals.

Talking about a conflict as a problem to be solved is a win-win approach to conflict management.

This kind of problem solving can produce satisfaction as we work through and successfully manage differences. We gain a sense that we are capable. We gain confidence and trust in the other person if the problem solving is han-dled supportively. You will learn how to follow this kind of strategy in the last section of this unit.

Society teaches us to use force as a conflict management strategy.

Using Forcing Strategies

Mary Anne Fitzpatrick and Jeff Winke′ examined how people address conflict in an interpersonal setting. They used the Kipnis Interpersonal Conflict Scale to determine factor categories, and then provided representative tactics for each conflict strategy. Their results are shown in table 24.1.

Notice that the first four strategies are related to forcing. The tactics involved in *manipulation* are attempts to use a particular behavior to get the other person in a good mood. Although such behavior is an attempt to build a climate that will permit less open conflict, it is manipulative because it puts on a false image to achieve a particular end.

Use of this strategy may not be particularly harmful to our relationships for it does not treat the other person badly. Obviously, when the other is sweet and charming, acting nicely, and seems to be doing you a favor, you may not mind giving that person what he wants. We all sense that we nourish a relationship by being helpful. This strategy can promote relational growth when the giving is not one-sided and the issues are not too important. Resentment can set in when we relent on an important issue in order to give the other person what she wants. Perhaps the other person will think that she is "forced" to give in because of the "obligation" created by the person being nice.

Table 24.1 Interpersonal Conflict Strategies and Representative Tactics

Strategy	Representative Tactics
Manipulation	Be especially sweet, charming, helpful and pleasant before bringing up the subject of disagreement Act so nice that later a person cannot refuse when you ask for your own way Make this person believe that he is doing you a favor by giving in
Non-negotiation	Refuse to discuss or even listen to the subject unless the other person gives in Keep repeating your point of view until the other person gives in Appeal until she changes her mind
Emotional appeal	Appeal to this person's love and affection for you Promise to be more loving in the future Get angry and demand that the other give in
Personal rejection	Withhold affection and act cold until the person gives in Ignore the other person Make the other person jealous by pretending to lose interest
Empathic understanding	Discuss what would happen if you each accepted the other's point of view Talk about why you do not agree Hold mutual talks without argument

Source: M. A. Fitzpatrick and J. Winke, "You Always Hurt the One You Love: Strategies and Tactics in Interpersonal Conflict," *Communication Quarterly* 27:1 (1979): 7.

The second strategy, *non-negotiation,* avoids open confrontation either by refusing to discuss the issue unless certain conditions are met or repeating a viewpoint until the other gives up. This strategy assumes that the other person will become so frustrated by the stalemate that he will give up to relieve the tension. This approach denies the other person's view by avoiding or ignoring the individual altogether. The attitude that the other person has no right to be in disagreement is often part of the tactic, too.

A strategy of non-negotiation can be especially damaging to a relationship because it is disconfirming. It says, in effect, that the view of the other person is not important. Insistence on having your way implies superiority, thus creating an imbalance in the relationship that may not be acceptable to the other person. If someone won't negotiate, you might give him what he wants because you have no alternative at the moment. Or, you may decide that the issue is more important than the relationship—at least, the relationship at that moment. You may engage in very hurtful behavior that may damage the relationship. On the other hand, you may just feel resentment and not engage in any hurtful behavior. Here, too, the relationship may suffer. In both cases, the communication has not promoted growth.

The strategy of *emotional appeal* relies on the use and abuse of the other person's affection. You may promise love and affection in return for achieving an end. One kind of emotional appeal is *displaying*. Its tactics include crying, pouting, or even venting anger to cause the other person to agree. An appeal might be, "If you really love me, you will give up studying for the test and go out to dinner with me." This is an attempt to force a viewpoint by demanding that you do what the person wants as a sign of affection.

In their least harmful form, strategies of emotional appeal are frustrating. It is difficult to know what to do or say when someone is pouting. This kind of behavior might not be damaging if it does not happen often. In contrast, behavior that says, "You would really give me what I want if you loved me," can be damaging. Giving in to the other's demands is a cheap definition of love. This strategy may get us what we want, but is likely to cause deep resentment if used regularly. Strategies of emotional appeal clearly can retard interpersonal growth.

Personal rejection is yet another forcing strategy. Fitzpatrick and Winke define this strategy as an "attempt to make their partner feel stupid, absurd, and worthless."[8] The message is, "You are not good enough for me to love, to give my attention to, or to be interested in, unless you give in to me." Thus, this strategy involves such tactics as attacking the other person's self-worth to achieve an end. Differences are not usually managed using this method. Instead, if we get what we want, we usually do so at the expense of a damaged relationship. The relationship will heal if we care for each other and if we do not employ this strategy too often. Frequent personal rejection can seriously damage a relationship.

Using a Confrontation and Problem-Solving Strategy

Empathic understanding is the fifth and final strategy presented by Fitzpatrick and Winke. This is a cooperative method that is similar to what Burke has called confrontation and problem solving. It is a win-win technique in that we attempt to understand each other and to accept the other person's point of view. Empathic understanding coincides with Carl Rogers's and Jack Gibb's ideas of supportive communication described earlier in this book. It requires that you express your thoughts, needs, and feelings directly and clearly, without judging the other person. Thus, an assertive style of communicating is usually appropriate to a confrontation or problem-solving strategy. Remember too that this is a cooperative effort to manage a difference—both parties must be willing to give a certain amount.

The goal of confrontation and problem-solving is to manage the conflict without damaging the relationship. You promote relational growth when you are able to do so. When using this strategy, discuss what would happen if you accepted your partner's view. Discuss why you seem to be disagreeing. Remain supportive. Avoid arguments based on personal opinion. You can learn to manage conflict in this way by carefully studying and implementing the plan we will present shortly.

Typical Use of Interpersonal Conflict Strategies

The title of the essay by Fitzpatrick and Winke, "You Always Hurt the One You Love: Strategies and Tactics in Interpersonal Conflict," summarizes their major discovery about use of conflict strategies: People hurt those they love. They use strategies that inflict pain more frequently than they use empathic understanding.[9] The people in their study who were involved in the most committed relationships were more likely to use emotional appeal or personal rejection to win their way than people who were less committed. People in less committed relationships were likely to use conflict avoidance techniques. They would divert attention by using a strategy of manipulation or non-negotiation.

The apparent inconsistency in always hurting the one you love is simple to understand. The bonds of a committed relationship are strong enough to withstand the risk of destroying it altogether. Less committed people are more concerned about their relationship. Think of a committed relationship you are experiencing. For example, do you or your parents use these tactics in relating to each other? How do you work out differences? Compare your style in these relationships to that in your dealings with friends. Is there a difference? We think, if you're honest, you'll find that Fitzpatrick and Winke were right.

In examining tactics used with same-sex best friends, Fitzpatrick and Winke found that typical patterns for males differ from typical patterns for females. Men were more likely to use non-negotiation strategies. Women use personal rejection, empathic understanding, or emotional appeals. Fitzpatrick and Bochner found that males rate themselves as more detached and controlling in their same-sex friendships.[10] Women, on the other hand, have greater social skill. Although generalizations, these may explain the differences. Non-negotiation techniques do offer a greater degree of control. In contrast, the techniques women seem to favor require the social skill of empathy.

One annoying problem remains. Why is the empathic understanding strategy not the most frequently used tactic for managing interpersonal conflict? Although not substantiated by research, it may be that forcing tactics are viewed as more likely to be successful, easier, and less time-consuming than empathic understanding or confrontation and problem solving. Forcing tactics that avoid direct conflict, or those used most often when the relationship is less committed, allow the participants to think about what they want. They also allow each person to hold fast to a viewpoint.

This kind of behavior occurs in dating relationships. Suppose, for example, that you are dating a person who is so set in his or her beliefs that the person finds it difficult to acknowledge any other point of view. Perhaps the person will not even discuss an issue that you do not see in the same way. We suspect that you would pick the time to discuss such an issue very carefully and that you would be helpful and pleasant before bringing up such an issue. It is as though you hope your behavior will keep your friend from rejecting you and from being emotional.

Amazingly, people seem to think such efforts will be more successful than if they actually tried to understand the other person's viewpoint. There is irony in the statement: "If you understood the other's view, you might be forced to give up your own view in favor of one that seems more reasonable!"

A strong desire to maintain a committed relationship appears to be the factor that makes forcing successful. It is difficult to withdraw from such a relationship since most people do not want to experience the pain of breaking up. So, they give in to the other person's view. In most instances, the only casualty appears to be a slightly damaged relationship and pain for one or the other. The damage is usually short-lived, but what accounts for the high rate of divorce? Is there a connection? If so, learning and practicing an alternative strategy—empathic understanding or confrontation and problem solving—can be very useful.

Managing Interpersonal Conflict

Confrontation and problem solving is a conflict *management* technique. It is not a conflict *resolution* technique. Management implies working with a conflict situation in a way that allows for a variety of solutions. Not all efforts will resolve a problem. Sometimes, in fact, differences cannot be settled satisfactorily. Understanding and empathy may be all that a pair can hope for. The following plan might resolve the difficulty. It might also lead to understanding the other's position in a way that allows for empathy. Either of these is a desirable alternative to hostility.

A Plan for Managing Conflict

1. *Begin by understanding your typical conflict management strategy and its consequences.* If you assume that your usual conflict behavior is not useful to you, and if you want to change that behavior, you need to know what you are trying to change. Although this prerequisite seems obvious, people do tend to engage in conflicts over and over again, sometimes using the same language and the same behavior.

For instance, a father and his son often experience conflict over the use of the family car. The father wants his son to be able to use the car, but he also wants the son to put some gas in the tank. And, of course, dad wants him to bring the car safely home by a reasonable hour. The son wants to use the car, but knows that he is often short on cash. Sometimes he forgets the time, and returns home after the gas stations are closed. Thus, the conflict episode between the father and the son over the use of the car often repeats itself.

"Dad, can I use the car tonight?" The son sees the muscles in his father's face tighten.

"Uh . . . well . . . uh . . . Son, I want you to be able to use the car, but I want you to bring it in at a reasonable time. And I want to find gas in the thing in the morning." The father sees his son's posture tense.

"Okay, Dad." The son heads for the doorway.

"Remember," says the father. "Come in at a reasonable hour. And put some gas in it." This sounded like a "zinger" to his son.

The son turns, asking a question that guarantees the same old conflict: "What time is 'reasonable'?"

"We've been all through that over and over." Dad is getting hot. "I think you know what 'reasonable' is. Can't you take some responsibility for yourself?" That does it. Father and son have the same fight again.

The key to managing such conflict behavior begins with knowing what you actually do. Otherwise it is impossible to *change* your behavior or to develop ground rules that might help you and the other person avoid the conflict.

Suppose that you and your best friend find that you often engage in the strategy of personal rejection. You treat each other to the "cold shoulder." You ignore each other when you engage in conflict. You might say to your friend, "It seems as if we tend to ignore each other when we are having a disagreement. When I do this, I feel frustrated afterward. I don't like the frustration. And besides, it doesn't do anything for the problem. What do you think?" If the other person agrees, you might offer, "I suggest that we try to sit down and understand each other, instead of ignoring each other. Would you be willing to do that?"

If you can agree to a basic rule like this, you are well on your way to changing your conflict style. You may need to go further and establish other agreements. If, for example, either or both of you engage in emotional appeals, you may have to agree to hold these back, also. Of course, rules are broken and sometimes hard to follow, and you may not be totally successful in sticking to your agreements. Nevertheless, agreements are an important first step to successful conflict management.

2. *Agree upon general, overriding goals.* Each party in a conflict has a goal for any particular disagreement. This goal probably centers around gaining the other person's agreement. If a goal is the motivating factor in your current conflict style, you are more likely to engage in one of the forcing behaviors we described. If you wish to avoid forcing, you can begin by stating your goals for the relationship: "We want to understand each other's positions and talk in ways that show that we value each other." You can also set goals to counter your previous, unwanted conflict strategy: "We will sit and hear each other out. We will avoid the ignoring behavior we engaged in before."

Don't despair if you and your friend are unable to keep your new goals always in sight. Sometimes the habits you have depended upon in conflict situations are very well learned. Even a much desired goal can get lost in the shuffle of words during a conflict. You have to replace such a pattern with a new and more desirable behavior. If you find that you have difficulty keeping your overall goals in mind during conflict episodes, write them down, carry them with you, and refer to them frequently.

This mechanical device was once recommended to a friend who often engaged in conflict with his wife over the same things. At first he thought the suggestion was silly. But repeating a conflict episode again and again, especially one that left both him and his wife unhappy and that they didn't want to repeat, was even sillier. He agreed to introduce the idea to his wife that weekend. Three years later, this friend said that he and his wife always write down their goals when they are in conflict, then share these goals with each other, making copies for each one to keep, and bring them out each time they find themselves falling into the trap of habit. They still have conflict, but, reports the friend, they do not play the same old tapes over and over. Both he and his wife agree that their relationship has matured and grown.

3. *Allow each person to describe her position on the issue.* Each person needs to be as clear and specific as possible. Stating positions is important because this can resolve misunderstandings.

Suppose your friend had committed himself to helping you study for a geography exam, but did not show up for the session. If you were a bit concerned about the outcome of the exam, and if you needed two pages of his notes, conflict might develop:

You: I am afraid to talk to you about this problem because I can't trust you anymore.

Your friend: I am surprised that you say that. I think we need to talk. Can we agree to hear each other's side of this?

You: O.K. You promised to bring your notes over last night and to help me study for geography. I am sure that I didn't pass the exam today. You broke your promise.

Your friend: I am really sorry about the test. I *am* willing to help you study, but I thought that I said that I would help you *if you wanted me to do so.* You didn't say anything, so I assumed that you didn't want help. I'm sorry.

Each person might go on to state the circumstances surrounding the conversation and the expected commitment, details that could be useful for future arrangements of this type.

The sample dialogue illustrates our point. If you believe your friend, it is clear that each of you had a different understanding of the commitment. Now you work out a way of being clearer about commitments. Perhaps your friend says, "Will you agree to call me next time something like this happens? I intend to do what I say I will. So if I fail to do it, it is because something beyond my control has happened or I do not understand what I am supposed to do."

4. *Engage in active listening.* Active listening encourages understanding because the other person must listen carefully enough to be able to repeat your position to you. You can also correct any apparent misunderstanding because you will hear the other person's interpretation of what you have said. Often errors in hearing and understanding surface when you take the time to

Table 24.2 A Plan for Managing Conlict

1. Begin by understanding your typical conflict management strategy and its consequences.
2. Agree upon general, overriding goals.
3. Allow each person to describe her own position on the issue.
4. Engage in active listening.
5. Suggest a range of ways of approaching or managing the differences you are experiencing.
6. Ask what would happen if each approach you have suggested were taken.
7. Implement the final plan by specifically stating who will do what, when, and where.

use this kind of feedback. Remember that active listening has some real advantages, so try to incorporate it as a step in conflict management. (You may want to review some of our suggestions for active listening in unit 7.)

5. *Suggest a range of ways of approaching or managing the difference you are experiencing.* You force yourself to think of various perspectives when you name several approaches to managing a conflict situation. Many people get stuck in a particular definition of a situation and are unable to achieve the necessary flexibility for productive discussion. Give yourself the freedom to adopt different positions by forcing yourself to consider alternatives to your favored plan (see table 24.2).

Consider also that your initial positions might be far apart. Other alternatives might be closer to what the other person can accept. When both persons are thinking of alternatives, you may be able to come up with some position that both are willing to accept. Win-win outcomes are related to discovering alternatives that allow both persons to accept the position without feeling as if it were necessary to give in to the other's position.

6. *Ask what would happen if each approach you have suggested were taken.* Visualizing the consequence of an action is an important step in making a decision. Sometimes what we are suggesting seems like it will work only because we have not thought of the implications. For example, a couple may decide that spanking children is not a good idea. In practice, however, they find that this kind of physical deterrent is necessary to keep their eighteen month old from running into the street. An attempt to visualize the result of their decision may have led them to another alternative.

7. *Implement the final plan by specifically stating who does what, when, and where.* Commitment involves action. It is an important step to decide what action will be taken by whom. Equally important are when and where. Some plans never are begun because there is no commitment as to when or where to start. Set a time. Set a place. Set a time to talk again with each other about how the plan is going.

Finally, in all conflict situations, you should keep your relationship in mind. One way to do this is to remember to include statements about the relationship. For example, you might say, ''I am feeling a little frustrated right now, but I know that we will be able to work out our differences. We have been good friends for a long time and have been able to settle problems." Or you might say, "I'm glad that we are able to talk about this without getting angry with each other." Comments like this make a positive statement about both you and the other person. They also help to keep the relationship at a conscious level. This can help both of you keep your differences under control so that you can avoid hurtful remarks.

When Agreement Is Not Possible

This is not a world of fantasy in which all differences can be managed through communication. Sometimes disagreements cannot be resolved. For example, one of the ongoing problems for some college students is a parent who is providing financial support and thus feels justified in imposing controlling behavior that treats the student as a child. Sometimes this relational problem is impossible to solve. Further discussion of the issue might only lead to a more impossible situation.

In cases like this, the decision to withdraw from the conflict may be the best answer. Avoid withdrawal, however, that is intended to hurt the other person. Some people part saying, "I am not going to listen to reason. I will move out and never see you again." This attitude says, "The conflict cannot be managed. The issue is impossible. The problem will never be solved. I will make sure of that by completely breaking off contact." This is both an unnecessary and an unfortunate announcement. Try to keep the communication channels open for the future. Saying, instead, something like: "It is clear that we can't agree on this. I love you, and because I do, I'm not willing to fight with you." Then, try to change the subject. Or, if you must walk way, find something positive to say to the other. "I'll be back soon. I just have to get away from this for a moment."

Summary

Interpersonal conflict takes place in both one-to-one and group settings. Sometimes this conflict is not useful and sometimes it is functional. Functional conflict manages the situation without damaging the relationship. Nonproductive conflict often damages the relationship. People employ various strategies for intervention in such conflict.

Lose-lose and win-lose strategies are often not productive. Forcing strategies are win-lose methods that are frequently employed to manage conflict. The major forcing strategies are manipulation, non-negotiation, emotional appeal, and personal rejection. In close relationships, you most often use strategies in this group that will hurt the other person and thereby allow you to gain your way. An alternative strategy is confrontation and problem-solving, a win-win strategy.

Discussion Questions

1. It has been noted that we frequently hurt the ones we love. Is this true in your experience? Why is this done? How might it be avoided?
2. Describe what you believe to be your most successful conflict management method. Would you describe this strategy as win-win, win-lose, or lose-lose? Why? Having studied this unit, how satisfied are you with your method? What do you like about the method? What do you dislike?
3. Which of the intervention techniques suggested in this unit would you be most comfortable using?
4. How does your method for managing conflict compare to those recommended in this unit?
5. Why is so much time spent giving yourself and others pain when trying to manage conflict?

Endnotes

1. J. L. Hocker and W. W. Wilmot, *Interpersonal Conflict,* 2d ed. (Dubuque, IA: Wm. C. Brown Publishers, 1985), 23.
2. M. Deutsch, "Conflicts: Productive and Destructive," in *Conflict Resolution Through Communication,* ed. F. E. Jandt (New York: Harper & Row Publishers, 1973), 158.
3. A. C. Filley, "Conflict Resolution: The Ethic of the Good Loser," in *Readings in Interpersonal and Organizational Communication,* eds. R. C. Huseman, C. M. Logue, and D. L. Freshley, 3d ed. (Boston: Holbrook Press, 1977), 234–35.
4. Ibid., 235.
5. R. Burke, "Methods of Resolving Superior-Subordinate Conflict: The Constructive Use of Subordinate Differences and Disagreements," in *Readings in Interpersonal and Organizational Communication,* eds. R. C. Huseman, C. M. Logue, and D. L. Freshley, 3d ed. (Boston: Holbrook Press, 1977), 234–55.
6. A. C. Filley, *Interpersonal Conflict Resolution* (Glenview, IL: Scott, Foresman and Company, 1975).
7. M. A. Fitzpatrick and J. Winke, "You Always Hurt the One You Love: Strategies and Tactics in Interpersonal Conflict," *Communication Quarterly* 27:1 (1979): 3–11.
8. Ibid., 7.
9. Ibid.
10. M. A. Fitzpatrick and A. Bochner, "Insider and Outsider Perspectives on Self and Other: Male-Female Differences in the Perception of Interpersonal Behaviors," *Sex Roles* 7:5 (1981): 523–35.

⟫⟩│⟨⟨ UNIT 25
Managing Relational Deterioration

Preview

Perhaps the most frustrating experiences are relationships that just do not work. In fact, some people insulate themselves from this by expecting only a few relationships to grow, mature, and prosper. But in spite of this emotional preparation, they are surprised and even saddened when they discover that a valued relationship is failing.

In this unit we describe the stages through which a deteriorating relationship will pass unless something is done. We also make suggestions about what can be done to intervene at each stage.

Objectives

1. Describe the major causes of relational deterioration.
2. Name and explain the stages of relational deterioration.
3. Specify behaviors that are helpful in managing the loss of a relationship.

Key Terms

avoiding
circumscribing
deterioration
differentiating
stagnating
terminating

There are many signs that relationships are coming apart. Our alarming divorce rate attests to the difficulty many people experience in maintaining healthy, growing relationships. In fact, by 1988, one of every two marriages ended in divorce.[1] If it is assumed that people do not enter marriage expecting failure, we must also assume that they attempt to manage their relationships in ways that will make them work. So why do half of American marriages fail? There is surely no simple answer to such a complicated question. Part of the answer lies in the fact that people do not understand the relational deterioration process and how to counter it. The last two units of this book will help you understand this process and how to combat it.

We begin this unit by discussing the major reasons that relationships stop working. Then we move to a description of the deterioration process. Finally, we will present several suggestions for managing the loss of a relationship.

Why Relationships Deteriorate

An attempt to discover why relationships deteriorate is a very ambitious undertaking. There may be nearly as many reasons as there are relationships.[2] However, the causes may be grouped into three general categories: loss of attractiveness, unfulfilled needs, and inability to manage differences.

Loss of Attractiveness

Attraction is based on physical attributes, social behavior, and task enjoyment. As time passes in our relationships, we discover that the physical attributes that originally caused us to engage have diminished. Loss of hair, added weight, changes in muscle tone, and lines in the face may all contribute to a different and less attractive appearance. Even though we may not want to admit it, research suggests that we emphasize physical appearance. When appearance slips, we may be less attracted.

Attention to the social presentation of self often changes as our relationship ages. We take extra care about how we present ourselves when we are courting a new friend. We make sure that we look just right. We are careful to be polite and observe all the social niceties. These are essential to nourishing the relationship during the initiating and experimenting stages. We drop some of this behavior as the relationship becomes more stable, when it moves to the "long-term" category. In a male-female relationship, this may mean not bothering to call when we will be late. We may give other people fewer signs and symbols of affection. All of these are significant indicators that the relationship has changed. We may accept these changes or they may serve as proof that we are falling apart and thereby decrease attraction.

We may lose our attraction to our partner because we spend less time enjoying tasks together. This may occur because we have become busier now

As time passes, physical attractiveness may diminish.

that our situation has changed. In a long-term, committed relationship such as marriage, we may take on a profession and perhaps have children to raise. These tasks take time—time that we used to spend with our spouse. Our interests may also have diverged as we grew older. Our spouse may not enjoy some new activity that we find interesting. We may find someone who does, which might contribute to our dissatisfaction with the troubled relationship. This development of separate activities reduces the stimulation that we can give each other and creates a feeling that we are different and that we are not receiving the kind of enjoyment we once did.

Unfulfilled Needs

We all enter relationships with expectations that the other person will fulfill our needs. Three of the more important needs are affection, inclusion, and control. We expect the other person to show signs of affection. If we are engaged in a sexual relationship, we have certain physical expectations. Display of affection is likely to change as a relationship becomes more commonplace. We take a person for granted and may no longer fulfill each other's needs.

We take each other for granted.

We have certain expectations about how we will be included in other people's lives. You may be disappointed if someone cancels a lunch appointment.

You may usually spend Friday nights with your friend but find that he or she is with someone else. You may notice that your friend has become more involved in his or her work. This takes time from your joint activities.

You may also find that the time you spend discussing and structuring your lives changes as your relationship goes on. Perhaps you had engaged in mutual planning and decision making. However, as relationships moves beyond the initial stages, we make assumptions and take things for granted. As a result, the other person may feel that he or she has lost some control. This can be a source of dissatisfaction.

The reverse side of this problem is too much control. You may enjoy being seen as a pair of friends or as a couple. Yet some of us do not want to feel like we are owned. Such a feeling interferes with your need for controlling your own life. Ownership restricts your personal freedom. It may place demands on you that make you uncomfortable. For example, in a dating relationship, you might be told that you cannot have any other opposite-sex friends. You might even feel that your friend resents time that you spend with same-sex friends. This problem is often characterized by language peppered with *my*—''*my* man,'' ''*my* woman,'' ''*my* wife,'' ''*my* husband.'' Inappropriate intimacy claims often produce stress because they make demands that we cannot fulfill. All of us need stimulation from other friends. We cannot always find enough time to be with our friends. Unwillingness to be controlled in this fashion can be a source of considerable discontent.

Sometimes we begin to feel as though we own and are owned by the other.

Either we or our friend may turn to a third person to meet needs if they are unfulfilled. Of course the likelihood that this will happen depends on whether these needs are strong enough to cause sufficient dissatisfaction to push us into new relationships. (We are likely to leave an existing relationship if we develop a new one in which our needs are more fully met.)

Inability to Manage Differences

Failure to manage our differences successfully is the final source of relational deterioration. Of course, a broad range of factors may create differences. Relational problems, financial problems, child-rearing problems, concerns over management of behavior problems like alcohol use, or even trivial problems related to doing various chores are some common sources of difficulty.

Ability to manage differences is related to three factors. First, we must have some level of commitment to be willing to put out the effort to manage the difficulty. Do you care enough? Is the relationship important enough? Strong commitment will push you to find ways to resolve your differences.

Second, we must know how to manage conflict productively. Many people do not. These skills for managing conflict can be learned, but knowing them will not guarantee success.

Third, we must practice conflict management skills. Success is related to a history of effective management in the relationship. Success yields greater confidence. Greater confidence yields a greater willingness to try to manage differences. It seems clear that people should become as skillful at managing differences as they can.

Each of the causes listed above creates some level of dissatisfaction in relationships. Relationships may begin to come apart if we do not manage them skillfully. What follows are two cases that illustrate what happens when partners begin to feel some of these problems and the accompanying dissatisfaction.

Case I: Kathy and Joe

Kathy and Joe had gone together during the year she was a sophomore and he was a junior. Both of them agreed that Kathy was the one who wanted to break up. She felt they were too tied to one another, and that Joe was too dependent and demanded her exclusive attention. Even in groups of friends he would draw her aside. As early as the spring, Joe felt that Kathy was no longer as much in love as he, but it took him a long time to reconcile himself to the notion that their relationship was ending. They saw less and less of each other over the summer months, until finally she began to date someone else. The first time the two were together after the start of the next school year, Kathy was in a bad mood, but wouldn't talk to Joe about it.

The following morning Joe told Kathy, "I guess things are over with us." Later, when they were able to talk further, he found out that she was already dating someone else. Kathy's reaction to the breakup was mainly a feeling of release—both from Joe and from the guilt she experienced because she was secretly dating someone else. But Joe had deep regrets about the relationship.

For some months afterward, he regretted that they didn't give the relationship one more chance. He really thought they might have been able to make it work. He said that he had learned something from the relationship, but hoped he hadn't become jaded by it. "If I fall in love again," he said, "it might be with the reservation that I'm going to keep awake this time. I don't know if you can keep an innocent attitude toward relationships and keep watch at the same time, but I hope so." Meanwhile, however, he had not begun to make any new social contacts, and instead focused on working through the old relationship, and in learning to be comfortable in her presence since Kathy and he sometimes see each other at school.[3]

Case II: David and Ruth

David and Ruth had gone together off-and-on for several years. David was less involved in the relationship than Ruth, but it is clear that Ruth precipitated the final breakup. According to Ruth, David was spending more and more time with his own group of friends, and this bothered her. She recalled one night in particular when they were showing *The Last Picture Show* in one of the dorms, and they went to see it.

"I was sitting next to him, but it was as if he wasn't really there. He was running around talking to all these people and I was following him around. I felt like his kid sister. So I knew I wasn't going to put up with that much longer." When she talked to him about this and other problems, he apologized, but did not change. Shortly thereafter, Ruth wanted to see a movie in Cambridge and asked David if he would go with her. He replied, "No, there's something going on in the dorm." This was the last straw for Ruth, and she told him she would not go out with him anymore. David started to cry, as if the relationship had really meant something to him, but at that point it was too late. At the time we talked to her, Ruth had not found another boyfriend, but she said she had no regrets about the relationship or about its ending.

"It's probably the most worthwhile thing that's ever happened to me in my twenty-one years, so I don't regret having the experience at all. But after being in the supportive role, I want a little support now. That's the main thing I look for." She added, "I don't think I ever felt romantic [about David]—I felt practical. I had the feeling that I'd better make the most of it because it won't last that long."[4]

The loss of a relationship can cause feelings of grief and guilt.

Table 25.1 Stages of Relational Deterioration

Stage	Representative Dialogue
Differentiating	"I just don't like big social gatherings." "Sometimes I don't understand you. This is one area where I'm certainly not like you at all."
Circumscribing	"Did you have a good time on your trip?" "What time will dinner be ready?"
Stagnating	"What's there to talk about?" "Right. I know what you're going to say, and you know what I'm going to say."
Avoiding	"I'm so busy, I just don't know when I'll be able to see you." "If I'm not around when you try, you'll understand."
Terminating	"I'm leaving you and don't bother trying to contact me." "Don't worry."

Source: M. L. Knapp, *Social Intercourse: From Greeting to Goodbye* (Boston: Allyn and Bacon, 1978), 13.

Many relationships slip somewhat during the process of evolving. Sometimes this happens intentionally. Of course, deterioration may also occur while we are totally unaware of what is going on. At still other times we know a relationship is coming apart, but either do not know how to stop it or are powerless to do so.

This section can be very helpful for two reasons. First, when you know the stages in the *deterioration* process, you will often find that you can reduce the chances of this happening without your awareness. Second, understanding this process and some of the options for reversing it can help you discover what to do when you want to counteract deterioration. You may thus be able to give new life to the relationship.

The Stages of Relational Deterioration

The process of coming apart, commonly referred to as relational *deterioration,* can be represented in stages, which have been given various names. Here we present the work of Mark Knapp[5] to illustrate how this process works. We have summarized the five stages with representative dialogue in table 25.1.

Differentiating

In *differentiating,* the first stage of deterioration, we make clear the differences we see in each other. Recall that in the later stages of the engagement process, the partners ignored their differences and focused on commonalities. They were preoccupied with creating new language patterns that showed unity. Differentiating, however, represents a shift in the relationship's focus from the couple to the individual. If you perceive yourself as separate from the other person and the relationship, you gain the distance necessary to differentiate effectively. If you have "glossed over" important differences, these differences may resurface and become the subjects of conflict during the differentiating stage.

Signs of differentiation are the opposite of what we witness in the integration stage. The "we," "us," and "our" language returns to "I," "me," and "mine." The shared possessions and friendships return to their "owners" or become less important. Conversation turns from the shared values, activities, and interests to questions about why we no longer share those values, activities, and interests. Too often, *why* isn't even asked. Rather than talk about our relationships, we privately dwell upon our awareness of them.

Circumscribing

If you are involved in a deteriorating relationship, you may engage in *circumscribing.* That is, you may tend to avoid both topics and intimacy because either might lead to self-disclosure. You may avoid the expected response by substituting some less appropriate topic for talk about your relationship. You can actually count a decrease in the number of your interactions, in the number of subjects you discuss, in the depth (intimacy) of those subjects, and in the length of the communications.[6] This is just the opposite of what occurs in the engagement process.

Knapp found that we try to avoid risky topics when circumscribing. But as the relational deterioration progresses, this becomes increasingly difficult to do. He points out that "any new topic becomes dangerous because it is not clear whether the new topic may, in some way, be wired to a previous area of static."[7]

Another characteristic of circumscribing is the lack of reciprocal behavior. While this is true of self-disclosure of all kinds, it is especially true of relational disclosure. The statement, "I know we are not agreeing, but I want you to know that I still like you," may be met by a neutral statement or perhaps even by silence. A statement about a concern may be similarly met. For example, we might say, "I feel bad about our disagreement last night. Let's talk about it." The other person might either reply, "I don't want to talk about it," or meet the suggestion with silence. Either way, the effect is to isolate, cut off, and disconfirm the other—something we would not do if the relationship were healthy.

Stagnating

Stagnating, the third stage of deterioration, is characterized by motionlessness and inactivity. Silence in the other's presence is indicative of this stage. Even though you may be physically together, you close off verbal communication. But nonverbal messages are not so easily extinguished. The other person still detects discomfort and negation.

Silence means that something is happening in the relationship. We carry on conversations in our heads, imagining how the other would respond. We make judgments about the other person. Many of these are negative judgments, which lead to further resentment and separation. We rarely confirm these thoughts with the other person because we want to avoid the potentially negative oucome. We say to ourselves, "I really can't bring any of this up because I know just what will happen, and I'll feel worse if I try."

Avoiding

The *avoiding* stage begins the process of ending the relationship. In this stage, you might hear, "Quit calling me. I don't want to talk to you anymore," or "Can't you see that it is all over? I don't even want to see you anymore." Statements can be as blunt as these, but they can also be quite subtle. For example, "I don't really have time to see you today," is avoidance. You might also hear, "I'm sorry, but I really can't stay long." Sometimes avoidance is evidenced in an evasion, as with, "I'm busy tonight." The other person then replies, "How about tomorrow?" That invitation is avoided with, "I told my boss I'd work late." The person persists, "When can I see you?" The avoiding answer is: "I'll call you when I'm free."

Terminating

It is not clear that *terminating* is a stage at all. It seems to be more an ending point or announcement. People physically separate. They may move to different parts of town or perhaps different cities. At this point, the relationship is usually dead, and both parties know it. They want to acknowledge this fact publicly. Generally, some parting statement about expectations regarding contact is made. This might be, "I want to make it clear that you are not welcome in my house," "We'll stay in touch by phone about the children. But don't come over to the house unless you call and I agree."

The relationship is over. When there has been a lengthy commitment, there is usually a grieving period. As with physical death, people experience loss when a relationship dies. We will frequently go through a period of intense negative feelings and blaming. Although painful, this seems to be a necessary part of the healing process for many people.

Managing the Loss of a Relationship

All of us have experienced the end of a relationship sometime in our lives. When the overwhelming feeling is relief, the loss of a relationship does not usually cause us much problem. However, we may experience considerable loss if it was a close, long-term relationship. We may not have done what we thought we should to manage the differences that finally brought the relationship to an end. The result may be a feeling of some guilt.

Here we do not address the issue of reversing this process, as that is a key topic of unit 26. Instead, our focus is on managing the feelings and circumstances associated with the end of a relationship.

Understanding and Coping with the Loss

The ending of a relationship can bring with it feelings of loss, emptiness, and loneliness. Perhaps you sit alone thinking about the times you had together. Thoughts may turn to sadness and then to depression.

Depression is a serious psychological problem. Usually the depression associated with the loss of a relationship is temporary. If it becomes debilitating get professional help. Consider talking with a counselor or clergy friend. One task in coping with this loss and the feelings that accompany it is to find ways to fill the void. Discover productive things to do during the time that you may have spent with this person. Avoid just sitting around. Idle time feeds such a depression. Feelings are related to the specific situation. You can change the situation by doing something else, you can eliminate or reduce your feelings of loneliness and depression.

Utilizing Your Support System

When we are grieving a personal loss, we often fail to realize that many people would be pleased to help. Who would not be willing to talk with and help a friend under similar circumstances? Consider who might be helpful. Some people seem to spend a lot of time being negative. In fact, Eric Berne described their behavior in the title of the game playing "Ain't It Awful."[8] Such people like to complain about their circumstances. Complaining has only limited therapeutic effect. It has a greater likelihood of making the situation seem worse. Our advice is to avoid these people.

Instead, turn to someone who can be positive. Many people get great satisfaction from being able to help their friends. Go to someone like this and describe your circumstances, to the extent you feel comfortable. Avoid dwelling

Many people get satisfaction from being able to help their friends.

on the negative: Extremely negative statements may feed your doubts about yourself and others instead of speeding the healing process.

Avoiding Reminders of the Relationship

When you are trying to move away from a hurtful relationship, encountering reminders of it does not help you redirect your focus. We recommend that you remove mementos of your relationship from your living space. Some people throw them away or burn them; resist this urge. You may feel differently about the situation later and wish you had these mementos. Avoid places where you spent time together. While you are attempting to redirect your attention it helps you to enjoy other places.

Engaging in Healthy Self-Talk

Sometimes when our relationships fail we think that we are partially to blame. When this happens it is very easy to feel guilty. We think that we should have behaved differently, perhaps been more tolerant. We may feel inadequate. Such feelings can lead to unhealthy self-talk. We carry on a conversation in our head that leads to the conclusion that we are somehow unable to manage relationships, that we are inadequate. Negative self-talk does nothing to help us begin anew. Instead it is discouraging.

You can help yourself by engaging in positive self-talk. Recognize that you still have a number of successful relationships and that you even managed the failed relationship quite well for some time. You are a skillful, likable person. Remind yourself of your successes.

Beyond this positive self-talk, you can take other actions to help bolster self-esteem. Take a few minutes to assess activities in which you have successfuly engaged. Perhaps they have included helping others. For some the act of helping others is rewarding and an excellent ego builder; it also tends to be noticed by others. This gives you a chance to interact with people under pleasant circumstances.

Finally, we often gain a positive experience by treating ourselves well. This might mean doing something you really enjoy or buying something you have wanted for a long time. Such activities can be rewarding. They help us focus on the positive.

Learning from the Experience

Try to learn from your experience. Although this is a difficult assignment, it is worth the effort. This book, or ones like it, can help you in this process.[9] You can engage in introspection and gain some insights. You can use the knowledge gained from studying interpersonal communication and gain even greater insights. As time passes what you have learned can fade from your memory. Using this book as a handbook to troubleshoot your relationships can help you discover how you might do things differently. We have included a Self-Help Guide at the back of the book to aid you in this process.

You may decide to model the relationships you are entering differently. You may try not to have the same expectations of the other person as you did in past relationships. You may also discover specific ways of encouraging growth in your relationships. You can learn a great deal about nourishing and maintaining relationships by carefully reading and taking some of the advice presented in the final unit of this book. This unit addresses the issue of promoting relational growth.

Summary

Relational deterioration is the weakening of the bonds that hold a relationship together. This may occur for a variety of reasons. Attraction for a partner may lessen because of changes in physical appearance, social presentation of self, or less enjoyment in doing tasks together. You may also find that your friend no longer fulfills your needs. There may be less affection and inclusion or problems related to the amount of control you have in your relationship. The coming apart process may result from not being able to manage differences. You may have neither sufficient commitment to the other person and the relationship nor the necessary information and skills to make a serious attempt at resolving problems.

Relational deterioration can be understood by knowing how the process progresses through its stages. First, we may focus primarily on *differentiating*. Then we may engage in *circumscribing* behavior. We talk around certain uncomfortable topics. After this we spend a great deal of time together in silence. This is described as *stagnating*. The silence becomes uncomfortable as we realize that the relationship is ending. We engage in *avoidance* during this stage. Successful avoidance moves us to the end, the *terminating* of the relationship.

We presented some suggestions for managing the loss associated with ending a relationship. Feelings of loss, emptiness, and loneliness may lead to depression. This can be helped by finding things to do, utilizing the support of your friends, and avoiding circumstances that remind you of the relationship. You can also try to engage in healthy self-talk by recognizing that you have been successful in other relationships and that you are a skillful and likable person. Helping others may also increase your self-esteem. You may also consider doing something positive for yourself. Finally, we recommended learning from your experience. After you have had time to gain some objectivity, use your knowledge of interpersonal communication, with this or a similar book serving as a handbook, to discover how to improve future relationships.

Discussion Questions

1. More than half the marriages in America end in divorce. Where do these relationships go wrong?
2. Suppose you were counseling young people who were engaged to marry. What advice would you give them with respect to avoiding relational deterioration?
3. This unit has presented several suggestions for managing the loss associated with the ending of a relationship. Can you offer others?

Endnotes

1. Source: National Center for Health Statistics, Public Health Service, Washington, D.C.
2. See, for example, M. L. Knapp, *Interpersonal Communication and Human Relationships* (Boston: Allyn and Bacon, 1984), especially Part IV.
3. G. Levinger and O. C. Moles, eds., *Divorce and Separation: Context, Causes and Consequences* (New York: Basic Books, 1979), 71–72.
4. Ibid., 72.
5. Knapp, *Social Intercourse: From Greeting to Goodbye* (Boston: Allyn and Bacon, 1978), 29–57.
6. Knapp, *Social Intercourse,* 24.
7. Ibid.
8. Eric Berne, *Games People Play* (New York: Grove Press, 1964).
9. For an excellent additional resource, we suggest W. J. Lederer, *Creating a Good Relationship* (New York: Norton, 1984).

>>|<< UNIT 26
Promoting Relational Growth

Preview

Relational growth occurs when we manage a relationship so that we keep a satisfying level of interest and meaningfulness. Growing relationships meet our needs. We can do a great deal to enhance the growth process if we know how. This unit presents six specific relational concerns that we can influence in our relationships.

Key Terms

affection
compatibility
cooperation
emotional support
intimacy
relational growth
role agreement
rule agreement
self-disclosure
stagnation
support

Objectives

1. Define "appropriate self-disclosure."
2. Explain and illustrate the concepts of roles and rules in interpersonal relationships, discussing their significance to relational growth.
3. Discuss the kinds of support that promote relational growth, illustrating each with an example.
4. Suggest ways to demonstrate affection and liking in various contexts.
5. Assess a relational problem using table 26.1.
6. Develop a plan for managing a relational difference.
7. Indicate what specific actions might be taken to guard against stagnation in a relationship.

Relational growth occurs when partners maintain a satisfying level of interest in each other and their relationship. Although most of us have learned from experience some of the basic skills needed to keep relationships healthy and growing, we sometimes have difficulty doing so. This unit is designed to help you sharpen existing skills and add some new ones. We will discuss six means of promoting relational growth: engaging in appropriate self-disclosure; achieving role and rule agreement; giving support; demonstrating affection and liking; managing relational problems constructively; and guarding against stagnation.

Engaging in Appropriate Self-Disclosure

Sidney Jourard said that we cannot possibly love another person unless that person fully discloses to us.[1] He meant that we must know a person in order to develop affection for that person. This knowledge is important for at least three reasons.

First, knowing provides a basis for discovering similarities, or common areas of interest. This is very important to the development and growth of a relationship. Obviously, you feel more comfortable with those who are similar to yourself. And you also trust the person because that person's behavior seems predictable

The act of self-disclosure promotes self-disclosure.

Second, the act of *self-disclosure* promotes self-disclosure. When a person shares with you and you see that disclosure as appropriate, you generally respond by disclosing yourself. Over time, this kind of talk maintains intimacy in a relationship. Greater intimacy can be achieved by greater self-disclosure. If you choose to deepen a relationship, you can reveal more of your experiences (breadth of disclosure) and more of the personal and private parts of those experiences (depth or intimacy of disclosure).

Finally, self disclosure stimulates the relationship. A stagnant relationship may be characterized in part as one in which nothing is new. When disclosure drops off to the point that we stop learning about each other, the relationship does not—cannot—grow.

Appropriate self-disclosure means that we tune into the kind of self-disclosure the other person is willing to give. Appropriate self-disclosure means balanced self-disclosure. Each person in a relationship should disclose at approximately the same depth and breadth as the other. Some questions may help in discovering what level of self-disclosure is appropriate. How well do I know the other person, especially in terms of his more private life? To what extent has the other person revealed his feelings, values and beliefs? How does my own self-disclosure compare to his? The breadth and depth of appropriate self-disclosure will also grow if we are in a relationship that we hope will move along the stages in engagement. (See unit 19.) Do you see progression through the stages? Do you see increased breadth and depth in disclosure over the life of the relationship?

Achieving Role and Rule Agreement

Satisfaction in a relationship is contingent upon achieving *role* and *rule agreement*. Once these are negotiated, continued satisfaction depends upon successfully changing as a relationship changes. As it matures, ideas of what is appropriate must mature as well. When change is not recognized, renegotiation of the relational roles and rules is unlikely; thus, adjustment and growth are not occurring. Although negotiation is the function of many of the skills discussed in previous units, the techniques of conflict management are especially important, for when we express our dissatisfaction with some role or rule, the potential for conflict is introduced into the relationship.

Giving Support

There are two kinds of *support* you can give a person in a relationship. First, the other person needs to be supported, affirmed, and valued. Carl Rogers called this "unconditional positive regard."[2] You can provide unconditional positive regard by telling the person directly that he or she is valued and needed. This creates a positive climate that promotes relational growth.

Second, a person needs support and confirmation when the pressures of daily living create a need for bolstering. Earlier you learned that people are motivated to engage others because of a need to share. You particularly need to share bad news so that you can be supported. It is psychologically much easier to handle a problem when you can share it with a friend. Active listening and empathy are the two main communication activities used to convey such support. Beyond these, it is important to reassure the person: "It must have been hard to deal with your boss today. You did a good job." Support is essential for maintenance and growth in a relationship, as it contributes directly to the psychological health of our partner.

Demonstrating Affection

One of the three primary interpersonal needs in William Schutz's model is *affection*.[3] Each person in a relationship has some particular need for being liked. If the relationship is to grow and prosper, we should try to meet this mutual need. The first step in being able to give affection is to discover the nature of this need in the other. For example, some people want affection to be demonstrated more frequently and more directly than others.

In Eric Berne's theory of transactional analysis, a display of affection is called stroking.[4] When you stroke an infant, you physically touch the child. Adult stroking does not always involve such overt acts as touching. Of course, stroking may happen in intimate relationships, but it does not usually occur in others. Instead, Americans tend to engage in verbal stroking. You might make it a point to remember to tell the other person from time to time how much you appreciate her. Be sure also to recognize the other's positive achievements. Noticing how good the other person feels is a powerful way of stroking. You might say, "I see that you are feeling really good about the report you have been working on all week. And then George liked it too. That's really neat!"

Therapist Muriel James suggests that good friends give each other this kind of stroking.[5] She recommends that you agree to help each other when necessary by directly signaling the need. You might say to a good friend, "I really feel beat down today. Things have just not gone right for me." Your friend then might reassure you about his affection by saying, "Let's talk. I want you to know that I care." This kind of reassurance is also very important to the relationship, since knowing that you can share your disappointments and still be liked will almost certainly enhance its growth. But keep in mind that the individual who repeatedly asks for support can become "needy." That is, this person may be seen as forever dependent, which the other may come to resent. Each pair must decide how much of this kind of sharing is healthy for their particular relationship.

Managing Relational Problems Constructively

People who are not successful in managing relational problems cannot expect their relationships to grow. In fact, problems that are not managed carefully can promote resentment and bitterness. A history of resentment and bitterness is a serious relational problem in itself. It can lead to movement through the stages of disengagement: differentiating, circumscribing, stagnating, avoiding, and, finally, terminating the relationship. Successful problem management, on the other hand, can provide a sense of accomplishment, growth, and optimism. It is important, therefore, to sharpen your relational diagnostic and problem management skills.

Assessing and Understanding Relational Problems

Problems are part of any relationship. We are sometimes frustrated because we do not know exactly what is happening and how to discover the difficulty. Here is a tool for diagnosing your relationship, followed by advice on developing a constructive course of action for managing relational difficulties.

Sometimes an effort to improve a relationship can be cooperative because both parties recognize a need and want to participate. Clearly, this is
the best situation for successful problem solving. But it is possible to work on
a relationship even under less-than-optimum conditions. If possible, both people
might fill out a diagnostic form (table 26.1). This will bring you closer to an
understanding of each other's view of the relationship. Only then are you ready
to develop a course of action.

Table 26.1 Diagnose Your Relationship

Step 1

Working separately, each person should place an initial on the continuum line in response to each statement.
Take as much time as you need to think about each item. Do not discuss your responses while you are
working. When you finish, proceed to Step 2.

1. Cooperation

A. We identify, define, and solve our problems together. We respect each other's competence.
Rarely < ---> Often

B. We work together as a team without competing or putting each other down.
Rarely < ---> Often

C. We make decisions together. We make the most of what each of us has to contribute.
Rarely < ---> Often

D. We share our opinions, thoughts, and ideas without becoming argumentative or defensive.
Rarely < ---> Often

E. Overall, I am satisfied with our mutual respect and cooperation in thinking, deciding, and working together.
Rarely < ---> Often

2. Compatibility

A. We accept and work through our differences to find a common life style with regard to our social and
public images.
Rarely < ---> Often

B. We accept and work through our differences to find common values with regard to religion, morality, social
concerns, and politics.
Rarely < ---> Often

C. We accept and work through our differences with regard to our social life and choice of friends.
Rarely < ---> Often

D. We accept and work through our differences so that we are able to share a basic approach to roles and
rules.
Rarely < ---> Often

E. Overall, I am satisfied with the way we deal with our differences, maintain a life style, and share values.
Rarely < ---> Often

3. Intimacy

A. We often play together. We put fun into what we do together.
Rarely < ---> Often

B. We express our emotions and feelings openly and freely. We say that we are scared, sad, hurting, angry,
or happy.
Rarely < ---> Often

C. We tell each other what we like and dislike. We ask openly for what we want from each other.
Rarely < --> Often

D. We "let go" with each other. We play, relax, and have fun with each other.
Rarely < --> Often

E. Overall, I am satisfied with the level of openness and intimacy in our relationship.
Rarely < --> Often

4. Emotional Support

A. We listen, understand, and empathize with each other's disappointments, hurts, or problems.
Rarely < --> Often

B. We encourage and support each other when one of us is making basic life changes or trying new behavior.
Rarely < --> Often

C. We take responsibility for nurturing when either of us is sick or hurting.
Rarely < --> Often

D. We are emotionally supportive of each other when either of us feels anxious, dependent, or in need of care.
Rarely < --> Often

E. Overall, I am satisfied with the nurturing and support we give and receive each other.
Rarely < --> Often

Step 2

A. Still working separately, review each item and analyze how *satisfied* you feel. You may have marked an item low on the continuum— and *like* it that way. Or you may have marked an item high but feel uncomfortable about it. One person's intimacy is another's anxiety. In the margin next to each item, put one of the following: S = satisfactory, OK = acceptable but not exceptional, or D = somewhat disappointing.
B. Take turns telling each other how and why you marked each item on the continuum.

Developing a Course of Action

Relational problem solving can be a difficult task because it usually involves conflict management. Each of the differences you uncover in a diagnosis of your relationship can be a source of negotiation. (We are assuming that the process of understanding each other did not alter the differences you originally uncovered.) The following suggestions may prove helpful in developing a course of action for managing your problems:

1. *Review what you have learned about conflict management.* The tools of conflict management are very important in an examination of relational problems.
2. *See if you can agree that change is important in the particular area.* This is important because unless you both agree that change is desirable, further discussion will only be frustrating. If you cannot agree at this time, you might agree to think more about it and to talk again later.
3. *List as many concrete proposals as you can for achieving the desired*

end. Suppose you discover that you and the other person want to share opinions, thoughts, and ideas more often, without becoming argumentative. Some techniques you might try are: (1) set aside a specific time for sharing, (2) write down what you think and make a date to discuss what you have written, (3) agree to discuss whatever is on your mind before the end of the day, and (4) wait until the other person says, "I've finished presenting my side," before you talk. List your ideas and even write them on a piece of paper if that will help. The more ideas you can generate for achieving your desired goals, the better.

4. *See if there are any particular ideas that the other person does not understand.* Exchange lists. Before you start talking about your ideas, you need to be sure that you understand each other. If one person does not understand an item on the list, she should mark it and return the list. Confer until all marks are eliminated.

5. *One person should now look over the list and make a proposal.* This proposal might even include a statement of expectations about the other's behavior. For example, you might say, "I'd be willing to set aside a time to talk, if you'd be willing to allow at least thirty minutes for us to do so."

Make a proposal about a desired change. Negotiation will go more smoothly if you are flexible.

6. *The other person should consider the proposal and respond.* It is helpful to limit the response to one of three types:

   a. an acceptance of the proposal
   b. a specific modification of the proposal
   c. a specific counterproposal of the proposal

7. *Continue modifying or making counterproposals until you can both agree.* Make sure that you fully understand any modification or counterproposal. A good way to do this is to engage in active listening. Usually, if partners are willing to stick with this kind of negotiation, they will be able to come to agreement.

The negotiation process will go much more smoothly if you are flexible and open to change. There is no magic formula that will *cause* you to be this way; you must resolve to be flexible. Begin your conversation by talking about the need for give and take. You might also talk about and try to agree that there is a need for change. If you can reach some agreement, you have laid the groundwork for successful negotiation.

You can also encourage agreement by avoiding extreme positions. As soon as one of you takes a position that involves absolutes, such as, "I want you to *guarantee* that you will *always* . . . ," the other person is likely to become defensive. When this happens, a counterproposal that is just as absolute and rigid will likely result.

Finally, recognize that you can agree to talk at another time if tempers flare. This is not *always* a good idea, of course, because avoidance can develop into a habit and does not solve the problem. Use it only to allow tempers to cool and to give you both time to think about the issue privately.

Guarding Against Stagnation

Stagnation occurs when a relationship ceases to be stimulating. The solution to this difficulty, therefore, is to find ways to increase stimulation. We could never offer a complete list of suggestions for increasing stimulation, but we can list five of the most important ones.

Set a Time for Sharing

You are often so busy that you do not spend enough time sharing and disclosing. Sometimes when you think you are sharing, you really are not. Joint activity often includes very little sharing at all. For example, going to a movie

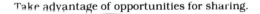

Take advantage of opportunities for sharing.

together, watching a favorite television program together, or taking classes together may not give you the opportunity to engage the other person interper-
sonally.

Sharing through disclosure is an important source of stimulation for relationships. Without it, a relationship will soon be in trouble. Conversations
become predictable, and, if there is no news, listening becomes almost impossible. Such conditions are deadly to relational growth. We can avoid this
by taking advantage of opportunities for sharing. Our recommendation is to
find activities that allow for time alone with the other person: have lunch together; walk together; go to the beach together; play a game that requires
interaction. When you are involved in such activities, you should try to share
yourself. However difficult this may seem, sharing is worth the effort, for it promotes reciprocal self-disclosure.

Agree to Do Something New Together

Another way to stimulate a relationship is to move in a new direction. Take
stock of potential interests and set aside time to plan something new. This can
prove to be a refreshing experience. The activity and challenges that go along
with new, joint experiences create numerous stories that can serve as a relational history that can establish the relationship as meaningful and unique.

Express Caring Frequently

Often we forget to say what we are thinking. This is especially true in long,
established relationships. We assume that the other person knows that we
care. However, there is no substitute for saying, "I care!"

Understand That It Is O.K. to Disagree

You cannot always agree with the other person. Most of us understand this
principle in the abstract, but applying it to a specific relationship is difficult. A
disagreement that we have been unable to resolve can create problems in our
relationships. Resentment or guilt may build. Managing a disagreement does
not directly prevent stagnation. It can, however, create a climate that helps us
focus on the positive and grow. (You can learn to manage internal conflict by
reviewing unit 23.)

Give Your Relationship a Periodic Check-Up

Use of the form presented in table 26.1 for diagnosing your relationships need
not be limited to relationships that are in trouble. You can use it to check up
on any relationship. Such a check can suggest ways to stimulate already healthy
relationships.

Summary

Relational growth occurs when people maintain a satisfying level of interest in each other and their relationship. Growth is encouraged by appropriate self-disclosure that is of about the same breadth and depth of your partner's disclosure. This self-disclosure provides a basis for discovering similarities, thereby promoting disclosure from the other person and stimulating the relationship. As the relationship grows we risk slightly more.

We also need to achieve role and rule agreement by discovering what kinds of behavior and tasks are appropriate for us at the various stages of our relationship.

We must likewise provide the type of support necessary to nourish the relationship. This involves affirming the other as a valued person. It also means that we will bolster each other during times of disappointment or discouragement.

Demonstrate affection. Doing so is crucial to relational growth. Give verbal and nonverbal signs of affection.

We must manage our relational problems constructively. A scheme for assessing rational problems and a plan for action were both presented.

Finally, we suggested that we can guard against stagnation in our relationships by engaging in certain activities: set a time for sharing, agree to do something new together, frequently express caring, understand it's O.K. to disagree, and give the relationship a periodic check-up.

Discussion Questions

1. How do we know what kind of self-disclosure is appropriate for a relationship? What are the possible outcomes of too much or too little self-disclosure?
2. Using a male/female relationship that is in the integrating stage of development as your frame of reference, speculate as to what kinds of role and rule agreements might be a part of this relationship.
3. How is it possible to give support when you are having a disagreement?
4. What kinds of demonstration of affection and liking would be appropriate in each of these relational stages: initiating, experimenting, intensifying, integrating, and bonding?
5. What have you found to be the most important aspects of managing a relational difference constructively?

Endnotes

1. S. M. Jourard, *The Transparent Self* (New York: Van Nostrand Reinhold Company, 1971), 5, 49–57.
2. C. R. Rogers, *On Becoming a Person* (Boston: Houghton Mifflin, 1961), 62, 283.

3. W. C. Schutz, *Firo: A Three-Dimensional Theory of Interpersonal Behavior* (New York: Holt, Rinehart and Winston, 1958).
4. One of the best treatments of Berne's idea of stroking is found in M. James and D. Jongeward, *Born to Win: Transactional Analysis with Gestalt Experiments* (Reading, MA: Addison-Wesley Publishing Company, 1971), 44–67.
5. M. James as cited in a lecture given by members of the staff of the Center for Transactional Analysis at Ghost Ranch Conference Center, Abiquin, NM, Summer 1982.

Epilogue

Interpersonal growth should be a constant, ongoing process. This text has detailed the basic skills for you to continue developing your relationships. Like most skills, you must practice daily to perfect them. Work at your relationships. Success will encourage you to continue your efforts.

By far the largest number of relationship problems among adults result from the inability to be open, honest, and constructive. Better communication is definitely needed. Our experience with students who complete a good interpersonal communication course is that they feel better about their ability to relate to other people. But they do not all relate to others more effectively. The difference lies in active practice. You have to work at making your relationships better, but it can be done.

We congratulate you on your growth and encourage you to continue growing. Your future will be brighter and more promising because of your improved interpersonal skills.

Experiences

Interpersonal Communication Levels

Unit 1: Interpersonal Effectiveness in Relationships

This experience is designed to illustrate the different levels on which people communicate. At the most superficial level we carry out rituals: "Hi! How are you?" "Just fine, thanks. And you?" Later we talk about "safe" subjects that exist outside the relationship and that do not require much self-disclosure. "What's your favorite food?" "This is going to be a neat course." Later still we begin to talk about the ideas that matter to us: "Here's where I stand on the issue of drug use. . . ." "Handguns should be abolished." Finally, with a few intimate friends, we disclose our feelings and wants. All of these levels of communication are bound and controlled by rules.

Begin this experience by moving the chairs in your classroom out of the way to create a large space where you can mill about. Begin to move through the room meeting people, until you come to someone with whom you think you might like to spend a moment. Engage that person in a conversation for a few minutes, using the following pointers:

1. Learn the person's name.
2. Try to discover something interesting about the person.
3. Try to find something the person values as important.
4. Try to find out how this person might like to be introduced to a stranger.
5. You will have to disclose yourself for the other person to be able to do this experience.

Now move about with your new acquaintance. Stop when you find another pair with whom you would like to talk. Make introductions all around. Remember to learn the things about this new pair that you learned about your partner. Spend about five minutes getting to know each other.

Continue the exercise by milling about with one of the two people you just met until you come upon another pair with whom you would like to repeat the experience.

Finally, arrange the chairs in groups of five or six. Take your seat, and discuss these questions for approximately fifteen minutes:

1. At what levels did you and the others communicate? Can you identify examples of talk that support your answer?
2. Did you disclose more than usual for a first meeting? Why or why not?
3. How do you feel about the experience? Are you generally relieved it is over? Are you glad you did it? Do you wish you had not been asked to participate? Why?

Discovering Communication Channels

Unit 1: Interpersonal Effectiveness in Relationships
Unit 2: Understanding the Interpersonal Communication Process

This experience is designed to help you discover the enormous complexity of our communication systems.

Prepare for this experience by working alone or with one other person out of class. Pretend that you wish to buy a used car. Determine where you will look and then travel to that place. It is unimportant whether you actually enter the car lot.

Beginning with the decision to look for a used car, you (and your classmate, if you work with one) should list every message communicated and every channel you use until you stop at the used car lot.

Bring your list to class and share it with members of a small group as you answer these questions:

1. Which messages required interpretation?
2. How would you classify the messages according to these categories?

   a. personal
   b. interpersonal
   c. one-to-many
   d. mass media

3. How is it possible to handle so much complexity in the communication system without experiencing overload?

Observing and Filtering

Unit 2: Understanding the Interpersonal Communication Process

This experience is designed to help you discover that you take in many different messages simultaneously and that you can find out a lot about another person without actually talking with that person.

Begin by agreeing to work with a classmate you do not know for about ten minutes. Move your chairs so that you can see each other well. *Do not talk with the other person during this activity.*

Answer the following questions based on your observations of your partner. Do not compare notes or check their accuracy now.

1. Age?
2. Gender?
3. Ethnic identification?
4. Marital status?
5. Full- or part-time student?
6. Is the person employed?
7. If so, what does this person do?
8. Can you identify anything that happened to the person before coming into the classroom?
9. How is the person feeling now (e.g., well, ill, tired, excited)?
10. What might happen to the person after leaving the classroom?

Now, compare notes with your partner. Check for accuracy, and share your thinking processes. What observations caused you to answer as you did?

Finally, discuss these questions as a class:

1. Were you able to draw inferences easily? Were you surprised by your accuracy or inaccuracy in doing so?
2. How do you account for your success rate in making inferences? What does this tell you about the communication process?

Communication Processes and Models

Unit 2: Understanding the Interpersonal Communication Process

This experience is designed to help you see that you already know and believe a good deal about the communication process.

Working in small groups, draw an original, visual model of the process of communication on the chalkboard. What are the components of the process? What influences the message exchange? How do we send and receive messages?

Now present each model and, as a class, discuss these questions:

1. Are the models complete?
2. Are the models process centered?
3. Are the models transactional?
4. How do the models show the *relationship* implied in every communication event?

Learning to Talk About Wants

Unit 3: An Agenda for Talking About Relationships
Unit 12: Talking About Feelings, Wants, and Expectations

This experience provides practice in talking about wants. Working with a partner, list at least six things that you each want from your relationships and from the people in your relationships. Discuss how you would describe these wants to someone in a relationship. Remember to include statements about the *observable behavior,* the *quantity* or *quality* criteria, and any *time frame* that might be involved. Finally, practice asking for the wants on your list, taking turns and helping each other to feel comfortable with the requests.

Talking About Feelings

Unit 3: An Agenda for Talking About Relationships
Unit 12: Talking About Feelings, Wants, and Expectations

This experience is designed to help you separate your feelings from the language you use to talk about your feelings.

Find a partner, and decide who will be Partner 1 and who will be Partner 2. Partner 1 should induce some pain in one hand by slapping it sharply on the table. Then try to describe that feeling to Partner 2.

Pointers:

1. Stay in the present tense.
2. Stay with descriptions.

Partner 2 should observe Partner 1's performance, counting the number of shifts from present tense to past tense and listing the metaphors used (look for the words "like," "as though," "as if," etc.). Share your observations, and then reverse roles and repeat the experience. Then discuss these questions as partners and as a class:

1. Was the speaker able to do the job easily? Was the present tense rule violated?
2. What features of language use were interesting? Why?
3. Did the speaker use a broad range of metaphors?
4. How can the task of describing feelings be made easier?

Communicating About Needs

Unit 4: Interpersonal Needs

Working through this experience provides an opportunity to identify and communicate needs. In small groups, identify the needs that might motivate a communication with a friend in the following situations. (Recall that the needs presented in this unit are physiological, safety, belonging, esteem, self-actualization, inclusion, affection, and control.)

1. You are short of cash to purchase books for the coming term.
2. You have two dates for Saturday night and must cancel one of your engagements.
3. You have just received a job promotion.
4. Your father and mother, who provide half of your school support, have just called to tell you that you will have to drop out of school because they are experiencing a temporary financial setback.
5. A close friend is moving to another city and you do not expect to see that person again.
6. You have won a week-long vacation.

After the needs have been identified, have one group member model communication to express the needs to a friend. Then have another member respond to the expressions. Answer these questions about each communication transaction:

1. Were the needs clearly stated? If not, how could they be clarified?
2. Was the response appropriate?
3. In what ways was the response satisfying or not satisfying to the person expressing the needs?
4. How could the response to the expression of needs be improved?

Improving Perception

Unit 5: The Perception Process

This experience is designed to help you learn how to improve your perception.

Sit comfortably where you will be undisturbed for about twenty minutes. Choose a spot slightly above your eye level and focus on it. As you focus, close your eyes, keeping your eyes raised slightly. Begin counting slowly backward from one hundred. As you count, you will find yourself becoming more and more relaxed. When you arrive at one, check how your body feels, starting with your feet and working up to the top of your head, including your jaws and forehead. You might tense slightly, hold, and then relax each part as you progress. Inhale deeply as you tense each part, and exhale slowly and steadily as you relax it. Focus on each body part for as long as it takes for you to feel comfortable with it. You may find that your back, shoulders and neck require greater attention. As you mentally climb your body, pay attention to what you are perceiving. Give some thought to each sense for every part of the body you relax.

You may get some images that seem unrelated to what you are doing, but this is O.K. It is important to accept whatever you think during the exercise and to go on. Do not try to change or avoid anything that comes to you. When you have finished this progressive relaxation, count down from twenty to one, recalling your environment as you go along. Remember the colors of the room, the arrangement of furniture, and what you expect to see when you open your eyes. When you reach one, you will open your eyes feeling relaxed and re-freshed, with an increased awareness of yourself because you have focused your perception.

After repeating this exercise several times, you may find that you can shorten, or even eliminate, the counting at the beginning and end of the ex-ercise. If this is true, you can spend this time becoming increasingly aware of your bodily processes through focused perception.

Once you have developed a routine of performing this exercise, you will be able to attend and concentrate on things outside yourself. For example, you might try this simple experience. Place a fresh orange in front of you. (It is important to start with a simple object that involves multiple senses.) After re-laxing, and with your eyes still closed, concentrate on the orange. Imagine its smell, taste, texture, and appearance. Think about what sounds the orange will make when it is squeezed or when its skin is peeled or cut. Work to make your images as vivid as possible.

Next, with your eyes still closed, pick up the fruit and validate your sen-sory predictions. Concentrate on one sense at a time. Feel the surface of the orange for its texture, smell it, then open your eyes and examine it. Tear it open and focus on the sounds that come with that action. Taste the fruit and get a sense of its internal texture as well.

Try this same experience with different objects. Over time the process of relaxing, predicting, and validating will strengthen your ability to perceive ob-jects. And although your perception of people is more complex than your per-ception of objects, this exercise, with some modifications, can help you in perceiving others too. After you feel comfortable using this process with ob-jects, apply your ability to create images to your experience of others.

As suggested before, relax and call to mind a familiar person. Exercise each of your senses as you concentrate on your image. The next time you see this person, verify your image, and you may be surprised at its accuracy. Having concentrated on this person, you may also find yourself paying more attention to your perception as you talk with and observe the individual.

When you feel comfortable creating images of people you know, try re-creating and studying your communication events with them. By remembering and concentrating on your various perceptions and the contributions of your senses to your action in the encounters, you can better understand how and why the exchanges went as they did. Through this method, you can better understand how perception functions in your relationships.

This regimen for building your receptive skills can take some time, but it is well worth the investment. The benefits are increased personal health and interpersonal skill.

Selective Attention

Unit 5: The Perception Process

The purpose of this exercise is to learn more about selective attention. Concentrate on your senses, one at a time:

What do you hear right now?
What do you see?
What do you taste?
What do you smell?
What does your skin sense?

Now, try the following:

1. Concentrate on the taste in your mouth. Notice its sweetness, bitterness, or saltiness.
2. Now, taste and smell at the same time. Is your experience flashing back and forth between the two sensations?
3. Next, taste, smell, and listen simultaneously. You may find that it is easier to hold your attention on what you are hearing.
4. Now, taste, smell, listen, and look at the same time. We expect you to find this very difficult.
5. Finally, try to taste, smell, listen, look, and feel the smoothness of this page at the same time.

   Were you able to focus on more than one sense at the same time? Try other combinations of senses. You will probably find it difficult to attend to more than one sense at a time.

Perception and Dating Preferences

Unit 5: The Perception Process
Unit 6: Perceiving Others Accurately

Your perceptions of others affect your evaluations of them. This experience will help you examine this relationship between perception and evaluation.

Working alone, rank order each of these characteristics, from 1 to 12, according to your estimate of their importance in selecting a romantic partner:

_____ religious
_____ well-dressed
_____ altruistic
_____ intellectually sophisticated
_____ sexually liberated
_____ socially equal
_____ quiet

_____ sexually attractive
_____ good conversationalist
_____ well-respected
_____ unconventional
_____ effervescent

Now, in a small group, without sharing your private work, arrive at a consensus about the order of the above characteristics. Avoid arguing. What is ''right'' is the best collective judgment. Everyone should be involved in the decision-making process.

_____ religious
_____ well-dressed
_____ altruistic
_____ intellectually sophisticated
_____ sexually liberated
_____ socially equal
_____ quiet
_____ sexually attractive
_____ good conversationalist
_____ well-respected
_____ unconventional
_____ effervescent

Discuss these questions when the rank orderings have been completed:

1. How do the private and group lists differ?
2. Can you identify any instance in which group members influenced the ranking of characteristics? Be specific. What kind of talk was influential? How was it characterized?

Finally, working alone, rank these characteristics again, without referring to your earlier list:

_____ religious
_____ well-dressed
_____ altruistic
_____ intellectually sophisticated
_____ sexually liberated
_____ socially equal
_____ quiet
_____ sexually attractive
_____ good conversationalist
_____ well-respected
_____ unconventional
_____ effervescent

Now, compare and contrast your first and second rankings. Are they the same? If not, why? How do you account for your answers to these questions?

Roles and Rules

Unit 6: Perceiving Others Accurately

This exercise is designed to help you think about your roles and the communication rules that go with them.

First list three roles that you very often assume. Working with a partner, share your lists. Then, for each situation below, each choose one of your roles and either role play or just describe how you would approach the situation in that role:

1. Your new secretary seems upset. She feels frustrated, and thinks that everyone expects her to do things the way your previous secretary did. How can you reassure her?
2. A friend borrowed one of your most prized books, which cannot be replaced. When it was returned, you found the cover was torn. What will you say to your friend?
3. A friend has asked you to help her husband find a new job as a decorator. You do not think very highly of his past work and do not especially want to put your reputation on the line by recommending him. What will you say to his wife?
4. Your new supervisor seems generally suspicious and is slow to come to trust people. You admire him and his work and would like to develop a positive working relationship. At your first evaluation, you have clearly done well, and your supervisor says so. What can you say to improve your relationship further?

Discuss how the communication rules that accompanied the roles helped to shape the interpersonal communication process in each situation. Then create your own situations, considering how communication rules and roles may either restrict or enhance interpersonal growth.

Active Listening

Unit 7: Listening to Others

This experience is designed to give you experience using active listening techniques.

Find a partner, and move so you can comfortably talk with each other. Next, decide who will make an initial statement and who will listen actively. The speaker begins by describing how the day started. The listener then paraphrases this statement. This feedback should include both the content and the feelings the speaker was trying to convey. Finally, the speaker either affirms or corrects the response. If there is a correction, the listener should paraphrase the new understanding of the statement.

   Now the roles are reversed and this process is repeated. A second and third round of active listening should be completed with topics chosen by both partners. Analyze the experience using these questions:

1. How easy was active listening?
2. How accurate was your first understanding of what the speaker said?
3. How easy was it to understand the feelings being conveyed? If it was difficult, why?
4. How did you feel after your partner had actively listened to you? Did your reaction differ from what you experience in the usual listening situation?
5. How do you think active listening might affect your relationships at work? home? with friends?

Role Playing Active Listening

Unit 7: Listening to Others

This experience gives you the opportunity to practice active listening through role playing. In small groups, act out each of the following situations for a few minutes. Designate one member to be the initiator and another to be the active listener. After role playing each situation, discuss as a group the effectiveness of the active listening. Rotate roles so that each member has an opportunity to listen actively.

1. You are single and would very much like to find someone to date seriously. You are telling your closest friend that you have met a very nice person who seems to be exactly who you have been looking for.
2. You were just told by your boss that the due date for a project you spent most of the night completing has been extended. You gave up tickets for a very special concert to finish this work, and your boss forgot to tell you that you had the extra time. You meet a close friend and coworker as you are walking down the hall.
3. You have just learned that the person who is both your academic advisor and friend has been fired. You go home and find your roommate (or spouse).
4. A good friend who has been engaged to marry for a year tells you that the engagement is off.
5. You have borrowed a car and accidentally backed into the concrete base of a light pole. You know the owner of the car will be very angry. A friend walks up as you are examining the damaged car.
6. You were counting on all A's this term. You received a C on the last

speech in your public speaking class, which you suspect will drop your grade for the course to B+. You decide to share your feelings with a friend.

7. You are depressed about living with your parents. You would like to move out but are not sure they will like the idea. You decide to talk with your mother about this issue.

8. A friend has had her car in the shop for over a week. You are tired of providing taxi service for her. She approaches you to ask for a ride to town.

9. Your marriage is not going well. You are not fighting, but all the excitement seems to have disappeared. You decide to discuss this with your spouse.

10. You are pretty tired of school. You have been in classes for almost two straight years with no summer vacation. You are facing an enormous paper that is especially depressing you. A close friend has noticed that you seem down.

After finishing your role playing, discuss these questions with your group and the class:

1. How successful was your active listening?
2. Why is active listening sometimes difficult?
3. What can be done to make active listening easier?
4. What would happen if you engaged in active listening every time someone tried to communicate to you?
5. Under what circumstances would you want to use active listening? Contrast these with the circumstances in which you would *not* want to practice active listening.
6. How did you feel when you were the active listener? Focus on the intensity of the feeling.
7. How did you feel toward the listener who paraphrased what you said?

Empathic Listening

Unit 7: Listening to Others
Unit 12: Talking About Feelings, Wants, and Expectations

This experience is designed to allow you to practice empathic listening and discuss the verbal and nonverbal cues that are associated with this kind of listening.

Divide the class into groups of three or four. Together, read the first statement in the following list, and spend two or three minutes thinking about a response. When all group members are ready, discuss the idea. *Each person should paraphrase the ideas of the previous speaker before making a new comment.* Repeat this process with the other statements.

1. People should limit the size of their family to two children.
2. Dependent college students whose parents make less than twenty thousand dollars per year should be granted a government scholarship of not less than five thousand dollars.
3. College courses not in a student's major area of study should be taken on a pass/fail basis.
4. For a tuition rebate of five hundred dollars, a student should be required to contribute one hundred hours of service to the university or college during an academic year.

After discussing each topic, answer these questions.

1. What nonverbal cues were displayed by the person doing the empathic listening?
2. What verbal cues were displayed by the person doing the empathic listening?
3. How did you feel about the other participants during the discussion? Did you feel any different in this group than in others? Why or why not?
4. When is empathic listening best used?

Beliefs

Unit 8: The Self-Concept and Relational Effectiveness

This experience is designed to allow you to compare your beliefs about yourself with those of others.

From the following list, select twenty characteristics that describe how you perceive yourself and how you believe others perceive you. How do these characteristics affect your interpersonal communication? Do you believe that others share this view of you? Test yourself. Ask a classmate or friend to look at your selections. How do these characteristics relate to your beliefs about yourself?

adaptable	diffident	loyal	skeptical
ambitious	direct	manipulative	self-confident
analytical	disagreeable	materialistic	self-conscious
argumentative	disorderly	officious	self-starter
arrogant	domineering	opportunistic	sensitive
articulate	driving	optimistic	shrewd
autocratic	earthy	outgoing	shy
belligerent	efficient	outspoken	sincere
calm	egotistical	overbearing	sneaky
candid	emotional	patient	stable
careless	enthusiastic	pensive	stern
cautious	flighty	persevering	stubborn
cold	frank	persuasive	sympathetic

competitive	friendly	pessimistic	systematic
complicated	garrulous	practical	tactful
conforming	genuine	pretentious	thorough
conservative	gregarious	probing	thrifty
considerate	guarded	prompt	truthful
cooperative	honest	proud	tyrannical
courageous	idealistic	rational	understanding
courteous	imaginative	relentless	vain
critical	impulsive	reliable	warm
decisive	independent	reserved	withdrawn
deferential	indifferent	resourceful	witty
dependable	kind	rude	
devious	lazy	ruthless	

Values

Unit 8: The Self-Concept and Relational Effectiveness

This experience gives you the opportunity to compare your values with those of another person.

Return to the Beliefs Experience, and *rank* the characteristics you selected from most important to least important. Next place a check (✓) by those that you perceive as positive characteristics. Compare your list with that of another person. How do they differ? Discuss both the differences and similarities with the other person to arrive at a better understanding of your own value system. Notice that some of your values are about you and what you want for yourself; others imply standards about the way things should be. You may also notice that some of your values are related to several beliefs. In fact, many values represent a synthesis of beliefs. Your values shape the images that you think are appropriate to present.

Thinking and talking about your values helps you to know more about who you are and who you want to be. A clearer idea about what is important to you enables you to express yourself more coherently and effectively.

A Discussion of the Self-Concept

Unit 8: The Self-Concept and Relational Effectiveness

Who we believe ourselves to be is the result of early and important messages we received from important others in our lives as well as how people react to us now. This exercise asks you to examine the bases of your concept of yourself as a professional person.

Divide the class into groups of six. Each group should select a leader who has the task of facilitating the conversation in the group. The leader should keep the group members focused on their images of themselves as adult members of the world of work.

As you think of yourself aspiring to the world of work, or already working, think about what early experiences with ''significant others'' (your parents, for example) have influenced your professional aspirations and accomplishments. Try to be as specific as possible in identifying who said what, when, and under what circumstances.

A Discussion of Self-Disclosure

Unit 9: Self-Disclosure and Relational Effectiveness

The purpose of this exercise is to focus your attention on how readily you and others disclose. Divide the class into groups of five or six. Each group should select a leader to facilitate the conversation and to keep it on track. Each member, in turn, should respond to these questions:

Do you have difficulty disclosing yourself to others? Under what circumstances is self-disclosure difficult? When is it easier? What kinds of behaviors by others make it easier for you to disclose yourself? Provide specific examples.

Self-Disclosure Models

Unit 9: Self-Disclosure and Relational Effectiveness

The purpose of this experience is to give you an opportunity to discuss how the quadrants in the Johari Window affect communication and relationships.

Examine the Johari Windows on page 377. Consider these questions, first alone and then with a group:

1. For each window pair, describe the communication that would occur.
2. Are there any kinds of relationships for which the window seems especially appropriate? If so, why?
3. Do you think this figure depicts a growing relationship?
4. What would you do to increase the openness in this relationship?

Language of Self-Disclosure

Unit 9: Self-Disclosure and Relational Effectiveness

On pages 377 and 378 is a series of semantic differential scale items for you to use in a self-discovery experience. Take a moment to produce two copies

How is communication affected by these Johari Windows?

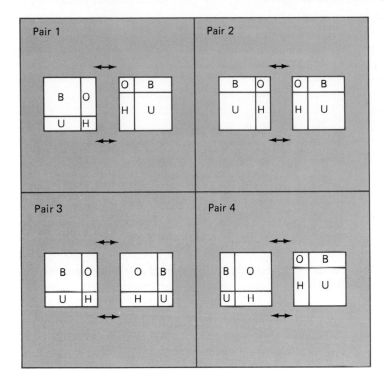

of this scale. On one copy, place a check on the continuum to represent the degree of the attribute you think you possess.

After you have marked all items, use a different color ink to mark the items to indicate how you believe others see you. Finally, give the unmarked copy of these scales to someone who knows you fairly well and ask that person to indicate how he or she sees you.

	7	6	5	4	3	2	1	
relaxed	____ : ____ : ____ : ____ : ____ : ____ : ____							tense
confidential	____ : ____ : ____ : ____ : ____ : ____ : ____							divulging
confident	____ : ____ : ____ : ____ : ____ : ____ : ____							ill-at-ease
enthusiastic	____ : ____ : ____ : ____ : ____ : ____ : ____							apathetic
trustworthy	____ : ____ : ____ : ____ : ____ : ____ : ____							untrustworthy
safe	____ : ____ : ____ : ____ : ____ : ____ : ____							dangerous
considerate	____ : ____ : ____ : ____ : ____ : ____ : ____							inconsiderate
friendly	____ : ____ : ____ : ____ : ____ : ____ : ____							hostile

involved	_____ : _____ : _____ : _____ : _____ : _____ : _____	detached
straightforward	_____ : _____ : _____ : _____ : _____ : _____ : _____	tricky
respectful	_____ : _____ : _____ : _____ : _____ : _____ : _____	disrespectful
reliable	_____ : _____ : _____ : _____ : _____ : _____ : _____	unreliable
secure	_____ : _____ : _____ : _____ : _____ : _____ : _____	insecure
sincere	_____ : _____ : _____ : _____ : _____ : _____ : _____	insincere
stimulating	_____ : _____ : _____ : _____ : _____ : _____ : _____	boring
sensitive	_____ : _____ : _____ : _____ : _____ : _____ : _____	insensitive
not deceitful	_____ : _____ : _____ : _____ : _____ : _____ : _____	deceitful
pleasant	_____ : _____ : _____ : _____ : _____ : _____ : _____	unpleasant
kind	_____ : _____ : _____ : _____ : _____ : _____ : _____	cruel
honest	_____ : _____ : _____ : _____ : _____ : _____ : _____	dishonest
skilled	_____ : _____ : _____ : _____ : _____ : _____ : _____	unskilled
informed	_____ : _____ : _____ : _____ : _____ : _____ : _____	uninformed
experienced	_____ : _____ : _____ : _____ : _____ : _____ : _____	inexperienced
bold	_____ : _____ : _____ : _____ : _____ : _____ : _____	timid

When you have collected data from all three ratings, transcribe the numbers associated with the spaces checked on the grid on page 379. When you have entered all the numbers, consider what they mean in terms of your self-concept.

Remember that self-concept is not necessarily static. If there are areas in which you would like to see change, you can. Remember, however, that *the rating from the other person is the perception of one (and only one) other person.* It is subject to selectivity and subjectivity.

Describing Relationships

Unit 10: The Nature of Language

Words that people use to describe their relationships include the following:

friend
associate
companion
acquaintance
person

Now write the answers to the questions below. Writing your responses will help you to think more thoroughly about the language you use to describe relationships.

1. Arrange the above words in order of increasing abstraction.
2. Examine each level of abstraction and list words or phrases that characterize relationships at that level. What behaviors are included at

Self Analysis Grid

Attribute Scale	Self-Rating	My Perception of Other's Rating	Other's Rating
Relaxed–tense			
Confidential–divulging			
Confident–ill-at-ease			
Enthusiastic–apathetic			
Trustworthy–untrustworthy			
Safe–dangerous			
Considerate–inconsiderate			
Friendly–hostile			
Involved–detached			
Straightforward–tricky			
Respectful–disrespectful			
Reliable–unreliable			
Secure–insecure			
Sincere–insincere			
Stimulating–boring			
Sensitive–insensitive			
Not deceitful–deceitful			
Pleasant–unpleasant			
Kind–cruel			
Honest–dishonest			
Skilled–unskilled			
Informed–uninformed			
Experienced–inexperienced			
Bold–timid			

each level? How do the characteristics and behaviors differ from level to level?

3. In what ways do intensity, involvement, and expectations of the other person differ from level to level?

4. Evaluate each level as more or less impersonal versus more or less interpersonal.

5. How would communication between two people be described at each level of abstraction?

6. How would communication between people be affected if they used different levels of abstraction in defining their relationship?

7. What words could you add to this list? Where would each fit into the abstraction ladder? What effect do these levels have on relational growth?

8. Construct a similar ladder of the levels of abstraction in describing a romantic relationship. Compare your descriptions with others in class.

The Word Is Not the Thing. Sometimes It Isn't Even the Word!

Unit 10: The Nature of Language

This experience is designed to provide insights into language use. The following statements all mean the same thing as common proverbs you have heard many times. Can you supply the more familiar version?

1. All articles that coruscate with resplendence are not truly suriferous.
2. Sorting on the part of mendicants must be interdicted.
3. Male cadavers are incapable of rendering testimony.
4. Abstention from elevatory undertakings precludes a potential escalation of a lucrative nature.
5. Freedom from undesirable incrustations—that is to say, undefiled and unadulterated—is contiguous to rectitude.
6. Avoid becoming lachrymose concerning precipitately departed lactile fluid.
7. Eschew the implement of correction and vitiate the scion.
8. Surveillance should precede saltation.
9. The individual presenting the ultimate cachinnation possesses thereby the optimal cachinnation.
10. Eleemosynary deeds have their incipience intramurally.
11. Conflagration occurs in context with visible vapors having their provenence in ignited carbonaceous material.
12. Refrain, all individuals whose residences may be characterized as vitreous edifices, from catapulting petrous projectiles.

Meanings Are in People

Unit 10: The Nature of Language
Unit 14: Problems with Language in Relationships

This exercise is designed to illustrate that meanings are in people, not in the language.

Step 1 (approximately 10 minutes; work alone)
In the space provided, write one sentence in response to each statement. Work rapidly and record your first reaction. Example:

Stimulus: Oak wood is the best kind for furniture.
Reaction: I think walnut is better.

1. Oak furniture is the best kind.

2. Hotels never have a thirteenth floor.

3. The color blue is the best one.

4. A statistics course should be required of everyone.

5. You are too short.

6. Everyone should eat fresh fruits and vegetables daily.

7. Chess is a fantastic sport.

8. The legal driving age should be lowered.

9. Fish is better for you than beef.

10. All undergraduates should complete a course in philosophy.

Step 2 (approximately 20 minutes)
Have two students working at the chalkboard: One records positive reactions to the above statements; the other records negative reactions. Ask students to read four comments for each item, until all forty responses are recorded.

Step 3 (approximately 10 minutes; work as a class)
Discuss these questions:

1. How do you account for the different responses to the above statements?

2. Do you find any patterns in the negative or positive responses? If so, how do you account for them?

3. Can you think of a single case in which the meaning of language obtains in the words rather than in the heads of the people who use the words?

Language and Relationships

Unit 11: Language and Relationships

This experience allows you to explore how language use is affected by particular kinds of relationships.

Write a letter to your family describing your progress this term. Be as specific as you can, but limit your description to two pages or less. Now write another letter on the same subject, this time to your best friend. Finally, imagine that you have been asked to orient an incoming freshman. Write to this person about what and how you are doing this term. Compare letters with other interpersonal communication students, and consider these questions:

1. What similarities and differences did you find among letters addressed to the same role relationships? Did the assignment reveal any consistency in the pools of language used?

2. What did the letters reveal about the breadth of each relationship for which they were written? Did some letters have more information than others? Did the levels of abstraction differ?

3. What language indicated the intensity of the relationship between the correspondents? Did this language vary from letter to letter?

Identifying Symmetrical and Complementary Language

Unit 11: Language and Relationships

This experience provides practice in identifying symmetrical and complementary language.

For each conversation below, determine each participant's view of the relationship. Identify specific remarks that led you to your conclusions.

Joan: I think that was a great film.

Bill: I think so too. The photography . . .

Joan: The photography was beautiful.

Bill: Yes, and the sound . . .

Joan: The sound was perfect.

Bill: The . . .

Joan: The whole film was a masterpiece.

Susan: I think it was a great film.

Cindy: Yes, great if you enjoy sleeping.

Susan: The photography was beautiful.

Cindy: The photography was fuzzy.

Susan: The sound track was perfect.

Cindy: The only things perfect about the sound track were the occasional moments of silence.

Dan: Well, Tom, what did you think?

Tom: I think it was a great film.

Dan: I didn't know what to make of the photography.

Tom: The tone of the photography really helped the theme of the film.

Dan: How about that sound?

Tom: It matched the imagery just right for me.

Dan: I guess it must be a masterpiece.

Tom: I think so.

Conclude by rewriting these conversations to make them reflect other views of the relationships presented.

Learning More Feeling Words

Unit 12: Talking About Feelings, Wants, and Expectations

This experience will help you use a broader range of language.

Begin by working alone to list at least five expressions of feelings for each of the following situations. Use any list of words you wish, including those provided in unit 12. Keep in mind that there are both verbal and nonverbal message systems.

1. You discover that someone has stolen your textbooks from your car.
2. You realize that you have spent too much time in one activity and are now late for an important appointment.
3. Someone important to you has behaved in a way that you do not approve of and in a context that you care about deeply.
4. Someone important to you has rejected your invitation to spend an evening together, using language you find offensive.
5. Someone you trusted has repeated a secret that you told in confidence.

6. Someone you love has just been recognized for an excellent accomplishment.
7. You have just been paid a very strong compliment by someone important to you.

Compare your responses with that of someone seated close to you. Expand your own list if you wish. Practice using the words on your list by role playing the situations with your partner. Remember that you are trying to expand your feeling vocabulary.

Finally, discuss these questions as a class:

1. Did you find this experience easy or difficult? Explain your answer.
2. How could you more easily learn more feeling words?

Creating Feeling Statements

Unit 12: Talking About Feelings, Wants, and Expectations

The goal of this experience is to give you practice in expressing feelings.

Form small groups and then select a situation from the left column below and a person to whom you will deliver the message from the right column. Role play the communication with another member of your group. Now role play the same situation with a different receiver. Analyze how the expressions of feelings differ. Allow each group member to role play at least one situation with two different receivers.

Situations

1. You have an appointment and the person did not show up.
2. The person next to you in class made sarcastic remarks about your test grade.
3. You have just been paid a compliment that you know you do not deserve. You are embarrassed, and the person who paid the compliment noticed your embarrassment.
4. A friend came up to you this morning and sensed that you were feeling depressed. The friend smiled, invited you to sit down, and then listened to your problems.

Receivers

1. A professor
2. Your mother, father, or spouse
3. An acquaintance of several months
4. A good friend

Identifying Assertive, Nonassertive, and Aggressive Language

Unit 13: Assertive, Nonassertive, and Aggressive Communication

This experience provides practice in identifying assertive, nonassertive, and aggressive language.

For each situation below, indicate what you might say in communicating assertively, nonassertively, or aggressively:

1. You are having a conversation with a friend who *never* makes eye contact when talking with you.
2. You have been offered a promotion at work, but the pay raise that comes with it is very small compared to the amount of increased work.
3. You were engaged last week, and today a person whom you find very attractive and would like to get to know as a friend, asks you for a date.
4. While visiting the local health spa, a stranger asks to borrow your towel.
5. You are sober, but your best friend is intoxicated and wants to drive home.
6. You are sober, but your friend, who is also sober, thinks you have had too much to drink. You want to drive home, and she protests.

Compare your statements with those of some of your classmates. Are there any common feelings or ideas among the responses? Did any issues about the relationship (such as trust or understanding) influence your decisions about appropriate assertive language?

Practicing Assertive Behavior

Unit 13: Assertive, Nonassertive, and Aggressive Communication

This experience provides practice in creating assertive responses to a variety of situations. You may either write scripts for these events or role play them in class. In either case, compare notes with your classmates to see if they have approaches to these problems that you may not have considered.

1. In a crowded movie theater, the person behind you is coughing so loudly that you cannot hear the film.
2. A professor is taking time from covering course material to express her views about university politics.
3. You see one of your neighbors taking materials from a construction site near your home.
4. Your television picture has been snowy for two weeks, and today it has

gone out altogether. The bill from the cable company arrives, and you do not feel it is correct.

5. You feel your spouse is taking you for granted by asking you to do more than your share of the housework.

6. At a lunch counter, the person after you in line ordered the same meal as you, a ham and cheese sandwich. When the cook calls out that the order is ready, this person goes quickly to the counter and takes your sandwich.

7. You want your best friend to stop smoking in your house.

8. You have learned that an acquaintance has said uncomplimentary things about you to another acquaintance.

9. Your neighbor visits frequently, uninvited, and installs himself in your kitchen to pass the time. You like him, but wish he wouldn't always stay so long.

10. Your supervisor has criticized you in a way that you think is only partially true and fair.

Personal Appearance and Communication

Unit 15: Body Communication and Relational Effectiveness

This experience demonstrates the impact of appearance on communication.

Step 1 (10 minutes; work alone)
Rank the following items in order of their importance to you for both men and women.

Women
_____ jewelry
_____ figure
_____ lipstick
_____ breath/teeth
_____ shoes
_____ pants/skirt
_____ perfume
_____ hair
_____ fingernails
_____ blouse
_____ legs
_____ eye make-up

Men
_____ breath/teeth
_____ facial hair
_____ cologne
_____ shoes
_____ hair
_____ pants
_____ physique
_____ accessories
_____ fingernails
_____ shirt
_____ shower
_____ other _____

Step 2 (30 minutes; work in groups of 5 or 6)
Arrive at a group consensus on rankings for the items on both lists. Record each group's rankings on the chalkboard.

Women	Men
_____ jewelry	_____ breath/teeth
_____ figure	_____ facial hair
_____ lipstick	_____ cologne
_____ breath/teeth	_____ shoes
_____ shoes	_____ hair
_____ pants/skirt	_____ pants
_____ perfume	_____ physique
_____ hair	_____ accessories
_____ fingernails	_____ fingernails
_____ blouse	_____ shirt
_____ legs	_____ shower
_____ eye make-up	_____ other _____

Step 3 (10 minutes; work as a class)

1. Why do some items seem more important than others?
2. What effect does physical appearance have on interpersonal communication?
3. Having seen the lists and heard the discussion, would you change any rankings on your personal list? If so, why?

Gestures and Meaning

Unit 15: Body Communication and Relational Effectiveness

Certain prevalent gestures are used in our society to make communication easier. This experience is designed to demonstrate the importance of gestures and body movement in communicating meaning.

Work in small groups to develop a list of commonly used gestures in several categories. We have begun the process to help get you started.

Gestures used by sports officials to communicate their decisions:

1. touchdown	6. _____
2. no score	7. _____
3. strike two	8. _____
4. _____	9. _____
5. _____	10. _____

Signals used on the job when noise inhibits the use of oral communication:

1. start engines	6. _____
2. left turn	7. _____
3. I want a ride.	8. _____
4. _____	9. _____
5. _____	10. _____

Gestures used to clarify and emphasize ideas:

1. show direction   6. _____
2. show size   7. _____
3. reject an idea   8. _____
4. _____   9. _____
5. _____   10. _____

Conclude the experience with each member selecting from the gestures recorded by the group and communicating a series of three messages, solely with signals. Others may wish to make notes. Check your levels of accuracy in sending and receiving these nonverbal messages. When everyone has had a turn, discuss these questions:

1. How accurately can the meaning of gestures be predicted?
2. Are stereotypical gestures (such as thumbing a ride) easier to understand than nonstereotypical gestures? Why or why not?

The Messages of Personal Space

Unit 16: Touching, Environmental Messages, Space, and Relational Effectiveness

This experience will help you understand your use of personal space. You will need to understand these definitions: *Freeze* means to stop all movement, including gestures, eye motion, and the like. *Melt* means to continue natural movements until "freeze" is called.

First, select a partner—someone from the class whom you do not know well. Stand facing each other, about ten feet apart. Move slowly toward or away from each other, until you find a comfortable distance for each of the following:

1. public distance—one that requires you to recognize the other person (between ten and eighteen feet)
2. social consultive distance—one that allows you to talk with each other comfortably but not to touch (between four and ten feet)
3. personal distance—one that allows you to tell secrets to each other and to touch (between two and four feet)

When you come to a comfortable distance, call "freeze." If your partner calls "freeze" before you do, stop all movement instantly.

Discuss these questions with your partner:

1. Did your experiences of each appropriate distance differ? Why or why not?
2. Was it difficult to "freeze" when asked to do so? Why or why not?

Now, face your partner again. Move slowly toward each other until one of you becomes so uncomfortable that you call "freeze." Stop all movement, study the distance between you, and then move to a comfortable distance and discuss these questions:

1. How close were you to each other?
2. Do any gender-related variables control how close you can get to each other?

Conclude this experience with a class discussion. Try to discover if women and men experience personal space differently. Are there any rules that control how closely two men can stand? A man and a woman? Two women? If so, how do you account for them? How do you suppose you learned them?

Vocalics and Communication

Unit 17: Silence, Time, and Vocalics

This experience will help you realize how much we depend upon vocalics for information about a speaker.

Have someone bring to class a tape recording (about ten minutes long) of any available speaker. After listening, complete the Vocalics Quiz on the next page.

As a class, discuss these questions:

1. How effective are vocal cues in sending messages about a speaker?
2. Which vocal cues provide information about each of the questions on the Vocalics Quiz?
3. Why is it possible to answer the questions correctly merely by hearing the speaker?

Form small groups of five or six to compare your data and experiences. Use this sheet to tabulate the responses of all group members:

introverted	: _____ : _____ : _____ : _____ :	extroverted
conservative	: _____ : _____ : _____ : _____ :	liberal
good leader	: _____ : _____ : _____ : _____ :	poor leader
beautiful	: _____ : _____ : _____ : _____ :	ugly
energetic	: _____ : _____ : _____ : _____ :	lazy
overweight	: _____ : _____ : _____ : _____ :	underweight
trustworthy	: _____ : _____ : _____ : _____ :	not trustworthy
articulate	: _____ : _____ : _____ : _____ :	inarticulate
happy	: _____ : _____ : _____ : _____ :	sad
friendly	: _____ : _____ : _____ : _____ :	distant
warm	: _____ : _____ : _____ : _____ :	cool
interesting	: _____ : _____ : _____ : _____ :	boring

Vocalics Quiz

1. What was the sex of the speaker? _____ male _____ female

2. What was the approximate age of the speaker?

    _____ under 10 years   _____ 30–39 years
    _____ 10–14 years   _____ 40–49 years
    _____ 15–19 years   _____ 50–59 years
    _____ 20–29 years   _____ 60 years and above

3. What part of the world does the speaker come from?

    _____

4. What educational level has this person attained?

    _____ elementary (1–6)   _____ college
    _____ junior high (7–9)   _____ graduate school
    _____ senior high (10–12)

5. Mark each continuum according to your experience of the speaker:

    introverted   : _____ : _____ : _____ : _____ : _____ :   extroverted
    conservative : _____ : _____ : _____ : _____ : _____ :   liberal
    good leader   : _____ : _____ : _____ : _____ : _____ :   poor leader
    beautiful   : _____ : _____ : _____ : _____ : _____ :   ugly
    energetic   : _____ : _____ : _____ : _____ : _____ :   lazy
    overweight   : _____ : _____ : _____ : _____ : _____ :   underweight
    trustworthy   : _____ : _____ : _____ : _____ : _____ :   not trustworthy
    articulate   : _____ : _____ : _____ : _____ : _____ :   inarticulate
    happy   : _____ : _____ : _____ : _____ : _____ :   sad
    friendly   : _____ : _____ : _____ : _____ : _____ :   distant
    warm   : _____ : _____ : _____ : _____ : _____ :   cool
    interesting   : _____ : _____ : _____ : _____ : _____ :   boring

As a class, discuss these questions:

1. Do you find a pattern in the group responses? If so, how do you account for it?
2. Does this experience suggest anything about your habits of drawing inferences? What are the implications for your choices of behavior in difficult, perhaps conflictual, conversations?

Examining Relational Development

Unit 18: Initiating Relationships
Unit 19: Relational Development

The purpose of this experience is to provide practice in analyzing a dialogue to discover various aspects of the relational development process.

Read the following dialogue that took place between Jill and Stephen, who are engaged to marry:

Steve: Jill, tell me what annoys you about me.

Jill: I get really upset when you sit in the living room and watch TV while I'm fixing dinner.

Steve: There wasn't any other place for me to sit. I wanted to watch the news anyway. You know I like to watch the news.

Jill: (interrupting) There was too a place to sit. And besides, I'm more important than watching news.

Steve: I didn't mean that you weren't more important than the news. I meant that I ought to get to watch the news for fifteen minutes.

Jill: I'm glad you are so considerate. You're nearly perfect—I guess.

Steve: Shut up! You're making fun of me.

Jill: You deserve it. Do you get mad when I make fun of you?

Steve: Yes.

Jill: I've changed my mind. You aren't even close to perfect.

Steve: Now it is my turn to tell you what annoys me! It annoys me when we are on a date and you make eyes at other guys.

Jill: It does?

Steve: Yes. It does.

Jill: You poor boy, you sure do have your problems.

Steve: There you go again. You can't carry on a serious conversation without teasing me. I hate it! I'm sorry you asked me over for dinner.

Examine this dialogue with these questions:

1. Speculate on why Steve and Jill might have initiated their relationship.
2. What stage of the relational development process do you think Steve and Jill are in? Why did you come to this conclusion?
3. Identify the self-disclosure in this communication. What effect did it have on relational development?
4. Identify the statements that positively or negatively affect the relationship. What effect did positiveness, or the lack of it, have on the relationship?

5. Did either person try to deal with potential conflict seriously? If not, speculate about how their attitudes affected the outcome of the relationship.

6. Assume that Steve and Jill would like their relationship to grow. Make a list of suggestions that would help them achieve this goal.

Role Playing Defensive and Supportive Communication

Unit 20: Defensiveness in Relationships
Unit 21: Supportiveness in Relationships

Form small groups, and have two members role play each of the following situations, first, using defensive behavior and then using supportive behavior. Remember that supportive behavior affirms the other person, but does not necessarily mean that you agree with that person's position. The other group members will act as observers. They should take notes so that they will be able to point out specific examples of defensive and supportive behavior.

After each role play, the observers should discuss with the actors how closely they kept to Gibb's categories. Continue to role play until all members have had an opportunity to practice both defensive and supportive behavior.

1. You have been bothered for three weeks by a member of the opposite sex who would like a date. You have no interest in the person. The person has caught up with you after class and is walking with you across campus, pressing you for a date.

2. You are living with someone who keeps an untidy apartment. You usually keep your belongings in their place. You have talked with this person several times. Your roommate's attitude is that she or he has a right to her or his own lifestyle and that you should move out if you don't like what is going on. Your parents are visiting in two days and you want the apartment cleaned. You do not have time to clean up your roommate's mess because you must study for an important final exam.

3. You and your roommate share the cost of food and the cooking. When your roommate is cooking, he or she frequently invites a friend or two and cooks for four instead of two. This happens about three times each week. You believe it is not fair to split the cost of groceries if this practice is to continue. Your roommate says that it is just part of living and being sociable, and that you are free to invite your friends when you cook. You might wish to do this once a week, but the paying arrangement still would not be fair.

4. You are selected as the leader of a group that is working on a class project. One member has missed a few meetings and is often late with his part of the work. The project is due next Monday. You have talked to this person before and he commented, ''You got it, didn't you? You're

lucky I had time to do it at all." You are concerned that his work will not be ready for the Monday deadline. You talk to him about the situation in hopes of getting some kind of firm commitment.

Assessing Supportiveness and Defensiveness

Unit 20: Defensiveness in Relationships
Unit 21: Supportiveness in Relationships

This experience provides practice in assessing supportiveness and defensiveness in a dialogue.

In small groups or as a class, analyze this dialogue for examples of defensive and supportive communication. Identify Gibb's category or categories that a statement illustrates and tell why the statement might produce defensive or supportive behavior in the other person. Then, if it is defensive, create an alternative statement that might be seen as supportive. If small groups are conducting the analysis, they should share their work with the class when they have completed the analysis.

This conversation takes place between Phil and John, who have been roommates for two years. They will both be seniors next year and are trying to decide whether to live together for their final year. Phil has some reservations about living together, while John thinks it is an excellent idea.

Phil: I really want to talk about our plans for sharing an apartment next year. But I know you won't want to talk about it.

John: I thought we made that decision last week. I don't have anything to say to you about this. There is nothing wrong with living together next year. You always want to talk.

Phil: I just want to find out how you think some things will go next year. We've had a few differences and I want to talk.

John: Things will go just fine. I don't see any reason to talk about this. Besides, when you decide we are going to "have a talk," we always end up having a fight. Why can't we just drop this whole "talk" idea and keep things as they are? You're trying to bump me out so Linda can move in. That's it.

Phil: That's not true. I did talk with Linda about living together, but that was in December. I can't believe that you are bringing that up now!

John: Well, you didn't tell me anything about it then. I had to find out from a friend of mine. Then I confronted you with it and you lied.

Phil: I'm telling the truth now. Can't you let the past be the past? I am sorry that I did that. I've told you that six times. I am telling you the truth.

John: I've noticed you hanging around Linda—I saw you talking in the corner of the snack bar yesterday. You didn't even notice me until I walked right up and grabbed a chair. You were talking to her about next year.

Phil: Linda is not trying to get me to let her move in here.

John: Then you are trying to convince her to move in.

Phil: I tell you there is nothing to this! This is one of the problems I wanted to bring up. You are *always* jealous of my friends. You think that being a roommate means that you have a right to impose decisions about my social life. I am sick of this!

John: Wow!

Phil: I am going to ask Linda to move in, and I expect you to get out.

John: Wait, Phil. We've roomed together for two years. We're good friends—or at least I thought we were. How can you just throw me out?

Phil: I don't know what you want me to say. I'm sick of this. I want you out. If you want to still be friends, we can try. I won't live with you—you can't change.

John: That does it! Forget that we ever roomed together. Every time you want to have one of these "talks" we have a fight. I'm leaving. I'll be back *when you're not here* to pick up my things. Linda can move in next week!

Assessing Your Areas of Power Wealth

Unit 22: Managing Power in Relationships

The purpose of this exercise is to identify your "power currencies" in a relationship. Power exists in every relationship, and it resides in the "currencies" that each person controls. What currencies do you control in a relationship with someone else? Work alone as you identify and list your sources of power in each of these categories.[1]

1. Expertise
    a. special knowledge _____
    b. skills _____

2. Resource control
    a. salary _____
    b. space _____
    c. equipment _____
    d. people _____
    e. budget _____
    f. energy _____
    g. time _____
    h. materials _____
    i. material rewards _____
    j. freedom/choice _____

3. Interpersonal linkages

    a. Do you serve as a liaison person between two people or factions?
    b. Do you hold a central position in formal/informal communication networks?
    c. Do you have access to important or sensitive information?
    d. Do you have indirect access to other sources of power?

4. Personal qualities

    a. attractiveness _____
    b. warmth _____
    c. conversational skill _____
    d. social status _____
    e. credibility _____
    f. trust _____
    g. reputation _____

5. Intimacy

    a. love _____
    b. sex _____
    c. caring _____
    d. nurturing _____
    e. bonding _____

A Closer Look at Threat as a Conflict Management Strategy

Unit 22: Managing Power in Relationships
Unit 24: Managing Interpersonal Conflict

The purpose of this experience is to focus your attention on threat as a conflict management tool.

Threat and threat-related conflict strategies may be the most common of all possible strategies in our society. They can be both productive and destructive. Here is a model based on the work of J. T. Tedeschi:[2]

	Source Controls the Outcome	Source Does Not Control the Outcome
Negative Sanction	Threat	Warning
Positive Sanction	Promise	Recommendation

Notice that a threat is only credible when:

1. the other party is in a position to follow through;
2. the other party is willing to follow through; and
3. the threat is something to be avoided.

Working in small groups, list four examples from your group's experiences of threat-related conflict management strategy for each of the four categories above (threat, warning, promise, and recommendation). Be sure to include two examples that are productive and two that are destructive in each category. Then, as a group, discuss how the destructive strategies might be avoided or managed, and prepare to make a recommendation to the class.

Stop and Reflect: Goal

Unit 23: Managing Intrapersonal Conflict

In this experience you will focus on goal conflicts you may be experiencing.

1. List your current goals:

   Today   This Week   This Year   Rest of My Life

   _____   _____   _____   _____
   _____   _____   _____   _____
   _____   _____   _____   _____

2. Which goals are suffering because you are not spending enough time and energy pursuing them?

   _____
   _____
   _____

3. What goal conflicts are causing you distress?

   _____ vs. _____
   _____ vs. _____
   _____ vs. _____

4. Is having too many goals a problem for you? How about too few? How does the number of goals you have to accomplish relate to intrapersonal conflict and its management?

   _____
   _____
   _____

A Self-Test Questionnaire

Unit 23: Managing Intrapersonal Conflict
Unit 24: Managing Interpersonal Conflict

This experience provides an opportunity for you to discover whether your attitudes about conflict are generally shared by your classmates. Begin by working alone.

In your opinion, which of the following statements is *most* accurate?

1. Avoidance of conflict leads to unhappy marriages and work relationships because it keeps important issues buried.
2. Avoidance of unnecessary conflict helps promote harmony and prevents unnecessary upsets.
3. The only effective way to manage conflict is to work through it by engaging the other person.
4. Engagement of conflict leads to escalatory spirals and hurt for all parties.

Compare your responses to those of other students. What similarities and differences do you find? How do you account for them?

Setting a Conflict Management Goal

Unit 24: Managing Interpersonal Conflict

The purpose of this exercise is to help you focus on setting an appropriate goal as part of managing conflicts.

Begin this exercise by identifying a relationship you have that is not going as smoothly as you might like. Find one in which you are experiencing some conflict. The key question is, "What do you want from the relationship that you are not getting?"

1. Write down what you want using whatever words best describe what you want from the other in the relationship.

   _____

   _____

   _____

2. Name the person: _____

   Describe what you would like the other person to *do*.

   _____

   _____

   _____

If some of your responses to the two questions are similar, eliminate the similar items from the second list.

3. Write a complete statement of each goal that remains in the list above. Specify what behavior you want, what amount (if you know it), and how you will measure that amount. Specify what quality criterion you hold and how you will measure that. Finally, specify a time frame—a date and time—by which you wish the goal to be accomplished.

Win as Much as You Can

Unit 24: Managing Interpersonal Conflict

The name of this game is "Win as Much as You Can."[3]

1. Divide the class into groups of eight students or more. Further divide these groups into pairs, and seat them as follows:

$$
\begin{array}{ccc}
 & \text{X X} & \\
\text{X X} & & \text{X X} \\
 & \text{X X} &
\end{array}
$$

Each pair is given a payoff schedule and scorecard and asked to study them for two or three minutes. The partners are asked to share their understanding of the game with each other—but not with their group.

Instructions: For ten successive rounds, you and your partner will choose either an *X* or a *Y.* Each round's payoff depends on the pattern of choices made in your cluster:

Payoff Schedule

4 *X*s: Lose $1 each
3 *X*s: Win $1 each 1 *Y*: Lose $3
2 *X*s: Win $2 each 2 *Y*s: Lose $2 each
1 *X*: Win $3 3 *Y*s: Lose $1 each
4 *Y*s: Win $1 each

You are to confer with your partner in each round and make a joint decision. In rounds 5, 8, and 10, you and your partner may first confer with the other pairs in your group before making your joint decision.

Scorecard

Round	Your Choice (circle)		Group's Pattern of Choices		Your Payoff	Your Balance
1	X	Y	___ X	___ Y		
2	X	Y	___ X	___ Y		
3	X	Y	___ X	___ Y		
4	X	Y	___ X	___ Y		
5 (bonus)	X	Y	___ X	___ Y	(x3)	
6	X	Y	___ X	___ Y		
7	X	Y	___ X	___ Y		
8 (bonus)	X	Y	___ X	___ Y	(x5)	
9	X	Y	___ X	___ Y		
10 (bonus)	X	Y	X	___ Y	(x10)	

2. The title of this activity is "Win as Much as You Can." Keep this goal in mind throughout the experience. There are three key rules:

   a. You are not to confer with other members of your group unless you are given specific permission to do so. Don't talk with them. Don't send nonverbal messages back and forth.

   b. Each pair must agree upon a single choice of X or Y for each round.

   c. You are to ensure that the other members of your group do not know your pair's choice until you are told to reveal it.

   There are ten rounds to the exercise. During each round you and your partner will have one minute to mark your choice of X or Y on the scorecard. You will now have one minute to mark your choice for round one. (After one minute, a facilitator should make sure that each pair has marked the scorecard.)

   Share your decision with the other pairs in your group. (Here, a facilitator can assist the groups by pointing to each pair and asking, in turn, "Have you marked your scorecard? What have you marked?") Now enter the score on the scorecard according to the payoff schedule. A facilitator will ask if there are any questions about the scoring. (Note that the purpose of the activity is stated in the title of the game, Win as Much as You Can.)

3. A facilitator should guide the game as follows:

    a. "You have one minute to mark your decision for round 2 . . . 3 . . . 4.
    b. "Has any pair not finished?
    c. "Share and score."

4. Round 5 is a bonus round. The scorecard shows that all amounts won or lost on this round will be multiplied by three. Before you mark your choice for this round, you may wish to discuss this experience with the other pairs in your group. You may have a moment to do that now. (Three minutes for this.)

5. After three minutes, please return to your pair positions. You now have one minute to mark the scorecard for round 5. Remember the rules are now in effect.

    Has any partnership not finished?

    Share and score.

    Rounds 6 and 7 are conducted like rounds 1 through 4. Round 8 is a bonus round, and is conducted like round 5. Round 9 is a standard round, and is conducted like rounds 1 through 4.

6. At round 10 remember that this round is a bonus round. It will increase the number of positive or negative points by ten. Thus, by itself, round 10 can change the balance in this game. Because that is so, you may wish to talk with the other pairs in your group. You can have three minutes to do that. (After three minutes proceed as in step 5.)

7. Each pair tallies its total points, and then each group tallies its total points from the combined pair scores.

Discuss the ideas of competition and cooperation in a conflict situation:

1. What are the usual outcomes of conflict situations? Is this the usual situation?

2. Why don't people cooperate? Under what circumstances might you have achieved cooperation in this experience?

3. Most people define this exercise as a win-lose experience. Is it necessary to define conflict situations as win-lose? Are most interpersonal situations really win-lose situations when conflict occurs?

4. How would you describe your feelings during this game? Do you think your feelings about the participants would affect your future relations with them if this were a real-world experience?

5. What implications might this experience have for your future conflict situations?

Making Some Changes

Unit 24: Managing Interpersonal Conflict

This is an experience in identifying habits that contribute to unwanted conflicts.

It is possible to change habitual behavior, but you have to replace a habit—you can't just break it! This means you must practice and practice until the new behavior feels as natural as the old. And, of course, you must first think about the habitual behavior you want to change.

Do you find yourself using habitual behavior in conflict situations that you want to change? For many, such habits center around child rearing, money, time, and sex.

1. Name a habit you would like to change and are willing to work on, then describe your behavior.

   _____

   _____

2. Describe, as specifically and positively as possible, the behavior you would like to substitute for the unwanted conflict habit.

   _____

   _____

3. What is the *worst* possible result from the habit you want to break?

   _____

   _____

4. How does the trouble caused by your habit usually start? That is, what behavior can you use to "trigger" your replacement?

   _____

   _____

5. What can you ask the other person to do to help you remember that you want to replace an unwanted conflict habit with the preferred choice?

   _____

   _____

Role Playing Conflict Management

Unit 24: Managing Interpersonal Conflict
Unit 22: Managing Power in Relationships
Unit 21: Supportiveness in Relationships

Practice role playing effective conflict management in each of the following situations. The actors should attempt to reach a decision about the problem.

After each case, answer the questions at the end of this experience before moving on to the next case.

1. Mary has been with her company for approximately five years and has a responsible position. She is intelligent, efficient, and capable. She is an excellent employee except for one problem that mars her record. Now and then she will antagonize her fellow workers by her defensiveness-producing behavior. For instance, one day she delivered material to a co-worker by just tossing it on the desk as she hurried by.

She has also left the impression that a person should have known better when they handed her work that contained an error. For example, the other day a co-worker asked her a perfectly reasonable question, but she walked on by as if she had not heard.

You and several of your fellow workers can no longer tolerate this situation and have decided to talk with Mary about it. She is usually a reasonable person—except, of course, when she has these occasional problems. She might become defensive.

2. James Irwin is a new professor. He has just given his midterm examination, which included sixty objective questions and six short-answer essay questions for a fifty-minute exam period. At the end of the fifty minutes, he called time and collected all of the papers. Only two students had finished the exam. The course for which the exam was being given is a prerequisite for all upper-level courses in the department. Irwin has indicated that any incomplete questions will be counted as incorrectly answered. At the urging of the department chairperson, you and four other students decide to go to him to discuss the problem. He has seemed reasonable on other matters related to the course, but you do not know how he will react to this inquiry.

3. Paul Holbrook has been the business manager for Midwest Chemical Company for fifteen years. During this time, he has developed a number of habits that are annoying to his subordinates. About two years ago, he started eating lunch alone in his office with his door closed. In fact, he keeps his door closed most of the time.

When members of the department have a question, they often get a brief and unsatisfactory answer. For example, Kay asked for the morning off to go to the dentist. Paul answered, "Two hours," without even looking up from his work. George put a note in Paul's mailbox asking how to submit a report. Two days later, he received a one-word reply, "Typewritten." Upon hearing George's story, Stan, another employee, told George how lucky he was. Several months ago Stan asked Paul a question as he passed through the office. Paul acted as if Stan hadn't said a word.

Four of you in the office have decided that you must speak to Paul. If the climate does not change, you have all agreed to ask to be transferred to another department.

4. Karl Lewis is a thirty-year-old recent graduate of Northeastern University. He worked for several years and then decided to return to school for a degree in organizational communication and management. Karl has been hired

by Southern Steel Corporation, a medium-sized producer, to direct their training and management development program.

The director of personnel, Margaret Goodyear, had been directing the training program along with her other duties. She hired Lewis, but had some reservations. She had wanted someone with at least five years of experience directing a training department, but for some reason, none of the other applicants seemed qualified.

Karl's academic record and recommendations were outstanding. In fact, Goodyear has no reason to believe that he cannot do well in the job. Nevertheless, she has assigned Karl only routine, predominately clerical duties. He has been given no real authority over the department he was hired to direct. Karl has scheduled a meeting with Goodyear to attempt to resolve this problem.

Discuss each case by answering these questions:

1. What conflict management strategy was followed?
2. How effective was this strategy for managing this conflict?
3. If the strategy was effective, how do you account for this?
4. If the strategy was ineffective, how do you explain this? What might be a better strategy? Why?

What Makes a Healthy Interpersonal Relationship

Unit 25: Managing Relational Deterioration
Unit 26: Promoting Relational Growth

This experience will help you understand the features of a healthy relationship by comparing your ideas with those of your classmates.

Step 1 (20 minutes)
Working as a group, discuss how to maintain a healthy relationship. After twenty minutes, list the group's ideas on the chalkboard, collectively rank ordered according to their relative importance.

Step 2 (approximately 10 minutes)
Still working as a group, discuss these questions:

1. Does the group share any ideas about healthy relationships? If so, what does this tell you?
2. Are there any notable differences in the listed ideas? If so, how do you explain them?
3. Based on the lists of other groups, would your group want to change its list? If so, how?
4. If you have made any changes in your list, rank order the top five, write them on the board, and erase everything else.

Step 3 (approximately 30 minutes)
Select one member of your group to work at the chalkboard. Select another

member to direct a conversation with the class. Identify at least one (or two, if this is easily done) implication for behavior for each item on the board.

Investigation of Male/Female Relational Differences

Unit 25: Managing Relational Deterioration
Unit 26: Promoting Relational Growth

This experience will allow you to explore interpersonal concerns that make relational development between males and females difficult. You can prepare for this assignment by listing those things that members of the opposite sex do, say, or think that impede meaningful interpersonal relationships.

Form two groups, one of men and one of women. If possible, they should work in separate rooms. Each group is to list ten things that members of the opposite sex do, say, or think that act as barriers to relational development. Rank order the items on each list, and then write them on the chalkboard.

The instructor will lead a discussion based on the following procedure:

1. The group will be asked to clarify each item, giving examples when requested.
2. The group about whom a statement is made will be asked if they believe it is true.
3. Class members should discuss what difference knowing this information might make in their effort to promote relational growth.[4]

Additional Dialogues for Analysis

Two Female Roommates

Roommate 1 (slamming the door): I thought I told you to clean this house. I went to work, I came back, and it's still a mess.

Roommate 2: Look—I just got home myself. I'm tired. I've had a long day and I don't have time to clean this whole apartment.

Roommate 1: Well, when I asked you to do it yesterday you sure seemed to have a lot of time. You were lying there watching TV.

Roommate 2: Look, I work full-time at two jobs. I go to school, you know, why should I . . .

Roommate 1: I have sympathy for you. I work too, and I go to school full-time. And, I have company coming in less than fifteen minutes, and this house is still a mess.

Roommate 2: Why should I have to clean this whole apartment?

Roommate 1: 'Cause you never clean! That's why! I'm sick of cleaning up after you.

Roommate 2: I *never* clean up? Now—I take out the trash, I stack the dishes every now and then. I do a little bit around here.

Roommate 1: Oh, maybe once a week—if I'm lucky to get even that much help.

Roommate 2: Now—who had that party this weekend?

Roommate 1: I had the party, but I believe more of your friends showed up at the end than mine. And they sure were wasted and making a mess.

Roommate 2: Well, look, you said it was an "open" party.

Roommate 1: Yeh—I said it was "open," but I didn't say you had to trash the place either.

Roommate 2: We didn't trash the place; there are just a few beer cans lying around. I can clean it up.

Roommate 1: You call this a few! Look around you! I can't even walk! And it smells bad. Look at those ashtrays. This place is gross!

Roommate 2: We can clean it together before your company comes tonight, I think. Let me finish watching . . .

Roommate 1: That's not the point. . . .

Roommate 2: my TV show here.

Roommate 1: This is how it always happens. This is just how it *always* happens, and I'm sick of always cleaning up the mess.

Roommate 2: I think we need to sit down and make some arrangements.

Roommate 1: This is just why it is a mess; you're sitting there watching TV.

Roommate 2: You're being too bossy. You know, I just can't do everything around here.

Roommate 1: Well, I wouldn't have to be if I didn't have to keep asking you this over and over. After a while I get sick of asking you.

Two Male Co-workers

First Version
Doug: Jim, dump that over there.

Ken: Doug, Doug—I got this call from a customer. He was irate. He received this entire shipment of a product and only some of it is right. He's just gone crazy! I wrote this order a week ago, and it means lots and lots of money to this company. And somehow it got screwed up. The only place I can see where that could have happened is down in shipping. You had all the parts, or you were suppose to have. . . .

Doug: Ken . . . Ken . . .

Ken: Yeh? Yeh?

Doug: People from your department come down here all of the time and complain about us. You can tell by that chart on the wall that we've had 572 man hours of perfect employment. Bill Phillips put that chart right there to inspire us. It sounds like you're just blowing off steam.

Ken: Well, maybe I am. I've got to get some answers for this customer. He's sitting there with a product he didn't order.

Second Version
Ken: Doug, I got this call, and this customer told me that he had ordered three

hundred of the 2400's and two hundred of the 2404's. The three hundred came in and the two hundred are only partial; and some of them are broken and some of them are bent, to the point that he can't use them. We've got to come up with some solution.

Doug: Is this your customer, Ken?

Ken: This is my customer. The one that I've been working on for years and years, and he finally placed his first order with us.

Doug: Well, you know how organized we are in the shipping department. It's a rare day when something is broken. But, let's face it, you know truckers are pretty violent. Maybe that's the cause of the problem? Have they filed a report with the trucking company yet?

Ken: We shipped those in our trucks!

Doug: We did?

Ken: Yeh—our truck. We delivered it on *our* truck.

Doug: Our truck? Who is that driver on that job? I'm going to have to talk to that guy! But I've inspected almost every package that goes out of here. 'Cause you know, that's my job. And I don't see what you could be talking about. I think your customer, you know, has some . . . well, I don't want to talk about your customer. But he has some problems. I think he's screwed up the material himself. We have had some customers do that when we've known for a fact that the material was put on their docks in perfect order.

Ken: Well, maybe we better go back and check our receipts and the signatures . . .

Doug: We'll check them at our end.

Ken: . . . and see that he's checked them and that they were in good shape.

Doug: But this is our third complaint this week from people in your department. I'm getting sick and tired of people coming down here and trying to tell me how to do my job.

Working Mother and College-Age Daughter

Mother (talking to herself): It's two o'clock in the morning, she said she was going to be here at twelve. Where in the world is she? Why didn't she even call? This is ridiculous! She is never going out again! Never, ever, ever—or she's moving out. I can't stand this!

[door closes]

Daughter: Oh, Mother—what are you doing up at this hour?

Mother: I could ask you the same question. Do you know what time it is, young lady?

Daughter: Yes, ma'am, I do!

Mother: Well, do you want to relay it to me?

Daughter: It's 2:15 A.M., but we were having such a good time. I thought for sure you'd be asleep. It wasn't hurting anybody.

Mother: What time did you tell me you'd be home?

Daughter: I don't remember.

Mother: What time did you tell me you'd be home?

Daughter: 1:30 A.M. Gee—I'm only forty-five minutes . . .

Mother: Wrong!

Daughter: Oh, Mom, go back to bed. You need your sleep.

Mother: I've never *been* to bed! I haven't been to bed yet. I was up reading, and then it happened to have been twelve o'clock and I expected you in. And then you didn't come, and you didn't come, and you didn't come, and now I'm worried.

Daughter: Well, I'm home now. I'm tired. Good night.

Mother: No, ma'am! You come right back here. You're not going to bed. Have you ever heard of a telephone? I mean, just call me and tell me you're not dead.

Daughter: Mom, you would have screamed holy murder . . .

Mother: I would not!

Daughter: . . . if I had awakened you at 1:15 A.M.

Mother: I would not.

Daughter: I was having such a good time.

Mother: I would not have screamed.

Daughter: Do you remember what it was like to have fun?

Mother: Oh, now, don't start that with me! Do not! I am the mother; you are the child.

Daughter: Mother, I could be a mother, too. Why don't we just be roommates? Do you always have to be the heavy and me the kid?

Mother: As long as I'm the mother, I'm going to be responsible for you. It doesn't matter if you're eighty years old, and God help me, if I'm still living, I will still worry about you.

Daughter: Well, you *should* worry about me; I worry about you.

Mother: Well, what if I'd stayed out all night and you were sitting home. Would you have cared? What if I came moseying on in about 3:30 in the morning? And you said, "Mom, where have you been?," and I said, "Out." Would you deserve—or would you feel like you deserved—some kind of explanation?

Daughter: Curiosity would have killed me! Where would you have been until . . . ha, ha!

Mother: Well, that's not the point! That's not the point!

Daughter: What *is* the point, Mother?

Mother: The point is . . .

Daughter: You're going to be tired, you're going to look like hell at work tomorrow—my class is at eleven tomorrow.

Mother: All right, Ms. Asterbuilt. That's what you do—you stay home and watch "The Young and the Restless" until it's time to go to school. You go to school; I work my butt off all day. I'm here by myself, the house is my responsibility. You don't even lift a finger to do anything around here.

Daughter: But that's your job.

Mother: Oh—no, ma'am! I have a full-time job elsewhere. You can help.

Daughter: Right now I'm going to school and that's my job.

Mother: Going to school from eleven to two—*big deal!*

Daughter: I can never eat here; why should I wash the dishes?

Mother: Fine—all right—if we're going to be roommates—you pay half the rent—(pause) how does that grab you?

Daughter: Can we have deferred payments?

Mother: No, ma'am! Now—half the bills; half the electricity; half the water. Hey! That's what roommates do! Half the telephone bill . . .

Daughter: So you want me to quit school.

Mother: God knows you love the telephone and calling your boyfriend in Alaska or wherever he lives.

Daughter: I call collect.

Mother: Well, it's a good thing. (pause) And back to the subject at hand. Where have you been from 6 P.M. to two o'clock in the morning?

Daughter: Do you want it minute by minute? I thought you were tired? You're fussing 'cause I'm keeping you all night.

Mother: You're not too old for me to slap you around a little bit. Tell me where you've been.

Daughter: All right. At 6:15 P.M. I went to Nancy's apartment . . .

Mother: Don't be smart—

Daughter: I was at Nancy's apartment until about 7:15 P.M., because we were waiting for Joann to come over, because we had to go to the cleaners. And then we had to—oh, let's see—umm—we went out for pizza. Nancy didn't want pizza 'cause she's on a diet, so we had to go get salad. Then we went to see what guys were hanging out at the 7-Eleven. And then we went to Adam's for a while. . . .

Mother: That's a good place. See, I want to know—I wonder how much money I've spent at Adam's and the Acapulco Club, when I've never even been in the place.

Daughter: Precious little mother. I don't drink like a wino.

Mother: You better not—you better not . . .

Daughter: We just socialize.

Mother: And I mean to tell you if I ever catch you coming in driving drunk—if you ever come home after you've had too much to drink—Honey—that will be the end of your automobile. *The end!*

Daughter: By whose standards—"too much to drink"?

Mother: By mine.

Daughter: You set pretty high standards for me, Mother.

Mother: Well, if you're going to live here that's the way it's going to be. I am worried about you. As long as you're my child—which will be forever—I will be worried about you.

Daughter: But what about your two martinis at lunch with the girls? Don't you drive home after that? What's the liquor content of that?

Mother: Let's get back to the point here.

Daughter: What I'm trying to say here, Mother, is that you should trust me. And I've never given you any reason to not trust me. I do everything by the book. I don't do drugs. I don't sleep around—my God, I even go to church with you!

Mother: And that is why I expect you to do what you say you are going to do. Because you are a good child. You have always been good, you have never given me any problems. You're right, until just this minute.

A Brother and Sister

Steven: I don't want you going out with Owen.

Jamie: Why not, Steven?

Steven: Because he is an SAE, and he's only got one thing on his mind, and I don't want him messing around with my sister.

Jamie: You're a Kappa Sigma. They think the same thing that SAEs do.

Steven: That's different. Kappa Sig is the biggest fraternity on campus. Everybody in Kappa Sig is O.K.

Jamie: He didn't go to South Alabama, he went to Auburn. That makes a difference.

Steven: No, it doesn't. . . .

Jamie: Why not?

Steven: You're not going out with him.

Jamie: Give me one good reason.

Steven: 'Cause he is no good. He's no good.

Jamie: That's not a good reason.

Steven: He's got nothing on his mind, and he's going nowhere.

Jamie: Nothing on his mind? *I'm* on his mind. I'm something.

Steven: No. That's beside the point.

Jamie: Steven, you're digging your own hole. *You're not going out with Owen!*

Steven: I'm not digging my own hole. You're not going out with Owen!

Jamie: And you're not big enough to stop me. What about that girl you went out with and I told you she was nothing but a slut. You went out with her anyway.

Steven: That's different. It's a double standard.

Jamie: Why?

Steven: 'Cause girls have to save themselves for marriage.

Jamie: So you just go ahead and take it from her so she can't save anything. Right?

Steven: I didn't take it from her, and that's none of your business. You are just not going out with Owen.

Jamie: Well, do you fear for your little sister?

Steven: Yes. You're not going out with Owen, because Owen . . .

Jamie: Well, have a talk with him.

Steven: You can't control Owen. And I can't be there on the date.

Jamie: Well, then, you talk to Owen and tell him to control himself.

Steven: It's not my place to . . .

Jamie: Well, then . . .

Steven: . . . talk to him.

Jamie: You can't stop me from going out with him. That should be Dad's job.

Steven: I'll tell Mom.

Jamie: Mother can't do anything. She went out with Daddy. (laughter)

Steven: I'll tell you what. I'll find you somebody to go out with.

Jamie: A Kappa Sig?

Steven: Kappa Sig is the best.

Jamie: No way! No, no, no! I've heard about them.

Steven: There's nothing wrong with them.

Jamie: I've heard about their games.

Steven: He's a freshman and in Kappa Sig. He's a nice guy.

Jamie: I had a class last quarter with a girl who used to date one. She had nothing but terrible things to say about him.

Steven: About a Kappa Sig?

Jamie: Yes!

Steven: I can't believe it.

Jamie: And his first name was Steve. I didn't think it was you.

Steven: You have a biased opinion here.

Jamie: You have a biased opinion against Owen as an SAE. And he went to Auburn. You don't know anything about that fraternity.

Steven: I know a guy you can go out with. His name is Gary. He's got glasses. He's a nice guy. He's a freshman.

Jamie: Glasses?

Steven: Well, they're neat looking. He's a nice Christian guy.

Jamie: Does he look like a bookworm?

Steven: No. He's a nice Christian guy.

Jamie: Don't be judging Owen. He may be also.

Steven: He's an SAE. None of those SAEs do that.

Jamie: In Auburn. He goes to South now.

Steven: An SAE is an SAE wherever they are.

Jamie: Are you going to be home Friday night?

Steven: No, I'm going out.

Jamie: See, you can't stop me then.

Steven: I can stop Owen.

Jamie: You wouldn't hurt him.

Steven: No. I'll cut his tires or something.

Jamie: You wouldn't do that 'cause then he'll take his dad's car.

Steven: I'll tie you up and put you in a closet.

Jamie: No, you're not big enough to tie me up and put me in a closet. Besides, I'm the one who took the rope-tying class. I could tie *you* up and put you in the closet. Where should we go on our date? Somewhere lighted?

Steven: You should go out with Gary.

Jamie: I've never met this Gary. And I hate blind dates. I hate them!

Steven: I'll set it up—he's not blind.

Jamie: You said he wore glasses.

Steven: It's just a vision impairment.

Jamie: Will he bring "Rover" with us?

Steven: Probably.

Jamie: A seeing-eye dog.

Steven: Gary is the ideal person for you to go out with.

Jamie: I'm not going out on another blind date.

Steven: You're not going out with Owen.

Jamie: The girl I tried setting you up with would have been nice. But you wouldn't go out with her.

Steven: That's different.

Jamie: No, it's not!

Steven: I can pick and choose whom I want to go out with. You are my little sister. You'll go out with whom I tell you to.

Jamie: How old are you now? One year older. Yeh. That makes you a real expert on dating.

Steven: It does. I've been around and seen more.

Jamie: When you were dating, I was double dating. And I wasn't double dating with your friends.

Steven: But you weren't going out with an SAE.

Jamie: Would you leave that aside.

Steven: I can't.

Jamie: That's not the point.

Steven: He's an SAE.

Jamie: He lives in Springhill.

Steven: He's too old. He's 27 years old.

Endnotes

1. After J. L. Hocker and W. W. Wilmot, *Interpersonal Conflict,* 2nd ed. (Dubuque, IA: Wm. C. Brown Publishers, 1985), 73.

2. J. T. Tedeschi, "Threats and Promises" in *Persuasion: New Directions in Theory and Research,* eds. M. E. Roloff and G. R. Miller (Beverly Hills, CA: Sage Publishing Company, 1980).

3. This experience has been widely disseminated. We have noticed variations of it in several sources. One version of it was formulated by William Gellerman. See W. Pfeiffer and J. E. Jones, eds., *A Handbook of Structured Experiences for Human Relations Training,* vol. 2 (La Jolla, CA: University Associates, 1974).

4. The basic idea for this experience may have originated with Joseph DeVito of Queens College, although we have seen it in several places.

Self-Help Guide

Interpersonal growth requires active practice, particularly since you will continuously encounter situations that require effective interpersonal communication. We know, however, that after you have completed this course, you may rarely have the opportunity to have a professional help you to improve your interpersonal skills. We have, therefore, constructed a self-help guide for you to consult when you feel you need help with a skill. The guide includes approximately ninety questions or statements about interpersonal communication and relational development. We have indexed them by page numbers so that you can turn to the appropriate spot in the text for the information you need.

Using the Question-Answer Index

1. Form a statement or question about the situation that is puzzling you. Try to word it using the terms you have learned from this text.
2. Look for key words in your statement or question. Then locate those words in the directory.
3. Turn to the key word in the guide and look at the questions and statements under it. Select the one that most closely resembles your concern.
4. Turn to the page in the text that addresses your need.
5. If the concern is not addressed by a key word in the directory, you may find an index entry that will help you.

Directory

Problem Category and Questions

agreement

I get frustrated when someone says they don't
  understand me, but what they really mean is they
  don't agree.   90, 92–93

assertiveness

I seem to be someone people like to push around.
  What can I do about this?   172–79

When I think I've been wronged, I act badly. What
  might be going on here? What is alternative
  behavior?   273–75, 284–90

attending

Why do I sometimes not even hear what another
  person has said?   56–60, 89–90

conflict

I fear conflict because it can be very destructive. What
  can be done to make conflict productive?   322–23, 329–35

Is there any relationship between how I fight and the
  likely outcome?   324–26

Sometimes, especially in an important relationship, I
  am particularly nasty to the other person. Why?   327–29, 330–31

I'd like to understand how to handle conflict better.
  What kind of management strategy should I follow?   329–35

decision making

Sometimes I have trouble making decisions. It is as
  though I don't know what's going on. Is there help?   313–18

defensive communication

At times I really feel the need to defend myself. Why?   274–75

interpersonal needs

language

listening

meaning

relational definition

I think of us as friends; my friend thinks of us as
   romantic partners. What's going on here?   73, 149–50, 250–53

relational deterioration

Everything was really great, but now that we're getting
   ready to marry, the relationship has fallen apart.
   Why?   266–68, 338–42

What are the signs that my relationship is
   deteriorating?   343–45

Suppose I know my relationship is in trouble. How can
   I save it?   351–58

relational engagement

Why are people attracted to some attempts at
   relationship initiation but not to others?   244–49, 257–66

relational rules

Sometimes it seems like a person I know is playing
   some sort of game. At other times my friend seems
   to act more naturally. I can't figure this out.   73, 149–50, 250–53

relationships

I have trouble meeting people.   249–50

Sometimes, especially in an important relationship, I
   seem to be particularly nasty to the other person.
   Why?   327–29, 330–31

Is there a checklist I can use for an agenda when I
   want to talk about my relationship with someone?   31–41

I need a single piece of good advice to help me
   manage one of my relationships.   38

I feel confused about my priorities and goals in several
   relationships.   353–55

I am upset when a coworker talks down to me. What
   could cause such behavior?   150–52

reification

roles

self-concept

self-fulfilling prophecy

Sometimes I get this feeling before an encounter that
things aren't going to go well. I'm usually right. Why
does this happen?   182–86

stereotyping

I am often criticized because of the clubs to which I
belong. What can I do about this?   182–86

supportive communication

What alternative do I have to returning the other
person's defensive behavior?   285–90

I'd rather be supportive than defensive when arguing.
How can I do this?   285–90, 293–94

Why be supportive? Isn't defensiveness more likely to
get me what I want?   290–93

symmetry and complementarity

I am upset when someone talks down to me. What
could cause this behavior?   150–52

understanding

What can I do to understand more fully what others
really mean when they talk to me?   38, 96–98, 131–33

Glossary

abdicrat   One of three personality types identified by William Schutz with regard to the interpersonal need to control. Abdicrats have little need to control, preferring to abdicate power and responsibility to the other person in a relationship.

absolute present   Principle that we can only live in the present and that our relationships are therefore always in the present.

abstraction   Process of moving, in language, farther from a referent; of perceiving and making sense of language; of translating experience into language. A general concept that partially represents some whole.

accommodation   Process of adjusting the frame of reference to integrate new information and experiences.

active listening   Technique that includes the skills of concentrating, frequent internal summarizing, interrupting, and paraphrasing what another has said.

adaptable-social   One of three personality types identified by William Schutz with regard to the need for inclusion. Adaptable-social people balance needs for inclusion and privacy.

adaptor   Movement or gesture displayed to alleviate psychological tension.

affect display   Movement or gesture that reflects a feeling or the intensity of feelings.

affection   Fondness for or devotion to someone or some thing; liking. One of three interpersonal needs identified by William Schutz. In this context, affection is the desire to be liked by others and to develop loving relationships. Schutz identified three personality types related to the interpersonal need for affection: (1) overpersonal, (2) personal, and (3) underpersonal.

agenda for talking about relationships   A list of all components of a relationship presented in an order that is convenient to follow in an interpersonal encounter. Included are observations, inferences, feelings, wants and expectations, intentions, openness, images, and check out.

aggressive   interactive style that is self-enhancing, belittling, controlling, and hurtful or damaging to others and to relationships.

ambiguity   Quality of a message that permits more than one interpretation.

analyst, the   Mnemonic device to assist in remembering a behavior that punishes talk about negative feelings. ("You feel that way because. . . .")

approach-approach conflict   Conflict over mutually exclusive but equally attractive outcomes.

approach-avoidance conflict   Conflict over outcomes that are both desirable and undesirable. The actor is attracted by one and put off by the other.

artifacts   Things people collect about themselves.

assertive   Interactive style that is self-enhancing, expressive, and self-supportive, while protective of the choices of others. Not aggressive and not shy.

assimilation   Process of changing what is perceived to fit a frame of reference.

attending   In listening, the selective act of attention.

attention   Process of responding to stimuli.

attitude   "Mental and neural state of readiness organized through experience, exerting a directive or dynamic influence upon behavior, the individual's response to all objects and situations to which it is related." (Gordon Allport) Predisposition to respond.

attraction   See "interpersonal attraction."

autocrat   One of three personality types identified by William Schutz with regard to the interpersonal need to control. Autocrats feel a need to dominate, to rise to the top of a hierarchy.

avoidance-avoidance conflict   Conflict that results when avoiding an undesirable outcome will yield a different undesirable outcome.

avoiding   Stage in relational deterioration characterized by overt efforts to break off contact and end the relationship.

balance   State of emotional calm that results when perceptions seem consistent with expectations or our image of reality.

belief   Statement about what is, developed from information outside the realm of personal experience. Three categories: primitive beliefs, surface beliefs, and derived beliefs.

bonding   One of five stages in a relationship in which the partners make a special, voluntary, ongoing commitment, usually, but not always, in a public ritual.

certainty   Defensive behavior characterized by a rigid viewpoint, and both verbal and nonverbal suggestions that the speaker is correct and the receiver is incorrect. Closed-mindedness that creates defensiveness. Behavioral opposite of provisionalism.

channel   The means of transmission; the vehicle through which messages are sent.

check out   Colloquial term used as mnemonic device to help remember the importance of getting and giving feedback when talking about relationships.

circumscribing   Stage in relational deterioriation characterized by avoidance of topics and intimacy that might lead to self-disclosure.

closure   Process of adding information to perceptions of otherwise incomplete events.

code   Set of symbols and signals used to convey messages. See "language."

coercive power   Power that derives from ability to remove another's actual choices or perception that choices are available. Power that derives from force or the threat of force.

cohesiveness   Sense, feeling, or property of wholeness, unity, or togetherness.

communication   Process of transmitting and interpreting messages.

compatibility   Ability to coexist in harmony.

competence   Perception that an individual is knowledgeable and able to perform in a given area. Language competence is knowledge of and ability to use the elements and rules of language. Communication competence refers to social skill and interpersonal effectiveness.

complementary relationship   Relationship, or view of a relationship, in which one person is superior and the other is subordinate, as in parent-child.

compromise   Conflict management strategy in which parties look for a position in which each gives and gets a little, splitting the difference if possible; no winners and no losers.

conditioning   Process of teaching or controlling behavior by making rewards and punishments contingent upon specific behavior.

conflict, interpersonal   Form of competition. Situation in which one person's behaviors are designed to interfere with or harm another.

conflict, intrapersonal   Condition or status of emotional tension. See approach-approach conflict, approach-avoidance conflict, and avoidance-avoidance conflict.

confrontation and problem solving   Conflict management strategy in which energies are directed toward defeating a problem and not the other person. Parties look for a mutually beneficial solution.

connotative meaning   Personal meaning of a word. Affective associations that an individual brings to a word. Connotation imbues language with value (right/wrong, good/bad), potency (hard/soft, hot/cold), and action (fast/slow).

consistency   Perceptual process that causes us to perceive what we expect to perceive and to be uncomfortable when this is not the case. In attribution theory, the expectation that an individual will exhibit the same behaviors in similar situations. We respond to consistency by attributing the behavioral cause to the individual, and to inconsistency by attributing the behavioral cause to circumstances outside the individual.

content dimension   Part of a communication event having to do with topics, objects, and events outside the relationship.

context   Physical, social, psychological, and temporal environment in which a communication event occurs.

control   (noun) Defensive behavior characterized by manipulation in an attempt to impose an attitude or viewpoint on another. One of three interpersonal needs identified by William Schutz. The degree of desire to exercise power and authority. Schutz identified two personality types related to the need to control: (1) abdicrat and (2) autocrat. Behavioral opposite of problem orientation. (verb) To exercise restraint, dominance, or direction over; to command.

cooperation   Process of working or acting together for a common purpose.

critical listening   Part of the listening process in which four questions are asked to discover closed-mindedness or bias: (1) position, (2) agreement, (3) feeling strength, and (4) importance.

cue   Message that is not symbolic.

culture   Assumptions and rules of a group that render patterns of thought and behavior appropriate or inappropriate.

decoder   Mechanism or agent that decodes. In interpersonal events, each individual decodes the messages sent by the other.

defensiveness   State of having assumed a position or attitude to protect against attack. In interpersonal communication, manifested in such behaviors as evaluation, superiority, certainty, control, neutrality, and strategy, each of which terms are defined in this glossary. Behavioral opposite of supportiveness.

democrat   One of three personality types identified by William Schutz with regard to the interpersonal need to control. Democrats are balanced and capable of taking charge or allowing others to be in control when appropriate.

denotation   The dictionary definition of a word. Meaning of a word, as agreed to by a speech community.

derived beliefs   Beliefs derived from other beliefs.

description   Supportive behavior characterized by factual information, absence of judgmental language, and straightforward questions.

differentiating   Stage in relational deterioration characterized by focus on the individual and perception of self as separate from the other person and the relationship.

disconfirmation   Process of ignoring or denying another's self-disclosure.

dissonance   Emotional discomfort resulting from conflict between related elements in the attitude-value-belief structure. In extreme form, dissonance and guilt are synonymous.

distortion   In the perception process, the actual changing of content to fit the frame of reference.

ego states   In Transactional Analysis, patterns of behavior reflecting the self-concept. There are three ego states: parent is the source of rules that govern behavior, adult is rational and conceptual, and child is emotional.

emblem   Deliberate movement that can be directly translated into words; discrete, categorical behavior that is generally known and accepted.

emotions   Physical feelings within particular contexts.

empathic listening   Part of the listening process; process of identifying one's observations of another's feelings, wants and expectations, intentions, openness, and images, and bringing them to the level of talk when they seem paramount or important.

empathy   Supportive behavior characterized by identification with experiences, feelings, and problems of others and affirmation of another's self-worth.

encoder   The component of the communication process that translates information from one form to another; in speech, that which translates ideas into spoken words. A telephone mouthpiece serves as an encoder when it translates spoken words into electronic impulses.

equality   Supportive behavior characterized by shows of respect for another, and efforts to minimize differences in ability, status, power, and intellectual ability. Behavioral opposite of superiority.

evaluation   Defensive behavior characterized by judgments, assessments, and questions about another's viewpoint or motive. Behavioral opposite of description.

expectation   Anticipation of an occurrence; prediction; assumption that an event is likely to occur. Anticipated response of another.

experimenting   One of five stages in interpersonal relationships in which an individual explores another and searches for common areas of interest.

expert power   Power that derives from knowledge.

fact-inference confusion   Process of making an observation, drawing an inference about the observation, and acting on the guess as though it were a fact.

feedback   Messages sent from a receiver to a source that correct or control error. Can take the form of talk, verbalized cues, and nonverbal cues.

feelings   Physical events of body experienced in the present tense. Body's responses to physical stimulation.

field of experience   Sum of an individual's experiences, plus all connections drawn among them, that allows a person to talk about and interact with the world. Some theorists believe that people cannot interact unless their fields of experience overlap.

filtering screen model   Model used to explain the process by which human selective behavior occurs.

forcing   Conflict management strategy that uses power to cause another to accept a position.

frame of reference   Interlocking facts, ideas, beliefs, values, and attitudes that give form to perceptions.

game   In game theory, a simulation with rules that govern the behavioral choices of players. Game may be played as win-win, win-lose, or lose-lose. In Transactional Analysis, a game is a dishonest, ulterior transaction in which the participant hides true feelings while manipulating another into providing a payoff.

General Semantics   Movement that began with the publication of *Science and Sanity* by Alfred Korzybski in 1933. Studies relationships among language, thought, and behavior.

gestures   Body movements that express an idea or emotion.

identity aspiration   Desire to be recognized as a particular kind of person.

illustrator   Deliberate movements used to reinforce and enrich verbal messages.

image   ·Mental representation, idea, or form. Description or conception of something.

inclusion   One of the interpersonal needs identified by William Schutz that includes an individual's desire to be accepted, to feel wanted, and to be a part of groups. He identified three personality types: see "undersocial," "oversocial," and "adaptable-social."

indiscrimination   Failure to recognize the uniqueness of a person. Interacting in terms of some class or category stereotype.

inference   Guess, conclusion, or judgment derived from observations.

information   In information theory, available data. The more available data, the more information and the greater uncertainty. More commonly used to mean anything that reduces uncertainty.

information overload   Condition in which the complexity or amount of available information is too great to manage effectively.

initiating   One of five stages in interpersonal relationships in which an individual observes another and decides whether to invite interaction.

integrating   One of five stages in interpersonal relationships in which partners move closer, talk more, and think of each other as a unit, using the terms "we" and "our" in reference to their relationship.

intensifying   One of five stages in interpersonal relationships in which intimacy and trust increase as partners commit more fully to each other.

intention   Will or determination to act or achieve some end.

interchangeability   Characteristic of language that makes it possible for individuals to function as both source and receiver.

interpersonal attraction   Willingness to communicate and develop a relationship with another.

interpersonal communication   Transactional process of exchanging messages and negotiating meaning to convey information and to establish and maintain relationships.

interview   Interpersonal communication context in which questions are asked and answered to achieve some goal.

intimacy   Characterization of a close, familiar, and usually affectionate relationship that results from self-disclosure and mutual acceptance.

irreversibility   Feature of communication process that makes it impossible to take back what has been said. Once a communication event has occurred it cannot be "uncommunicated."

Johari Window   Illustration designed by psychologists Joseph Luft and Harrington Ingham to explain the relationships between self-concept and self-presentation. Includes four sections: (1) open self—things about the self that are known both to self and others; (2) blind self—things known to others but not to self; (3) hidden self—things known to self but not to others; and (4) unknown self—an area inferred to exist but not known to self or others.

judge, the   Mnemonic device used to help remember one way that clear talk about negative feelings is punished in our society. ("You have no right to feel that way.")

language   Body of words and symbols, governed by rules, commonly used to communicate.

legitimate power   Power that derives from position.

leveling   Process of message distortion by omitting details from what is perceived.

liking   To regard with favor. To have kindly, friendly feeling for someone or some thing. Related to "affection."

linguistics   Study of language that focuses on the rules of word usage and the relationships between words, meanings, and behavior. Sometimes subdivided into semantics (study of meanings), syntax (study of rules), and pragmatics (study of language–behavior relationships).

listening   Active process of receiving verbal and nonverbal messages.

map-territory confusion   Substitution of language for experience. Treating a symbol as an object that can be manipulated. Sometimes called "reification."

material me   Part of self-concept that focuses on body, home, and physical objects.

message   Any sign, symbol, or combination thereof that functions as stimulus material for a receiver.

metacommunication   Communication about communication.

model   Physical representation of something. A metaphor that allows examination of some object or process in a particular way but also limits what can be observed in that way.

naming   Assignment of labels to objects, phenomena, events, and especially people.

negative reinforcement   Removal of an aversive stimulus to strengthen behavior. Removal is contingent on the behavior.

neutrality   Defensive behavior characterized by treating another as an object having only one or a limited set of functions or without showing concern for that individual's problems or viewpoint. Behavioral opposite of "empathy."

noise   Any interference or distortion in message exchange. Noise exists in the communication process to the extent that message fidelity is damaged. Three broad categories: (1) physical, or channel, noise, (2) semantic, or psychological, noise, and (3) systemic, or system-centered, noise.

nonassertive   Interactive style characterized by self-denial, which allows or encourages others to choose and receive what they want, even at the expense of self. Sometimes called "shy."

nonverbal communication   Communication other than words.

observations   In interpersonal communication, the results of noticing or perceiving the behavior of others. Process of taking in information about another person. One component of the relationship dimension of communication.

openness   Willingness to receive and consider ideas from another. Sometimes called "latitude of acceptance."

operant conditioning   Process of strengthening or weakening behavior by making rewards and punishments contingent upon the change desired.

optimist, the   Mnemonic device used to help remember one of the ways to punish clear talk about negative feelings. ("Everything will be all right.")

overpersonal   One of three personality types identified by William Schutz regarding the need for affection. Overpersonal people take special pains to avoid being disliked by anyone. They may spend great amounts of time talking about their feelings or inquiring about the feelings of others.

oversocial   One of three personality types identified by William Schutz regarding the need for inclusion. Oversocial people continually seek to join and feel a part of many groups.

paraverbal cues   Variations in rate, pitch, force, and formation of suprasegmental elements of language that constitute "how" a word is spoken.

passive listening   Attending to what is being said without actively providing feedback. Does not interrupt the speaker, but may provide subtle, nonverbal feedback.

perception   Process of becoming aware of sensory stimuli through which we select from available information.

perceptual accentuation   Feature of perception process that distorts perceptions in the direction of wants. For example, we tend to see people we like as smarter and more beautiful than those we do not like.

personal   One of three personality types identified by William Schutz regarding the interpersonal need for affection. Personal people can balance situations to be liked when affection is desirable or maintain distance when it is not desirable.

personalizing   Using language that places responsibility for judgments and opinions upon oneself.

person perception   Process of perceiving another, characterized by mutuality, clarity, and number of expectations. Derives from summary evaluation, and includes and is influenced by feelings about self and others.

persuasion   Process of influencing attitudes and behaviors.

persuasive power   Power that derives from ability to argue logically and persuasively.

polarization   Use of language in pairs of opposites without allowing any middle ground.

positive reinforcement   Process of strengthening behavior by making reward contingent upon that behavior.

posture   Carriage or position of the body as a whole.

power   Ability or potential to influence others. J. R. P. French and B. H. Raven identified six bases of power—referent, expert, legitimate, reward, and coercive—each of which is defined in this glossary.

problem orientation   Supportive behavior characterized by a desire to collaborate with another in defining and solving a problem. Behavioral opposite of control.

process   Ongoing activity. Continuous changing in pursuit of a goal.

productivity   Feature of language that makes it possible to create original sentences that will be understood and to talk about new ideas.

projection   Process of attributing one's own feelings, attitudes, values, and beliefs to others.

provisionalism   Supportive behavior characterized by willingness to be tentative, to share information, to suggest that additional information might change one's mind, and to work jointly with another. Behavioral opposite of certainty.

proximity   Nearness in space that makes it possible for two people to develop a relationship. Part of interpersonal attraction.

punctuation   Arbitrary assignment of beginnings and endings in the continuous process of communication, thus identifying separate sequences. One means of interpreting events.

receiver   Person or thing that takes in messages.

referent   Object, phenomenon, person, or event to which a symbol refers. Part of the triangle of meaning developed by C. K. Ogden and I. A. Richards.

referent power   Power that derives from liking.

reflexiveness   Feature of language that permits it to be used to refer to itself.

regulator   Body movement that fosters interaction. Gesture system that controls turn-taking in the flow of communication.

reification   See "map-territory confusion."

reinforcement   Strengthening of another's behavior or self-concept.

relational definition   Perception each person carries in language about a relationship at a particular moment.

relational deterioration   Disintegration or wearing down of a relationship resulting from loss of attractiveness, unfulfilled needs, inability to manage differences.

relational growth   Result of maintaining a satisfying, interesting, and meaningful relationship.

relational rules   Societal assumptions and interpersonal agreements arrived at through self-disclosure that allows the prediction of behavior.

relationship dimension   Part of a communication event, usually nonverbal, that allows interpretations about the nature of the relationship.

remembering   Process of recalling by an effort of memory. Fourth component of the listening process.

response   Any behavior that results from stimulation.

reward power   Power that derives from ability to mediate another's rewards through possession of something valued.

rigidity in naming   Process of fixing or hardening a label to some person, object, phenomenon, or event.

rip-off artist, the   Mnemonic device used to remember one way that clear talk about negative feelings is punished in our society. ("This happened to me.")

risk   Exposure to a hazard, danger, or loss.

role   Behavior evidenced by an individual and sanctioned by others. Expectations of someone's dual behavior. Pattern of behavior. Routine associated with an individual in a particular context.

rule   Pattern of behavior expected from a certain role situation, or context.

script   In Transactional Analysis, the life plan an individual feels compelled to act out. Characterized by four basic themes, or life positions: (1) I'm O.K., you're O.K. (2) I'm O.K., you're not O.K. (3) I'm not O.K., you're O.K. (4) I'm not O.K., you're not O.K.

selective attention   Process of choosing one or more of the stimuli to which we are exposed.

selective exposure   Process of choosing certain stimuli while disregarding or avoiding others.

self-concept   Sum of perceptions, ideas, and images about oneself.

self-disclosure   Revealing one's thinking, feelings, beliefs, and the like to another.

self-esteem   Value of oneself. Self-love. Self-respect.

self-expression   Feature of language usage by which word choice reflects the status of speaker. Sometimes strong language that was not intended literally.

self-fulfilling prophecy   Process of making a prediction come true.

sensing   Receiving stimuli through the five senses.

Shannon and Weaver model   Model of the communication process.

shared beliefs   Beliefs derived through experience and acknowledged by others.

sharpening   In perception, process of focusing on details that reinforce the frame of reference while discarding the rest.

shy   See "nonassertive."

sign   Token. Indication. Something that stands for or announces the presence of something else when a natural relationship exists.

significant other   Person who influences the formation of the self-concept. Person to whom one looks for information about appropriate behavior.

silence   Absence of sound. Background upon which all spoken language is structured. Thomas Bruneau identified three forms: (1) psycholinguistic (part of the temporal sequence of speech), (2) interactive (pause or interruption used for decision making), and (3) sociocultural (culturally sanctioned or mandated silences).

similarity   Perception that someone is like ourselves. Part of interpersonal attraction.

smoothing   Conflict management strategy of minimizing differences and emphasizing positive, common interests, or of avoiding issues that might cause conflict.

social comparison   Comparison of oneself to others.

social me   Part of self-concept that focuses upon how others perceive and experience oneself.

source   Location of an idea. Originator of a message.

spiritual me   Part of self-concept that focuses upon awareness of oneself as a thinking and feeling person.

spontaneity   Supportive behavior characterized by the candid, straightforward, and uncomplicated presentation of the self.

stagnating   Stage in relational deterioration characterized by inactivity, verbal silence, discomfort, and negation of one's partner.

stereotype   Application of a fixed set of beliefs about a group or subgroup to an individual member that ignore the uniqueness of the individual.

strategy   Defensive behavior characterized by attempts to trick another into thinking that he is making a decision that in fact has already been made or that his best interests are being considered when they are not.

superiority   Defensive behavior characterized by suggestions that another is inadequate or inferior and thus unable to entertain feedback or share in problem solving.

supportiveness   Interpersonal behavior characterized by description, problem orientation, spontaneity, empathy, equality, and provisionalism, each of which is defined in this glossary.

surface beliefs   Flexible beliefs. Least central of all elements in the belief structure, such as those dealing with matters of taste.

symbol   Something that stands for something else when no natural relationship exists. In language, words, phrases, and sentences that stand for thoughts.

symmetrical relationship   Relationship, or view of a relationship, in which partners are essentially similar in status, responsibility, and the like.

terminating   Result of relational deterioration. End of a relationship. Severance of contact, sometimes codified, as in a divorce decree.

territoriality   Tendency for individuals to claim, "own," and use space as an extension of their own personal space. Lyman and Scott described four categories: (1) public (area that individuals may enter freely), (2) interactional (area marked by participants as theirs while they are interacting), (3) home (private space occupied by legal sanction), and (4) body (space immediately surrounding one's physical person).

thought   Result of mental activity. Perception and interpretation of a referent, including feelings, past experiences, and related perceptions. Mental image of a referent.

time   Cultural system of temporal or sequential relationships between and among events that has message potential. Some cultures are monochronic because they use time arbitrarily. Others are polychronic because they emphasize people and interactions rather than an arbitrary understanding of time.

touching behavior, friendship/warmth   Casual and spontaneous touching that signals mutual acceptance and positive regard (but excluding love or sexual touching), as in congratulatory back patting.

touching behavior, functional/professional   Touching to deliver professional service, as between a physician and patient.

touching behavior, love/intimacy   Touching that signals a special, or bonded, relationship, or that assumes or confirms intimate access to be appropriate, as in handholding or lap sitting.

touching behavior, sexual arousal   Touching that is pleasant because of the sexual meaning it conveys or the sexual stimulation it produces, as in petting and sexual intercourse.

touching behavior, social/polite   Ritual touching to acknowledge someone's personhood or essential humanity and/or acknowledge or neutralize status differences, as in handshaking or kissing a cardinal's ring.

transactional   Mutual negotiation of meaning. Mutual influence.

Transactional Analysis   System developed by Eric Berne for analyzing relationship behavior as it is occurring.

triangle of meaning   Figure developed by C. K. Ogden and I. A. Richards that depicts the relationship among words, their referents, and thoughts.

trust   Feeling of comfort that derives from ability to predict another's behavior. A belief that the other can be relied on.

turn-taking   Process of passing initiative for talk back and forth between or among participants in conversation; signaled by various nonverbal cues.

two-valued orientation   Behaving or tending to experience a phenomenon or event in polarized terms, but without allowing any middle ground. See "polarization."

underpersonal   One of three personality types identified by William Schutz regarding the interpersonal need for affection. Underpersonal people have little need for affection and avoid giving it to others.

undersocial   One of three personality types identified by William Schutz regarding the need for inclusion. Undersocial people have little need for inclusion, isolating themselves from group involvement.

understanding   Third component of the listening process. Interpretation and evaluation of what is sensed.

values   What a person considers important, composed of wants, goals, and guidelines. Characterized by statements of what should be.

vocalics   Variations in rate, pitch, force, and formation of suprasegmental elements of language that constitute "how" a word is spoken.

wants   Wishes, needs, and desires that one holds of a relationship.

withdrawal   Conflict management strategy of retreating from the conflict.

Credits

Name Index

Subject Index